Marks of
London Goldsmiths
and Silversmiths
1837–1914

Marks of London Goldsmiths and Silversmiths

1837–1914

JOHN P. FALLON

BARRIE & JENKINS

LONDON

First published in Great Britain in 1992 by
Barrie & Jenkins Ltd
20 Vauxhall Bridge Road, London SW1V 2SA

A catalogue record for this book is available
from the British Library.

ISBN 0 7126 5406 2

Design by Behram Kapadia
Typeset by Edna A Moore, ⊼ Tek-Art, Addiscombe, Croydon, Surrey
Printed in England by Clays Ltd, St Ives plc

Contents

Acknowledgements

The author wishes to thank the Wardens and Court of the Worshipful Company of Goldsmiths for granting access to their records. Equal thanks are due to Susan Hare and David Beasley of the Company's library, who gave their invaluable assistance in the compilation of this book.

Introduction

For many years, there has been considerable interest in Victorian and Edwardian goldsmiths and silversmiths with a corresponding desire to identify the makers' or sponsors' marks stamped on their silverware. Unfortunately, there was a great lack of published information on the subject. Then, in 1987, John Culme's book, *The Directory of Gold & Silversmiths, Jewellers & Allied Traders 1838–1914*, was published in two volumes and immediately became the standard work on manufacturers and retailers of this period. However, there still remained a demand for a pocket-sized edition covering the better-known makers which could be carried around auctions, etc. and serve as a useful reference book for all who have an interest in antique silver.

Following the format of its predecessor, *Marks of London Goldsmiths and Silversmiths c.1697–1837*, this book has been arranged in three main sections: makers' names, including individuals, manufacturers and retailers, together with their marks and biographical information; lists of London Assay marks from 1697 to the present day; and lastly, an index of makers' marks, or sponsors' marks as they are now called. (The current name of 'sponsor' was created by the provisions of the 1975 Hallmarking Act.)

To trace a maker by means of a mark, locate it in the index by looking up the first letter of the mark; this will give the name of the maker or sponsor, which can then be located alphabetically in the makers' section. Where more than one maker has the same name, numerical classification has been used for reference purposes. It must be remembered that, although this book illustrates over 1,300 marks registered from *circa* 1837 to 1914, this is only a small portion of the 15,000 marks that were recorded in the Goldsmiths' Company's registers during that period.

Unless otherwise stated, all makers' marks illustrated in the book are accurate drawings of those entered in the records at Goldsmiths' Hall, London. All these drawings are from approximately one-and-a-half times to twice the size of the original punch marks. This means that, where two or more different makers have used very similar marks to one another during the same period – for example, the same initials in a rectangular surround – the only really conclusive check on the true maker is to compare the punch mark for size as well as shape with its original counterpart registered at Goldsmiths' Hall.

In addition to the illustrated marks being accurate drawings of those entered at Goldsmiths' Hall, all text alongside these marks has been transcribed directly from the registers.

Generally, the marks illustrated in this book were registered at Goldsmiths' Hall from 1837 onwards, although some earlier ones are included in order to provide continuity where certain makers were working before that date. This will assist the reader to relate these makers to their pre-1837 marks, already illustrated in the previous book, *Marks of London Goldsmiths and Silversmiths c.1697–1837*.

Throughout the eighteenth and nineteenth centuries, the maker's mark became an increasingly misleading symbol. Generally it was representative of the firm of manufacture and not of the individual silversmith. Even when the mark included a person's initials, they were usually those of the firm's partner or director. Sometimes this anomaly was stretched still further by the retailer stamping his own registered mark on the silverware under the guise of it being a maker's mark. For example, in the 1780s and 1790s, pieces of domestic silverware manufactured in the Bateman workshops were frequently bought and retailed by George Giles with the makers' marks of Hester Bateman and Peter and Ann Bateman overstruck with that of George Giles. By the middle of the nineteenth century, this practice of retailers entering their own marks as makers' marks had grown considerably. Many of the larger retailing firms of goldsmiths, silversmiths and jewellers who placed orders for silverware with manufacturing silversmiths and jewellers ensured that the makers' marks stamped on these goods were their own marks and not those of the manufacturer. One such example of this practice was the twelve-light candelabrum, depicting Britannia, exhibited at the Great Exhibition of 1851 by Lambert & Rawlings (illustrated in the 1851 *Art Journal* catalogue). The candelabrum was stamped with the Lambert & Rawlings maker's mark as being of their own manufacture, whereas it was actually manufactured by Edward Barnard & Sons for Lambert & Rawlings.

As a manufacturer, Edward Barnard & Sons appears to have supplied silverware to most of the better-known retailing firms throughout the country from the early nineteenth century up to the latter half of the twentieth century. The majority of these firms often had their own maker's mark stamped on the goods they bought from Barnards, the punches even being held by Barnards in their own workshops. Some of the firms for whom Edward Barnard & Sons manufactured over the years were: Asprey & Co.;

J. W. Benson Ltd; Boodle & Dunthorne (Liverpool); Bruford & Son (Eastbourne); Critchon Brothers; James Dixon & Sons (Sheffield); Garrard & Co.; Hamilton & Co. (Calcutta); R. Hennell & Sons; Hunt & Roskell; Lambert & Rawlings; Lowe & Sons (Chester); Mappin & Webb; H. H. Plante & Co. (Birmingham); Reid & Sons (Newcastle); Serle & Co.; Walker & Hall (Sheffield); West & Son (Dublin); and Wilson & Sharp (Edinburgh).

Makers and their Marks

Since 1773 all makers' marks registered at Goldsmiths' Hall have been recorded in two ways: as ink impressions in the record books and as stamped impressions on metal plates. With the first, in use since 1697, the tip of the actual punch to be used on the silverware was coated with a special ink and then pressed on to the appropriate page in the record book, thus leaving an ink impression of the punch mark. This was not always done very carefully, with the result that some entries are smudged and blurred, while others are indistinct or have missed printing in part due to insufficient ink. With the other method of recording, first introduced in 1773, flat plates of lead or brass, approximately 203mm × 254mm, were marked out into rows of small rectangles. In each rectangle was stamped an impression of the actual punch used on the silverware together with a code number relating the impression to the correct maker's name in the record book.

Methods of Entry to the Goldsmiths' Company

Becoming a member or Freeman of the Goldsmiths' Company could be achieved in any of three possible ways: by Service; by Redemption; by Patrimony.

1. Service: to serve and complete an apprenticeship to a Freeman of the Goldsmiths' Company. The period was generally seven years, sometimes more.
2. Redemption: to be nominated and seconded by members of the Goldsmiths' Company and then pay an entrance fee if elected by the Company's Court of Assistants.
3. Patrimony: to receive the freedom of the Company automatically upon application, provided that the applicant's father, at the time of the applicant's birth, was already a Freeman. If the father became free after the birth, then the applicant could not claim freedom by Patrimony.

On occasions, particularly in more recent times, freedom was granted by Special Grant. It was granted by the Company's Court of Assistants, usually for services rendered to the Company or to the art of gold and silversmithing.

Occasionally a member of a Goldsmiths' Company in another part of the country wished to work in London and become a member of the London Company. Transference of membership was arranged through a Letter of Attorney giving proof to the new Company of existing freedom.

Structure of the Goldsmiths' Company

The general members of the Company were called Freemen. Above them was the Livery which, during the nineteenth century, was composed of some 160 Liverymen elected from the Freemen of the Company. Above this group, and governing the whole of the Goldsmiths' Company, was the Court of Assistants. In 1827, membership of the Court was fixed at twenty-five, and this appears to have remained constant ever since. Within the Court, four assistants were elected annually to act as Wardens and serve as senior members of the Court. These Wardens were also placed in order of seniority, namely 4th, 3rd, 2nd and Prime Warden. This Board also appointed a Deputy Warden who was in charge of the Assay Office and its workings. Before being elected to either the Livery or the Court of Assistants, a member asked to be nominated and then paid an entrance fee upon election; a procedure that is still followed today.

Originally, any craftsman or tradesman working within London's city boundaries was required to be a member of one of the city Companies representing a craft or trade, e.g. Goldsmiths, Watchmakers, Grocers, etc. The fact that a craftsman was a member of a Company different from the one representing the craft or trade in which he worked did not matter. Once he had gained the Freedom of a Company and thereby had become a Citizen of London, he was at liberty to work within the city boundaries at any craft or trade of his choice. However, throughout the eighteenth century, the city Companies found it increasingly difficult to enforce this regulation and, by the early nineteenth century, membership of one of the city Companies was optional rather than a necessity in order to trade within the city boundaries. Hence, many esteemed city goldsmiths and silversmiths included in this book were not Freemen of a city Company or Citizens of London.

In the biographical notes within the main body of this book, the trades of individuals, if known, are stated in brackets. Where the stated trade commences with a capital letter, it indicates that the person so named was a Freeman of that particular Company. Where the word 'Citizen' is included in brackets, it indicates that the person so named was a Freeman of the City of London. Thus, Francis Lambert (No. 2) (silversmith, Citizen and

Goldsmith) indicates that he traded as a silversmith, was a Citizen of London and was a Freeman of the Goldsmiths' Company.

Assaying

Then, as now, all articles of silver were required to be sent to the Assay Office for testing to ensure that the correct standard of silver had been used. The minimum standard, known today as Stirling Standard, was 92.5 per cent pure, i.e. 925 parts of pure silver in every 1,000. An alternative higher standard, called Britannia Standard, was also acceptable, but was used only occasionally. This was 95.84 per cent pure, i.e. 958.4 parts of pure silver in every 1,000.

In order to test the standard of silver used, scrapings were removed from the submitted article, weighed, wrapped in lead foil and then heated in a small cup called a cupel. This cupel, being made of bone ash, absorbed all the alloy metals leaving a residue of pure silver. The residue was weighed and the result compared with the weight of the original scrapings. If the difference was more than a certain amount, it meant that the silver used was below standard, and consequently the article was rejected. Thus procedure has now been superseded by the more accurate volumetric method, whereby the silver is assayed by titration with either chloride or thiocyanate solution.

In the Goldsmiths' Company, each assay year ran from 19 May (St Dunstan's Day) to 18 May of the following year. This meant that with each May a new date letter was introduced for the coming year which partially spanned two normal calendar years. This procedure continued to apply until the end of 1974, except that for some years prior to 1974 the changeover was variable, simply occurring at a convenient date in mid-May. From 1 January 1975 the changeover was standardised for all Assay Offices. It now occurs on 1 January of each year.

Makers and their Marks

George William Adams

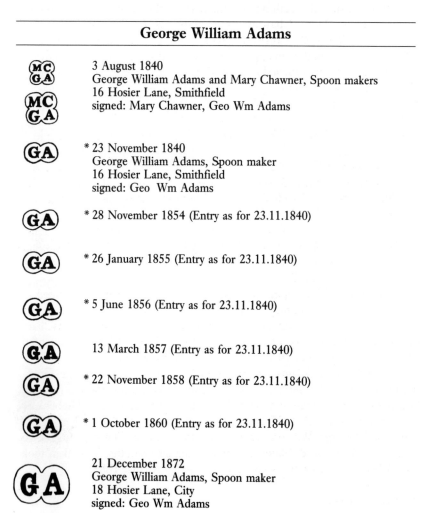

3 August 1840
George William Adams and Mary Chawner, Spoon makers
16 Hosier Lane, Smithfield
signed: Mary Chawner, Geo Wm Adams

* 23 November 1840
George William Adams, Spoon maker
16 Hosier Lane, Smithfield
signed: Geo Wm Adams

* 28 November 1854 (Entry as for 23.11.1840)

* 26 January 1855 (Entry as for 23.11.1840)

* 5 June 1856 (Entry as for 23.11.1840)

13 March 1857 (Entry as for 23.11.1840)

* 22 November 1858 (Entry as for 23.11.1840)

* 1 October 1860 (Entry as for 23.11.1840)

21 December 1872
George William Adams, Spoon maker
18 Hosier Lane, City
signed: Geo Wm Adams

* 26 May 1873 (Entry as for 21.12.1872)

* 17 August 1877 (Entry as for 21.12.1872)

* 21 November 1881 (Entry as for 21.12.1872)

This firm was the continuation of that previously run by William Chawner (No. 2). Following his death on 20 March 1834, the business was continued by his widow, Mary Chawner (see *Marks of London Goldsmiths and Silversmiths c.1697–1837*, revised edition 1988, p. 71). Their son, William Chawner (No. 3), had been apprenticed to his father in 1831 but, following his father's death, was turned over to Mary to complete his apprenticeship. He obtained his freedom in 1838 but there is no record of him having assumed a position of responsibility within the firm.

In 1840 Mary Chawner entered into partnership with her son-in-law, George William Adams. They registered their joint marks at Goldsmiths' Hall on 3 August but within four months these marks were superseded by the registration of G. W. Adams' own mark at Goldsmiths' Hall. However, since the London street directory for 1844 still recorded the firm as 'Mrs M. Chawner & Co., 16 Hosier Lane, Smithfield', it seems likely that she was still a partner, if only with a financial interest in the firm.

George William Adams was born on 12 September 1808. He obtained his freedom of the Clockmakers' Company in 1829, was elected a member of the Court of Assistants in 1854 and twice became Master of the Company. He died on 27 November 1895.

On 4 April 1855 his son, William Herbert Adams, was apprenticed to William Ledger (silversmith, Citizen and Goldsmith) of 16 Hosier Lane. This was the business address of Chawner & Co., so presumably William Ledger was an employee of the firm. George William Adams's residential address at the time was 10 Royal Crescent, Notting Hill.

William Herbert Adams eventually took up his freedom of the Goldsmiths' Company by Service on 4 December 1872, a few days before the firm registered a change of address from 16 to 18 Hosier Lane. He became a Liveryman in March 1877 and died on 21 January 1910.

In 1883 George William Adams sold the firm of Chawner & Co. to Holland, Aldwinckle & Slater, manufacturing silversmiths. This firm took over Adams' premises at 18 Hosier Lane on 13 August 1883.

*Mark entered in two sizes.

James Aitchison

JA ** 18 October 1877
James Aitchison, Gold worker
23 Princes Street, Edinburgh
residence: 15 Queens Crescent, Newington, Edinburgh

JA ** 16 November 1897
James Aitchison, Gold and Silver worker
80 Princes Street, Edinburgh
residence: 7 Regent Terrace, Edinburgh

JA * 10 May 1898

JA * 14 May 1901

JA ** 27 January 1902 (Entry as for 16.11.1897)

JA * 23 November 1904 James Aitchison, Gold and Silver worker
80 Princes Street, Edinburgh
residence: 7 Regent Terrace, Edinburgh
partner: James Aitchison

Although James Aitchison was a Scottish silversmith, presumably he had his marks registered at Goldsmiths' Hall, London, because of his continuous supplying of silverware to the London market.

He seems to have specialised in manufacturing Scottish jewellery, mostly inlaid with native pebbles and cairngorm.

*Mark entered in two sizes.
**Mark entered in three sizes.

George Aldwinckle

30 August 1876
George Aldwinckle, Small worker
282 Fulham Road, Brompton, SW

15 January 1879

16 January 1889
Removed to 2 Newcastle Place, Clerkenwell
residence: 81 Lichfield Grove, Church End, Finchley, N

He was not apprenticed through the Goldsmiths' Company, nor was he a Freeman of the Company.

His brother was John Aldwinckle of Holland, Aldwinckle & Slater, manufacturing silversmiths.

John Angell & Son

19 June 1840
John (Charles) Angell (No. 2) and George Angell, Plate workers
51 Compton Street, Clerkenwell
signed: John C. Angell, George Angell

15 July 1844
John Angell (No. 3) and George Angell, Plate workers
51 Compton Street, Clerkenwell
signed: John Angell, George Angell

15 January 1850
George Angell, Plate worker
51 Compton Street, Clerkenwell
signed: George Angell

14 August 1861 (Entry as for 15.1.1850)

10 September 1875 (Entry as for 15.1.1850)

(Marks) Defaced 2.10.1884

This firm was taken over by Frederick Courthope who entered his own mark on 2 October 1884.

John Charles Angell (No. 2) and George Angell were sons of John Angell (No. 1), goldsmith. John Angell (No. 1) had been in partnership with his brother, Joseph Angell (No. 1) at 55 Compton Street since 1831 (see *Marks of London Goldsmiths and Silversmiths c.1697–1837*, revised edition 1988, pp. 28–9). Then, in 1840, Joseph Angell (No. 1) entered a new mark from 55 Compton Street in partnership with his own son, Joseph Angell (No. 2). Meanwhile, John Charles Angell (No. 2) and George Angell, the two sons of John Angell (No. 1), entered their first partnership mark from 51 Compton Street.

John Charles Angell (No. 2) was apprenticed to his father, John Angell (No. 1), on 5 October 1825 and obtained his freedom by Service on 7 November 1832. He died in the autumn of 1850.

George Angell obtained his freedom by Patrimony on 5 October 1842, was made a Liveryman in 1851 and died on 24 July 1884.

A third brother, Walter Angell, became a silverplate engraver and obtained his freedom by Patrimony on 4 December 1850.

Following the death of John Charles Angell (No. 2) in 1850, George Angell took over the firm, renaming it George Angell & Co. With the death of George Angell on 24 July 1884, the firm was taken over by Frederick Courthope.

The signatures of John C. Angell and John Angell accompanying the 1840 and 1844 entries do not appear to be by the same hand. Because of this, the latter signature has been referred to as John Angell (No. 3), although the existence of another John Angell within the firm at this time has yet to be verified.

Joseph Angell (No. 2)

6 July 1840
Joseph Angell (No. 1) and Joseph Angell (No. 2), Plate workers
55 Compton Street, Clerkenwell

Removed to 25 Panton Street, Haymarket, 13 October 1842

20 October 1849
Joseph Angell (No. 2), Plate worker
10 Strand, London
manufactory: 25 Panton Street, Haymarket

Joseph Angell (No. 2) was the son of Joseph Angell (No. 1), a goldsmith with his own business, working from 55 Compton Street (see *Marks of London Goldsmiths and Silversmiths c.1697–1837*, revised edition 1988, pp. 28–9).

Joseph Angell (No. 2) was born in 1815 and obtained his freedom of the Goldsmiths' Company by Patrimony on 3 February 1836. His first mark, in partnership with his father, was entered at Goldsmiths' Hall in July 1840, although it is likely that he had been working with his father for some time prior to this date. He was made a Liveryman on 20 April 1842 and died on 13 September 1891.

He had two sons who became Freemen of the Goldsmiths' Company: Edmund Frank Angell and Robert Angell. Edmund F. Angell became a goldsmith, obtaining his freedom by Patrimony on 3 December 1873. He was elected a Liveryman on 21 March 1877 and died on 23 February 1892. Robert Angell became an architect, obtaining his freedom by Patrimony on 7 December 1904.

The firm's premises at 25 Panton Street had previously been occupied by Wakelin & Taylor, James Crespel, Robert Garrard (No. 1) and Robert Garrard (No. 2) before being leased to Joseph Angell. Joseph Angell (No. 2) eventually purchased the premises in 1856 for £1,050 (see Culme, *Directory of Gold & Silversmiths, Jewellers & Allied Traders 1838–1914*, vol. 1, p. 12, col 3).

20 March 1855
Charles Asprey (No. 1), Small worker
166 New Bond Street

5 February 1876
Charles Asprey (No. 1) and Charles Asprey (No. 2), Small
workers
166 New Bond Street and 22 Albemarle Street
C. Asprey (No. 1)'s residence: Beechlands, Caterham, Surrey
C. Asprey (No. 2)'s residence: Wendy Lodge, Putney

31 October 1879 (Entry as for 5.2.1876)

* 20 February 1891
Charles Asprey (No. 2) and George Asprey, Small workers
166 New Bond Street and 22 Albemarle Street
C. Asprey (No. 2)'s residence: Beechlands, Caterham, Surrey
G. Asprey's residence: Lancaster Lodge, Amersham Road, Putney

9 March 1891 (Entry as for 20.2.1891)

17 July 1896 (Entry as for 20.2.1891)

13 February 1900 (Entry as for 20.2.1891)
manufactory: 8 Sherwood Street, W

20 February 1900 Charles Asprey (No. 2) and George Asprey,
Gold and Silver workers
166 New Bond Street and 22 Albemarle Street
manufactory: 8 Sherwood Street, W
C. Asprey (No. 2)'s residence: Beechlands, Caterham, Surrey
G. Asprey's residence: Court Lodge, Chelsfield, Kent

13 November 1900
Charles Asprey (No. 2) and George Asprey, Gold and Silver
workers
166 New Bond Street and 22 Albemarle Street

manufactory: 8 Sherwood Street, W
C. Asprey (No. 2)'s residence: Beechlands, Caterham, Surrey
G. Asprey's residence: Lancaster Lodge, Amersham Road, Putney

(CA·GA) * 4 April 1901 (Entry as for 13.11.1900)

(CA·GA)

Removed to 19 and 21 Heddon Street, Regent Street, W, 10
April 1902

(CA·GA) 7 May 1902
Charles Asprey (No. 2) and George Asprey, Gold and Silver
workers
166 New Bond Street and 22 Albemarle Street
19 & 21 Heddon Street, Regent Street
C. Asprey (No. 2)' residence: Beechlands, Caterham, Surrey
G. Asprey's residence: Court Lodge, Chelsfield, Kent

(CA·GA) 10 June 1903 (Entry as for 7.5.1902)

(CA·GA)

(CAGA) 18 September 1907
C. and G. Asprey, Gold and Silver workers
166 New Bond Street and 22 Albemarle Street
19 & 21 Heddon Street, London, W
residences: Beechlands, Caterham, Surrey
Court Lodge, Chelsfield, Kent
partners: Charles Asprey (No. 2), George Asprey

[A&C°LT᪲] 1 November 1909
Asprey & Co. Ltd, Gold and Silver workers
163–167 New Bond Street and 22 Albemarle Street, W
[A&C°LT᪲] 6 Bird Street, Oxford Street, W
G. K. Asprey's residence: West Lodge, Pinner
chairman: George Edward Asprey
directors: Lionel C. Asprey, George K. Asprey, Arthur W.
Hilling

Charles Asprey (No. 1) was born in 1813. *Circa* 1840 he entered into
partnership with Francis Kennedy, a stationer and dressing-case manufacturer. This partnership was dissolved in 1843, following which Charles
Asprey (No. 1) set up on his own as a stationer, dressing- and travelling-
case manufacturer, cutler and card-plate and seal engraver.

19

When his son, Charles Asprey (No. 2), joined him in partnership, *circa* 1872, the firm was renamed Charles Asprey & Son. Later his other son, George Edward Asprey, joined the partnership and the firm was then renamed Asprey & Sons. Charles Asprey (No. 2) was born in 1845 and George Edward Asprey in 1851.

The firm's first mark for use on gold and silverware was entered at Goldsmiths' Hall by Charles Asprey (No. 1) in 1855. This mark was not replaced until 1876 when Charles Asprey (No. 1) and Charles Asprey (No. 2) entered a partnership mark.

In 1891 the two brothers, Charles Asprey (No. 2) and George Edward Asprey, entered their own partnership mark. Presumably this was due to Charles Asprey (No. 1) having retired. He died in 1892.

Charles Asprey (No. 2) retired as senior partner in 1909 and died in 1916. George Edward Asprey became chairman in 1909 and died in 1918.

Both brothers had sons who became partners in the firm. Charles Asprey (No. 2)'s son, Lionel Charles Asprey, was born in 1874 and became a director in 1909. He retired in 1922 and died in 1943.

George Kenneth Asprey, the son of George Edward Asprey by his first marriage, was born in 1880 and became a partner in 1909. He was made chairman in 1922 and died in 1947.

George Edward Asprey's two sons by his second marriage were Philip Rolls Asprey and Eric Arthur Rolls Asprey. Philip, born in 1894, became a director *circa* 1922, while Eric, born in 1902, became one *circa* 1927. Both obtained their freedom of the Goldsmiths' Company by Redemption on 18 June 1947.

In 1902 Arthur W. Hilling, an employee of the firm, was taken into the partnership and became a director in 1909. He was born in 1851 and died in 1937. His son, Julian Hilling, became a director *circa* 1922.

*Mark entered in two sizes.

Atkin Brothers

---

 4 November 1843
Henry Atkin, Spoon maker
32 Howard Street, Sheffield

 9 March 1859
Harry Wright Atkin, Plate worker
39 Ely Place, Holborn (London)
manufactory: Matilda Street, Sheffield

18 July 1883
Removed to 11 Charterhouse Street

** 4 July 1884

3 March 1887

29 June 1892

8 March 1894

This worker having died, the next entry is that of his son Harry Atkin

* 23 March 1905
Atkin Brothers, Silver workers
Truro Works, Matilda Street, Sheffield
11 Charterhouse Street, London, EC
Harry Atkin's residence: Muswell Lodge, Brincliffe Crescent, Sheffield
partners: Edward Atkin, Edward T. Atkin, Oliver Atkin, Harry Atkin

* 19 May 1905 (Entry as for 23.3.1905)

9 June 1909
Atkin Brothers, Silver workers
Truro Works, Sheffield
11 Charterhouse Street, London, EC
Harry Atkin's residence: Muswell Lodge, Brincliffe Crescent, Sheffield
partner: Harry Atkin

Circa 1841 Henry Atkin dissolved his partnership with John Oxley and commenced trading in Sheffield under the name of Henry Atkin & Co. He entered his first mark at the Sheffield Assay Office on 22 March 1841. Following his death in 1853, his three sons, Harry Wright Atkin, Edward Thomas Atkin and Frank Shaw Atkin, took over the firm, renaming it Atkin Brothers.

Harry Wright Atkin subsequently moved to London where he ran the firm's London retail outlet. He died in May 1896 leaving a widow and five sons, including Edward and Harry Atkin who later became partners in the firm.

Frank Shaw Atkin died in May 1901. This left his son, Frank Atkin, together with Edward Thomas Atkin and the two nephews, Edward and Harry Atkin, to continue running the firm.

Frank Atkin left the partnership in 1902 and died in 1925. Edward Thomas Atkin retired in 1906 and died in October 1907, while Edward and Harry Atkin died in 1935 and 1940 respectively.

In 1925 the firm was converted into a limited liability company, trading as Atkin Brothers (Silversmiths) Ltd. It was acquired by C. J. Vander Ltd, manufacturing silversmiths of London and Sheffield, in 1958.

*Mark entered in two sizes.
**Mark entered in three sizes.

Ball & Macaire

R·B GM	31 December 1806 Richard (John) Ball and Gideon (Paul) Macaire, Case makers 6 St James Street, Clerkenwell

Removed to 33 Rosoman Street, Clerkenwell, 11 January 1809

RB GM	* 21 November 1812

Removed to 32 Northampton Square, Clerkenwell, 6 June 1814

R B G M	24 July 1818

Removed to 17 Myddleton Street, 4 June 1821

R B GM	* 25 February 1829 Richard (John) Ball and Gideon (Paul) Macaire, Case makers 17 Myddleton Street, Clerkenwell
RB G·M	* 31 October 1833 Richard (John) Ball and Gideon (Paul) Macaire, Gold case makers 26 Myddleton Street, Clerkenwell
RB GM	22 December 1840
RB GM	17 April 1847 Richard (John) Ball and Gideon (Paul) Macaire, Case makers 25 & 26 Myddleton Street, Clerkenwell 31 Sudeley Street, Islington
R B GM RB	3 June 1853 Richard (John) Ball, Gideon (Paul) Macaire and Richard (Macaire) Ball, Case makers 25 & 26 Myddleton Street, Clerkenwell 31 Sudeley Street, Islington

Richard John Ball and his partner, Gideon Paul Macaire, entered their first partnership mark at Goldsmiths' Hall in December 1806, trading as Ball & Macaire, watch-case makers. In 1853 they were joined by Richard Macaire Ball. He was probably the son of Richard John Ball and, in view of his second Christian name being Macaire, it is likely that he was the godson of Gideon Paul Macaire.

In June 1854 their partnership was dissolved, possibly as a result of the retirement or death of Richard John Ball. Richard Macaire Ball then continued in business under his own name at 31 Sudely Street, entering his mark at Goldsmiths' Hall on 13 July 1854 (see Richard Macaire Ball).

Meanwhile, Gideon Paul Macaire continued working under his own name from 26 Myddleton Street, entering his mark at Goldsmiths' Hall on 11 July 1854 (see Gideon Paul Macaire). His final mark was entered in partnership with Hunter Charles Dewar on 8 July 1867.

Following Gideon Paul Macaire's death in April 1871, Hunter Charles Dewar continued working at 26 Myddleton Street, entering his own mark on 18 August 1871.

*Mark entered in two sizes.

Richard Macaire Ball

RB GM RB	3 June 1853 Richard (John) Ball, Gideon (Paul) Macaire and Richard (Macaire) Ball, Case makers 25 & 26 Myddleton Street, Clerkenwell 31 Sudeley Street, Islington
RB	13 July 1854 Richard Macaire Ball, Case maker 31 Sudeley Street, Nelson Terrace, City Road
RB	9 March 1876
RB	27 November 1886

Richard Macaire Ball was probably the son of Richard John Ball. In 1853 he joined the partnership of Richard John Ball and Gideon Paul Macaire, watch-case makers, trading under the name of Ball & Macaire (see Ball & Macaire). This triple partnership was dissolved in June 1854, possibly due to the retirement or death of Richard John Ball. Richard Macaire Ball then continued in business on his own at 31 Sudeley Street, while Gideon Paul Macaire continued to trade from 26 Myddleton Street.

J. M. Banks & Co.

JMB * 8 January 1891
John Millward Banks, Plate worker
6 Northampton Street, Birmingham
residence: Heathfield Road, Birmingham

J.M.B 4 January 1895

J.M.B 20 May 1897

J·M·B 3 September 1903
J. M. Banks & Co., Gold and Silver worker
12 & 14 Beak Street, Regent Street, London, W
6 & 7 Northampton Street, Birmingham
partner: John Millward Banks

This entry was cancelled June 1904

J.M.B * 7 January 1905
John Millward Banks & Co., Gold and Silver worker
12 & 14 Beak Street, Regent Street, London, W
6 & 7 Northampton Street, Birmingham
residence: 50 Carpenter Road, Edgbaston, Birmingham
partner: John Millward Banks

John Millward Banks built up a considerable business as a manufacturing goldsmith, silversmith and diamond mounter, specialising in jewellery and small articles of gold and silverware. Although based at Birmingham, he entered marks at both the Chester and Sheffield Assay Offices as well as Goldsmiths' Hall, London.

When J. M. Banks died in February 1911, the firm was continued by his son, Francis M. Banks, until *circa* 1925 when it closed down with its stock, plant, etc. being sold by auction.

Occasionally the firm's silverware was struck with the mark of a flower in an oval surround in addition to the usual hallmarks.

 Taken from a card case by J. M. Banks, hallmarked, Chester 1898.
The reason for this mark is unknown.
It may have been a trade mark.

*Mark entered in two sizes.

[J.B]

[J.B]

13 October 1862
Jes Barkentin, Gold and Silver worker
manufactory: 23 Berners Street, W
residence: 3 St Pauls Villas, St Pauls Road, Camden Town

Removed to 291 Regent Street, 25 November 1865

[J.B]

*5 September 1873
Jes Barkentin
manufactory: 24 Berners Mews, Oxford Street

[C.K]

28 November 1883
Carl (Christof) Krall, Plate worker
289–291 Regent Street
residence: 14 Eaton Villas, Haverstock Hill, NW

[C.K]

20 October 1890
Carl (Christof) Krall

[C:K]

24 July 1902
Carl (Christof) Krall, Plate worker
289–291 Regent Street, W

Neither Jes Barkentin nor Carl Christof Krall became Freemen of the Goldsmiths' Company.

Jes Barkentin, a Danish immigrant, was born *circa* 1800 and died in 1883. In 1865 he was in partnership with George Slater trading as Barkentin & Slater, goldsmiths, but this partnership appears to have been dissolved *circa* 1867.

Carl Christof Krall, a Czech immigrant, joined Jes Barkentin *circa* 1868 and subsequently took over the running of the business following Jes Barkentin's death in 1883. Carl Christof Krall died in 1923 aged 79 years and the firm ceased trading *circa* 1933.

The firm produced a considerable amount of ecclesiastical silverware from the designs of various designers of the day, including the architect, William Burgess (b. 1827, d. 1881). In 1867 the firm was appointed manufacturer to the Ecclesiological Society as part of its scheme for the manufacture of church plate. At the time, William Burgess was super-intendent of the Society's scheme. However, although the Society was disbanded the following year, William Burgess continued to design articles for Barkentin & Krall to manufacture.

The firm also made the Milton 'Paradise Lost' shield in Westminster

Abbey and the Wanamaker gold and silver altar plate at Sandringham Church.

In the 1920s, Walter Stoye, managing director of the firm and former apprentice of Carl Christof Krall, designed an altar crucifix and two candlesticks, now held in the Goldsmiths' Company collection of plate.

*Mark entered in two sizes.

Edward Barnard & Sons

** 25 February 1829
Edward (No. 1), Edward (No. 2), John (No. 1) and William Barnard, Plate workers
Amen Corner

Removed to Angel Street, St Martins-le-Grand, 18 June 1838

*** 7 December 1846
Edward (No. 2), John (No. 1) and William Barnard, Plate workers
Angel Street, St Martins-le-Grand
residences: John (No. 1): 8 Cross Street, Islington
William; 23 Great Percy Street, Lloyd Square

** 4 November 1851
Edward (No. 2) and John Barnard (No. 1), Plate workers
Angel Street, St Martins-le-Grand
residence: John (No. 1); 8 Cross Street, Islington

* 15 May 1861 (Entry as for 4.11.1851)

† 9 June 1868
John (No. 1), Edward (No. 3), Walter and John Barnard (No. 2), Plate workers
manufactory: Angel Street, St Martins-le-Grand
residences: John (No. 1): 12 Compton Terrace, Islington
Edward (No. 3): 10 King Edward Street, City
Walter: Marquis Grove, Marquis Road, Lower Road, Islington
John (No. 2): Eleanor Villas, Tollington Park

2 June 1874 (Entry as for 9.6.1868)

†† 9 April 1877
Walter and John Barnard (No. 2), Plate workers
manufactory: Angel Street, St Martins-le-Grand
residences: Walter: 8 Cannonbury Place, N
John (No. 2): 20 Drayton Park, Highbury, N

10 July 1882 (Entry as for 9.4.1877)

†† 22 June 1896
Barnard, Plate workers
Angel Street, St Martins-le-Grand
residences: Stanley: 12 Ribblesdale Road, Hornsey
Walter: 60 Leigh Road, Highbury
John (No. 2) and/or Michael Barnard and/or Robert Dubock: 43
Baelbeck Road, Highbury
72 Onslow Gardens, Highgate
21 Stoke Newington Common

†† 17 August 1903
Edward Barnard & Sons
Walter, John (No. 2),
Michael and Stanley Barnard, Plate workers
22–24 Fetter Lane, Holborn, EC
residence: Walter: 60 Leigh Road, Highbury

*** 3 March 1910
Edward Barnard & Sons Ltd, Gold and Silver workers
22–24 Fetter Lane, Holborn, EC
residence: Stanley: 12 Ribblesdale Road, Hornsey
directors: Walter Barnard, John Barnard (No. 2), Michael
Barnard, Stanley Barnard
secretary: Stanley Barnard

14 April 1910 (Entry as for 3.3.1910)

14 August 1913
Edward Barnard & Sons Ltd, Gold and Silver workers
22 Fetter Lane, London, EC
residence: Michael: 12 Thyra Grove, North Finchley
directors: Walter Barnard, John Barnard (No. 2), Michael
Barnard, Stanley Barnard, George Joynes[1]

28 November 1913 One new punch

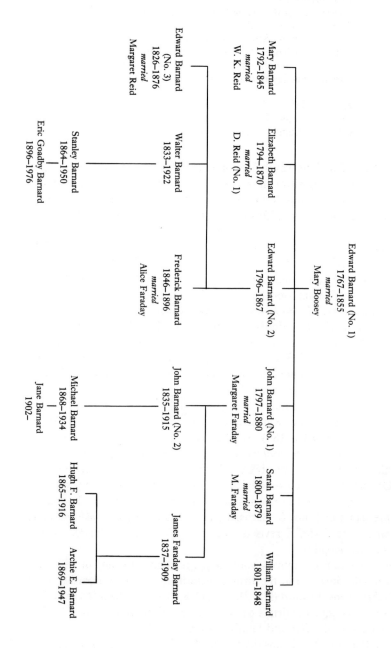

Edward Barnard (No. 1)
1767–1855
married
Mary Boosey

Mary Barnard
1792–1845
married
W. K. Reid

Elizabeth Barnard
1794–1870
married
D. Reid (No. 1)

Edward Barnard (No. 2)
1796–1867

John Barnard (No. 1)
1797–1880
married
Margaret Faraday

Sarah Barnard
1800–1879
married
M. Faraday

William Barnard
1801–1848

Edward Barnard
(No. 3)
1826–1876
married
Margaret Reid

Walter Barnard
1833–1922

Frederick Barnard
1846–1896
married
Alice Faraday

John Barnard (No. 2)
1835–1915

James Faraday Barnard
1837–1909

Stanley Barnard
1864–1950

Eric Goadby Barnard
1896–1976

Michael Barnard
1868–1934

Jane Barnard
1902–

Hugh F. Barnard
1865–1916

Archie E. Barnard
1869–1947

28

* 17 February 1914
Edward Barnard & Sons Ltd, Gold and Silver workers
22 Fetter Lane, London, EC
33 Northampton Street, Birmingham
residence: Michael: 12 Thyra Grove, North Finchley
directors: Walter Barnard, John Barnard (No. 2), Michael
Barnard, Stanley Barnard, George Joynes

25 May 1920
Removed to 54 Hatton Garden, London, EC
residence: Stanley: 8 Barrington Road, Hornsey

Edward Barnard & Sons was the continuation of an already well-established firm of manufacturing silversmiths previously owned by Thomas, William and Henry Chawner and John Emes respectively (see *Marks of London Goldsmiths and Silversmiths c.1697–1837*, revised edition 1988, p. 70, 72, 73, 122).

Thomas Chawner and his brother, William, founded the firm *circa* 1763. Their partnership remained in existence until 1773, following which Thomas Chawner continued working on his own at 60 Paternoster Row. In 1783 he apparently took over the silversmithing business of Charles Wright together with Wright's premises at 9 Ave Maria Lane. Then, in 1786, Thomas Chawner's son, Henry, assumed control of the firm and subsequently took John Emes, an engraver, into partnership in 1796. Henry Chawner retired *circa* 1798, leaving John Emes to continue running the firm. However, Henry Chawner still retained a financial interest by leaving monies invested in the business.

When John Emes died intestate in June 1808, Letters of Administration were granted to his widow, Rebecca, and his brother, William Emes (Public Record Office, PROB/6/184). At the same time, Rebecca and William Emes entered into a temporary partnership, registering their mark at Goldsmiths' Hall on 30 June 1808. This mark was subsequently cancelled on 14 October 1808 when she registered a new one in partnership with her leading journeyman and works manager, Edward Barnard (No. 1), trading under the name of Emes & Barnard (see *Marks of London Goldsmiths and Silversmiths c. 1697–1837*, revised edition 1988, p. 35, for marks entered under this partnership).

When Rebecca Emes retired from the partnership at the end of 1828, she still left monies invested in the firm. Meanwhile, Edward Barnard (No. 1) took his three sons, Edward (No. 2), John (No. 1) and William Barnard, into partnership, changing the firm's name to Edward Barnard & Sons. The firm then remained in the Barnard family until it was sold in 1974.

Edward Barnard (No. 1) was the son of Mary (née Gastineau) and Edward

Barnard (silver flatter) of Aldersgate, London. He was born on 30 November 1767, apprenticed to Charles Wright (goldsmith, Citizen and Goldsmith) on 5 December 1781 and, following Wright's retirement, turned over to Thomas Chawner (goldsmith, Citizen and Goldsmith) on 4 February 1784. He obtained his freedom of the Goldsmiths' Company by Service on 4 February 1789 and was made a Liveryman on 14 June 1811.

On 18 January 1791 he married Mary Boosey, a cousin of William Boosey who founded the firm of music publishers, Boosey & Hawkes. Mary and Edward Barnard (No. 1) had ten children: Mary, Elizabeth, Edward (No. 2), John (No. 1), Sarah, William, Jane, Charlotte, George and Thomas.

At some date prior to April 1842, Edward Barnard (No. 1) retired from the firm, leaving his three sons, Edward (No. 2), John (No. 1) and William to continue running the business. Edward (No. 1) died on 4 January 1855 when over 87 years old. His wife, Mary, died on 12 January 1847. Of their five daughters, Mary, Elizabeth and Sarah are notable for their marriages.

Mary Barnard was born on 25 April 1792 and married William Ker Reid, a London silversmith, on 11 February 1812. He was the son of Christian Ker Reid, the well-known Newcastle upon Tyne silversmith. Mary and William Ker Reid had thirteen children, including Edward Ker Reid who became a silversmith and subsequently married Anna, the daughter of John Barnard (No. 1). Mary died on 24 October 1845 but her husband, William Ker Reid, did not die until 1 February 1868.

Elizabeth Barnard, born on 4 May 1794, married William Ker Reid's brother, David Reid (No. 1) on 26 August 1815. He was a silversmith working in his father's firm at Newcastle upon Tyne. Elizabeth and David (No. 1) had ten children, including Christian John Reid who became a silversmith and, in 1868, senior partner in the family firm at Newcastle. Elizabeth died on 8 June 1870 and David Reid (No. 1) on 7 February 1868, only six days after the death of his brother, William Ker Reid.

Sarah Barnard, born on 7 January 1800, married the scientist, Michael Faraday, on 12 June 1821. Unfortunately, although very keen on children, they were unable to have any of their own. Instead, they helped to raise Margaret Reid who was one of their nieces. Most of their married life was spent living in rooms at the Royal Institution where Michael worked. He was made Director of the Laboratory in 1825, and from 1826 onwards spent all his time on original research. He first produced induced electricity in August 1831 and a steady current of electricity through magnetism in October 1831. Due to overwork he suffered a mental breakdown in 1840, following which he took two years to return to a reasonable state of health. In 1858, in recognition of his scientific work, Queen Victoria granted him a 'grace and favour' house on Hampton Court Green.

Gradually Michael Faraday's health deteriorated, so Jane Barnard, another niece, came to live with the Faradays and help care for him. Michael died on 25 August 1867 and his wife, Sarah, on 6 January 1879.

Returning to Edward Barnard (No. 1)'s five sons, Thomas, the youngest, died when 17 months old and George, born on 11 March 1807, became a landscape artist and art master at Rugby School. He exhibited his watercolours at the Royal Academy and the British Institution, and illustrated W. B. Cooke's *Richmond and its Surrounding Scenery*. Also, he was the author of several books: *Switzerland, Scenes and Incidents of Travel in the Bernese Oberland; Theory and Practice in Landscape Painting; Handbook of Foreground Painting; Drawing from Nature* and *Trees in Nature*. On 2 April 1828 he obtained his freedom of the Goldsmiths' Company by Patrimony, and in February 1831 he was made a Liveryman. He married Emma Hillhouse on 16 April 1840 and died on 29 September 1890.

Edward Barnard (No. 2), born on 1 February 1796, was apprenticed to his father, Edward Barnard (No. 1), on 7 February 1810. He obtained his freedom of the Goldsmiths' Company by Service on 5 March 1817 and was made a Liveryman on 23 January 1822. On 26 September 1822 he married Caroline Chater, by whom he had twelve children. These included Edward (No. 3) and Walter, both of whom became silversmiths and subsequently partners in the family firm, and Frederick[2] who became a black-and-white illustrator of *Punch, The Illustrated London News* and Charles Dickens' books. Edward Barnard (No. 2) died on 26 December 1867.

John Barnard (No. 1) was born on 11 December 1797 and apprenticed to his father, Edward Barnard (No. 1), on 1 January 1812. He obtained his freedom of the Goldsmiths' Company by Service on 6 January 1819 and was made a Liveryman on 23 February 1831. On 14 March 1826 he married his sister-in-law, Margaret Faraday. She was the sister of Michael Faraday the scientist. Margaret and John (No. 1) had fourteen children, including John (No. 2) who became a silversmith and future partner in the firm of Edward Barnard & Sons, and James Faraday[3] who became an engraver and founded his own engraving firm, later known as James F. Barnard & Son. John Barnard (No. 1) retired at some date prior to 1877 and subsequently died on 1 December 1880. His wife, Margaret, died on 7 June 1910.

William Barnard, born on 26 June 1801, was apprenticed to his father, Edward Barnard (No. 1), on 5 July 1815 and obtained his freedom of the Goldsmiths' Company by Service on 5 February 1823. On 24 October 1832 he married Martha Lyon, by whom he had three children. He died on 20 October 1848 when only 47 years old.

The next generation of Barnards to become partners in the family firm were Edward Barnard (No. 1)'s grandsons, Edward Barnard (No. 3), Walter Barnard and John Barnard (No. 2).

Edward Barnard (No. 3), born on 23 June 1826, was the son of Edward Barnard (No. 2). He obtained his freedom of the Goldsmiths' Company by Patrimony on 5 July 1848 and was made a Liveryman on 28 March 1855. On 5 July 1853 he married Margaret Reid, daughter of the silversmith David Reid (No. 1), his uncle by marriage. They had only one child, Sarah, who remained a spinster. Edward Barnard (No. 3) died in tragic circumstances on 14 August 1876. While on holiday in the Lake District, he became lost on the Cumbrian mountains and, although his relatives made every effort to find him alive, they found his body only after a prolonged search.

Walter Barnard, born on 7 May 1833, was another son of Edward Barnard (No. 2). He obtained his freedom of the Goldsmiths' Company by Patrimony on 13 December 1854 and was made a Liveryman on 20 December 1865. On 12 July 1859 he married Ellen Rutt, by whom he had nine children, including Stanley who became manager and later partner in the firm. Walter Barnard's name was listed as a partner for the first time when the firm's mark was registered in 1868. He eventually died on 25 September 1922 when over 89 years old.

John Barnard (No. 2), born on 29 June 1835, was the son of John Barnard (No. 1). He was apprenticed to his father on 3 October 1849, obtained his freedom of the Goldsmiths' Company by Service on 3 December 1856 and was made a Liveryman on 20 December 1865. On 25 July 1860 he married Fanny Proctor, but she died on 17 November 1869, only forty-three days after the birth of their fifth child. On 9 April 1875 he married Ruth Blaikley who gave him a further three children. John Barnard (No. 2) died on 27 January 1915. One of his children by his first marriage was Michael who became a silversmith and, later, a partner in the firm.

Michael Barnard, a great-grandson of Edward Barnard (No. 1), was born on 28 January 1868 and obtained his freedom of the Goldsmiths' Company by Patrimony on 6 April 1892. On 24 June 1896 he married Alice Louise Miller, but of their eleven children, only Jane, born on 13 August 1902, worked within the firm. This was in the capacity of artist, designer and modeller from 1923 to 1938 when she retired. She was 35 years old when she married Dennis Quinton Sandeman on 9 October 1937. Meanwhile, with the death of Michael Barnard on 10 March 1934, this branch of the family disappeared from the firm's partnership.

The other great-grandson to become a partner was Stanley Barnard, the son of Walter Barnard. Stanley was born on 6 May 1864, obtained his freedom of the Goldsmiths' Company by Patrimony on 3 January 1894 and was made a Liveryman on 12 April 1905. On 20 June 1895 he married

Agnes Ethel Goadby. They had only two children, a stillborn daughter and Eric Goadby who became a silversmith and partner in the firm. Agnes died on 21 March 1907 when only 38 years old. Eventually Stanley Barnard was remarried, on 4 September 1919, to Mrs Rosa Edith Besley (née Lee). Stanley Barnard died on 7 February 1950.

Eric Goadby Barnard, Stanley's son and the great-great-grandson of Edward Barnard (No. 1), was born on 10 June 1896. He was apprenticed to his father on 5 March 1913 and obtained his freedom of the Goldsmiths' Company by Service on 5 December 1917. By 1933 he had joined the firm's board of directors, and in January 1938 he was made a Liveryman. On 2 April 1921 he married Gladys Lucy Besley, the daughter of his stepmother by her previous marriage. They had no children. Following his wife's death in 1960, he married Gracie Bent on 11 August 1961.

In 1967 he retired, and then, in 1974, he and other members of the Barnard family sold their controlling financial interest in the business to an American firm which, in 1977, sold Edward Barnard & Sons Ltd to Padgett & Braham Ltd, a London firm of manufacturing silversmiths. Eric Goadby, the last of the silversmithing Barnards, died on 14 May 1976 aged 79 years.

1. George Joynes joined the firm in 1860 and subsequently became one of its travellers. He was made a director in 1913 and died in 1915.

George William Joynes, the son of George Joynes of 10 Jenner Road, Stoke Newington, was apprenticed to Michael Barnard of Angel Street on 6 October 1897. He obtained his freedom of the Goldsmiths' Company by Service on 2 November 1904 and was made a Liveryman on 11 May 1921. In 1915 he became a director at Edward Barnard & Sons Ltd and died on 10 October 1963.

His son, George Frederick Joynes, joined Edward Barnard & Sons Ltd in 1927, was made a director in 1939 and retired in 1983. He obtained his freedom of the Goldsmiths' Company by Patrimony on 6 April 1932 and was made a Liveryman in January 1944.

2. Frederick, the son of Edward Barnard (No. 2), was born on 25 May 1846. Having definite artistic leanings, he studied at Heatherley's Art School in Newman Street and later under Léon Bonnat in Paris. He first exhibited at the Royal Academy in 1858 when only 12 years old, and then, in 1863, he made his first contribution as an illustrator to *Punch* magazine. This was followed by many more of his drawings being used to illustrate such magazines as *Good Words, Once a Week* and *The Illustrated London News*. He also illustrated an edition of Bunyan's *Pilgrim's Progress* in 1880. However, he is probably best known for his illustrations in the household

edition of the works of Charles Dickens from 1871 to 1879. These drawings are usually signed in one corner with an intertwined *FB* in script lettering. It seems that he specialised in portraying domestic scenes, many of which depicted Victorian interiors of the period in considerable detail.

On 11 August 1870 he married 23-year-old Alice Faraday (b.1.3.1847), a great-niece of Michael Faraday. Alice and Frederick Barnard had three children: Geoffrey (b.28.10.1871), Marian Alice (b.30.6.1873) and Dorothy (b.2.11.1877).

In 1885 Frederick Barnard and his family temporarily vacated their London home and moved to Broadway in the Cotswolds to join their artist friend, Edwin Austin Abbey, for the summer. Through him, they met and became firm friends of Francis Davis Millett and his family, then living in Broadway, and their guest, John Singer Sargent (1856–1925), one of the most successful portraitists of the time. Besides painting an excellent portrait of Alice Barnard, John Singer Sargent used the two Barnard daughters, Marian and Dorothy, as his models for the well-known painting *Carnation, Lily, Lily, Rose*, which he commenced in late August 1885. Set in Millett's garden at Farnham House, Broadway, the painting depicted the two girls dressed in white, lighting Chinese paper lanterns hung among the rose trees and lilies. As the twilight effect being illustrated lasted only for about ten minutes after sunset, the painting progressed very slowly. With the coming of autumn, the two Barnard girls wore vests and pullovers under their white dresses to keep out the cold, but eventually the picture had to be stored away until the following year. With the return of the Barnard family the following summer, John Singer Sargent was able to complete the painting. In the spring of 1887 he exhibited it at the Royal Academy to much acclaim, and two years later he sold it for £700 to the Chantry Bequest. It now resides in the Tate Gallery.

On 18 December 1891 Alice and Frederick Barnard's son, Geoffrey, died when only 20 years old. Then, on 17 September 1896 at the age of 50, Frederick Barnard tragically died from suffocation in a fire at a friend's house in Wimbledon.

After Frederick Barnard's death, his widow and daughters maintained their friendship with Edwin Austin Abbey, John Singer Sargent and the Millett family. From 1906 to 1914 they frequently joined John Singer Sargent on his continental summer holidays, usually taken in Austria, Switzerland or Italy.

John Singer Sargent died in his sleep on 19 April 1925, and in his will he bequeathed £5,000 to Alice Barnard, Frederick Barnard's widow.

3. James Faraday Barnard, son of John Barnard (No. 1), was born on 11 March 1837. He was apprenticed to Francis Sampson Manaton of White

& Manaton, engravers, of 27 Brooke Street, Holborn, and obtained his freedom of the Goldsmiths' Company by Patrimony on 1 December 1858. He then set up his own firm of heraldic engravers, later known as James F. Barnard & Son, which continued to trade until *circa* 1939.

On 2 June 1863 he married Elizabeth Cooper Jennings, by whom he had seven children: Edith, Hugh Faraday, Harold Leslie, Archie Evelyn, Jessie, Grace and Dorothea. Of these, Hugh Faraday and Archie Evelyn became engravers working within their father's firm.

Hugh Faraday Barnard, born on 23 October 1865, was apprenticed to his father on 5 November 1879. He obtained his freedom of the Goldsmiths' Company by Service on 2 March 1887 and died in 1916.

Archie Evelyn Barnard, born on 4 August 1869, was apprenticed to his father on 3 October 1883. He obtained his freedom of the Goldsmiths' Company by Service on 7 January 1891 and died on 8 May 1947.

Of the other children, Edith Barnard, born in 1864, was married in 1889 to Sydney Reid, grandson of the silversmith, David Reid (No. 1) of Newcastle upon Tyne, and Harold Leslie Barnard, born in 1868, became a surgeon to the London Hospital.

*Mark entered in two sizes.
**Mark entered in three sizes.
***Mark entered in four sizes.
†Mark entered in five sizes.
††Mark entered in six sizes.

Z. Barraclough & Sons

 *** 29 November 1894
James Henry Barraclough and Herbert Barraclough, Gold and Silver workers
54 Briggate, Commercial Street, Leeds

 3 October 1896

29 April 1897

** 24 October 1907
Z. Barraclough & Sons, Gold and Silver workers
54 Briggate, Leeds
H. Barraclough's residence: 6 St Mary's Road, Newton Park,
Leeds
partners: James Henry Barraclough, Herbert Barraclough

 13 July 1914
Z. Barraclough & Sons
(Entry as for 24.10.1907)

Z. Barraclough & Sons was an old-established Leeds firm of watch and clock makers, jewellers and silversmiths. The firm's mark, bearing the initials of J. H. Barraclough and H. Barraclough, was registered at the Sheffield Assay Office on 15 December 1888 under the name of Z. Barraclough & Sons of 54 Briggate, Leeds.

James Henry Barraclough died in 1917 aged 57 years, and Herbert Barraclough died in 1941 when 78 years old.

**Mark entered in three sizes.
***Mark entered in four sizes.

James Beebe

 16 August 1811
James Beebe, Spoon maker
30 Red Lion Street, Clerkenwell

(Removed to) 26 Wilderness Row, 1 October 1817

 11 September 1826

Removed to 65 Red Lion Street, Clerkenwell, 18 July 1827

 21 October 1829

 3 August 1839

6 January 1844
65 Red Lion Street, Clerkenwell

James Beebe was the son of John Beebe (brewer's servant deceased) of Compton Street, Clerkenwell, and was apprenticed to William Seaman (silversmith, Citizen and Goldsmith) of Pear Tree Street, Goswell Street, Middlesex on 4 July 1804. He obtained his freedom of the Goldsmiths' Company by Service on 7 August 1811 and appears to have ceased trading *circa* 1847.

James William Benson

7 October 1874
James William Benson, Plate worker
58 and 60 Ludgate Hill
residences: Fairlawn, Oaklands Park, Weybridge
57 Addison Road, Kensington

5 February 1880

26 July 1882

20 August 1884

* 19 January 1885

* 10 December 1885

** 1 December 1890

* 31 August 1893
James William Benson, Plate worker
62 and 64 Ludgate Hill
25 Old Bond Street
28 Royal Exchange
residence: Walton Oaks, Walton on the Hill, Epsom

Next entry under Hunt & Roskell, 25 August 1897

J.W.B

circa July 1912
James William Benson, Gold and Silver worker
62 and 64 Ludgate Hill
28 Royal Exchange, London, EC
The Registration of this Punch was not proceeded with, as a letter
was received from J. W. Benson Limited, stating their intention of
entering new Marks. (dated) 25 July 1912

J.W.B.L

15 October 1912
J. W. Benson Ltd, Gold and Silver workers
62 Ludgate Hill
28 Royal Exchange, London, EC
G. B. Whitworth's residence: The Avenue, Datchet, Near
Windsor
directors: A. W. Benson, Alfred Benson, G. B. Whitworth,
Douglas Benson
secretary: E. J. S. Mills

J.W.B.L

6 November 1912
J. W. Benson Ltd, Gold and Silver workers
62 & 64 Ludgate Hill, London, EC
28 Royal Exchange, London, EC
G. B. Whitworth's residence: 3 The Avenue, Datchet, Near
Windsor
directors: Alfred Benson, A. H. Benson, G. B. Whitworth,
Douglas Benson
secretary: E. H. Mills

James William Benson was a co-founder of the firm of S. S. & J. W. Benson,
watchmakers, gold and silversmiths, established *circa* 1847. In 1855 he and
Samuel Suckley Benson dissolved their partnership, following which J. W.
Benson set up on his own at 33 Ludgate Hill. In 1861 he was listed as a
chronometer, watch and clock manufacturer, gold and silversmith.

In 1889 the firm of J. W. Benson acquired Hunt & Roskell, manufacturing and retail jewellers and silversmiths of 156 New Bond Street. Then, in
1897, they became two separate limited liability companies known as J. W.
Benson Ltd and Hunt & Roskell Ltd, with J. W. Benson remaining as
director of J. W. Benson Ltd. Today J. W. Benson is part of Mappin &
Webb Ltd, which is itself a subsidiary of Sears Holdings Ltd.

*Mark entered in two sizes.
**Mark entered in three sizes.

William Arthur Smith Benson

| W.A.S.B | 10 November 1898 |

William Arthur Smith Benson, Silver worker
82 and 83 New Bond Street
Eyot Works, Hammersmith
residence: 39 Montague Square, W
signed: William A. S. Benson

This Worker having turned his business into a Limited Company, a new punch was registered, (dated) 30 November 1901

| W.A.S.B &Cº LD | 2 December 1901 |

W. A. S. Benson & Co. Ltd, Silver workers
82 and 83 New Bond Street, W
Eyot Works, Hammersmith
H. C. Marillier's residence: Kelmscott House, Hammersmith
signed: H. C. Marillier, director

14 January 1905
J. Lovegrove's residence: 14 Prebend Gardens, Chiswick
signed: John Lovegrove, director

| WB | * 2 June 1909 |

W. A. S. Benson & Co. Ltd, Gold and Silver workers
82 and 83 New Bond Street, London, W
Eyot Works, St Peters Square, Hammersmith
W. A. S. Benson's residence: Windleshaw, Withyham, Sussex
partner: William Arthur Smith Benson, director
signed: W. A. S. Benson, director

William Arthur Smith Benson was born in 1854 and died in 1924. He was an architect who, in about 1880, commenced designing and manufacturing metal work commercially under the name of W. A. S. Benson & Co.

In 1887 he set up his own factory called Eyot Works and opened showrooms at 82 and 83 New Bond Street for the sale of metalwork, lamps, candleholders and gas and electric fittings. The firm was listed as metalworkers, electrical engineers and electroplaters.

From 1902 onwards it was also listed as silversmiths and makers of 'Benson' electrical and gas fittings, oil lamps and acetylene fittings.

In 1920 the firm was bought by Allen-Liversidge Ltd, manufacturers of plant for oxyacetylene welding and cutting.

*Mark entered in two sizes.

Edward & John Septimus Beresford

11 December 1869
Edward & John S. Beresford, Plate workers
7 Chapel Street, Pentonville
189 Oxford Street, Stepney

6 April 1872
Edward & John S. Beresford

30 June 1873
Edward Beresford, Plate worker
7 Chapel Street, Pentonville
residence: 38 Barnsbury Road, Islington

30 June 1873
John S. Beresford, Plate worker
37 Theberton Street, Islington

22 January 1886
John S. Beresford
Removed to 7 Meredith Street, Clerkenwell

Both Edward and John Beresford were silversmiths and silver chasers. Following the dissolution of their partnership in 1873, Edward Beresford remained at 7 Chapel Street, Pentonville. Meanwhile, John Beresford set up on his own at Theberton Street, Islington, where he later entered into partnership with William West, trading as Beresford & West. This partnership was dissolved in 1880, following which John Beresford continued working on his own until *circa* 1888.

George Betjemann & Sons

15 February 1872
George Betjemann, George William Betjemann and John Betjemann, Small workers
36 and 38 Pentonville Road
residence: 4 Loraine Place, Holloway Road
signed: G, G. W. and John Betjemann

27 June 1876

3 December 1900
George Betjemann and Sons, Silver workers
36 and 38 Pentonville Road
residence: 114 Hillfield Avenue, Hornsey
signed: Mr Candland, partner in G. Betjemann and Sons

26 March 1902
George Betjemann and Sons, Gold and Silver workers
36 and 38 Pentonville Road, Clerkenwell
residences: 114 Hillfield Avenue, Hornsey
15 Highbury Hill, N
signed: G. W. Betjemann, partner in G. B. & Sons

* 6 January 1904
George Betjemann and Sons, Gold and Silver workers
36 and 38 Pentonville Road, London, W
residence: 34 Gondar Gardens, West Hampstead, NW
partners: John George Betjemann, Ernest Edward Betjemann,
William Candland
signed: John G. Betjemann, partner in G. B. & Sons

12 January 1909
G. Betjemann and Sons, Gold and Silver workers
36 to 40 Pentonville Road, N (Remainder of entry as for
6.1.1904)

This firm was established by George Betjemann, dressing-case maker, in 1851. About 1858, his two sons, George William and John Betjemann joined him, the firm's name being changed to George Betjemann & Sons. The firm gradually expanded until it was probably the largest manufacturer of fancy goods in the country. It was known for making desk and dressing cases, envelope cases, blotting books, inkstands, letter balances, clock cases, photographic frames, candelabra and engraved or gilded mounts in antique medieval or ornamental metalwork. It was also known for enamelling, working in decorative marbles and manufacturing the Tantalus spirit stand which George Betjemann invented *circa* 1880.

41

George Betjemann died in 1886. His two sons, George William Betjemann and John Betjemann, died in 1903 and 1893 respectively. John Betjemann's two sons, John George and Ernest Edward Betjemann, became directors following their uncle's death in 1903.

The firm eventually closed down in 1939. Ernest Edward Betjemann and his wife Mabel *née* Dawson had one son, John (1906–84), who subsequently became Sir John Betjeman, Poet Laureate. The family dropped the last 'n' from the surname during the First World War due to its German connotations.

*Mark entered in two sizes.

Barnabus Blackburn

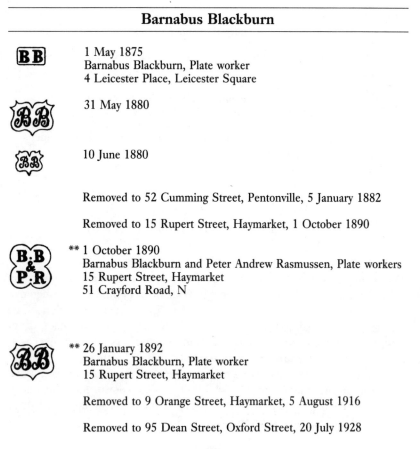

1 May 1875
Barnabus Blackburn, Plate worker
4 Leicester Place, Leicester Square

31 May 1880

10 June 1880

Removed to 52 Cumming Street, Pentonville, 5 January 1882

Removed to 15 Rupert Street, Haymarket, 1 October 1890

** 1 October 1890
Barnabus Blackburn and Peter Andrew Rasmussen, Plate workers
15 Rupert Street, Haymarket
51 Crayford Road, N

** 26 January 1892
Barnabus Blackburn, Plate worker
15 Rupert Street, Haymarket

Removed to 9 Orange Street, Haymarket, 5 August 1916

Removed to 95 Dean Street, Oxford Street, 20 July 1928

Barnabus Blackburn was a manufacturing silversmith and electroplate worker located at 4 Leicester Place from 1875 to 1881, at 49 Rupert Street from 1882 to 1890, then at 15 Rupert Street from 1890 to 1916. In 1916 he moved his business to 9 Orange Street. Then, in 1928, it moved to Dean Street where it survived until about 1933.

In 1890 Barnabus Blackburn entered into partnership with Peter Andrew Rasmussen, but this was dissolved in January 1892.

His private address was listed in 1882 as 52 Cumming Street, Pentonville. The private address of 51 Crayford Road, Holloway, listed in 1890, was probably that of Peter Rasmussen.

**Mark entered in three sizes.

Blunt & Wray

** 31 October 1888
Sidney Blunt and Frederick Dendy Wray, Plate workers
Great Sutton Street
S. Blunt's residence: 25 Albion Grove, Barnsbury
F. D. Wray's residence: 33 Beresford Road, Canonbury

6 June 1893

The partnership between Sidney Blunt and Frederick Dendy Wray was dissolved in April 1900, the business being afterwards carried on by the said F. D. Wray

** 11 May 1900
Frederick Dendy Wray
trading as Blunt & Wray, Silver workers
7 Great Sutton Street, Clerkenwell, EC
residence: 80 Queens Road, Finsbury Park

2 December 1909
Blunt & Wray, Gold and Silver workers
51A Red Lion Street, Holborn, WC
residence: 80 Queens Road, Finsbury Park
partner: Frederick Dendy Wray

This worker died early in 1916 and the next entry is that of Julius Foreman, 6 July 1916

This firm of silversmiths and church plate manufacturers was established in 1888 by Sidney Blunt and Frederick Dendy Wray, trading as Blunt, Wray & Co. In 1900 they dissolved their partnership, leaving F. D. Wray to continue trading on his own as Blunt & Wray. Following F. D. Wray's death early in 1916, the firm was continued by Julius Foreman, still trading as Blunt & Wray, church metalworkers and manufacturers of communion plate.

Circa 1920 the firm was converted into a limited liability company, trading as Blunt & Wray Ltd. *Circa* 1970 Anthony Elson became director and the firm's name was changed to Blunt & Wray, Anthony Elson Ltd. The company went into voluntary liquidation in 1981.

**Mark entered in three sizes.

Boardman, Glossop & Co. Ltd

** 28 March 1895
Boardman, Glossop & Co. Ltd, Silver workers
Clarence Works, Pond Street, Sheffield
16 Eley Place, Holborn, London

18 September 1902
Boardman, Glossop & Co. Ltd, Silver workers
Clarence Works, Pond Street, Sheffield
78 Bartletts Buildings, Holborn
W. P. Davis's residence: 3 Endcliffe Vale, Sheffield
signed: W. P. Davis, director

This was a Sheffield firm of manufacturing silversmiths apparently founded by Charles Boardman. He first entered a mark at the Sheffield Assay Office on 11 January 1844, giving his address as 48 Pond Street.

Later the business became Boardman & Glossop of Clarence Works, Pond Street, and a new mark, containing the initials of C. Boardman and A. O. Glossop, was entered at Sheffield on 13 March 1871.

On 4 July 1883 a further mark was entered at Sheffield bearing the initials of William P. Davis, director. His private address was listed as 3 Endcliffe Vale, Sheffield, in 1902.

With the opening of subsidiary premises at Eley Place, London, a new mark was entered at Goldsmiths' Hall in March 1895.

The firm was bought by Frank Cobb & Co. of Howard Street, Sheffield, *circa* 1924.

**Mark entered in three sizes.

Charles Boyton & Son

(CB)
30 November 1825
Charles Boyton (No. 1), Spoon maker
12 Europia Place, St Lukes

(CB)
10 September 1830

Removed to 26 Wellington Street, St Lukes, 29 October 1830

(C·B)
30 December 1830

(CB)
4 February 1834

(CB)
29 June 1838

(CB)
11 March 1840
Charles Boyton (No. 1), Spoon maker
26 Wellington Street, St Lukes

(CB)
9 February 1841

(CB)
18 March 1841

(CB)
9 December 1842

Removed to 19 Upper Charles Street, Northampton Square, 29 January 1849

(CB)
29 October 1849
Charles Boyton (No. 2), Spoon maker
19 Upper Charles Street, Northampton Square

(CB)
17 March 1851

CB   19 December 1854

CB   17 May 1855

C·B   16 May 1861

CB

CB   28 October 1862

CB

CB   11 April 1872

CB   7 July 1874

CB   ** 11 August 1884
Charles Boyton (No. 2), Plate worker
19 Upper Charles Street, Northampton Square

CB

CB   * 6 December 1887

CB   4 January 1889

CB   *

CB   * 29 August 1889

CB   27 July 1893

CB

CB

23 April 1894 and again on 5 November 1894

CB

C.B

27 January 1897
Charles Boyton (No. 2), Plate worker
19 Upper Charles Street, Northampton Square
120 Highbury New Park

(Marks) Defaced 9.9.1898

CB

9 September 1898

CB

This worker died early in the year 1900 and the next registration
is that of his son, Charles Boyton.
(Note: This date is incorrect. Charles Boyton (No. 2) died on 2
November 1899 and was succeeded by his son, Charles Holman
Boyton (No. 3))

CB

* 11 May 1900
Charles (Holman) Boyton (No. 3), Silver worker
19 Upper Charles Street, Northampton Square, EC

Charles (Holman) Boyton (No. 3) died early in 1904 and the
business was afterwards carried on by his widow, Marien Beatrice
Boyton.

C&B S

** 21 September 1904
Charles Boyton & Son, Silver workers
19, 21 & 22 Upper Charles Street, Northampton Square,
Clerkenwell
residence: Sussex House, 61 Highbury New Park, N
partner: Marien Beatrice Boyton, sole partner in the firm of
Charles Boyton & Son

20 February 1906
Charles Boyton, partner in the firm of Charles Boyton & Son

C&B S

19 November 1908
Charles Boyton & Son, Silver workers
19, 21 & 22 Upper Charles Street, Northampton Square, EC
residence: Sussex House, 61 Highbury New Park, N
partners: Marien Beatrice Boyton, Charles Boyton (No. 4)

20 July 1914
Charles Boyton & Son, Silver workers
19, 20 & 22 Upper Charles Street, Northampton Square, EC
Mrs Boyton's residence: Sussex House, 61 Highbury New Park, N
C. Boyton's residence: Oakdene, 25 Oakhill Avenue, Hampstead
partner: Charles Boyton (No. 4)

Charles Boyton (No. 1), the son of George Boyton (baize weaver) of Braintree, Essex, was apprenticed to William Seaman (silversmith, Citizen and Goldsmith) of Hull Street, St Lukes, on 4 November 1807. From the records, he was clearly illiterate when he commenced his apprenticeship but obviously had overcome this problem by the time he took up his freedom of the Goldsmiths' Company on 4 April 1827. Prior to this date, he had set up in business as a spoon maker, entering his first mark at Goldsmiths' Hall in November 1825.

Two of his sons, George and Charles Boyton (No. 2), became silversmiths. George Boyton was apprenticed to John William Figg (silversmith, Citizen and Goldsmith) of 5 Wellington Street on 2 December 1846. Although he never became a Freeman of the Goldsmiths' Company, he entered into partnership with a James Boyton in 1854 working as plate workers at 39 King Square.

Charles Boyton (No. 2) was born in 1829 and obtained his freedom of the Goldsmiths' Company by Patrimony on 5 October 1853. He remained working with his father and eventually took over the firm. From their signatures in the records at Goldsmiths' Hall, it would appear that Charles (No. 2) entered the firm's marks from 29 October 1849 onwards. He was made a Liveryman in July 1890 and died on 2 November 1899 according to the Liveryman records at Goldsmiths' Hall, although the register of marks states that he died in early 1900. He was buried on 6 November 1899 at Highgate.

Charles Boyton (No. 2) had two sons who became silversmiths: Frederick William Boyton and Charles Holman Boyton (No. 3). Frederick William Boyton obtained his freedom by Patrimony on 1 July 1891 and it seems that he continued working with his father and brother until 1904 when he started his own business under the name of F. Boyton & Co. Following his brother's death in May 1904, he entered his own mark at Goldsmiths' Hall, giving his address as 47 Hatton Garden. He remained in business until *circa* 1910.

Charles Holman Boyton (No. 3) remained working in his father's business. On the death of his father in 1899, he became head of the firm and subsequently bought his freedom of the Goldsmiths' Company by

Redemption on 3 October 1900. On 20 April 1904 he was accepted as a Liveryman of the Company, but died on 12 May 1904 before he could be formally admitted to the Livery. He was buried on 17 May at St Marylebone Cemetery, Finchley. His widow, Marien, carried on the family business as sole partner until their son, Charles Boyton (No. 4), had completed his apprenticeship to become a silversmith.

Charles Boyton (No. 4) was born on 15 November 1884 and apprenticed to his father on 6 February 1901. Following his father's death, he was turned over on 5 July 1904 to George Edmund Jarvis (Citizen and Goldsmith), an employee in his father's firm, to complete his apprenticeship. He obtained his freedom of the Goldsmiths' Company on 7 February 1906, and on 20 February he joined his mother as a partner of the firm. He was made a Liveryman of the Company on 17 December 1919 and died on 8 October 1958.

As a result of increasing debts, the firm was forced to close down *circa* 1933, but a new company, named Charles Boyton & Son, was formed and operated from the same premises. This firm remained in existence until 1977.

Meanwhile, in 1934, Charles Boyton (No. 4), ex-director of the defunct firm of C. Boyton & Son Ltd, set up on his own as a wholesale silversmith at 114 and 116 Marylebone Lane where he produced contemporary silverware to his own designs. These were marketed from the firm's shop at 98 Wigmore Street until 1939 when the firm closed down.

*Mark entered in two sizes.
**Mark entered in three sizes.

George Boyton

* 2 February 1854
George Boyton and James Boyton, Plate workers
39 King Square, St Lukes

* 18 February 1854
George Boyton and James Boyton

20 April 1855
George Boyton, Plate worker
39 King Square, Goswell Road

Removed to 16 King Street, Clerkenwell, 14 July 1855

George Boyton was the son of Charles Boyton (No. 1), silversmith, of 26 Wellington Street, St Lukes, and was apprenticed to John Wilmin Figg (silversmith, Citizen and Goldsmith) of 5 Wellington Street on 2 December 1846. Although he never became a Freeman of the Goldsmiths' Company, presumably he completed his apprenticeship before setting up in partnership with a James Boyton in 1854.

*Mark entered in two sizes.

James Boyton

* 2 February 1854
George Boyton and James Boyton, Plate workers
39 King Square, St Lukes

* 18 February 1854
George Boyton and James Boyton

7 April 1855
James Boyton, Spoon maker
39 King Square, St Lukes

23 February 1858
Removed to 11 Upper Rosoman Street, Clerkenwell

3 January 1862

James Boyton was not apprenticed through the Goldsmiths' Company, nor was he a Freeman of the Company. He and George Boyton may have been brothers. Following the dissolution of their partnership in March 1855, they both continued working from their old address at 39 King Square. George Boyton moved to 16 King Street in July 1855, but James Boyton remained until February 1858 when he moved to 11 Upper Rosoman Street. Here he continued to be listed as a silversmith until 1868. In April 1864 he filed a petition for bankruptcy, from which he was discharged in June 1864.

*Mark entered in two sizes.

Thomas Bradbury & Sons

* 26 July 1860
Joseph Bradbury (No. 1) and Edward Bradbury, Plate workers
manufactory: 24 Arundel Street, Sheffield
warehouse: 12 Gough Square, Fleet Street, London
residence: Broomhall Park, Kenwood Road, Sheffield
signed: Joseph Bradbury (No. 1), Edward Bradbury

Removed warehouse to 29 Golden Square, Regent Street, W (no date given)

Joseph Bradbury dead, see new entry (24.5.1878)

** 24 May 1878
Thomas Bradbury (No. 3) and John S. Henderson, Plate workers
24 Arundel Street, Sheffield
29 Golden Square, Regent Street, London
residences: 23 Westbourne Road, Sheffield
Woodlands, Tapton Villa, Sheffield
signed: Thomas Bradbury (No. 3), John S. Henderson

Removed to 26 Bartletts Buildings, Holborn, London, 24 June 1880

Removed to 15 Charterhouse Street, EC, 13 March 1883

30 May 1889
Turner Bradbury
Plate worker
15 Charterhouse Street
* 33 Duke Street, St James
signed: Turner Bradbury

51

This worker died during 1906, the (next) entry is that of Thomas Bradbury and Sons Ltd

* 9 October 1906
Thomas Bradbury & Sons Ltd
Gold and Silver workers
22 & 24 Arundel Street, Sheffield
15 Charterhouse Street, London, EC

** J. Bradbury (No. 2)'s residence: Mosborough Hall, Derbyshire
partners: Joseph Bradbury (No. 2), Frederick Bradbury
secretary: G. H. Cottam, 27 Meersbrook Road, Sheffield
signed: J. Bradbury, director

14 March 1907
Thomas Bradbury & Sons Ltd, Gold and Silver workers
22 & 24 Arundel Street, Sheffield
15 Charterhouse Street, London, EC
J. Bradbury (No. 2)'s residence: Mosborough Hall, Derbyshire
partners: Joseph Bradbury (No. 2), Frederick Bradbury
secretary: G. H. Cottam
signed: J. Bradbury, director

Thomas Bradbury & Sons Ltd was an old-established Sheffield firm of platers and silversmiths. In the late eighteenth century it traded as Fenton, Creswick & Co., entering its mark at the newly opened Sheffield Assay Office in 1773. Following Fenton's death it was sold to Thomas Watson, who took on Thomas Bradbury (No. 1) as his partner in 1795. It was known as Watson & Co., then as Watson & Bradbury, with Thomas Watson, his nephew William Watson, Thomas Bradbury (No. 1) and his son Thomas Bradbury (No. 2) as partners. Following William Watson's retirement in 1831, the Bradburys assumed control of the business and the firm's name was changed to Thomas Bradbury & Son. The firm entered its first mark under this name at the Sheffield Assay Office on 16 February 1832, giving its address as Arundel Street.

Thomas Bradbury (No. 1) died in 1838 and, with the death of his son, Thomas Bradbury (No. 2), in 1855, his two grandsons, Joseph Bradbury (No. 1) and Edward Bradbury, assumed control of the firm. They renamed the firm Thomas Bradbury & Sons.

Joseph (No. 1) and Edward Bradbury were the sons of Thomas Bradbury (No. 2). They entered their first mark at Goldsmiths' Hall, London, in July 1860. With the death of Joseph Bradbury (No. 1) in 1877, new marks were entered at Goldsmiths' Hall by his brother, Thomas Bradbury (No. 3) and John Sutherland Henderson.

When this partnership was dissolved in 1886, the firm of Thomas

Bradbury & Sons was continued by the three sons of Joseph Bradbury (No. 1). They were Walton Turner Bradbury, recorded as Turner Bradbury in the entry of 30 May 1889, Joseph Bradbury (No. 2) and Frederick Bradbury, the author of *A History of Old Sheffield Plate*.

Walton Turner died in 1906, leaving Joseph Bradbury (No. 2) and Frederick Bradbury to continue running the firm until their retirement *circa* 1943. The firm was then closed down and its dies and goodwill were sold to Atkin Brothers (silversmiths) Ltd.

*Mark entered in two sizes.
**Mark entered in three sizes.

Frederick Brasted

JB FB
23 May 1857
John Bell and Frederick Brasted, Plate workers
6 President Street, Goswell Road
Brasted's residence: 16 Pownall Road, Dalton
signed: John Bell, Frederick Brasted

FB
* 24 June 1862
Frederick Brasted, Plate worker
6 President Street, Goswell Road
signed: Frederick Brasted

FB
* 10 January 1865

FB
* 18 February 1873
Defaced 6 October 1886

FB
** 6 October 1880
These marks defaced 20 June 1888

This firm was known as Bell & Brasted from 1857 to 1862. Thereafter Frederick Brasted worked on his own at President Street until his death on

53

1 June 1888.
Following his death, the firm continued to operate under his widow, Susannah, and later under his son, Harry Brasted.

*Mark entered in two sizes.
**Mark entered in three sizes.

Harry Brasted

 *** 31 December 1895
Harry Brasted, Silver worker
37 President Street, Goswell Road, EC
residence: 61 Kelvin Road, Highbury

Harry Brasted was the son of Frederick and Susannah Brasted. Following his father's death on 1 June 1888, his mother continued running the family business until Harry Brasted took over in 1895.
In 1908 the firm was taken over by F. C. Britten and F. W. Britten.

***Mark entered in four sizes.

Susannah Brasted

 ** 20 June 1888
Susannah Brasted, Plate worker
37 President Street, Goswell Road

Susannah Brasted was the widow of Frederick Brasted. Following his death on 1 June 1888, she continued running the business until their son, Harry Brasted, took over the firm in 1895.

**Mark entered in three sizes.

Bristol Goldsmiths Alliance

23 July 1884
Francis James Langford and George Langford, Plate workers
30 College Green, Bristol
F. J. Langford's residence: Craignethan, Waverley Road, Clifton
G. Langford's residence: Pensford, Somerset

** 20 October 1902
George Langford, Gold and Silver workers
30 College Green, Bristol

Trading as Bristol Goldsmiths Alliance

This firm was previously known as William Langford & Sons, but following its amalgamation with the firm of John J. Peters & Co. (see Charles Taylor & Son), it was renamed the Bristol Goldsmiths Alliance, with Francis James Langford and George Langford as partners.

In 1893 George Langford and his then partner, James Henry Mole, dissolved their partnership, leaving George Langford as sole partner in the firm.

It seems likely that the firm's marks were registered at Goldsmiths' Hall as the result of it having a London outlet for its goods.

**Mark entered in three sizes.

Brockwell & Company

19 July 1859
Frederick Henry Brockwell, Small worker
79 & 80 Leather Lane, Holborn

Removed to 8 Brook Street, Holborn, 30 November 1871

2 October 1874
Henry Titterton Brockwell, Plate worker
8 Brook Street, Middleton Square

55

HTB   18 October 1875

H.T.B   28 November 1883
Removed to Crescent Place, NW

HTB   31 January 1884

H.T.B   14 July 1884

H·T·B   21 August 1884

H.T.B   12 January 1885

HTB   15 August 1889

HTB   2 April 1895
Henry Titterton Brockwell, Silver worker
27 Brook Street, EC
residence: 47 Philbeach Gardens, SW

This firm was listed in 1860 as silver mounters and manufacturers of cut glass, smelling bottles, flasks and ink glasses. Prior to this date, the firm's premises at 80 Leather Lane were occupied by Henry Brockwell, spoon maker, in 1821; John Wheeler, glass cutter and mounter, in 1841; and William Wheeler & Co., glass cutters and mounters, in 1859.

Frederick Henry Brockwell appears to have retired or died *circa* 1873. The firm of Brockwell & Son was then continued by Henry Titterton Brockwell who was probably his son. Henry T. Brockwell subsequently entered into partnership with John Elwin Evered, but this was dissolved in 1894. The firm eventually closed down *circa* 1910.

Edward Brown

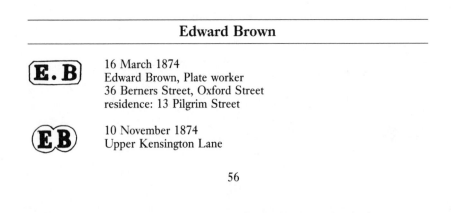

E.B   16 March 1874
Edward Brown, Plate worker
36 Berners Street, Oxford Street
residence: 13 Pilgrim Street

EB   10 November 1874
Upper Kensington Lane

Removed to 19 Poland Street, Oxford Street, W, 11 December 1874

EB 29 November 1878
Removed to 13 Greek Street, Soho Square
residence: 14 Leicester Place, Leicester Square
Defaced (mark) 16 October 1879

Removed to Blackhorse Yard, Rathbone Place, W, 10 May 1879
residence: 24 Charlotte Street, Fitzroy Square

EB 3 September 1879

EB 16 October 1879

EB 28 October 1881
Edward Brown, Plate worker
Blackhorse Yard, Rathbone Place
24 Charlotte Place, Fitzroy Square

EB 24 March 1882
Edward Brown, Plate worker
44 Greek Street, Soho, W

Removed to 16 Greek Street, Soho, W
12 October 1883

E.B 4 March 1885

EB 22 July 1887

Removed to 13 Bateman Street, Soho, W
23 January 1891

EB 12 February 1892

Edward Brown entered his first mark at Goldsmiths' Hall in March 1874 where he was described as a plate worker. By 1876 he was known as a silversmith, electroplater and manufacturer.

His last mark was entered at Goldsmiths' Hall in 1892, but he remained working until 1895, following which his business was continued by Mrs Ada Brown. The firm was subsequently taken over by Harris Brothers.

William Brown (No. 1)

 24 January 1823
William Brown (No. 1), Plate worker
54 Little Bartholomew Close

Removed to 13 Silver Street, Wood Street, 31 August 1823

 * 10 April 1839
William Brown (No. 1) and William Somersall, Plate workers
53 Bartholomew Close

* 18 May 1843
William Brown (No. 1), Plate worker
53 Bartholomew Close

This may have been the William Thomas Brown who was a son of William Brown (silversmith) of Langbourn Chambers, Fenchurch Street. If this is the case, he was apprenticed on 2 February 1814 to George Munro (working silversmith) of John Street, St George in the East. There is no record of him obtaining his freedom of the Goldsmiths' Company.

He was in partnership with William Somersall from 1839 to 1843 when the partnership was dissolved (see William Somersall). He then continued on his own at Bartholomew Close until *circa* 1845.

*Mark entered in two sizes.

William Brown (No. 2)

 15 January 1847
William Brown (No. 2), Gold worker
20 North Street, Red Lion Square

Removed to 18 Newman Street, Oxford Street, 25 June 1853

William Brown (No. 2) was a manufacturing jeweller and was first recorded in partnership with Edward Moss Shew, trading as Brown & Shew at 20

North Street. His only mark was entered at Goldsmiths' Hall in January 1847. The partnership was dissolved in September 1847 leaving William Brown (No. 2) to continue working on his own. From *circa* 1855 to *circa* 1861 he was in partnership with Charles Pembroke Gearing, trading as Brown & Gearing, manufacturing jewellers.

Carrington & Company

** 28 June 1880
John Bodman Carrington, Plate worker
130 Regent Street, W
57 Cambridge Street, Birmingham
residence: 20 Porchester Terrace, Hyde Park, W

* 23 September 1880

3 February 1881

*** 28 February 1890

5 November 1891

19 August 1895

The whole of the above marks (from 28.6.1880) defaced, 8 October 1895

8 October 1895

†

59

** 16 October 1895

 16 June 1897

 * 26 May 1899
John Bodman Carrington, Plate worker
130 Regent Street, London, W
57 Cambridge Street, Birmingham
residence: 14 Netherhall Gardens, Hampstead

 *** 7 July 1902

 *** 13 March 1903

All these marks defaced 25.1.1909

 † 28 May 1906
Carrington & Co., Silver workers
130 Regent Street, London, W
W. C. Smith's residence: The Hermitage, Harrow Weald
sole partner: William Carrington Smith

††† 17 September 1906 (Entry as for 28.5.1906)

 * 8 May 1907
John Bodman Carrington, Silver worker
business: 14 Netherhall Gardens, Hampstead
residence: 14 Netherhall Gardens, Hampstead
signed: John Bodman Carrington

* 10 June 1907

John Bodman Carrington, the son of John Carrington, obtained his freedom of the Goldsmiths' Company by Redemption on 6 May 1891. His occupation at the time was recorded as goldsmith and jeweller. On 16 January 1895 he was made a Liveryman of the Goldsmiths' Company and on 12 February 1896 he became an Assistant. He became 4th Warden in 1900, 3rd Warden in 1901, 2nd Warden in 1902 and Prime Warden in 1903. He retired from business on 1 January 1906 and died on 23 September 1926.

His two sons, Arthur John Bodman Carrington and Hugh Bodman Carrington, obtained their freedoms of the Goldsmiths' Company by Special Grant. Arthur obtained his freedom on 1 May 1907 (occupation: undergraduate), was made a Liveryman on 13 March 1907 and died on 9 November 1916. Hugh obtained his freedom on 2 May 1917 (occupation: paper maker), was made a Liveryman on 17 December 1919 and died on 18 April 1954.

In 1873 the firm of Carrington & Co. was first recorded as being under John Carrington, manufacturing silversmith, electroplater, goldsmith and jeweller of 130 Regent Street.

In 1880 his son, John Bodman Carrington, appears to have taken over the business, entering his first mark at Goldsmiths' Hall and giving his business addresses as 130 Regent Street, London, and 57 Cambridge Street, Birmingham. At the time he already controlled G. R. Collis & Co., a Birmingham firm of manufacturing silversmiths and electroplaters, whose factory was at 57 Cambridge Street, Birmingham, with showrooms at 130 Regent Street, London (see G. R. Collis & Co.). It seems that both his companies were sharing the same London premises while trading as separate firms.

In 1882 John Bodman Carrington, as senior partner of G. R. Collis & Co., entered into some form of partnership with Samuel Watton Smith, senior partner of S. W. Smith & Co., silversmiths and electroplaters, also of 57 Cambridge Street, Birmingham (see S. W. Smith & Co.). This partnership was dissolved on 31 December 1888, leaving John Bodman Carrington apparently in control of S. W. Smith & Co. as well as G. R. Collis & Co. and Carrington & Co.

G. R. Collis & Co. and Carrington & Co. continued to trade as separate firms at 130 Regent Street until *circa* 1893 when G. R. Collis & Co. appears to have been absorbed by Carrington & Co. The partners of Carrington & Co. at the time were John Bodman Carrington, William Carrington Smith of S. W. Smith & Co. and George Bruford. George Bruford retired on 31 December 1895 and John Bodman Carrington on 1 January 1906, leaving William Carrington Smith as sole partner to continue running the firm.

Meanwhile, in 1907, John Bodman Carrington entered his own marks as a private individual from his home address.

William Carrington Smith, the son of Thomas Smith, obtained his freedom of the Goldsmiths' Company by Redemption on 2 January 1901. He was made a Liveryman in April 1904 and died on 25 March 1924. In 1922 the firm was converted into a limited liability company, and it is now a subsidiary of The Collingwood Group Ltd.

*Mark entered in two sizes.
**Mark entered in three sizes.
***Mark entered in four sizes.
†Mark entered in five sizes.
†††Mark entered in seven sizes.

Cartier

 *** 20 July 1914
Gold and Silver worker
175 New Bond Street, London, W
13 Rue de la Paix, Paris
712 Fifth Avenue, New York
J. Cartier's residence: 90 Seymour Street, Connaught Square, W
director: Jacques Cartier

This firm of manufacturing and retail jewellers was founded by Louis François Cartier in Paris in 1859. His son, Alfred Cartier, assumed control of the firm in 1874 and subsequently passed it on to his own three sons, Louis J. Cartier, Pierre C. Cartier and Jacques Cartier.

A London branch was opened at 4 New Burlington Street in 1904. From here it moved to 175 New Bond Street in 1909 under the management of Jacques Cartier. This was followed by the opening of an American branch at 712 Fifth Avenue, New York, in 1912.

In 1919 the firm was converted into a limited liability company, trading as Cartier Ltd, with Louis J. Cartier, Pierre C. Cartier and Jacques Cartier as directors.

***Mark entered in four sizes.

Catchpole & Williams

** 19 August 1880
Charles Johnston Hill, Plate worker
223 Oxford Street
residence: 13 Colville Gardens, W

15 August 1893

This Worker, who succeeded the firm of Catchpole and Williams, died in the year 1895 and the business was then floated as a Limited Liability Company under the old name of Catchpole and Williams, 17 January 1900

** 16 January 1900
Catchpole and Williams Ltd, Gold and Silver workers
508 and 510 Oxford Street, London, W
residence: 141 Alexandria Road, St Johns Wood
director: Alston Thompson Smith

The firm of Catchpole and Williams Ltd succeeded Charles Johnston Hill who died in 1895 of 223 Oxford Street (previous street numbering)

Removed to 22 Acol Road, West Hampstead, 22 February 1901 (A. T. Smith's residence)

Removed to 8 Mapesbury Road, Brondesbury, 22 November 1911 (A. T. Smith's residence)

24 April 1912
Catchpole & Williams Ltd, Gold and Silver workers
510 Oxford Street, London, W
A. T. Smith's residence: 8 Mapesbury Road, Brondesbury
directors: Alston T. Smith, A. T. Jannaway, Leslie Alston Smith

Mr A. T. Jannaway retired December 1919

The partnership between James Catchpole and Charles Williams commenced *circa* 1836. It was dissolved in 1846 and, at the time, the firm was described as goldsmiths and jewellers trading from 120 Regent Street.

Following the dissolution of their partnership, James Catchpole commenced trading on his own from 40 Conduit Street. His firm's name subsequently changed to James Catchpole & Son and remained in existence until *circa* 1865.

Meanwhile, Charles Williams commenced trading on his own under the name of Charles Williams & Co. (late Catchpole & Williams). This continued until *circa* 1872 when Charles Johnston Hill joined Charles Williams in partnership and the firm was renamed Williams & Hill (late Catchpole & Williams).

In 1874 Charles Williams died and the current partnership between Charles Williams, his brother Henry Richard Williams and Charles Johnston Hill was dissolved. Charles J. Hill then continued to run the firm under the name of Charles Johnston Hill (late Catchpole & Williams).

Following Charles J. Hill's death on 6 August 1895, the firm was turned into a limited liability company under the name of Catchpole & Williams Ltd, its directors being Arthur Thomas Jannaway and Alston Thompson Smith. Arthur Thomas Jannaway retired from the firm in December 1919. In the 1930s, the firm moved from 510 Oxford Street to 14 Grafton Street where it closed down *circa* 1966.

**Mark entered in three sizes.

Chapple & Mantell

 *** 17 September 1880
John Chapple and John Mantell, Plate workers
32 Strand
Chapple's residence: Lubeck House, Brixton Hill Street

 15 June 1887
Mantell's residence: Havard Lodge, Havard Road, Chiswick

 4 September 1900
This entry not being completed, the punch was destroyed

This firm of retail silversmiths commenced with the partnership of John Chapple and John Mantell *circa* 1860. John Chapple was born in 1838 and died in 1905.

The firm was still trading in the 1930s, but from premises at 55–57 Maddox Street, New Bond Street.

***Mark entered in four sizes.

Child & Child

---

21 February 1888
Walter Child and Harold Child, Plate workers
1 Seville Street, SW

2 August 1888

Removed to 35 Alfred Place West, SW, 21 March 1892

This firm dissolved partnership, 20 June 1899

(Note: At this point in the records, the following entry of 26.6.1899 is referred to as having been entered by Sir Harold Child)

** 26 June 1899
Gold and Silver worker
35 Alfred Place West, SW

Walter and Harold Child entered their first mark at Goldsmiths' Hall in February 1888, although they were already trading prior to this date as jewellers and silversmiths. They dissolved their partnership on or before 20 June 1899, following which Harold Child continued trading on his own until his death in Milan in 1915.

Child & Child often stamped their goods with their own trade mark of a sunflower with a 'C' on each side.

**Mark entered in three sizes.

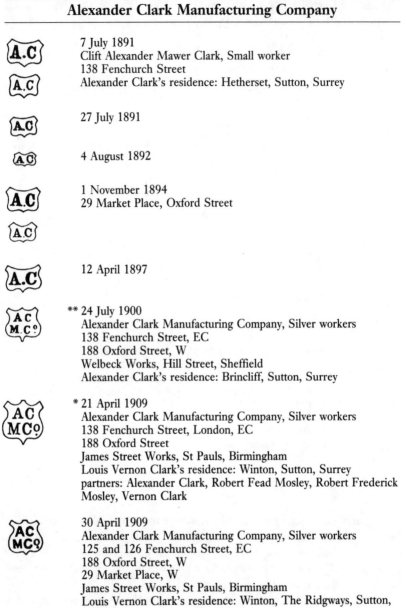

7 July 1891
Clift Alexander Mawer Clark, Small worker
138 Fenchurch Street
Alexander Clark's residence: Hetherset, Sutton, Surrey

27 July 1891

4 August 1892

1 November 1894
29 Market Place, Oxford Street

12 April 1897

** 24 July 1900
Alexander Clark Manufacturing Company, Silver workers
138 Fenchurch Street, EC
188 Oxford Street, W
Welbeck Works, Hill Street, Sheffield
Alexander Clark's residence: Brincliff, Sutton, Surrey

* 21 April 1909
Alexander Clark Manufacturing Company, Silver workers
138 Fenchurch Street, London, EC
188 Oxford Street
James Street Works, St Pauls, Birmingham
Louis Vernon Clark's residence: Winton, Sutton, Surrey
partners: Alexander Clark, Robert Fead Mosley, Robert Frederick
Mosley, Vernon Clark

30 April 1909
Alexander Clark Manufacturing Company, Silver workers
125 and 126 Fenchurch Street, EC
188 Oxford Street, W
29 Market Place, W
James Street Works, St Pauls, Birmingham
Louis Vernon Clark's residence: Winton, The Ridgways, Sutton,
Surrey
partners: Alexander Clark, Robert Fead Mosley, Robert Frederick
Mosley, Vernon Clark

9 June 1910
Alexander Clark Manufacturing Company, Gold and Silver
workers
(Remainder of entry as for 30.4.1909)

The above punch (9.6.1910) and those previously entered were
cancelled 24 April 1912 as the firm was registered as a Limited
Company

** 24 April 1912
Alexander Clark Manufacturing Company Ltd, Silver workers
125 and 126 Fenchurch Street, London, EC
188 Oxford Street, London, W
James Street Works, St Pauls, Birmingham
residences: West Wood, West Hill, Sydenham
45 Parklands Road, Streatham
directors: Clift A. M. Clark, Robert Mosley, Walter S. Littlewood
secretary: Walter Sidney Littlewood

Circa 1891 Clift Alexander Mawer Clark commenced business as a purse
and dressing-bag manufacturer, silversmith and cutler. By 1 November
1894 he had his own factory at 29 Market Place, Oxford Street, London.

He subsequently entered into a business arrangement with the Sheffield
firm of R. F. Mosley & Co. Ltd, manufacturing silversmiths, whereby he
used their Welbeck Works in Sheffield for his manufacturing purposes.
Presumably the connections between these two firms strengthened for, by
21 April 1909, both Robert Fead Mosley and Robert Frederick Mosley,
directors of R. F. Mosley & Co. Ltd, had joined Alexander Clark and Louis
Vernon Clark as partners of the Alexander Clark Manufacturing Co. Also
by this date, the firm's manufactory had been transferred from Sheffield to
James Street Works, Birmingham.

In 1912 the firm was turned into a limited liability company.

Alexander Clark died *circa* 1938 while still managing director of the
company.

*Mark entered in two sizes.
**Mark entered in three sizes.

G. R. Collis & Company

8 April 1840
George Richmond Collis, Plate worker
28 Church Street, Birmingham

When Sir Edward Thomason retired in 1835, his business at 28 Church Street, Birmingham, was taken over by George Richmond Collis who then proceeded to enter his own mark at the Birmingham Assay Office in November of that year.

Edward Thomason was born in 1769 and apprenticed to Matthew Boulton in 1785. In 1793 Edward Thomason set himself up as a manufacturer of plated and gilt buttons. The firm expanded over the years so that when George Collis assumed control in 1835, it was manufacturing gold and silverware of every description.

In 1840 George Collis entered his mark at Goldsmiths' Hall, London, and *circa* 1847 the firm opened showrooms at 1 Langham Place, Regent Street, London. These showrooms were moved to 130 Regent Street in about 1854, where they remained until the firm's demise *circa* 1893. In about 1868 G. R. Collis & Co. moved its Birmingham factory to 57 Cambridge Street, Birmingham.

In 1873 John Carrington, manufacturing silversmith, electroplater, goldsmith and jeweller, was also trading from 130 Regent Street. It appears that both of these firms were trading separately from the same showrooms (see Carrington & Co). In 1880 John Carrington's son, John Bodman Carrington, took over his father's firm of Carrington & Co., entering his mark at Goldsmiths' Hall on 28 June 1880. At the same time he appears to have acquired G. R. Collis & Co. Even so, the two firms continued to trade separately from 130 Regent Street until about 1893 when the name of G. R. Collis & Co. disappeared, leaving Carrington & Co. as sole occupier of the premises.

Meanwhile, *circa* 1882, G. R. Collis & Co. entered into some form of partnership with the Birmingham silversmithing firm of S. W. Smith & Co. based at 57 Cambridge Street. This partnership was dissolved on 31 December 1888 by John Bodman Carrington representing G. R. Collis & Co. and Samuel Watton Smith representing S. W. Smith & Co. (see S. W. Smith & Co.). Following this dissolution, G. R. Collis & Co. ceased to be listed at 57 Cambridge Street.

William Comyns & Sons

 * 26 January 1859
William Comyns, Plate worker
2 Carlisle Street, Soho Square

Removed to 1 Percy Mews, Rathbone Place, 6 December 1869

Removed to 16 Silver Street, Golden Square, 6 June 1878
residence: Lena Villa, Highgate Rise, Highgate

 * 13 June 1878

Removed to 41 Beak Street, Regent Street, W
(undated, entry made between 1.12.1800 and 2.3.1888)

 2 March 1888

 12 November 1890
William Comyns, Plate worker
41 Beak Street, Regent Street, W

 19 January 1892

*** 3 March 1894

 6 February 1901

* 13 February 1901
William Comyns, Silver worker
Beak Street, Regent Street, W

*** 4 April 1903
William Comyns, Silver worker
41–47 Beak Street,
54 Marshall Street, London, W
residence: The Hermitage, Silver Hill Park, St Leonards-on-Sea

3 March 1905
William Comyns and Sons, Silver workers
41–47 Beak Street, Regent Street, W
residence: The Hermitage, Silver Hill Park, St Leonards-on-Sea

William Comyns died in January 1916 and the business was
afterwards carried on by his sons, C. and R. Comyns

William Comyns was the son of Charles Comyns (gentleman) of 5 Wilmot Place, Camden Town. On 3 January 1849 he was apprenticed to George John Richards (silversmith, Citizen and Goldsmith), senior partner of Richards & Brown of 26½ Sekforde Street, Clerkenwell. William Comyns obtained his freedom of the Goldsmiths' Company by Service on 6 February 1856.

Possibly he remained with Richards & Brown until December 1858 or January 1859 when he acquired the silversmithing business of Robert Tagg at 2 Carlisle Street, Soho Square, and entered his own mark at Goldsmiths' Hall on 26 January 1859. In about 1888 he took two of his sons, Charles Harling Comyns and Richard Henry Comyns, into partnership, changing the firm's name to William Comyns & Sons, manufacturing silversmiths. He continued as head of the firm until his death in January 1916 when about 79 years old.

William Comyns had three sons who became silversmiths and Freemen of the Goldsmiths' Company. They were Charles Harling Comyns, Richard Henry Comyns and Francis Harling Comyns.

Charles H. Comyns was apprenticed to his father on 3 December 1879 and obtained his freedom of the Goldsmiths' Company by Patrimony on 7 November 1888. He was made a Liveryman in December 1899 and died on 15 December 1925 while attending a sale at Christie's.

Richard H. Comyns was apprenticed to his father on 1 December 1880 and obtained his freedom of the Goldsmiths' Company by Patrimony on 7 November 1888, the same day as his brother, Charles. He was made a Liveryman in January 1895 and died on 5 April 1953.

Francis H. Comyns was apprenticed to his father on 4 December 1889 and obtained his freedom of the Goldsmiths' Company by Service on 6 July 1897.

With the death of William Comyns in January 1916, his two sons, Charles and Richard, continued running the firm.

In about 1953 the firm was acquired by Bernard Copping who transferred it to Dean Street and later to Comyns House, Tower Street.

*Mark entered in two sizes.
***Mark entered in four sizes.

G. L. Connell Ltd

---

27 April 1893
William George Connell, Plate worker
83 Cheapside
residence: 14 Doughty Street, NC

This worker died in 1902 and the business was carried on by
George Lawrence Connell

*** 1 September 1902
George Lawrence Connell, Gold and Silver workers
83 Cheapside, EC
residence: 50 Tierney Road, Streatham

Died 27 January 1933

This firm was founded, *circa* 1839, by William Connell, a chronometer and watch maker. In 1846 he was at 83 Cheapside as a chronometer and watch maker to the Royal Navy. In about 1876 his son, William George Connell, took over the business.

In 1878 William George Connell was listed as a chronometer, watch and clock maker, gold and silversmith and jeweller. Following his death on 5 May 1902, his son, George Lawrence Connell, took over the firm.

In 1917 the firm became a limited liability company under the name of G. L. Connell Ltd. Its directors were George Lawrence Connell, Christine Connell (his wife) and Hermann Julius Siemssen.

When George Lawrence Connell died on 27 January 1933, Christine Connell took control of the firm.

***Mark entered in four sizes.

Frederick Courthope

2 October 1884
Frederick Courthope, Plate worker
51A Compton Street, Clerkenwell
residence: 17 Lichfield Grove, Finchley, N

Removed to 27 Amwell Street, Clerkenwell, 13 May 1885

12 October 1887

7 June 1900
residence: 119 Lordship Road, Stoke Newington

Removed to 59 Highbury Park, N, (residence), 26 January 1904

20 September 1907
Frederick Courthope, Silver worker
27 Amwell Street, Clerkenwell
residence: 59 Highbury Park, N

Removed to 1A Aubert Park, Highbury, 20 June 1916

Frederick Courthope, full name George Frederick Courthope, acquired the silversmithing business of George Angell following the latter's death on 24 July 1884 (see John Angell & Son). Frederick Courthope entered his first mark at Goldsmiths' Hall in October 1884, but continued to trade under the name of George Angell & Co.

He was a practising silversmith able to design, model and chase silverware. In recognition of his services to the trade generally and to the Goldsmiths' Company in particular, he was made a Liveryman of the Goldsmiths' Company by Special Grant in December 1928. He died on 8 October 1935.

Cox & Sons

TC

9 March 1860
Thomas Cox, Small worker
28–29 Southampton Street, Strand
manufactory: Belvidere Road, Lambeth
residence: Oakenshaw, Surbiton, Surrey

T . C

20 July 1865

TC
EC

10 July 1866
Thomas and Edward Cox, Small workers
28–29 Southampton Street, Strand
manufactory: Belsize Road, Lambeth
residences: Thomas Cox: Hazelbourne, near Dorking
Edward Cox: Ewell Road, Surbiton

72

E.Y.C
19 October 1880
Edward Young Cox, Small worker
28–29 Southampton Street, Strand
residence: 74 Pentonville Road

This firm was founded *circa* 1837 by Thomas Cox, a clerical tailor and robe maker. About 1853 he took his son, Edward Young Cox, into partnership and changed the firm's name to Cox & Son. By 1859 he had widened the firm's field of manufacture to include church furniture, official robes, church carvings and stained glass. In about 1866 he changed the firm's name to Cox & Sons, which is how it remained until it was amalgamated with Buckley & Co. in 1881.

Circa 1870 Cox & Sons absorbed the silversmithing business of John Keith together with his staff (see John James Keith).

When Thomas Cox retired in 1876, Edward Young Cox assumed control of the firm. At the time Cox & Sons were known as robe makers, embroiderers, engravers, bronze statue founders, monumental sculptors and manufacturers of church furniture, stained glass and church plate.

Edward Young Cox appears to have retired or died in 1881, this being when Cox & Sons amalgamated with Buckley & Co. to create the firm of Cox, Sons, Buckley & Co. A mark representing this new firm was entered at Goldsmiths' Hall on 29 July 1881.

Crespel & Parker

AC
29 September 1858
Andrew Crespel (No. 2), Plate worker
manufactory: 1 James Street, Haymarket
residence: 7 Green Street, Leicester Square

Mark defaced 22 July 1863

A.C T.P
* 22 July 1863
Andrew Crespel (No. 2) and Thomas Parker, Plate workers
manufactory: 1 James Street, Haymarket
residences: Crespel: 7 Green Street, Leicester Square
Parker: 84 Stanhope Street, Hampstead Road

11 May 1875
Thomas Parker, Plate worker
1 James Street, Haymarket
residence: 192 Stanhope Street, NW

This firm was founded by Sebastian Crespel (No. 2) in 1820 at 11 James Street, Haymarket (see *Marks of London Goldsmiths and Silversmiths c. 1697–1837*, revised edition 1988, pp. 99, 382). Sebastian Crespel (No. 2) was born on 11 April 1786, the son of Mary and James Crespel (No. 1) (silversmith). James Crespel (No. 1) had worked extensively for John Wakelin and William Taylor, silversmiths of Panton Street, during the 1770s and 1780s and then for their successor, Robert Garrard (No. 1). In addition to Sebastian (No. 2), James Crespel (No. 1) had three other sons who became silversmiths. They were Honorius Crespel, Andrew Crespel (No. 1) and James Crespel (No. 2) (see *Marks of London Goldsmiths and Silversmiths c. 1697–1837*, revised edition 1988, pp. 98, 99, 382).

Sebastian Crespel (No. 2) was apprenticed to his brother, Honorius Crespel (silver flatter, Citizen and Goldsmith) on 3 June 1801. Following his brother's death in the spring of 1806, he was turned over to Robert Garrard (No. 1) (silversmith and Grocer) on 7 May 1806. Having obtained his freedom of the Goldsmiths' Company by Service on 3 May 1809, he continued working for Robert Garrard (No. 1).

In 1815 his wife, Jane, gave birth to their son, Andrew Crespel (No. 2). At the time of Andrew's baptism on 18 June 1815, Sebastian Crespel (No. 2) was recorded as silversmith of 25 Panton Street. This was the address of Robert Garrard's working premises.

In 1820, some two years after the death of Robert Garrard (No. 1), Sebastian Crespel (No. 2) set up in business on his own at 11 James Street, Haymarket, entering his mark at Goldsmiths' Hall on 3 August 1820. From here he moved to 11 White Hart Court, Castle Street, Leicester Square, in October 1836.

On 3 July 1839 Thomas Parker, the son of Joseph William Parker (watch-case maker) of 7 Skinners Street, Clerkenwell, was apprenticed to Sebastian Crespel (No. 2) of White Hart Court to learn the trade of silversmith. Having obtained his freedom of the Goldsmiths' Company by Service on 7 April 1847, he presumably continued working for Sebastian Crespel (No. 2). Meanwhile, Andrew Crespel (No. 2) (silversmith) of Green Street obtained his freedom of the Goldsmiths' Company by Patrimony on 6 May 1846. He likewise continued working with his father in the family business.

In the Census return for the night of 30 March 1851, the residents of 7 Green Street, Leicester Square, included Sebastian Crespel (No. 2), aged 64, and Andrew Crespel (No. 2), aged 35, working silversmiths. Also residing at this address were William Pairpoint, water gilder and founder of William Pairpoint & Sons Ltd, his wife Maria and their children: Maria, aged 23; Alfred, aged 21; Emma, aged 18; Walter, aged 14; Thomas, aged 12; Fanny, aged 10; and Caroline, aged 6. William Pairpoint's eldest son, Edward James Pairpoint, silversmith, is recorded in the Census as residing at 44 Greek Street, Leicester Square. He was the founder of Pairpoint Brothers (see Pairpoint Brothers).

On 25 August 1858 Sebastian Crespel (No. 2) died of chronic bronchitis at 7 Green Street. Following his death, Andrew Crespel (No. 2) took over his father's business, entering his own mark at Goldsmiths' Hall. In 1863 he took Thomas Parker into partnership, renaming the firm Crespel and Parker, working silversmiths.

Andrew Crespel (No. 2) died on 10 March 1875. Thomas Parker continued running the firm of Crespel and Parker, working silversmiths, until it ceased trading *circa* 1878.

*Mark entered in two sizes.

Creswick & Co.

---

* 26 March 1852
Thomas, James and Nathaniel Creswick, Plate workers
manufactory: Paternoster Row, Sheffield
17 Craven Street, Strand, London
residences: T. Creswick: Eccleshall Grange, Sheffield
J. Creswick: Crooksmoor, Sheffield
N. Creswick: Easthill, Sheffield

By virtue of a Power of Attorney I enter three marks of Thomas Creswick, James Creswick and Nathaniel Creswick, Plate workers of London and Sheffield this 26th day of March 1852.
William Potter, Attorney to the said firm

** 11 March 1853
James and Nathaniel Creswick, Plate workers
Paternoster Row, Sheffield
17 Craven Street, Strand, London

By virtue of a Power of Attorney I enter six marks of James Creswick and Nathaniel Creswick, Plate workers of London and Sheffield this 11th day of March 1853. William Potter, Attorney to the said firm

16 February 1874
Rupert Favell, Plate worker
111 Arundel Street, Sheffield
17 Craven Street, Strand
residence: 12 Grays Inn Square

 10 July 1879
Charles Favell, Plate worker
111 Arundel Street, Sheffield
17 Craven Street, Strand

Creswick & Co. was an old-established Sheffield firm of silversmiths and platers. Thomas and James Creswick entered their first mark, consisting of the script letters 'T & J C' in a rectangle, at the Sheffield Assay Office on 29 October 1810. At the time, the firm was known as T. & J. Creswick.

In 1819 Nathaniel Creswick joined the partnership and a new mark, consisting of 'T J & N C' in a rectangle, was entered at the Sheffield Assay Office on 25 October. The firm's name was amended accordingly to T. J. & N. Creswick. A further mark was entered at Sheffield on 18 December 1832.

On 26 March 1852 the Creswicks entered their first mark at the London Assay Office, following it with a similar mark at the Sheffield Assay Office on 18 August 1852.

By March 1853 Thomas Creswick had retired and new marks of similar appearance were entered at both the London and Sheffield Assay Offices. These entries indicated James and Nathaniel Creswick as the senior partners with William Potter, silversmith and plater, the London representative at the Craven Street showrooms.

Following Nathaniel Creswick's death in November 1855, the firm's name was changed to Creswick & Co. with Nathaniel Irving, Charles Favell and Frederick Potter as its partners. A mark enclosing their three surname initials 'I F P' over 'C & Co' was entered at Sheffield on 1 September 1858.

Frederick Potter retired in 1860 and Nathaniel Irving in 1862, leaving Charles Favell to continue running the firm in partnership with Rupert Favell at 111 Arundel Street, Sheffield, and 17 Craven Street, London. On 31 March 1879 Rupert and Charles Favell dissolved their partnership, following which Rupert commenced trading as R. Favell & Co., New Oxford Street, London (see Rupert Favell & Co.)

Meanwhile, Charles Favell entered his own mark at the London Assay Office. He continued trading as Creswick & Co. until 1887, but then changed the firm's name to Charles Favell & Co., entering his own 'C F' mark at the Sheffield Assay Office on 6 May 1887. On 15 March 1901 he entered a further mark, 'C F & Co', at the Sheffield Assay Office, but in 1902 the firm was acquired by William Hutton & Sons Ltd of Sheffield.

*Mark entered in two sizes.
**Mark entered in three sizes.

Crichton Brothers

LAC   4 February 1895
Lionel Alfred Crichton, Silver worker
22 Old Bond Street, W
29 Church Street, Kensington, W
residence: 2 Bolingbroke Road, West Kensington

LAC   12 March 1904
Crichton Brothers, Silver workers
22 Old Bond Street, W
29 Church Street, Kensington
residence: 18 Hamilton Terrace, NW
partner: Lionel Alfred Crichton

LAC   15 March 1904 (Entry as for 12.3.1904)

LAC   * 13 July 1909
Crichton Brothers, Silver workers
22 Old Bond Street, W
residence: 18 Hamilton Terrace, NW
partner: Lionel Alfred Crichton

LAC   29 January 1910 (Entry as for 13.7.1909)

LAC   30 April 1910 (Entry as for 13.7.1909)

LAC   25 June 1910 (Entry as for 13.7.1909)

LAC   * 28 January 1911 (Entry as for 13.7.1909)

LAC   1 March 1911 (Entry as for 13.7.1909)

LAC   * 20 May 1911 (Entry as for 13.7.1909)

LAC   * 21 July 1911 (Entry as for 13.7.1909)

LAC * 3 July 1912
Crichton Brothers, Gold and Silver workers
22 Old Bond Street, London, W
636 Fifth Avenue, New York, USA
residence: 17 Portman Street, London, W
partner: Lionel Alfred Crichton

This retail firm traded in reproduction and antique silver. It was established *circa* 1890 by Lionel Alfred Crichton, whose first mark was presumably for marking newly manufactured silverware sold in the firm's shop at 22 Old Bond Street. By 1916 the firm had expanded to include branch showrooms in New York and Chicago.

L. A. Crichton was 72 years old when he died in 1938, but the firm continued to trade until it closed down in 1950.

*Mark entered in two sizes.

Alexander Crichton

---

 * 12 November 1872
Alexander Crichton, Plate worker
47 Great Russell Street
residence: 7 Little Russell Street

 28 February 1876
33 Gerrard Street, Soho
residence: 321 Kings Road, Chelsea

Removed to 45 Rathbone Place, W,
14 October 1880
residence: 25 Wingate Road, Hammersmith

Failed, business taken by Messrs E. Dimes (no date recorded, but probably 1893)

As well as being a silversmith, Alexander Crichton was a designer of silverware. About 1880 he entered into partnership with Charles John Curry, trading as Crichton & Curry, but this partnership was dissolved in 1883 and the remaining business was taken over by the silversmith, Edward Dimes.

Edward Dimes entered his first mark at Goldsmiths' Hall on 13 April

1893, probably as a result of having taken over Crichton's business (see Edward Dimes).

Alexander Crichton was declared bankrupt in December 1886 and subsequently moved to Sheffield. He applied for a discharge from bankruptcy in 1899.

*Mark entered in two sizes.

Henry William Curry

H.W.C   * 1 January 1868
Henry William Curry, Plate worker
21 Great Sutton Street, Clerkenwell

H·W·C   ** 13 March 1869
residence: 4 Luccombe House, Pellatt Road, Wood Green
(Mark) defaced 28.3.1882

H·W·C

H·W·C   ** 23 March 1882

When Augustus George Piesse, manufacturing silversmith of 21 Great Sutton Street, died in November 1867, his business was taken over by Henry William Curry. Curry was a manufacturing silversmith who traded additionally in second-hand silverware.

Although Curry's last mark was entered at Goldsmiths' Hall in March 1882, he continued working from 21 Great Sutton Street until 1889 when the premises were taken over by Charles Stuart Harris (No. 2), manufacturing silversmith (see Charles Stuart Harris (No. 2)).

*Mark entered in two sizes.
**Mark entered in three sizes.

William Frederick Curry

* 13 March 1873
Frederick Perry and William Frederick Curry, Plate workers
39 St John Street Road, Clerkenwell
residences: F. Perry: 18 Sudeley Street, City Road
W. Curry: 7 St George's Terrace, Liverpool Road
Manufactory removed to 1 Upper Gloucester Street, Clerkenwell
(undated)

24 March 1879
William Frederick Curry, Plate worker
1 Upper Gloucester Street, Clerkenwell

Circa 1874 Frederick Perry and William Frederick Curry, trading as Perry & Curry, silversmiths, vacated their working premises at 39 St John Street Road, Clerkenwell, and moved to 1 Upper Gloucester Street, Clerkenwell. Although they dissolved their partnership in September 1875, neither of them entered new marks at Goldsmiths' Hall for some years. William Frederick Curry remained at the old premises in Upper Gloucester Street. When Frederick Perry entered his mark in 1880, he gave his address as 25 Thornhill Road, Barnsbury (see Frederick Perry).

*Mark entered in two sizes.

Thomas De La Rue & Co.

T.D.L.R   27 June 1878
Thomas De La Rue, Small worker
110 Bunhill Row
residence: 8 Upper Wimpole Street

17 July 1878

6 February 1879

7 February 1879

20 October 1879

29 January 1880

80

ⓣⓓⓛⓡ ** 5 January 1894

ⓣⓓⓛⓡ *

These marks (6.2.1879 to 5.1.1894) cancelled 1 February 1898

ⓣⓓⓛⓡ ** 1 February 1898
ⓣⓓⓛⓡ * Thomas De La Rue, Small worker
110 Bunhill Row
residence: 8 Upper Wimpole Street, W
The business of Thomas De La Rue having been turned into a
Limited Company under the title of T. De La Rue Ltd, new
punches were entered.

ⓓⓛⓡⓟ * 1 December 1904
Thomas De La Rue Ltd, Gold and Silver workers
110 Bunhill Row, EC
secretary: Stuart Andros De La Rue
residence: 52 Cadogan Square, SW
directors: Evelyn, Andros De La Rue, Ivor Andros De La Rue,
Stuart Andros De La Rue, William Palmer Fuller, William Auld

(no mark) 28 July 1909
Gold and Silver workers
110 Bunhill Row, EC
P. W. Potter's residence: 110 Bunhill Row, EC
directors: Sir T. Andros De La Rue, Bart., Evelyn Andros De La
Rue, Ivor Andros De La Rue, Stuart Andros De La Rue
secretary: Percy William Potter

Frank Aubrey Powell appointed secretary, February 1911
Henry Walter Scarlett appointed secretary, 10 November 1919

The firm of Thomas De La Rue was founded *circa* 1813 to manufacture
and print playing cards. In 1827 it was additionally listed as a straw hat
manufacturer of 65 Crown Street, Finsbury Square. By 1832 the firm was
known as De La Rue, Cornish & Rock, cardmakers of 29 Wilson Street,
Finsbury; and in 1835 as James De La Rue, cardmakers of 20 Finsbury
Place. The following year it was James De La Rue & Rudd, cardmakers,
embossers and wholesale fancy stationers of 20 Finsbury Place.

In 1837 the firm moved to 110 Bunhill Row, where it remained until the
premises were destroyed during a German air raid in 1940. In 1848 and

again in 1854, the firm of Thomas De La Rue & Co. was listed as playing card makers and wholesale stationers.

When Thomas De La Rue died in 1866, the firm was continued by his sons, Warren and Frederick De La Rue.

Although the firm's mark was entered at Goldsmiths' Hall, London, in June 1878, it was not until 5 June 1881 that its mark was first entered at the Sheffield Assay Office. This mark consisted of 'T' over 'DLR', all contained within an oval surround.

In 1898, when the firm was turned into a limited liability company, it was known as printers of postage and other stamps for various governments and colonies, engravers and printers of bank notes and securities and manufacturers of playing cards, stationery, railway tickets, labels, account books, albums, fancy leather goods, writing ink and fountain pens.

*Mark entered in two sizes.
**Mark entered in three sizes.

Deakin & Francis Ltd

---

29 September 1882
Stephen Henry Deakin, Gold worker
S. H. Deakin's residence: 69 Hagley Road, Regent Place, Birmingham

Mark defaced 20.6.1894

14 June 1894
Stephen Henry Deakin, John Horace Francis, Gold and Silver workers
15 and 17 Regent Place, Birmingham
S. H. Deakin's residence: 335 Hagley Road, Birmingham
J. H. Francis' residence: 59 Stanmore Road, Edgbaston, Birmingham

10 November 1896
Removed to 28 Hatton Garden, London
S. H. Deakin's residence: 21 Portland Road, Birmingham
J. H. Francis' residence: 26 Bolton Park Road, Birmingham

27 August 1902
Deakin & Francis Ltd, Gold and Silver workers
15 and 17 Regent Place, Birmingham

S. H. Deakin's residence: 283 Hagley Road, Birmingham
partners: Stephen Henry Deakin, John Horace Francis, Arthur
Salisbury Cox, Robert Hutton, William Lillie Jordan, Joseph Law

28 July 1905
Deakin & Francis Ltd, Gold and Silver workers
15 and 17 Regent Place, Birmingham
J. Law's residence: 8 Mayfield Road, Handsworth
partners: Stephen Henry Deakin, John Horace Francis, William
Lillie Jordan, Robert Hutton, Arthur S. Cox, Joseph Law
(secretary)

In 1848 Charles Washington Shirley Deakin and his partner, C. W. B.
Moore, purchased the Birmingham firm of C. & H. Woolfield, manufactur-
ing jewellers and silversmiths, renaming it Deakin & Moore. When C. W.
B. Moore retired in 1879, C. W. S. Deakin took his nephew, Stephen Henry
Deakin, into partnership, changing the firm's name to Deakin & Nephew.
In December 1881 C. W. S. Deakin retired and S. H. Deakin, together
with another nephew, John Horace Francis, continued running the firm,
renaming it Deakin & Francis.

Although Birmingham based, the firm entered its mark at Goldsmiths'
Hall, London, in 1882 and opened a London office at 28 Hatton Garden
in 1896.

In 1902 the firm was turned into a limited liability company with a board
of six directors including S. H. Deakin and J. H. Francis. Another member
of the board was Robert Hutton, who in 1907 became a director of his
father's silversmithing firm, William Hutton & Sons of Sheffield.

J. H. Francis died in January 1932, aged 71, and S. H. Deakin in March
1936 when 82 years old.

James Deakin & Sons

26 May 1888
John Deakin and William Deakin, Plate workers
Sidney Works, Matilda Street, Sheffield
48 Holborn Viaduct, EC

(no mark) 14 July 1891. Removed to: Sidney Works, Matilda Street,
Sheffield
14 Charterhouse Street, London

34 St Enoch Square, Glasgow
7 Queen Street, Belfast
J. Deakin's and/or W. Deakin's residence: Nether Edge, Sheffield

 10 December 1894
John Deakin and William Deakin, Silver workers
Sidney Works, Sheffield
J. Deakin's residence: Ashland Road, Sheffield
W. Deakin's residence: Moncrief Road, Sharlon

** 6 July 1896
John Deakin and William Deakin, Gold and Silver workers
Sidney Works, Matilda Street, Sheffield
14 Charterhouse Street, London
34 St Enoch Square, Glasgow
7 Queen Street, Belfast
J. Deakin's residence: Osborne Road, Sheffield
W. Deakin's residence: Nether Edge, Sheffield

** 15 April 1909
James Deakin & Sons Ltd, Silver workers
Sidney Works, Sheffield
14 Charterhouse Street, London, EC
34 St Enoch Square, Glasgow
7 Queen Street, Belfast
J. Deakin's residence: Elmleigh, Osborne Road, Brincliffe, Sheffield
directors: William P. Deakin, John Deakin

This Sheffield firm of silversmiths, platers and cutlers was founded by James Deakin, *circa* 1865. On 31 January 1878 the firm's mark was entered at the Sheffield Assay Office for the first time. It consisted of the initials 'J D' over 'W D' and possibly represented those of James Deakin and his son, William Pitchford Deakin. By 1886 two further sons, John and Albert Deakin, had joined the firm, which was then known as James Deakin & Sons.

With the opening of subsidiary offices and showrooms at 48 Holborn Viaduct, London, in 1888, the firm's mark was entered at Goldsmiths' Hall in May of that year by two of the sons, William and John Deakin.

James Deakin retired in January 1893, leaving William, John and Albert to continue running the firm.

In 1897 the firm was turned into a limited liability company, its directors being William Pitchford Deakin, John Deakin and Albert Deakin. John Deakin died prior to 1927, William between 1927 and 1937 and Albert in 1937. The company, James Deakin & Sons Ltd, closed down *circa* 1940.

**Mark entered in three sizes.

James Dewsnap Ltd

J.D

27 August 1880
James Dewsnap, Small worker
10 St Thomas Street, Sheffield
35 Ely Place, Holborn, London, EC
residence: 348 Glossop Road, Sheffield

This mark erased 7 March 1893

TB WA

7 March 1893
Joseph Thomas Bolsover and William Henry Appleby,
Plate workers
10 and 27 St Thomas Street, Sheffield
35 Ely Place, Holborn, London
J. T. Bolsover's residence: 32 Beech Hill Road, Broomhill
W. H. Appleby's residence: 26 Clarke Street, Sheffield

J.D Lᴰ

29 January 1896
James Dewsnap Ltd, Silver worker
10 and 27 St Thomas Street, Sheffield
35 Ely Place, Holborn
W. H. Appleby's residence: 26 Clarke Street, Collegiate Crescent,
Sheffield
managing director: W. H. Appleby

J.D Lᴅ

6 October 1896

J.D.Lᴰ?

19 May 1897
James Dewsnap Ltd, Silver worker
10 St Thomas Street, Sheffield
35 Ely Place, Holborn, EC

J·D Lᴾ

23 August 1902

J·D Lᴰ

4 March 1904
James Dewsnap Ltd, Gold and Silver workers
10 St Thomas Street, Sheffield
35 Ely Place, London EC
W. W. Knowles's residence: 26 Peveril Road, Sheffield
W. W. Knowles, secretary

In a letter to the Deputy Warden (Goldsmiths' Company) dated
12.3.1909, James Dewsnap & Co. advise the appointment of J.
Revill as secretary

This Sheffield firm was founded by James Dewsnap in 1841. Following the opening of a subsidiary office at 35 Ely Place, London, the firm's mark was entered at Goldsmiths' Hall for the first time in August 1880.

When James Dewsnap retired or died *circa* 1885, the firm was continued by Joseph Thomas Bolsover, William Henry Appleby and Richard Parker Greenland. Following Greenland's retirement in January 1892, Bolsover and Appleby continued running the firm, entering a new mark at Goldsmiths' Hall in March 1893.

In 1895 the firm was turned into a limited liability company with W. H. Appleby as managing director. The company closed down in 1941.

Francis David Dexter

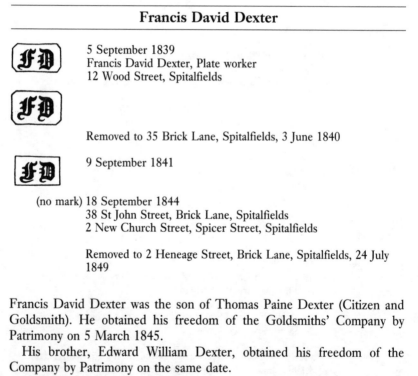

5 September 1839
Francis David Dexter, Plate worker
12 Wood Street, Spitalfields

Removed to 35 Brick Lane, Spitalfields, 3 June 1840

9 September 1841

(no mark) 18 September 1844
38 St John Street, Brick Lane, Spitalfields
2 New Church Street, Spicer Street, Spitalfields

Removed to 2 Heneage Street, Brick Lane, Spitalfields, 24 July 1849

Francis David Dexter was the son of Thomas Paine Dexter (Citizen and Goldsmith). He obtained his freedom of the Goldsmiths' Company by Patrimony on 5 March 1845.

His brother, Edward William Dexter, obtained his freedom of the Company by Patrimony on the same date.

Another brother, John Peter Dexter, obtained his freedom of the Company by Patrimony on 2 October 1844, was made a Liveryman in February 1850 and died in 1871.

Robert Dicker & Co.

* 5 March 1873
Robert Dicker, Plate worker
8 Vigo Street, Regent Street, W
R. Dicker's residence: 23 Warwick Gardens, Kensington

* 10 July 1873 (Mark) defaced 15.7.1886

* 14 July 1886

** 5 June 1914
Robert Dicker & Co., Gold and Silver worker
8 Vigo Street, Regent Street, London, W
F. Parkes's residence: Grangemuir, Wimbledon Common, Surrey
sole partner: Fraser Parkes

Robert Dicker and John Dicker were in partnership as silversmiths and pawnbrokers at 43 High Street, Poplar, until late 1862. Then, in 1863, Robert Dicker appears to have taken over the existing business of Walter Tarrant, silversmith, at 8 Vigo Street, Regent Street. For the rest of his working life, Robert was listed as a silversmith and jeweller.

Following his death in 1900, aged 73, the firm continued trading, and in June 1914 new marks depicting Robert Dicker & Co. were entered by Fraser Parkes, sole partner in the firm. By 1916 the premises had been taken over by Hancock & Co. Ltd, silversmiths and jewellers.

*Mark entered in two sizes.
**Mark entered in three sizes.

Edward Dimes

* 13 April 1893
Edward Dimes, Plate worker
3 King Square, Goswell Road

Also (at) 42 Charterhouse Square, EC, 21 January 1903

Removed to 170 St John Street, EC, 30 June 1904
residence: 4 Marquess Grove, Canonbury, N

This worker in 1905 went into the employment of Elkington &
Co. Ltd but left and again started in June 1906

(ED) * 11 June 1906
Edward Dimes, Silver worker
23 Rahere Street, Goswell Road, EC
residence: 17 Oakley Road, N

Removed to Blue Lion Court, 25 Aldersgate Street, EC, 3 June
1909
residence: 39 Mysore Road, Lavender Hill, SW

Removed to 4 Upper Charles Street, Clerkenwell, EC, 20 March
1911

Removed to 10 Northampton Street, Clerkenwell, 29 August 1916
(Note: This last 'removed' entry has been signed by a different
'Edward Dimes' to the two previous 'removed' entries which have
feebly written 'Edward Dimes' signatures against them.
Presumably the 1916 entry was signed by the son, Edward Ernest
Dimes)

Edward Dimes, the son of Samuel Dimes (silversmith, Citizen and
Goldsmith), obtained his freedom of the Goldsmiths' Company by
Patrimony on 3 February 1869. He was a member of a large family, many
of whom were Freemen of the Goldsmiths' Company. His grandfather, John
Dimes (silversmith), was apprenticed to Charles Chesterman (No. 2)
(silversmith, Citizen and Goldsmith) in 1781 and obtained his freedom in
1788.

His father, Samuel Dimes (silversmith), was apprenticed to grandfather
John Dimes (silversmith, Citizen and Goldsmith) in 1815, was turned over
to Joseph Angell (No. 1) (silversmith, Citizen and Goldsmith) in 1821 and
obtained his freedom in 1823. In 1841 he was working at 139 Old Street
for the firm of C. T. & G. Fox.

Two of Edward Dimes's uncles, William and John Dimes (silversmiths),
obtained their freedoms in 1811 and 1829 respectively, while two of his
cousins, James and Thomas Dimes (silver chasers), obtained their freedoms
in 1853 and 1865 respectively.

Edward Dimes's own son, Edward Ernest Dimes (silversmith), was
apprenticed to Horace Reginald Savory (silversmith, Citizen and Goldsmith)
of 18 Red Lion Street on 2 March 1886 and obtained his freedom of the
Goldsmiths' Company by Patrimony on 5 March 1895. At the time of his

apprenticeship in 1886, his father, Edward Dimes, gave his address as 18 Red Lion Street, so it would appear that he was working for the Goldsmiths' Alliance Ltd, previously known as A. B. Savory & Sons.

Another of Edward Dimes's sons, Henry Bertram Dimes (chaser), obtained his freedom of the Goldsmiths' Company by Patrimony on 6 November 1895.

Edward Dimes presumably worked for many years as an employee of the Goldsmiths' Alliance Ltd until it was voluntarily wound up and its stock sold at Christie's on 7–10 March 1893. He then set up on his own and acquired the failed business of Alexander Crichton (silversmith), entering his own mark at Goldsmiths' Hall in April 1893.

In 1905 he ceased trading and became an employee of Elkington & Co. Ltd, but he again started up on his own in 1906, re-entering his mark. He had probably retired or died by 29 August 1916, the date of the last entry, since it seems to have been signed by his son, Edward Ernest Dimes.

*Mark entered in two sizes.

James Dixon & Son

*** 3 July 1873
James Willis Dixon (No. 2), Plate worker
Cornish Place, Sheffield
37 Ludgate Hill, London
residence: Oakfield House, Sheffield

5 November 1883
J. W. Dixon (No. 2)
residence: Hillsborough Hall, Sheffield

** 9 February 1897
Removed to Cornish House, 14 St Andrews Street, Holborn, EC

* 26 May 1905
James Dixon & Sons, Silver workers
Cornish Place, Sheffield
Cornish House, 14 St Andrews Street, Holborn Circus, London, EC
J. W. Dixon (No. 2)'s residence: Shire House, Sheffield
partners: James Willis Dixon (No. 2), James Dixon, Lennox Burton Dixon, Ernest Dixon Fawcett

16 February 1910 (Entry as for 26.5.1905 except James Willis Dixon is the only partner listed)

 30 April 1910 (Entry as for 26.5.1905, but with the addition of James Kenneth Dixon to the previous list of four partners)

 *** 22 November 1912
James Dixon & Sons, Gold and Silver workers
Cornish Place, Sheffield
Cornish House, 14 St Andrews Street, Holborn Circus, EC
Carson Place, Little Collins Street, Melbourne
420 George Street, Sydney
L. B. Dixon's residence: More Hall, Bolsterstone
partners: James Willis Dixon (No. 2), James Dixon, Lennox B. Dixon, Ernest Dixon Fawcett, James K. Dixon

** 9 October 1914
James Dixon & Sons, Silver workers
Cornish Place, Sheffield
14 St Andrew Street, London
L. B. Dixon's residence: More Hall, Bolsterstone, Sheffield
partners: James Willis Dixon (No. 2), James Dixon, Lennox Burton Dixon, James Kenneth Dixon, Ernest Dixon Fawcett

James Dixon and a Mr Smith founded the firm of Dixon & Smith, Britannia metal workers of Silver Street, Sheffield, *circa* 1804. In 1823 James Dixon took his eldest son, William Frederick Dixon, into partnership, renaming the firm James Dixon & Son.

On 1 September 1826 the firm's mark was entered for the first time at the Sheffield Assay Office, the firm's business address being given as Silver Street. The mark entered comprised the initials 'D & S' in a rectangular surround. At about this time the firm moved to new premises at Cornish Place, Sheffield, and soon afterwards the works were extended to include silversmithing and plating trades.

In 1835 James Dixon's second son, James Willis Dixon (No. 1), was taken into the partnership, the firm's name being changed to James Dixon & Sons. The following year the firm commenced manufacturing nickel silver spoons and forks.

James Dixon died in 1842, leaving his three sons, William Frederick Dixon, James Willis Dixon (No. 1) and Henry Isaac Dixon, together with his son-in-law, William Fawcett, to continue running the firm. William Fawcett died in 1864 and James Willis Dixon (No. 1) in January 1876.

On 13 August 1866 a further mark was entered at the Sheffield Assay Office. This consisted of the initials 'J D & S' in an ogee-shaped rectangular

90

surround. In July 1873 the firm's mark was entered for the first time at Goldsmiths' Hall, London, by James Willis Dixon (No. 2). He was the son of James Willis Dixon (No. 1) and a partner in the firm.

When Henry Isaac Dixon retired in December 1892, the remaining partners were James Willis Dixon (No. 2), James Dixon (great-grandson of James Dixon), Lennox Burton Dixon, James Dixon Fawcett and Ernest Dixon Fawcett. James Dixon Fawcett died in 1900 and James Willis Dixon (No. 2) in 1917. Between 1910 and 1912 James Kenneth Dixon became a partner.

In 1920 the firm became a limited liability company with Lennox Burton Dixon and Ernest Dixon Fawcett as directors. Lennox Burton Dixon died in 1941.

In 1930 the company took over the firm of William Hutton & Sons Ltd, manufacturing silversmiths and platers of Sheffield.

*Mark entered in two sizes.
**Mark entered in three sizes.
***Mark entered in four sizes.

Dobson & Sons

---

* 10 April 1851
Henry Holmes Dobson (No. 1), Plate worker
32 Piccadilly, London

*** 7 December 1877
Thomas William Dobson and Henry Holmes Dobson (No. 2), Plate workers
32 Piccadilly
T. W. Dobson's residence: 149 Abbey Road, St Johns Wood
H. H. Dobson's residence: Holmsdale, Grange Park, Ealing, Middlesex

*** 22 March 1886
Thomas William Dobson, Plate worker
32 Piccadilly
T. W. Dobson's residence: 149 Abbey Road, St Johns Wood

(Marks) defaced 1.4.1886

*** 1 April 1886

22 August 1895

9 February 1898
T. W. Dobson's residence: Gothic House, Chislett Road, N.
Hampstead

T. W. Dobson died in 1905, the business being afterwards carried
on by P. H. & C. W. Dobson

** 28 June 1905
Percy Holmes Dobson and Charles Westcott Dobson, Gold and
Silver workers
200 Piccadilly, W
P. H. Dobson's residence: 62 Marlborough Mansions, Cannon
Hill, Hampstead, NW
C. W. Dobson's residences: 34 Goldhurst Terrace, South
Hampstead
4 Parsifal Road, West Hampstead

22 August 1907

Removed to 110 New Bond Street, W, 9 March 1912

1 December 1913
Dobson & Sons, Gold and Silver workers
110 New Bond Street, London, W
P. H. Dobson's residence: 49 Hollycroft Avenue, Hampstead,
NW
C. W. Dobson's residence: 4 Parsifal Road, West Hampstead

5 January 1914
Dobson & Sons, Gold and Silver workers
110 New Bond Street, London, W
P. H. Dobson's residence: 49 Hollycroft Avenue, Hampstead,
NW
C. W. Dobson's residence: 4 Parsifal Road, West Hampstead
partners: Percy Holmes Dobson, Charles Westcott Dobson

This firm of retail silversmiths and jewellers was founded *circa* 1814 by
Thomas Wilkinson. Following his retirement or death *circa* 1845, the firm
was continued by his son, John Wilkinson, in partnership with Henry
Holmes Dobson (No. 1) under the name of Wilkinson & Dobson. John
Wilkinson was born in 1819 and Henry Holmes Dobson (No. 1) in 1798.

On 1 January 1851 their partnership was dissolved, leaving Henry Holmes
Dobson (No. 1) to continue trading under his own name as a retail

silversmith and jeweller at 32 Piccadilly. He and his wife, Mary, are known to have had three sons and a daughter: Thomas William, born 1824; Henry Holmes (No. 2), born 1826; Talbot, born 1829; and Margaret, born 1833.

In 1877 the firm's name was changed to Dobson & Sons, its partners being two of the sons, Thomas William Dobson and Henry Holmes Dobson (No. 2). Henry Holmes Dobson (No. 2) had two sons who were apprenticed to George Lambert (Citizen and Goldsmith). They were Arthur Edwin Dobson, apprenticed on 2 January 1878, free by Service on 7 January 1885, and Robert Holmes Dobson, apprenticed on 6 November 1878, free by Service on 3 March 1886.

By March 1886 Henry Holmes Dobson (No. 2) had died, leaving Thomas William Dobson to continue running the firm. Following Thomas's death in 1905, the firm was carried on by Percy Holmes Dobson and Charles Westcott Dobson.

*Mark entered in two sizes.
**Mark entered in three sizes.
***Mark entered in four sizes.

Drew & Sons

SSD

27 January 1887
Samuel Summers Drew, Small worker
33 Piccadilly Circus, W
residence: 76 Cromvell Avenue, Highgate Hill, N

(Mark) defaced February 1888

S S D / E D

10 December 1887
Samuel Summers Drew and Ernest Drew, Small workers
156 Leadenhall Street
S. S. Drew's residence: 76 Cromwell Avenue, Highgate
E. Drew's residence: 12 Harringay Road, Crouch End, N

SSD / ED

21 January 1892

S S D / E D

5 February 1892

S.S.D / E.D

22 February 1898

 13 November 1900
Samuel Summers Drew and Ernest Drew, Gold and Silver workers
33 Piccadilly Circus, W
156 Leadenhall Street, EC
S. S. Drew's residence: Leawood, Highgate, N
E. Drew's residence: Langland Gardens, Hampstead

 * 25 November 1903
Drew and Sons (Entry as for 13 November 1900)

15 January 1914
Drew and Sons, Gold and Silver workers
33, 35, 37 Piccadilly Circus, London, W
156 Leadenhall Street, London, EC
E. Drew's residence: 18 Cornwall Terrace, NW
J. S. Drew's residence: Charfield, Oakley Avenue, Whetstone, N
partners: Ernest Drew, John Summers Drew

This firm, founded *circa* 1844, specialised in the manufacture of dressing bags and cases, portmanteaux, trunks, baskets and leather goods. The firm's marks, as entered at Goldsmiths' Hall, are to be found on gold and silver mounts and fittings used on articles manufactured by the firm.

Samuel Summers Drew retired or died at some date prior to 15 January 1914, this being when a further mark was entered at Goldsmiths' Hall excluding his name. The firm was then continued by Ernest Drew in partnership with John Summers Drew.

*Mark entered in two sizes.

Elizabeth Eaton

---

 3 December 1845
Elizabeth Eaton, Spoon and fork maker
16 Jewin Crescent, City

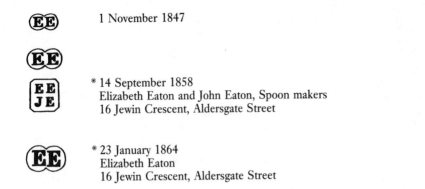

1 November 1847

* 14 September 1858
Elizabeth Eaton and John Eaton, Spoon makers
16 Jewin Crescent, Aldersgate Street

* 23 January 1864
Elizabeth Eaton
16 Jewin Crescent, Aldersgate Street

Elizabeth Eaton was the widow of the silversmith, William Eaton (No. 2). He had traded as a plate worker at 16 Jewin Crescent from 1825 to 1828, then as a plate worker and spoon maker at 2 Lovell's Court, Paternoster Row, from 1828 to 1837 and at 16 Jewin Crescent from 1837 until his death in 1845 (see *Marks of London Goldsmiths and Silversmiths c. 1697–1837*, revised edition 1988, pp. 111, 112).

Following his death, Elizabeth continued running the firm, specialising in the manufacture of silver spoons and forks. In September 1858 she entered a mark at Goldsmiths' Hall in partnership with her son, John Eaton, but this partnership was terminated by January 1864 when she entered her final mark. Her signature against this mark is very shaky indeed, indicating a lack of hand control probably due to old age. She appears to have retired or died within the next two years for, between 16 February and 7 July 1866, the firm was taken over by Henry Holland & Son, manufacturing silversmiths of 14 Northampton Square (see Holland, Aldwinckle & Slater).

*Mark entered in two sizes.

James Charles Edington

6 February 1828
James Charles Edington, Plate worker
43 Berwick Street, Soho

10 November 1837 Removed to 23 Leicester Square

22 January 1845

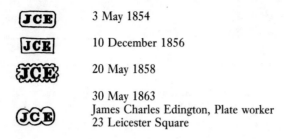

	3 May 1854
	10 December 1856
	20 May 1858
	30 May 1863 James Charles Edington, Plate worker 23 Leicester Square

James Charles Edington was the son of James Edington (Plasterer) of Berwick Street, Soho. On 5 November 1817 he was apprenticed to William Ker Reid (silversmith, Citizen and Goldsmith) who, at the time, was in partnership with Joseph Cradock. James Charles Edington obtained his freedom of the Goldsmiths' Company by Service on 1 December 1824, but apparently did not commence in business on his own account until 1828.

In 1837 he moved to new premises at 23 Leicester Square where he remained for the rest of his working life. In the 1861 Census, he was listed as 59 years old, unmarried and living at 23 Leicester Square, together with his father, James Edington, widower, aged 84 years.

He appears to have retired or died by 9 June 1869, this being when Henry Stokes entered a mark at Goldsmiths' Hall giving Edington's address of 23 Leicester Square as his own.

George Edward & Sons

*** 13 May 1880
David Edward and George Sherwood Edward, Plate workers
1 Poultry, Cheapside
residences: D. Edward: Heather Hill, The Park, Highgate
G. S. Edward: 1 Poultry, Cheapside

All defaced 16.10.1891

* 16 October 1891
David Edward and George Edward, Gold workers
1 Poultry, EC
92 Buchanan Street, Glasgow
residence: Elmslie, Glasgow

4 February 1892

19 March 1892

23 November 1907
Edward & Sons, Gold and Silver workers
92 Buchanan Street, Glasgow
D. H. Edward's residence: 20 Queensborough Gardens, Glasgow, W
partners: George Edward, David Herbert Edward

** 2 April 1909
Edward & Sons, Gold and Silver workers
92 and 96 Buchanan Street, Glasgow
D. H. Edward's residence: Senga, Helensburgh
partners: George Edward, David Herbert Edward

This firm, founded in Glasgow by George Edward *circa* 1838, had established itself at 92 Buchanan Street by 1863. A London branch was opened at 19 Poultry, Cheapside, *circa* 1874, but subsequently moved to 1 Poultry. It was from here that the firm's mark was first entered at Goldsmiths' Hall in May 1880 by George Edward's sons, David Edward and George Sherwood Edward. David Edward was born in 1838 and died in 1913.

In December 1888 George Sherwood Edward left the firm, and in July 1889 commenced trading on his own account. He entered his mark at Goldsmiths' Hall on 22 May 1890 (see George Sherwood Edward).

Meanwhile, the firm continued under the partnership of David Edward and his son, George Edward, a new mark being entered at Goldsmiths' Hall in October 1891. At the time, the firm was listed as manufacturing goldsmiths and silversmiths, watch and clock makers and gem merchants.

When David Edward retired *circa* 1907, another of his sons, David Herbert Edward, became a partner. With the death of David Herbert Edward in 1925, the firm was made into a limited liability company named Edward & Sons Ltd. Eventually, it was taken over by Mappin & Webb Ltd in the late 1960s.

*Mark entered in two sizes.
**Mark entered in three sizes.
***Mark entered in four sizes.

George Sherwood Edward

*** 13 May 1880
David Edward and George Sherwood Edward, Plate workers
1 Poultry, Cheapside
residences: D. Edward: Heather Hill, The Park, Highgate
G. S. Edward: 1 Poultry, Cheapside

All defaced 16.10.1891

22 May 1890
George Edward, Plate worker
62 Piccadilly
residence: 17 Coolhurst Road, Crouch End

George Sherwood Edward and David Edward were the sons of George Edward who, *circa* 1838, founded the Glasgow-based firm of George Edward & Sons. Both sons worked in their father's firm where, by May 1880, they had become partners.

In December 1888 George Sherwood Edward left the family firm, and in July 1889 commenced trading on his own account at 13 Poultry, Cheapside, London. By 22 May 1890, when he entered his mark at Goldsmiths' Hall, he was established in premises at 62 Piccadilly as a manufacturing goldsmith and silversmith, watch and clock maker and diamond merchant. In 1892 he was declared bankrupt and the business closed.

***Mark entered in four sizes.

Edwards & Son

* 14 April 1874
Elizabeth Martha Edwards and Francis Philip Edwards, Plate workers
34 Great Sutton Street, Clerkenwell

This firm was founded by Robert Morley Edwards, electroplater, *circa* 1846. Following his death in about 1872, it was continued by his widow, Elizabeth, and son, Francis, under the name of Edwards & Son. The firm, listed as gilders, electroplaters, silver repairers and polishers, appears to have continued trading until about 1884.

*Mark entered in two sizes.

Elkington & Co. Ltd

 ** 30 September 1851
George Richards Elkington, Plate worker
20 and 22 Regent Street, London
45 Moorgate Street, London
Newhall Street, Birmingham

By virtue of a Power of Attorney I enter three marks of George Richards Elkington, Plate worker of London and Birmingham this 30 September 1851.
John Castelfrane Cheveley, Attorney to the said George Richards Elkington

 *** 11 February 1858

 ** 24 May 1869
Frederick Elkington, Plate worker
22 Regent Street, W
45 Moorgate Street, City
Newhall Street, Birmingham
Church Street, Liverpool
residence: North Field, near Birmingham
signed: Frederick Elkington

Manufactory (acquired) 15 Myddleton Street, Clerkenwell, EC, 6 April 1881

Four marks sent (to Goldsmiths' Hall) and were defaced this day 10 March 1890

 ** 6 March 1890
Elkington & Co. Ltd, Plate workers
128 Newhall Street, Birmingham
Brearley Street, Birmingham
22 Regent Street, London
73 Cheapside, London
15 Myddleton Street, London

25 Church Street, Liverpool
St Ann's Square, Manchester
signed: Henry Rollason, managing director, Elkington Co. Ltd

 13 December 1895

 ‡ 26 January 1897
These six marks withdrawn (refers to those entered on 6.3.1890
and 13.12.1895) and fifteen new marks entered (refers to those
entered on 26.1.1897)

 ‡ 12 February 1897 (Entry as for 6.3.1890)

 † 17 February 1897
H. Rollason's residence: Holbeach, Balham

 ** 18 June 1897
Elkington & Co. Ltd, Plate workers
120 Newhall Street, Birmingham
Brearley Street, Birmingham
22 Regent Street, London
73 Cheapside, London
15 Myddleton Street, London
25 Church Street, Liverpool
St Ann's Square, Manchester
residence: Holbeach, Balham, London
signed: Henry Rollason, managing director, Elkington & Co. Ltd

 ** 16 July 1897 (Entry as for 18.6.1897)

 31 August 1900
Elkington & Co. Ltd, Gold and Silver workers
120 Newhall Street, Birmingham
22 Regent Street, London
73 Cheapside, London
13 Hatton Wall, Hatton Garden, London
25 Church Street, Liverpool
St Ann's Square, Manchester
residence: Holbeach, Balham
signed: H. Rollason, director of Elkington & Co. Ltd

 14 December 1904
Elkington & Co. Ltd, Gold and Silver workers
Newhall Street and Brearley Street, Birmingham
22 Regent Street, 73 Cheapside,

and 1 Hatton Wall, London
27 Lord Street, Liverpool
St Ann's Square, Manchester
84 St Vincent Street, Glasgow
32 Northumberland Street, Newcastle
residence: Chines, Wentworth Road, Sutton Coalfield
directors: Frederick Elkington, Herbert Frederick Elkington, Hyla
Garrett Elkington, Sir George Scott Robertson, William Lee
Matthews
signed: Herbert F. Elkington

These and previous punches were all cancelled 23 May 1906

† 23 May 1906
Elkington & Co. Ltd, Gold and Silver workers
Newhall Street, Birmingham
Brearley Street, Birmingham
22 Regent Street, SW
73 Cheapside, EC
Lord Street, Liverpool
St Ann's Square, Manchester
St Vincent Street, Glasgow
Northumberland Street, Newcastle
residence: 19 Randolph Road, Maida Vale
directors: Herbert F. Elkington, Gerard B. Elkington, Hyla
Garrett Elkington, William Lee Matthews, Andrew Binnie
signed: Gerard B. Elkington

† 8 June 1906 (Entry as for 23.5.1906)

* 23 December 1909
Elkington & Co. Ltd, Gold and Silver workers
Newhall Street, Birmingham
22 Regent Street and 73 Cheapside, London
Watts and Rumball Ltd,
2 Ridgemount Street, WC
Lord Street, Liverpool
St Ann's Square, Manchester
Buckanan Street, Glasgow
Northumberland Street, Newcastle
residence: Kingstone, Trinity Road, Handsworth
signed: T. B. Read, secretary

12 December 1910
Elkington & Co. Ltd, Gold and Silver workers
Newhall Street, Birmingham

22 Regent Street, W
73 Cheapside, London
Lord Street, Liverpool
St Ann's Square, Manchester
Buckanan Street, Glasgow
Commerce Street, Glasgow
Northumberland Street, Newcastle
residence: Kingstone, Trinity Road, Birchfields, Birmingham
directors: H. F. Elkington, H. G. Elkington, G. B. Elkington, G.
M. Elkington, W. L. Matthews, N. H. Gibson, J. Clayton, F. de
Escofet
secretary: T. B. Read
signed: J. Clayton, managing director

18 December 1913
Elkington & Co. Ltd, Gold and Silver workers
* 22 Regent Street, London
73 Cheapside, London
50 King Street, Manchester
27 and 29 Lord Street, Glasgow
34 Buchanan Street, Birmingham
Brierly Street, Birmingham
residences: 33 Trinity Road, Handsworth
Birch Street, Langley Green, Birmingham
directors: Herbert F. Elkington, Hyla G. Elkington, James
Clayton, C. C. Chipman, Edwin Wocker
signed: T. B. Read, secretary

This firm of electroplaters and manufacturing silversmiths was founded *circa* 1836 by George Richards Elkington and his cousin, Henry Elkington. G. R. Elkington, the son of James Elkington (a gilt-toy maker), was born on 17 October 1801 at St Pauls Square, Birmingham. He was apprenticed to his uncles, Josiah Richards and George Richards, and eventually joined them in partnership. George Richards was a jeweller, silversmith, gilt-toy maker and glass cutter.

In about 1824 G. R. Elkington inherited his father's manufactory at St Pauls Square, Birmingham, producing gilt-toys, scent bottles and spectacle cases. Meanwhile, his partnership with his uncle, George Richards, continued until 1840 under the name of Richards & Elkington, toy manufacturers of 24 Bartletts Buildings, Holborn, London and 44 St Pauls Square, Birmingham.

G. R. Elkington maintained other partnerships concurrent with that of Richards & Elkington. One, with Joseph Taylor, a gilt-toy maker of Birmingham, was dissolved in 1839. Another, with his cousin Henry

Elkington, commenced *circa* 1836 and eventually became the firm of Elkington & Co. Within this partnership, G. R. Elkington and Henry Elkington experimented with new ways of gilding base metals. As a result of these experiments, they took out patents for improved gilding methods in 1836 and 1837, and by 1840 they had so perfected an innovative method of electroplating that they were able to commence production at their factory recently completed at Newhall Street, Birmingham. In 1842 they obtained further financial backing by entering into partnership with Josiah Mason, a successful steel pen-nib manufacturer, consequently renaming the firm Elkington, Mason & Co. At about this time, G. R. Elkington opened a showroom at 74 Hatton Garden, London, as a manufacturer of gold, silver and gilt ornaments. Then, between 1848 and 1851, Elkington, Mason & Co. opened another factory, this time at Brearley Street, Birmingham, for electroplating cutlery.

Initially there was resistance to Elkington's electroplating process from other Sheffield plating firms, but before long a number of firms were using the process under licence from Elkington. These included Chirstofle & Cie in France, William Carr Hutton in Sheffield and Edward Barnard & Sons in London. Elkington's agreement in 1842 with Edward Barnard & Sons allowed the firm to plate goods on its own premises under the supervision of an Elkington workman. In return, Barnards agreed to pay Elkington the sum of £200 plus a percentage payment on all goods plated over a period of fourteen years.

In 1840 G. R. Elkington entered into an agreement to supply plated goods to the London silversmith, Benjamin Smith (No. 2). From the sale of these goods, Elkington was to receive two-thirds of the proceeds. In 1841 it was agreed that Smith would manufacture and sell electroplated goods in London, giving Elkington two-thirds of the profits, while Elkington would establish premises in Birmingham for the same purpose, giving Smith one-third of the profits. This led to the opening of electroplating workshops at 45 Moorgate Street, London, and a retail shop at 22 Regent Street, London. Other agreements were made between the two parties, but unfortunately Smith failed to keep them and in 1849 G. R. Elkington terminated all agreements between them, taking control of both London premises. Following this separation, Benjamin Smith (No. 2) became bankrupt early in 1850 and subsequently died in May of that year.

In 1849 G. R. Elkington's daughter, Emma Elizabeth, married Apsley Smith, the son of Benjamin Smith (No. 2). Apsley's occupation was listed at the time as copper smelter, and later as that of country gentleman. Emma died in 1893 and Apsley in 1905.

From 1853 Elkington's design staff was headed by Pierre-Emile Jeannest who had come to England *circa* 1845, initially being employed as a ceramic modeller by Mintons of Stoke-on-Trent. Following his death in 1857, his position at Elkington, Mason & Co. was filled by the recruitment, two years later, of the designers, Leonard Morel-Ladeuil and Auguste Adolphe Willms. Both men died while still in the firm's employment: Morel-Ladeuil in 1888 and Willms in 1899.

In 1852 Henry Elkington died. Then, in 1861, the partnership between G. R. Elkington and Josiah Mason was terminated, the firm being renamed Elkington & Co.

G. R. Elkington died on 22 September 1865, aged 64 years, leaving the firm to be continued by his four sons: Frederick, James Balleny, Alfred John and Howard. Frederick obtained his freedom of the Goldsmiths' Company by Redemption on 7 January 1885, his occupation being listed as silversmith. He was made a Liveryman in July 1890 and died on 2 January 1905. He had two sons, Herbert Frederick and Gerard Bartlett, who became directors of the firm. Gerard Bartlett Elkington obtained his freedom of the Goldsmiths' Company by Redemption on 4 May 1904, was made a Liveryman in May 1907 and died on 1 August 1933. His occupation is listed in the records as metallurgist.

James Balleny Elkington died on 27 June 1907. His son, George M. Elkington, became a director of the firm and died on 18 February 1913.

Howard Elkington died in 1899 and Alfred John Elkington in 1910.

Thomas Henry Rollason joined the firm in 1846 when 15 years old. He eventually became a director of the firm and died in 1908.

*Mark entered in two sizes.
**Mark entered in three sizes.
***Mark entered in four sizes.
†Mark entered in five sizes.
‡Mark entered in eight sizes.

Charles Elkington

 13 June 1854
Charles Elkington, Plate worker
14 Hall Street, City Road, London
The Parade, Birmingham

Initially, Charles Elkington appears to have been in partnership with Alfred Tunstall as electroplate manufacturers at 14 Hall Street, London. With the dissolution of this partnership in 1854, he continued working on his own from the same London address, but with additional premises at The Parade, Birmingham. He entered his mark at Goldsmiths' Hall in June 1854, but was declared bankrupt in December of that year and ceased trading, leaving a considerable number of creditors.

E. & E. Emanuel

* 31 May 1859
Emanuel Emanuel (No. 1) and Ezekiel Emanuel, Plate workers
The Hard, Portsea
101 High Street, Portsmouth

* 16 August 1864
Emanuel Emanuel (No. 1), Plate worker
101 High Street, Portsmouth
residence: Sydney House, Southsea

Retired from business and now carried on by Emanuel his son

* 21 May 1875
Emanuel Emanuel (No. 3), Plate worker
27 Old Bond Street
residence: 20 Westbourn Square

This Portsmouth firm of retail silversmiths and jewellers was probably founded by Moses Emanuel. Following his death on 21 April 1859, the business was continued by his two sons, Emanuel Emanuel (No. 1) and Ezekiel Emanuel.

With the death of Ezekiel on 30 October 1860, Emanuel (No. 1) entered into partnership with Ezekiel's son, Emanuel Emanuel (No. 2). This partnership was dissolved in June 1862, leaving Emanuel (No. 1) to continue trading from 101 High Street, Portsmouth, and Emanuel (No. 2) from 3 The Hard, Portsea.

Circa 1867 Emanuel (No. 1) entered into partnership with his son, Emanuel Emanuel (No. 3), trading as E. & E. Emanuel, jewellers, silversmiths and watchmakers, opening a shop at 1 Burlington Gardens, New Bond Street, London.

With the retirement of Emanuel (No. 1) on 31 December 1870, the firm was continued by his son, Emanuel (No. 3), at Burlington Gardens under the name of Emanuel & Co. Meanwhile, the premises at 101 High Street,

105

Portsmouth, were taken over by a George Dimmer, silversmith and jeweller. By May 1875 Emanuel (No. 3) had moved to 27 Old Bond Street, and by 1881 he had moved to 45 Albemarle Street. In 1891 he was dealing in jewellery and diamonds at 40 Old Bond Street. In 1899 he was at 170 New Bond Street, and in 1900 at 37 Old Bond Street.

*Mark entered in two sizes.

Emanuel Emanuel (No. 2)

6 July 1863
Emanuel Emanuel (No. 2), Plate worker
3 The Hard, Portsea

21 September 1868

20 March 1871

31 March 1871

29 April 1908
E. & E. Emanuel, Gold and Silver worker
3 The Hard, Portsea
residence: 3 The Hard, Portsea
director: Emanuel Emanuel (No. 2)

Emanuel Emanuel (No. 2) was the son of Ezekiel Emanuel and grandson of Moses Emanuel, the probable founder of the Portsmouth firm of E. & E. Emanuel, retail silversmiths and jewellers. When Moses died in April 1859, his business was continued by his two sons, Ezekiel and Emanuel (No. 1). With the death of Ezekiel in October 1860, Emanuel (No. 1) entered into partnership with Ezekiel's son, Emanuel (No. 2), who had inherited his father's portion of the business. This partnership was dissolved in June 1862, leaving Emanuel (No. 1) to continue trading from 101 High Street, Portsmouth, and Emanuel (No. 2) from 3 The Hard, Portsea. Emanuel (No. 2) entered his first mark at Goldsmiths' Hall in July 1863. At the time of his last mark, entered on 29 April 1908, he was listed as E. & E. Emanuel, silversmiths. He died on 20 October 1918.

25 November 1825
Morris and Michael Emanuel, Plate workers
1 Belvis Marks, Camomile Street

29 July 1828

25 October 1830

28 April 1843
Michael and Henry Emanuel, Plate workers
5 Hanover Square

29 November 1855
Harry Emanuel, Plate worker
5 Hanover Square

* 14 August 1858

(no mark)   22 January 1859
manufactory: 6 Riding House Street, Langham Place

* 30 March 1870
Removed to 18 New Bond Street
residence: 23 Great Cumberland Place, Hyde Park

This firm was founded by Joel Emanuel, *circa* 1801. Joel was the brother of Moses Emanuel who is believed to have founded the Portsmouth-based firm, E. & E. Emanuel, retail silversmiths and jewellers. Joel had four sons, Edward, Morris, Michael and Henry, who worked in the family business. When Joel semi-retired *circa* 1818, Edward and Morris continued running the firm as hardwaremen, jewellers and silversmiths.

In August 1825 the partnership between Joel and Morris was dissolved and in November of that year, Morris entered his first mark at Goldsmiths' Hall in partnership with his brother, Michael.

With the retirement of Morris in October 1839, Michael and Henry continued running the firm under the name of Emanuel Brothers. *Circa* 1841 they occupied additional premises at 5 Hanover Square, to which they subsequently moved from their Bevis Marks premises *circa* 1843. In January 1846 Michael and Henry were filed bankrupts, but in the subsequent Court of Bankruptcy hearings, it transpired that Henry was to blame for all their debts, amounting to some £120,000. Michael was cleared of any offence, but Henry was described as one of the most fraudulent men that had ever appeared before the Court. Michael continued running the firm until his retirement or death in 1855 at the age of 50, following which his son, Harry, took over the firm and entered his own mark at Goldsmiths' Hall in 1855.

Harry, born *circa* 1830, continued to sell diamonds, jewellery and silverware from 5 Hanover Square, but in January 1859 he, together with Francis Higgins (No. 3) and others, set up a secondary firm called Portland Co. Ltd at 6 Riding House Street. This company produced cutlery by an improved method of manufacture. Unfortunately, it did not prove to be a financial success and went into voluntary liquidation in 1863.

Meanwhile, *circa* 1860, Harry Emanuel's own firm moved to new premises at 70–71 Brook Street, Hanover Square, and then to 18 New Bond Street and 18 Clifford Street *circa* 1864. Harry retired in 1873, selling the lease of his premises to his former manager, Edwin W. Streeter. While in retirement, Harry was created Baron de Almeda and moved to Paris where, in 1880, he was appointed the Minister Plenipotentiary of the Dominican Republic in France. He died in Nice on 17 January 1898, his body being returned to England for burial at Balls Pond Cemetery, London.

*Mark entered in two sizes.

C. Fabergé

(AB)   7 July 1904
Arthur Bowe, Gold and Silver worker
Portman House, 415 Oxford Street, W
A. Bowe's residence: Portman House, 415 Oxford Street, W

(CF)   * 7 March 1911
Charles Fabergé
(CF)   * Gold and Silver worker
48 Dover Street, Piccadilly, London, W
residence: 48 Dover Street, Piccadilly, W
By Virtue of a Power of Attorney dated 27 January 1911, I enter
the Marks of Charles Fabergé.
(signed) Henry C. Bainbridge, his Attorney

(CF) 24 May 1911
Charles Fabergé (Entry as for 7.3.1911)

17 July 1911
Removed to 173 New Bond Street, London, W
H. C. Bainbridge's residence: Charnside, Wargrave on Thames

27 November 1915
By Virtue of a Power of Attorney dated 20 October and
2 November 1915, I enter the Marks of Charles Fabergé.
(signed) Charles William Stones
residence: Hey Tor, Carshalton, Surrey

This firm of manufacturing and retail jewellers, goldsmiths and silversmiths was founded by Gustav Petrovitch Fabergé in St Petersburg in 1842. He died in 1893, when 78 years old. His son, Peter Carl Fabergé (b.30.5.1846), took control of the firm in 1870 when only 24 years old. In 1872 he married Augusta Julia Jacobs (b.25.12.1851, d.27.1.1925). Augusta and Peter Carl Fabergé had four sons: Eugène (1874–1960), Agathon (1876–1951), Alexander (1877–1952) and Nicholas (1884–1939). All four sons eventually joined the family firm.

By 1887 the firm had expanded sufficiently to justify opening a branch in Moscow. Then, in 1903, Fabergé sent Arthur Bowe from Moscow to open a branch in London. Arthur Bowe, together with his brothers, Allen and Charles, were all associated with the House of Fabergé. Allen Bowe was one of the firm's partners, a post he held until his retirement in 1906.

Initially Arthur Bowe operated from an office he set up at the Berners Hotel, 6–7 Berners Street. Then, in 1904, he moved the London branch to Portman House, 415 Oxford Street, from where he entered his mark at Goldsmiths' Hall on 7 July. He retired from the firm of Fabergé in 1906, and then, in June 1908, entered a new mark at Goldsmiths' Hall in partnership with William Crump, trading as Noble and Company, importer of gold and silver wares.

Following the retirement of Arthur Bowe, the London branch of Fabergé moved to St Petersburg House, 48 Dover Street, Piccadilly, under the joint management of Henry Charles Bainbridge and Nicholas Fabergé, the youngest son of Peter Carl Fabergé. In 1911 new marks were entered at Goldsmiths' Hall by Henry Charles Bainbridge acting as attorney for the firm of Fabergé. By 17 July 1911 the London branch had moved to its final address at 173 New Bond Street. It officially ceased to trade in 1915, but unofficially continued until 1917 under a Power of Attorney granted to Charles William Stones. Eventually, the firm of Fabergé was closed down by the Bolsheviks in 1918.

In September 1918 Peter Carl Fabergé escaped from Russia and eventually reached Wiesbaden, Germany. He subsequently moved to Lausanne, Switzerland, and died on 24 September 1920 at Hotel Bellevue, La Rosiaz, Lausanne.

*Mark entered in two sizes.

Rupert Favell & Co.

* 28 April 1879
Rupert Favell
Removed to 11 Bucknall Street, New Oxford Street

6 July 1880

3 April 1883
Rupert Favell and Henry Elliott, Plate workers
5 Bucknall Street, New Oxford Street
residence: 65 Gloucester Crescent, Regents Park

The above punches (entered 3.4.1883) were not used until September 1887

24 July 1891
Rupert Favell, Plate worker

Bedford Walk, Bucknall Street, New Oxford Street
residence: 45 St Johns Park, Blackheath

Rupert Favell is first recorded in 1862 as a partner with Charles Favell in the firm of Creswick & Co., silversmiths and platers of 111 Arundel Street, Sheffield, and 17 Craven Street, London. On 16 February 1874 Rupert

Favell entered a mark at Goldsmiths' Hall, London, on behalf of Creswick & Co. (see Creswick & Co.) but then, on 31 March 1879, Rupert and Charles Favell dissolved their partnership, following which Rupert commenced trading from Bucknall Street, New Oxford Street as Rupert Favell & Co., silver and electroplate manufacturers. Meanwhile, Charles continued trading as Creswick & Co., entering his own mark at Goldsmiths' Hall (see Creswick & Co).

In 1883 Rupert took Henry Elliott into partnership, renaming the firm Favell, Elliott & Co. However, following Elliott's retirement in December 1890, the firm's name reverted to Rupert Favell & Co. In 1893 the firm was then taken over by William Hutton & Sons of Sheffield.

*Mark entered in two sizes.

Fenton Brothers

17 June 1875
John Frederick Fenton and Frank Fenton, Plate workers
South Moor Works, Earl Street, Sheffield
22 Bartletts Buildings, Holborn Circus
residences: J. Fenton: 230 Eccleshall Road, Sheffield
F. Fenton: 232 Eccleshall Road, Sheffield

(This mark was entered by Joseph Andrews Barton, 22 Bartletts Buildings, Holborn Circus, London, under a Power of Attorney dated 16.6.1875)

3 September 1881

*** 13 November 1883
Frank Fenton and Samuel Fenton, Plate workers
South Moor Works, Earl Street, Sheffield
residences: F. Fenton: Chambord House, Pontac, Jersey
S. Fenton: Thorn Bank, Spring Hill Road, Sheffield

(These marks were entered by Joseph Andrews Barton, 22 Bartletts Buildings, Holborn Circus, London, under a Power of Attorney dated 30.10.1883)

*** 23 April 1888
Samuel Fenton and Alfred John Fenton, Plate workers
South Moor Works, Earl Street, Sheffield
residences: S. Fenton: Thorn Bank, Spring Hill Road, Sheffield

111

A. J. Fenton: 242 Eccleshall Road, Sheffield
(These marks were entered by Joseph Andrews Barton, 22
Bartletts Buildings, Holborn Circus, London, under a Power of
Attorney dated 23.4.1888)

 *** 22 November 1893
Samuel Fenton and William Stainforth, Plate workers
South Moor Works, Earl Street, Sheffield

22 Bartletts Buildings
residences: S. Fenton: Thorn Bank, Spring Hill Road, Sheffield
W. Fenton: Westmorland Villa, 221 Upper Thorpe, Sheffield

** 18 December 1896
Fenton Brothers Ltd, William Stainforth, managing director,
Silver workers
South Moor Works, Earl Street, Sheffield
22 Bartletts Buildings, EC
residence: W. Stainforth: 221 Upper Thorpe, Sheffield

New London address: 89 Hatton Garden, London, EC, 4 March
1914

This firm of manufacturing silversmiths and platers commenced as Hukin
& Fenton of Cadman Lane, Sheffield, its mark being entered at the
Sheffield Assay Office on 7 February 1856. However, on 28 July 1856 John
Frederick Fenton entered his own mark of 'J F F' from the same address.
Then, on 5 November 1860, he and his brother, Frank Fenton, entered a
partnership mark of 'F Brs' from 14 Norfolk Lane, Sheffield. On 13 August
1868 they entered a new mark of 'J F F' over '& F F', and on 26 June 1875
one of 'J F F' over 'F F'. Both of these entries listed their address as South
Moor Works, Sheffield.

On 17 June 1875 they entered their first mark at the London Assay
Office, giving 22 Bartletts Buildings as the address of their London
showrooms. By November 1883 John F. Fenton had either retired or died
and his brother, Frank Fenton, had retired to Jersey, leaving John F.
Fenton's son, Samuel Fenton, to continue running the firm.

At some date prior to 23 April 1888, Samuel Fenton took Alfred John
Fenton into partnership. Then, on 17 November 1891, Samuel entered a
new mark at the Sheffield Assay Office in partnership with William
Stainforth. This same mark was entered at Goldsmiths' Hall, London, in

1893. *Circa* 1896 the firm was made a limited liability company with William Stainforth as managing director.

In March 1914 the London showrooms at 22 Bartletts Buildings were transferred to 89 Hatton Garden.

**Mark entered in three sizes.
***Mark entered in four sizes.

John Wilmin Figg

* 31 July 1834
John Wilmin Figg, Plate worker
25 St John Street, Clerkenwell
signed: John Figg (No. 1)

* 10 May 1838
Removed to 5 Wellington Street, St Lukes

10 July 1848
Removed to 6 Denmark Street, St Giles

8 December 1882
John Wilmin Figg, Plate worker
6 Denmark Street, St Giles
signed: John Figg (No. 2)

This firm was founded by John Wilmin Figg (No. 1) in 1834. John Wilmin Figg (No. 1), the son of William Figg (farmer) of Kenton, Middlesex, was apprenticed to William Elliott (Citizen and Goldsmith) of Compton Street, Clerkenwell, on 1 February 1826. He obtained his freedom on 5 June 1833. Later, he moved to 5 Wellington Street and then, some ten years afterwards, to 6 Denmark Street.

Two of his apprentices were Frederick Yonge Fox, apprenticed to him in

1845, and George Boyton, apprenticed in 1846. His son, John Wilmin Figg (No. 2), was apprenticed to him on 3 July 1861 but never obtained his freedom of the Goldsmiths' Company, although he continued to work in his father's firm. It was John Wilmin Figg (No. 2) who entered the firm's mark at Goldsmiths' Hall in 1882.

Following the death of John Wilmin Figg (No. 1) on 7 May 1886, the firm was taken over by Walter Keith of Keith & Co., silversmiths. Keith continued running the firm as Figg & Co. from its existing premises at 6 Denmark Street until *circa* 1892.

*Mark entered in two sizes.

C. J. Fox & Co. Ltd

C.J.F   16 June 1884
Charles James Fox, Small worker
31 Sekforde Street, Clerkenwell
residence: 182 Downham Road, Islington

Removed to 23 St James Walk, Clerkenwell, 27 June 1887

Removed to 18 St John Street Road, 8 January 1890

C.J.F   6 December 1893
Defaced 30.4.1896

Removed to 21 and 22 Great Sutton Street, EC, 23 January 1896

CJF   30 April 1896
Charles James Fox, Small worker
21 and 22 Great Sutton Street, EC

Removed to 17 and 19 Great Sutton Street, Clerkenwell, EC, 27 April 1898

CJF   1 September 1898

CJF   9 March 1899

CJF   17 November 1899

Removed to 40 Great Pulteney Street, W, 7 September 1903

CJF

28 February 1907
Small worker
40 Great Pulteney Street, London, W
residence: 16 Park Avenue, Wood Green
director: Charles James Fox

CJF

28 February 1910
Gold and Silver workers
40 Great Pulteney Street, Golden Square
residence: 16 Park Avenue, Wood Green, N
managing director: Charles James Fox

Charles James Fox appears to have founded this firm in 1884, entering his first mark as a manufacturing silversmith on 16 June of that year. In 1888, when he entered into partnership with William Fox, the firm was known as Charles James Fox & Co.

In June 1889 the firm was converted into a limited liability company, its directors being listed as C. J. Fox and W. H. Hazard. Then, in December 1889, the partnership between Charles James Fox and William Fox was dissolved with C. J. Fox moving to 18 St John Street Road, where he continued to trade as a manufacturing silversmith.

William Fox, meanwhile, remained at 23 St James Walk, where he continued to trade on his own (see William Fox).

The firm of C. J. Fox & Co. Ltd was still in existence in 1916.

C. T. & G. Fox

26 July 1841
Charles Thomas Fox and George Fox, Plate workers
139 Old Street
* signed: Charles Thomas Fox, George Fox

20 August 1841
signed: Charles Thomas Fox, George Fox

*

29 September 1843
signed: Charles Thomas Fox, George Fox

115

Removed to 13 Queen Street, Soho, 9 January 1852
signed: George Fox

* 11 March 1861
George Fox, Plate worker
residence: 14 Albion Terrace, Canonbury Square, Islington
signed: George Fox

Removed to 13 Queen Street, Soho Market, now called Bateman
Street (no date)
residence: 5 Tufnell Park Road, Holloway

1 January 1869
signed: George Fox

25 March 1891
Removed to 50 Berwick Street
residence: 104 Hammersmith Road
signed: Robert Frederick Fox

George Fox died and the next entry is that of his son, Robert
Frederick Fox, 15 September 1910

20 September 1910
Robert Frederick Fox
Silver worker
50 Berwick Street, Oxford Street, W
residence: 50 Berwick Street, Oxford Street, W
signed: Robert Frederick Fox

This firm of manufacturing silversmiths was established in 1801 by James
Turner and Charles Fox (No. 1) at 3 Old Street. With the dissolution of
their partnership in 1804, Charles Fox (No. 1) moved into premises at 139
Old Street, where he continued trading as a manufacturing silversmith. In
1822 his son, Charles Fox (No. 2), appears to have taken over the firm,
entering marks at Goldsmiths' Hall from 1822 to 1838 (see *Marks of London
Goldsmiths and Silversmiths c. 1697–1837*, revised edition 1988, pp. 137–8).

Charles Fox (No. 2) and his wife, Catherine (née Goodson),[1] are known
to have had five children who survived infancy. They were: Yonge William;
Mary; Charles Thomas, born 1801; Frederick, born 1810; and George,
born 1816. Frederick Fox became a corn chandler, but in 1852 he
apparently set up as a silversmith and probably entered into partnership with
his silversmith son, Frederick Yonge Fox.

Charles Thomas and George Fox, meanwhile, took over the family firm
when their father, Charles Fox (No. 2), retired. They entered their first

partnership mark at Goldsmiths' Hall in July 1841. Charles Fox (No. 2) subsequently died on 14 March 1850 when 73 years old.

Charles Thomas Fox retired from the firm in December 1860 and subsequently died on 6 June 1872. Following his brother's retirement, George Fox continued running the firm, entering the first of his own marks in March 1861. His last mark was entered in March 1891 when he was 75 years old. It was entered by his son, Robert Frederick Fox, born in 1845, who presumably had taken over the running of the firm some years previously. With the death of George Fox in 1910, Robert Frederick Fox entered his own mark. He continued trading as C. T. & G. Fox until 1921 when the firm closed down.

[1] For details of Catherine Fox's will, see *Marks of London Goldsmiths and Silversmiths c.1697–1837*, revised edition 1988, pp. 383, 384.

*Mark entered in two sizes.

Frederick Fox

* 5 August 1852
Frederick Fox, Plate worker
75 Goswell Road, Clerkenwell
signed: Frederick Fox

12 October 1852

Removed to 21 High Street, Camden Town, 24 October 1854

Born in 1810, Frederick Fox was the son of Catherine (née Goodson) and Charles Fox (No. 2) (silversmith) of 139 Old Street (see *Marks of London Goldsmiths and Silversmiths c. 1697–1837*, revised edition 1988, pp. 137–8). In 1852 Frederick Fox was listed as a corn chandler of 75 Goswell Road, although he appears to have been working as a silversmith, having entered marks at Goldsmiths' Hall under his own name on 5 August. On the other hand, his son, Frederick Yonge Fox, had just obtained his freedom of the Goldsmiths' Company by Service on 3 March 1852, and it may be that Frederick Fox entered into partnership with his son at the time just to give him financial backing in his silversmithing business.

Frederick Fox apparently resigned *circa* December 1867, leaving his son, Frederick Yonge Fox, to continue running the business and enter his own marks at Goldsmiths' Hall (see Frederick Yonge Fox).

Frederick Fox is listed as living at 6 Regina Road, Tollington Park, in 1882 where presumably he remained until his death on 1 April 1884.

*Mark entered in two sizes.

Frederick Yonge Fox

---

* 31 January 1868
Frederick Yonge Fox, Plate worker
12 Panton Square, Coventry Street
signed: F. Y. Fox

25 August 1868

These marks were withdrawn, 2 September 1870

Frederick Yonge Fox was the son of Frederick Fox (corn chandler) of 75 Goswell Road, Clerkenwell, and was apprenticed to John Wilmin Figg (No. 1) (silversmith, Citizen and Goldsmith) on 5 February 1845. He obtained his freedom of the Goldsmiths' Company by Service on 3 March 1852, following which he apparently worked as a silversmith either for his father or in partnership with him. If it was the latter, it is possible that his father was a sleeping partner. On 5 August 1852 marks were entered at Goldsmiths' Hall under Frederick Fox's name, followed by a second mark some two months later.

With the retirement of Frederick Fox, *circa* December 1867, Frederick Yonge Fox continued running the business, entering his own marks at Goldsmiths' Hall in 1868. Since these marks were withdrawn on 2 September 1870 and no further marks were entered at Goldsmiths' Hall, it seems likely that he ceased trading as a silversmith from this date.

His son, Frederick William Fox, became an armourer in the Royal Navy and obtained his freedom of the Goldsmiths' Company by Patrimony on 4 November 1896.

*Mark entered in two sizes.

William Fox

8 January 1890
William Fox, Small worker
23 St James Walk, Clerkenwell

20 April 1898
15 Kingsgate Street, Holborn

In 1888 William Fox joined Charles James Fox in partnership in the firm of Charles James Fox & Co., manufacturing silversmiths of 23 St James Walk, Clerkenwell. With the dissolution of their partnership in December 1889, Charles James Fox moved to 18 St John Street Road (see C. J. Fox & Co.), while William Fox remained at 23 St James Walk from where he entered his own mark in 1890.

Frederick Francis and Thomas Henry Francis

F·F

3 June 1852
Frederick Francis, Plate worker
manufactory: 26 Wells Street, Oxford Street
residence: 23 Wells Street, Oxford Street

Removed to 5 Market Street, Oxford Street, 22 April 1853

T·H·F & F·F

* 23 January 1854
Thomas Henry Francis and Frederick Francis, Plate workers
5 Market Street, Oxford Street

Removed to 24 Poland Street, Oxford Street, 10 October 1854

Thomas Henry Francis, born in November 1824, and Frederick Francis, born in May 1829, were the sons of Jane and Thomas Francis (silversmith) of 5 Salisbury Street, Fleet Street. Frederick Francis entered his first mark as a manufacturing silversmith on 3 June 1852. Later, he was joined by his brother, Thomas Henry Francis, and they entered a partnership mark at Goldsmiths' Hall in 1854.

They continued to trade as manufacturing silversmiths at 24 Poland

Street until April 1866 when the business was closed down due to Frederick Francis becoming a debtor and filing a Deed of Composition.

*Mark entered in two sizes.

R. & S. Garrard & Co.
---

29 June 1847
Robert Garrard (No. 2), Plate worker
29 Panton Street

† 14 October 1881
James (Mortimer) Garrard, Plate worker
29 Panton Street, Haymarket
residences: 103 Westbourne Terrace, Pinner Place, Pinner

The above worker, a member of the Court died March 1900, the next registration is that of his son Sebastian Henry Garrard

25 April 1900
Sebastian Henry Garrard
Gold and Silver workers
25 Haymarket
†† 29–31 Panton Street, London, W
residence: Pinner Place, Pinner

It having been decided not to accept any Makers Mark with a Crown, the above were cancelled, 19 April 1901. (Marks) all defaced 24 April 1901

‡ 19 April 1901 (Entry as for 25.4.1900)

* 12 February 1914
Garrard and Co. Ltd
* Gold and Silver workers
24 Albemarle Street
17 Grafton Street
1, 2 and 3 Avery Row, London, W
residence: Welton Place, Daventry
partner: Sebastian Harry Garrard

This firm was founded in 1722 by George Wickes (Citizen and Goldsmith). It then continued to operate for the remainder of the eighteenth century under the following names: Craig & Wickes, George Wickes, Wickes & Netherton, Parker & Wakelin, Wakelin & Tayler, Wakelin & Garrard and, from August 1802, Robert Garrard. This was when Robert Garrard (No. 1) acquired complete control of the firm, a position he held until his death on 26 March 1818. Under the terms of his will, proved on 4 April 1818, his three eldest sons, Robert (No. 2), James and Sebastian, aged 24, 22 and 19 respectively, had been bequeathed his business and were directed by him to become partners in the firm (see *Marks of London Goldsmiths and Silversmiths c.1697–1837*, revised edition 1988, Will of Robert Garrard (No. 1), pp. 384–8; also see Robert Garrard (No. 1) and Robert Garrard (No. 2), pp. 146–8, for the firm's marks prior to 1847). Being senior partner, Robert (No. 2) inherited 40 per cent of the firm while James and Sebastian were each bequeathed 30 per cent. As a result of this reorganisation and the setting up of the new partnership, the firm's name was changed to R. J. & S. Garrard.

Circa 1835 the firm's name was altered to R. & S. Garrard due to James Garrard retiring from the firm, although he continued to be an active member of the Goldsmiths' Company.

In 1843 the firm's name was modified to R. & S. Garrard & Co. and remained as such until March 1909 when the firm was made into a limited liability company. During this period there were other partners in the firm beside Robert (No. 2) and Sebastian: Samuel Spilsbury in the 1840s, Robert Sewers in the 1850s and John Peter Dexter *circa* 1870.

During November 1870 both James and Sebastian Garrard died, leaving Robert (No. 2) as head of the company. Then, with the death of Robert (No. 2) on 26 September 1881, his nephew, James Mortimer Garrard, took control of the company, entering his own mark at Goldsmiths' Hall. When he died in March 1900, his son, Sebastian Henry Garrard, took over as senior partner, the other partners at the time being Henry C. Pearson, Henry J. Bell and Maurice Whippy Garrard.

In 1911, after occupying premises in Panton Street since about 1735, the firm of Garrard & Co. Ltd moved to a new building at 24 Albemarle Street and 17 Grafton Street. On 24 June 1952 the company was taken over by the Goldsmiths & Silversmiths Co. Ltd and transferred to 112 Regent Street, where it continued to trade under the name of Garrard & Co. Ltd. However, on 13 November 1959, both Garrard's and the Goldsmiths & Silversmiths Co. Ltd were taken over by Mappin & Webb Ltd, then a division of Sears Holdings Ltd.

Returning to individual members of the Garrard family, biographical information is as follows.

Robert Garrard (No. 1) (1758–1818) and his wife, Sarah (née Crespel) (1767–1824), had ten children, of whom eight were still living at the time of Robert (No. 1)'s death. They were Robert (No. 2), James, Sebastian, Stephen, Henry, Sarah, Miriam and Caroline.

Robert (No. 2), born on 13 August 1793, was apprenticed to his father (silversmith, Citizen and Grocer) on 1 June 1809 and obtained his freedom of the Grocers' Company by Service on 4 July 1816. He was made a Liveryman of the Grocers' Company in May 1818, 3rd Warden in 1844 and again in 1845, 2nd Warden in 1852 and Prime Warden or Master in 1853. He died on 26 September 1881. On 11 June 1825, he married Ester Whippy who gave him three sons and three daughters. The eldest son, Robert (1831–1896), became a Captain in the 5th Dragoon Guards.

James Garrard, born on 13 June 1795, obtained his freedom of the Goldsmiths' Company by Redemption on 1 June 1825. He was made a Liveryman of the Goldsmiths' Company in March 1829, an Assistant in January 1842, 4th Warden in 1844, 3rd Warden in 1845, 2nd Warden in 1846 and Prime Warden in 1847 and 1850. He married Emily Van der Zee and died in November 1870.

Sebastian Garrard was born in 1798. He married Harriet Fletcher but they were unable to produce any children. Sebastian died on 11 November 1870 and Harriet in 1873.

Henry Garrard, born in 1808, emigrated to New England, Australia, where he became a farmer. In 1831 he married Mary Mortimer who gave him four sons and seven daughters. Their four eldest children, of whom James Mortimer was the third, returned to England where they were adopted and educated by their childless aunt and uncle, Harriet and Sebastian Garrard. Henry Garrard died in 1862, and Mary, his wife, in 1873.

James Mortimer Garrard, born in Australia in 1834, was apprenticed to George Withers (silversmith, Citizen and Goldsmith) of 32 Panton Street on 6 March 1850. He obtained his freedom of the Goldsmiths' Company by Service on 1 April 1857, was made a Liveryman in November 1860, an Assistant in March 1891, 4th Warden in 1893, 3rd Warden in 1894, 2nd Warden in 1895 and Prime Warden in 1896. In 1865 he married Mary Holloway who gave him a daughter, Ethel Mary, and two sons, Sebastian Henry and James Robert Lindsey. James Mortimer Garrard died on 3 March 1900 and his wife, Mary, in the same year.

Sebastian Henry Garrard, born in 1868, obtained his freedom of the Goldsmiths' Company by Patrimony on 4 December 1889 and was made a Liveryman in January 1895. He married Mary Eleanor Cazenove in 1894, by whom he had six daughters, and died on 23 February 1946.

James Robert Lindsey Garrard, born in 1871, became a 2nd Lieutenant in the 5th Dragoon Guards. He obtained his freedom of the Goldsmiths' Company by Patrimony on 5 July 1892 and was made a Liveryman in June 1897. He married Ada Bain-Brown, by whom he had two daughters, and died on 11 July 1935.

*Mark entered in two sizes.
†Mark entered in five sizes.
††Mark entered in six sizes.
‡Mark entered in eight sizes.

George Gillett

 * 12 October 1880
George Gillett, Small worker
1 Upper Gloucester Street, Clerkenwell

 19 June 1883

 8 September 1890

He was the son of George Gillett (Citizen and Goldsmith) and obtained his freedom of the Goldsmiths' Company by Patrimony on 3 June 1874. In 1897 he was recorded as a silversmith trading from 46 Gloucester Street, Clerkenwell.

*Mark entered in two sizes.

Goldsmiths & Silversmiths Co. Ltd

 ** 22 June 1882
William Gibson and John Langman, Plate workers
112 Regent Street
Langman's residence: 9 Patshull Road, NW
signed: Wm Gibson, John Langman

17 April 1883

2 September 1890

24 May 1894

*** 13 July 1894
William Gibson and John Langman, Plate workers
112 Regent Street
residences: W. Gibson: 47 Albion Street, Hyde Park
J. Langman: 6 Stanhope Terrace, Hyde Park
signed: Wm Gibson, John Langman

14 July 1894
Nineteen marks produced and defaced this day some which had been in use but never registered.

Impressions of three marks found to have been in use but not
* registered. (Example of these three marks is illustrated here)

* 19 January 1895

The above marks cancelled 31 May 1897

†† 31 May 1897
William Gibson and John Langman, Plate workers
112 Regent Street, W
signed: Wm Gibson, John L. Langman

All these marks are cancelled (21.6.1898)

†† 21 June 1898
William Gibson and John Langman, Gold and Silver workers
110–112 Regent Street, W
48 Glasshouse Street
48 and 49 Warwick Street, W
residences: W. Gibson: 47 Albion Street, Hyde Park, W
J. Langman: 6 Stanhope Terrace, Hyde Park, W
signed: Wm Gibson, John L. Langman

27 September 1899
Goldsmiths & Silversmiths Co. Ltd, Gold and Silver workers
110–112 Regent Street, W
48 Glasshouse Street, W
48–49 Warwick Street, W
MaGinnis's residence: 29 Carmalt Gardens, Putney, SW
signed: A. Gordon MaGinnis

These workers are previously entered in the books under the
name of Gibson and Langman. The Goldsmiths and Silversmiths
Company was floated as a Limited Company in 1898.

16 February 1900
110–112 Regent Street, W
MaGinnis's residence: 29 Carmalt Gardens, Putney, SW
signed: A. Gordon MaGinnis

27 February 1900

27 January 1904
Goldsmiths & Silversmiths Co. Ltd, Gold and Silver workers
110–112 Regent Street, W
MaGinnis's residence:
Caerwys, Putney Common, SW
director: Alexander Gordon MaGinnis

10 August 1906
Goldsmiths & Silversmiths Co. Ltd, Gold and Silver workers
110–112 Regent Street, W
47–49 Warwick Street
48 Glasshouse Street, W
MaGinnis's residence: Caerwys, Putney Common, SW
director: A. Gordon MaGinnis

29 October 1908
Goldsmiths & Silversmiths Co. Ltd, Gold and Silver workers
112 Regent Street
Warwick Street
Glasshouse Street, London, W
Rice's residence: 28 Eland Road, Lavender Hill
directors: William Gibson, William Henry Willoughby,
Courtauld Thompson, Charles L. Graff, Eugene Henry Posen
secretary: James William Rice

12 October 1911
Goldsmiths & Silversmiths Co. Ltd, Gold and Silver workers
112 Regent Street
47 Warwick Street, London
Rice's residence: 12 Mysore Road, Lavender Hill, SW

directors: William Gibson, Courtauld Thompson, Charles L.
Graff, Eugene Henry Posen, W. S. Salisbury
secretary: James W. Rice

17 June 1913
Goldsmiths & Silversmiths Co. Ltd, Gold and Silver workers
112 Regent Street
47–49 Warwick Street, London
Rice's residence: 12 Mysore Road, Lavender Hill, SW
directors: Sir Courtauld Thompson, Charles L. Graff, Eugene H.
Posen, Walter S. Salisbury, Albert T. Rice, William Gibson
secretary: James W. Rice

This firm, trading as the Manufacturing Goldsmiths and Silversmiths Co.,
was established in 1880 by William Gibson and John Lawrence Langman
at 112 Regent Street, London, for the manufacture and retailing of jewellery
and gold and silver goods. William Gibson, born *circa* 1839, was a jeweller
and had already established his own firm of W. Gibson & Co. in Belfast.
He died on 1 November 1913 when 74 years old. John Lawrence Langman,
born on 24 June 1846, was created a baronet on 21 July 1906 and died on
30 October 1928.

The firm's mark was first entered at the Sheffield Assay Office by W.
Gibson and J. L. Langman on 15 February 1881. The mark consisted of
the initials 'W.G' over 'J.L' in a rectangular surround. It was not until 22
June 1882 that they entered the firm's mark at Goldsmiths' Hall, London,
for the first time. A second mark was entered at the Sheffield Assay Office
on 30 April 1883 under the names of both W. Gibson and J. L. Langman
and the Manufacturing Goldsmiths & Silversmiths Company. This mark
was similar to those registered at Goldsmiths' Hall on 17 April 1883.

In 1889 Gibson and Langman bought the ailing firm of Mappin Bros
from Frederick Crockford and Charles Hickson (see Mappin Brothers),
following which, in January 1890, they entered their joint 'WG' and 'JLL'
marks at the Sheffield Assay Office under the name of Mappin Bros of
Bakers Hill, Sheffield. Then, in 1893, they took over the Goldsmiths'
Alliance Ltd (previously A. B. Savory & Sons) of Cornhill, London.

In 1898 they converted the Goldsmiths & Silversmiths Co. into a limited
liability company with themselves as its first directors. Later, other directors
were appointed, including Alexander Gordon MaGinnis. Born in 1861, he
joined the firm as an employee in 1882, became a director by 1889 and
eventually left the firm in 1908. He was drowned when the ship *Empress of
Ireland*, in which he was returning from Canada to England, sank on 29 May
1914.

In 1903 the Goldsmiths & Silversmiths Co. Ltd sold its controlling interest in Mappin Bros to Mappin & Webb Ltd (see Mappin Brothers and Mappin & Webb). Then, in 1952, the Goldsmiths & Silversmiths Co. Ltd took over Garrard & Co. Ltd of 24 Albemarle Street and transferred the firm to its own premises at 112 Regent Street. However, on 13 November 1959 Mappin & Webb Ltd, then a subsidiary of Sears Holdings Ltd, took over both the Goldsmiths & Silversmiths Co. Ltd and Garrard & Co. Ltd of Regent Street, thus bringing together three of the largest retailers in the jewellery and precious metals trade. Other firms also acquired by Mappin & Webb Ltd include J. W. Benson Ltd, Ollivant & Botsford Ltd and Walker & Hall Ltd.

*Mark entered in two sizes.
**Mark entered in three sizes.
***Mark entered in four sizes.
††Mark entered in six sizes.

Gorham Manufacturing Co.

(J·H·B) 17 September 1894
John Henry Buck, Silver worker
32 Essex Street, Strand
Gorham Manufacturing Co., Broadway and 19th Street, New York and Mount Vernon, NY

(G·M·Co) * 20 June 1904
Gorham Manufacturing Co., Gold and Silver workers
Broadway and 19th Street, New York, USA
Audrey House, Ely Place, Holborn Circus
Cotton's residence: 137 Alexandra Road, Hampstead, NW
partner: Abraham Cotton, London manager, by virtue of a Power of Attorney

(G·M·Co) 20 July 1904 (Entry as for 20.6.1904)

(G·M·Co) ** 3 October 1910
Gorham Manufacturing Co., Silver workers
5th Avenue and 36th Street, New York Providence, Rhode Island
Audrey House, Ely Place, Holborn Circus
Time Works, Barr Street, Birmingham
Cotton's residence: 146 Goldhurst Terrace, Hampstead, London
partners: Edward Holbrook, president: John Swift Holbrook, vice president: Abraham Cotton, by power of attorney

Established in 1831, this American firm of manufacturing silversmiths was based at Providence, Rhode Island. However, in 1894 the firm's first English agency was opened at 32 Essex Street, Strand, London, by John Henry Buck who, acting on the firm's behalf, entered a mark bearing his own initials at Goldsmiths' Hall. Then, in June 1904, the firm opened its own showrooms at Audrey House, Ely Place, London with Abraham Cotton as manager.

By 1910 the firm had set up a factory at Barr Street, Birmingham, thereby avoiding having to import the majority of its goods from the Providence factory. The Birmingham factory continued to operate until *circa* 1914.

*Mark entered in two sizes.
**Mark entered in three sizes.

Gough & Silvester

* 12 August 1864
William Gough, Plate worker
11 & 12 Parade, Birmingham
Gough's residence: 75 Monument Lane, Edgbaston, Birmingham

This Birmingham firm of silver plate manufacturers was established by William Gough *circa* 1837, but it was not until 1840 that he entered his first mark at the Birmingham Assay Office.

In about 1859 he entered into partnership with John Bartlett Silvester, trading as Gough & Silvester. With the dissolution of this partnership in March 1870, William Gough's son, John, continued to run the business until its closure *circa* 1885.

*Mark entered in two sizes.

George Gray

21 August 1876
George Gray, Gold worker
34 Percy Street, Rathbone Place

11 June 1879
Removed to 114 Great Russell Street, Bloomsbury

12 August 1887

16 June 1898
Removed to 34 Percy Street, Rathbone Place, W

George Gray was listed as a manufacturing goldsmith of 34 Percy Street when he entered his first mark at Goldsmiths' Hall. He moved to 114 Great Russell Street in 1879, but subsequently returned to 34 Percy Street in 1898, where he was listed as a manufacturing jeweller. By 1907 he was trading from 29 Mornington Crescent, but he had moved to 69 Albany Street by 1913.

John Grinsell & Sons

(T.B.G) 6 April 1883
Thomas Bywater Grinsell, Plate worker
Upper Tower Street, Birmingham
Ely House, Charterhouse Street (London)
T. B. Grinsell's residence: Camden Villa, Heathfield Road, Birmingham

This mark defaced 1 November 1892

(J.G&S) *** 1 November 1892
John Grinsell & Sons, Plate workers
57 Tower Street, St George's, Birmingham
13 Charterhouse Street, Holborn
residence: Anchorage Road, Sutton Coalfield

(J.G&S) *** 22 November 1892

These marks cancelled 22.9.1905 (refers to 1.11.1892 and 22.11.1892 marks)

The firm of John Grinsell and Sons was turned into a limited company in September 1905

(J.G&S) * 22 September 1905
John Grinsell & Sons Ltd, Silver workers
Tower Street, Birmingham

13 Charterhouse Street, Holborn Circus
Costigan's residence: 126 Ombersly Road, Sparkbrook,
Birmingham
directors: James Erazmus Grinsell, James Reginald Hugh Grinsell
secretary: Philip James Costigan

Mr J. H. Grinsell was appointed secretary 26.9.1906 in place of
Mr P. J. Costigan resigned. Mr Marcel Martin appointed
secretary 18.11.1907

This Birmingham firm was established in 1871 by John Grinsell in
partnership with his sons, Thomas Bywater, James Erazmus, Lorenzo and
Joseph Charles Grinsell. *Circa* 1880 they opened showrooms at Ely House,
Charterhouse Street, London. Then, in 1883, Thomas Bywater Grinsell
entered his mark at Goldsmiths' Hall on behalf of the firm. In 1887 the firm
was listed as silversmiths, electroplate manufacturers and fancy cabinet
makers, while in 1905 it was recorded as silversmiths, electroplate
manufacturers and glass cutters.

John Grinsell retired in December 1887, followed by Thomas Bywater
Grinsell in June 1894. The remaining sons, James Erazmus Grinsell,
Lorenzo Grinsell and Joseph Charles Grinsell, continued trading until June
1905 when they dissolved their partnership. The firm was then turned into
a limited liability company. Eventually the firm was taken over by Barker
Ellis & Co. Ltd.

*Mark entered in two sizes.
***Mark entered in four sizes.

Guild of Handicraft

29 January 1896
Guild of Handicraft
Essex House, Mile End Road
Ashbee's residence: Magpie & Stump House, 37 Cheyne Walk,
Chelsea, SW
signed: Charles Robert Ashbee

** 14 December 1900
Guild of Handicraft, Gold and Silver workers
Essex House, 401 Mile End Road, E

16A Brook Street, Bond Street, W
Osborn's residence: 23 Warner Place, Hackney Road
signed: W. Osborn, secretary

Removed to Essex House, Chipping Campden, Gloucestershire,
see letter sent to Deputy Warden, 3 February 1903

James Thomas Webster appointed secretary, 13 July 1906

George Vickery, secretary, 13 January 1908

(Q|H)

(G|H)

22 July 1908
Guild of Handicraft, Gold and Silver workers
Essex House, Chipping Campden, RSO, Gloucestershire
Hart's residence: Elm Tree House, Campden
partners: George Henry Hart, John Kirsten Baily, George Edward
Horwood, William Mark
signed: George Henry Hart, on behalf of Guild of Handicraft

This firm dissolved 28 November 1912
(Marks) cancelled 21.11.1912

(G|H)

(G|H)

5 December 1912
Guild of Handicraft, Gold and Silver workers
Essex House, Campden, Gloucestershire
Hart's residence: Holly Bush Farm, Campden, Gloucestershire
partner: George Henry Hart

The Guild of Handicraft was founded by Charles Robert Ashbee in 1888. Born on 17 May 1863, C. R. Ashbee was educated at Wellington College and Kings College, Cambridge. Upon his leaving Cambridge, he was articled to the architect G. F. Bodley, a friend of William Morris.

In 1888, when 25 years old, he set up the School of Handicraft at Toynbee Hall in the East End of London. This was soon followed by the Guild of Handicraft with C. R. Ashbee as its director and supervising designer. The Guild was intended to concentrate on all aspects of design, but it was only in metal work and jewellery that it achieved reasonable commercial success. In 1891 C. R. Ashbee moved the Guild to Essex House in the Mile End Road, where in July 1898 it was converted into a limited liability company with William James Osborn as secretary. By this time it had opened its own London showrooms at 16A Brook Street.

In 1902 C. R. Ashbee moved the Guild, together with its members and families totalling some 150 people, to Chipping Campden, Gloucestershire. However, the Guild continued to have difficulties in marketing its products, and on 30 September 1908 it was agreed by all members that the Guild should be voluntarily wound up by reason of its liabilities.

Following its liquidation, some of the workmen remained at Essex House, Chipping Campden, where they set up a separate business named the Guild of Handicraft with George Henry Hart, John Kirsten Baily, George Edward Horwood and William Mark as its partners.

When this partnership was dissolved in November 1912 G. H. Hart remained at Essex House, where he continued to run the business under its existing name. G. H. Hart, the son of Thomas Hart, was born in 1878. He obtained his freedom of the Goldsmiths' Company by Special Grant on 13 February 1929, was made a Liveryman on 12 April 1933 and died on 21 October 1973.

Meanwhile, C. R. Ashbee returned to working as an architect, developer and town planning adviser from his premises at Cheyne Walk, Chelsea, London. He and his wife, Janet, had four daughters, the eldest being born in 1911. C. R. Ashbee died in 1942.

**Mark entered in three sizes.

R. H. Halford & Sons

* 18 October 1894
Robert Hosier Halford & Sons, Gold and Silver workers
69 St Martins Lane, WC
43 Fenchurch Street, City, EC
R. H. Halford's residence: High Street, Rotherfield, Sussex
signed: Robert Hosier Halford

11 July 1895
signed: Robert Hosier Halford

24 June 1896
signed: R. C. Halford

9 October 1896
signed: R. C. Halford

15 January 1902
Robert Hosier Halford & Sons, Gold and Silver workers
69 St Martins Lane, WC

43 Fenchurch Street, EC
signed: R. C. Halford, partner

 ** 13 October 1902
Robert Hosier Halford & Sons, Gold and Silver workers
69 St Martins Lane, WC
43 Fenchurch Street, EC
R. C. Halford's residence: The Chestnuts, Horsell Common,
Woking
signed: R. C. Halford, partner

*** 23 November 1907
R. H. Halford & Sons, Gold and Silver workers
41 Pall Mall, SW
129 Fenchurch Street, EC
W. J. Halford's residence: Holly Dene, Horsell Common, Woking
partners: Robert Hosier Halford, William John Halford, Robert
Collins Halford
signed: Wm John Halford, partner

The firm of R. H. Halford & Sons having been converted into a
Limited Company, new punches were registered, 7 July 1910

† 7 July 1910
R. H. Halford & Sons Ltd, Gold and Silver workers
41 Pall Mall, SW
129 Fenchurch Street, EC
H. W. Halford's residence: Holly Dene, Horsell Common,
Woking
partners: William John Halford, Harold W. Halford, Robert C.
Halford
secretary: Henry T. Mann
signed: H. W. Halford, partner

It seems that this firm was established *circa* 1852 by Charles Frederick
Wassell, a jeweller and silversmith. Later he entered into partnership with
Robert Hosier Halford, trading as Wassell & Halford, jewellers, silversmiths
and watchmakers of 43 Fenchurch Street. Following the dissolution of this
partnership in December 1879, R. H. Halford continued trading on his own
from the same address, but later he took his sons into partnership, renaming
the firm R. H. Halford & Sons.

He entered his mark at Goldsmiths' Hall in October 1894 and again in
July 1895, but subsequent marks were entered by Robert Collins Halford.

At the time, the firm was listed as watchmakers, jewellers, silversmiths and appraisers.

The firm was converted into a limited liability company in February 1910, following which new marks were entered at Goldsmiths' Hall.

In 1912 the Fenchurch Street premises were vacated, leaving the entire firm located at 41 Pall Mall. The firm then transferred to 86 Piccadilly in 1930, where it went into voluntary liquidation in September 1934.

*Mark entered in two sizes.
**Mark entered in three sizes.
***Mark entered in four sizes.
†Mark entered in five sizes.

Hamilton & Co. (Calcutta)

10 November 1908
Hamilton & Co., Gold and Silver workers
8 Old Court House Street, Calcutta
Allenville, Simla (India)
16 Eastcheap, London, EC
Davies's residence: 32 Hamilton Road, Ealing
partners: Walter Davies, William Smith

6 October 1909
Hamilton & Co. (Entry as for 10.11.1908)

22 November 1912
Gold and Silver workers
8 Old Court House Street, Calcutta
Allenville, Simla
16 Eastcheap, London, EC
Davies's residence: Downhurst, Castle Bar Road, Ealing
partners: Walter Davies, William Smith, John MacLaren

Hamilton & Co. was an old-established Calcutta firm of retailing and manufacturing silversmiths and jewellers, thought to have been established by Robert Hamilton *circa* 1815. Throughout the nineteenth century, one of its major suppliers of silverware was the London firm of Edward Barnard

& Sons, manufacturing silversmiths. During the latter half of the nineteenth century, it was supplied additionally by Charles Boyton & Son of London and George Unite of Birmingham.

In 1908 Hamilton of Co. set up an English agency through the firm of Remfrey, Davies & Co. of 16 Eastcheap, London. At the time, the partners in this firm were Walter Davies and William Smith. Originally, Walter Davies had joined Hamilton & Co. as an assistant in Calcutta in 1891. He subsequently became a partner in the firm and later in Remfrey, Davies & Co. He retired in 1929 and died during the winter of 1941–2.

Hamilton & Company (Regent Street)

9 April 1902
Hamilton & Company, Gold and Silver workers
202 Regent Street, W
Duveen's residence: 22 Avenue Mansions, Finchley Road, NW
signed: Edward J. Duveen, sole partner

6 June 1902

17 October 1902
Hamilton & Company (Entry as for 9.4.1902)

* 6 June 1903
Hamilton & Company, Gold and Silver workers
202 Regent Street, W
E. J. Duveen's residence: 22 Avenue Mansions, Finchley Road, NW

The firm of Hamilton & Company having decided to discontinue business, the registration of these three punches was not proceeded with. See letter to the Deputy Warden dated January 1905. (date) 11 January 1905

In 1901 Hamilton & Company, jewellers, took over the firm of Incorporated Goldsmiths' Realization Co. Following this acquisition, its first mark was entered at Goldsmiths' Hall by its sole partner, E. J. Duveen. The firm continued to trade until the end of 1904 when it closed down and its stock was sold off.

*Mark entered in two sizes.

Hancocks & Co.

* 11 April 1850
Charles Frederick Hancock (No. 1), Plate worker
39 Bruton Street, corner of Bond Street
manufactory: Little Bruton Street
signed: C. F. Hancock

* 22 January 1870
Charles Frederick Hancock (No. 1), Plate worker
38–39 Bruton Street
152 New Bond Street
manufactory: Little Bruton Street
residence: Hendon Hall, Hendon, Middlesex
signed: C. F. Hancock

These marks defaced 1 April 1890

* 1 April 1890
C. F. Hancock & Co., Plate workers
38–39 Bruton Street
152 New Bond Street
manufactory: Little Bruton Street
signed: Henry John Dore

* 23 July 1898
Hancocks & Co., Silver workers
38–39 Bruton Street, W
152 New Bond Street, W
H. H. Dore's residence: 39 Bruton Street, W
signed: H. Hancock Dore, partner

* 22 August 1899
Hancocks & Co. (Entry as for 23.7.1898 except signed: Alfred Dore, partner, residing at 39 Bruton Street, W)

⟨C.F.H&C⟩

29 September 1914
Hancocks & Co., Gold and Silver workers
38 and 39 Bruton Street
152 New Bond Street, London W
A. G. Dore's residence: 39 Bruton Street, London W
partners: Henry Hancock Dore, Alfred George Dore

This firm was founded by Charles Frederick Hancock (No. 1) in 1849. C. F. Hancock (No. 1), the son of Sophia and Charles Hancock, was born in November 1807. For a while he was a partner in the firm of Hunt & Roskell, goldsmiths, silversmiths and jewellers of 156 New Bond Street. He retired from the firm in January 1849 and soon after opened his own shop at 39 Bruton Street with adjoining premises for manufacturing gold and silverware, jewellery and works of art. Then, on 13 August 1849, he received a Royal Warrant of Appointment from Queen Victoria.

On 1 February 1854 he obtained his freedom of the Goldsmiths' Company by Redemption, and in June 1864 he was made a Liveryman of the Company.

By 1862 he had extended his premises to include 38 and 39 Bruton Street and 152 New Bond Street.

In 1866 he semi-retired, leaving the business to be run by one of his sons, Mortimer Hancock, together with Horatio Stewart and Henry John Dore. Meanwhile, the firm's name was changed to Hancock, Son & Co. Although C. F. Hancock fully retired from the firm officially on 31 December 1869, he still entered the firm's new marks at Goldsmiths' Hall in January 1870 and signed the record of entry. He died on 10 February 1891 when 83 years old.

Following his retirement on 31 December 1869, a new partnership deed was drawn up and signed on 4 January 1870, changing the firm's name to Hancocks & Co. and listing his two sons, Mortimer Hancock and Charles Frederick Hancock (No. 2), together with Horatio Stewart and John Henry Dore, as its partners.

Mortimer Hancock was apprenticed to his father on 6 October 1858, obtained his freedom of the Goldsmiths' Company by Service on 1 November 1865 and was made a Liveryman in January 1872. He retired from the firm on 31 December 1883 and died aged 57 on 15 July 1901.

His son, Mortimer Pawson Hancock, obtained his freedom of the Goldsmiths' Company by Patrimony on 5 January 1893 and became a Lieutenant in the Royal Fusiliers.

Charles Frederick Hancock (No. 2) was apprenticed to his father on 5 November 1862 and obtained his freedom of the Goldsmiths' Company by Service on 6 March 1872. He retired from the firm on 12 April 1876 and died in 1909. His son, Charles Granville Hancock, born in 1885, became a barrister and eventually obtained his freedom of the Goldsmiths' Company by Patrimony on 2 May 1951.

When Horatio Stewart retired on 1 October 1885, Henry John Dore, the sole remaining partner, continued running the firm. He took his two sons, Henry Hancock Dore and Alfred George Dore, into partnership on 1 May 1895. Then, when Henry John Dore died aged 63 on 27 November 1895, his widow, Louisa Mary Dore, and their two sons continued running the firm. Louisa retired on 31 December 1904.

Henry Hancock Dore had been apprenticed to Mortimer Hancock on 7 April 1880 and had obtained his freedom of the Goldsmiths' Company by Service on 9 May 1887. Following the death of Henry Hancock Dore in July 1926, Alfred George Dore took his own two nephews, John Addley Bourne and Gerald L. Hancock Dore, into partnership. When Alfred George Dore died in November 1935, the firm was converted into a limited liability company named Hancocks & Co. (Jewellers) Ltd with Gerald L. Hancock Dore and John A. Bourne as directors and W. H. J. Wixley as chairman.

*Mark entered in two sizes.

Robert Harper & Co.

---

 * 19 February 1853
Robert Harper, Plate worker
10 St Johns Street, Clerkenwell

Removed to 35 Whiskin Street, Clerkenwell, 14 May 1853

 * 31 January 1856

RH   2 May 1856

Removed to 3 James Street, Goswell Road, 4 October 1859

Removed to 16 Red Lion Street, Clerkenwell, 9 January 1868

RH   19 February 1869

RH   2 July 1869
Robert Harper, Plate worker
16 Red Lion Street, Clerkenwell

RH   1 June 1874

RH   28 March 1877

Removed to 17 Red Lion Street, Clerkenwell, EC, 2 August 1883

JRH   *** 21 February 1884
John Robert Harper, Plate worker
17 Red Lion Street, Clerkenwell

JH   ** 6 January 1885
Joseph Harper, Plate worker
17 Red Lion Street, Clerkenwell

This firm of manufacturing silversmiths was founded *circa* 1853 by Robert Harper, a former employee of Joseph Angell of Panton Street.

In 1869 he took his son, John Robert Harper, into partnership, at the same time changing the firm's name to R. Harper & Son. This partnership was dissolved in December 1880, but the firm's name still remained as R. Harper & Son.

Robert Harper was declared bankrupt in 1883, following which the firm continued trading under its new name of R. Harper & Co. with John Robert Harper, Joseph Harper, George Augustus Peacock and Ralph Francis Close as its partners.

John Robert Harper entered his mark as representative of the firm in February 1884, but he then retired on 2 July 1884, followed by George Augustus Peacock on 26 November 1884. This left Joseph Harper to enter his mark on behalf of the firm in January 1885.

The firm appears to have ceased trading *circa* 1889.

*Mark entered in two sizes.
**Mark entered in three sizes.
***Mark entered in four sizes.

Harris Bros

* 10 April 1896
Arthur Stuart Harris and Ernest Stuart Harris, Silver workers
13 Bateman Street, Soho
A. S. Harris's residence: Bush Lodge, Southgate
E. S. Harris's residence: 49 Alexandra Road, Swiss Cottage
signed: Ernest Stuart Harris

The above marks defaced 8 December 1897 on account of the
amalgamation of the firm with that of C. S. Harris Ltd

Arthur Stuart Harris and Ernest Stuart Harris were the sons of Charles
Stuart Harris (No. 1), manufacturing silversmith of 41–42 Hatton Garden.
In 1896 the two sons established their own firm of manufacturing
silversmiths at 13 Bateman Street, but in December 1897 they amalgamated
with their father's firm, Charles Stuart Harris. Following this amalgamation,
the parent firm was renamed C. S. Harris & Sons Ltd. Arthur Stuart Harris
continued to work for the firm. He died in 1935 when 70 years old.

*Mark entered in two sizes.

Charles Stuart Harris (No. 1)

(CSH)

24 December 1852
Charles Stuart Harris (No. 1), Spoon maker
29 Kirby Street, Hatton Garden
signed: C. S. Harris

(CSH)

9 July 1859

C S
H

24 January 1871

13 April 1881

*

 1 March 1884

(no mark)   29 March 1886
24 Red Lion Street, Clerkenwell
C. S. Harris's residence: Avenue House, Southgate, North
London

 9 January 1891

 27 March 1896
Charles Stuart Harris (No. 1), Silver worker
41 and 42 Hatton Garden
29 Kirby Street, City
24 Red Lion Street, Clerkenwell
C. S. Harris's residence: Avenue House, Southgate
signed: C. S. Harris

 ** 9 December 1897

 ** 16 August 1899 (Entry as for 27.3.1896)

The business of C. S. Harris was turned into a Limited Co. about 1899. Afterwards in 1904 new marks were entered

* 7 December 1904
C. S. Harris & Sons Ltd, Silver workers
41–42 Hatton Garden, EC
28–29 Kirby Street, Hatton Garden, EC
23–24 Red Lion Street, Clerkenwell
13–14 Bateman Street, Soho
F. S. Harris's residence: Avenue House, Southgate, N
partners: Henry Stuart Harris, Walter Stuart Harris, Edwin Stuart Harris, Alfred Stuart Harris, Frederick Stuart Harris
signed: Frederick Stuart Harris, secretary C. S. Harris & Sons Ltd

Born in 1830, Charles Stuart Harris (No. 1) was probably the son of John Harris and brother of John Robert Harris, both of whom were silversmiths and spoon makers.

John Harris had established his own business as a silversmith and spoon maker in 1817. Then, in December 1850, he apparently acquired the business of John Robert Harris together with its premises at 29 Kirby Street. John Harris seems to have retired or died by December 1852, this being when his business was taken over by Charles Stuart Harris (No. 1).

Charles Stuart Harris (No. 1) entered his first mark from 29 Kirby Street in December 1852 when 22 years old. For a while he was in partnership with John Masters, trading as Harris & Masters, silversmiths and electroplate manufacturers of 29 Kirby Street, but this partnership was dissolved in April 1860, following which he continued trading as Charles Stuart Harris.

In 1885 he purchased the firm of D. J. & C. Houle, silversmiths, acquiring their workshops at 24 Red Lion Street. Then, in December 1897, he absorbed the business of Harris Bros, manufacturing silversmiths, together with its premises at 13–14 Bateman Street. This business had been established by two of his sons, Arthur Stuart Harris and Ernest Stuart Harris, in 1896. *Circa* 1897–9 he converted the firm of Charles Stuart Harris into a limited liability company, renaming it C. S. Harris & Sons Ltd. He retired from the firm between 1899 and 1904 and died in September 1918 when 88 years old.

Meanwhile, the firm continued to trade until 1934 when it was taken over by I. Freeman & Son Ltd, manufacturing silversmiths and dealers in antique silver of 23 Hatton Garden.

*Mark entered in two sizes.
**Mark entered in three sizes.

Charles Stuart Harris (No. 2)

14 February 1890
Charles Stuart Harris (No. 2), Plate worker
21 Great Sutton Street, Clerkenwell
residence: Poplar Villa, Chase Side, Southgate
signed: C. S. Harris junior

Removed to 7 Meredith Street, Clerkenwell, 29 June 1891

Removed to 11 President Street, Goswell Road, 24 April 1896

Charles Stuart Harris (No. 2) was the son of Charles Stuart Harris (No. 1). In 1889 Charles Stuart Harris (No. 2) took over the premises of Henry William Curry, manufacturing silversmith, at 21 Great Sutton Street, from where he traded as Charles Stuart, manufacturing silversmith. He became bankrupt in 1891, but subsequently recommenced trading from premises at 7 Meredith Street. Later, he entered into partnership with Henry William Curry, trading as C. S. Harris & Co., manufacturing silversmiths (not to be confused with his father's firm of C. S. Harris & Sons Ltd). This partnership with Curry was dissolved in June 1896.

John Harris

15 January 1818
John Harris, Spoon maker
146 Aldersgate Street

9 February 1820
Removed to 12 Well Street, Cripplegate

25 January 1822

Removed to 16 Red Lion Street, Clerkenwell, 2 January 1823

Removed to 32 Charles Street, Goswell Street, 10 June 1823

 12 July 1825

 25 May 1827
John Harris, Spoon maker
43 Leather Lane

Removed to 5 West Place, John Row, City Road (no date)

Removed to 27 Nelson Street, City Road, 21 January 1831

 22 November 1831
John Harris, Small worker
27 Nelson Street, City Road

 27 August 1834

 18 September 1839

21 July 1840

15 August 1840

23 January 1851
Removed to 29 Kirby Street, Hatton Garden

Apparently, John Harris commenced working as a spoon maker at 146 Aldersgate Street in 1817, entering his first mark at Goldsmiths' Hall the following year. He entered further marks at regular intervals over the next 33 years, during which time he worked from various premises. In 1831 he was recorded at Goldsmiths' Hall as a small worker, which could indicate that a descendant of the same name took over the business at this point in time. However, since the signatures against all the entries from 1818 to 1851 appear to be by the same person, it has been assumed that they all belong to the same John Harris.

In January 1851 John Harris moved to 29 Kirby Street, where he apparently took over the business of John Robert Harris, spoon maker, and amalgamated it with his own. John Robert Harris was probably his son and may have retired or died at this time.

However, by December 1852 John Harris seems to have likewise retired or died, this being when Charles Stuart Harris (No. 1) entered his own mark at Goldsmiths' Hall, listing 29 Kirby Street as his business address. Presumably Charles Stuart Harris (No. 1) was another of John Harris's sons.

John Robert Harris

(J R H)
17 June 1842
John Robert Harris, Spoon maker
24 Bridge Street, Covent Garden
manufactory: 29 Kirby Street, Hatton Garden
signed: John Robt Harris

IRH
8 December 1842

(IRH)
28 April 1847

IRH
28 November 1848

John Robert Harris was probably the son of John Harris, silversmith and spoon maker, and brother of Charles Stuart Harris (No. 1), silversmith. In 1842 John Robert Harris commenced working as a spoon maker with his own manufactory at 29 Kirby Street.

He appears to have retired or, more likely, died *circa* December 1850, since John Harris moved into his premises at 29 Kirby Street in January 1851 and entered his own mark from there on 23 January. Probably John Harris took over his business at the same time and amalgamated it with his own. However, by December 1852 John Harris seems to have likewise retired or died, this being when Charles Stuart Harris (No. 1) took over the business, entering his own mark at Goldsmiths' Hall on 24 December 1852 and listing 29 Kirby Street as his business premises.

Joseph Hart & Son (later Hart, Son, Peard & Co.)

C H
3 August 1857
Charles Hart, Small worker
manufactory: 53–58 Wych Street, Strand

C. Hart's residence: 3 College Terrace, Finchley Road, St John's Wood
signed: Charles Hart

 18 January 1861
Charles Hart, Small worker
53–58 Wych Street and 20 Cockspur Street
C. Hart's residence: Oak Villa, Woodridings, Pinner
signed: Charles Hart

 6 September 1906
Hart, Son, Peard & Co. Ltd, Silver workers
138–140 Charing Cross Road, London, WC
Grosvenor Works, Birmingham
C. J. Hart's residence: Highfield Gate, Birmingham
T. Peard's residence: 13 Princes Avenue, Finchley
directors: Charles Joseph Hart, Thomas Peard

11 July 1911
Hart, Son, Peard & Co. Ltd, Gold and Silver workers
138–140 Charing Cross Road, London, WC
Grosvenor Works, Grosvenor Street West, Birmingham
W. J. Peard's residence: Ermynville, Fortis Green Road, East Finchley, London, N
director: William James Peard

10 June 1914
Removed to Commerce House, 70–86 Oxford Street, W
W. J. Peard's residence:
40 Fortis Green Avenue, East Finchley, N

11 November 1920
Removed to 28 Berners Street, W1
signed: William James Peard

Joseph Hart started his own business as a wholesale and retail ironmonger *circa* 1842. He traded as Joseph Hart & Sons from 1845 to *circa* 1855, then as Joseph Hart & Son until 1866 when he amalgamated with the firm of Peard & Jackson, manufacturers of medieval art metal works at 159 High Holborn (see Peard & Jackson).

In 1852 Joseph Hart & Sons were listed as wholesale and retail ironmongers, brass finishers, bellhangers, gasfitters and lock manufacturers. However, in 1857 and again in 1861, marks were entered at Goldsmiths' Hall by Joseph's son, Charles Hart. These entries gave the address of the firm's manufactory as 53–58 Wych Street and that of its showrooms as 20 Cockspur Street. Charles Hart was particularly interested in ecclesiastical metal work, and in 1863 he became a member of the Ecclesiological Society.

Having amalgamated with Peard & Jackson in 1866, the new firm was called Hart, Son, Peard & Co. with Charles Hart overseeing the Grosvenor Works at Birmingham, Thomas Peard the London manufactory and showrooms, and Frederick Jackson the firm's finances (see Peard & Jackson).

Circa 1905 the firm was converted into a limited liability company, trading as Hart, Son, Peard & Co. Ltd with Thomas Peard and Charles Joseph Hart as directors. The firm was still in existence in 1920 at 28 Berners Street, Oxford Street.

Judah Hart

24 February 1847
Judah Hart, Spoon maker
31 Bevis Marks, Camomile Street
manufactory: 65 Crown Street, Finsbury

Judah Hart is first listed as a jeweller at 17 Camomile Street in 1828, then as Judah Hart & Co., jewellers and silversmiths of 31 Bevis Marks in 1830 and 1841, and as a wholesale goldsmith in 1852.

In February 1847, he gave the address of his manufactory as 65 Crown Street, Finsbury. This was the address of Charles Lias from 1837 to 1847 and of William Smily from 1853 onwards.

Hawksworth, Eyre & Co.

21 April 1866
Charles Hawksworth and John Eyre, Plate workers
Nursery Street, Sheffield
22 Bouverie Street, Fleet Street
C. Hawksworth's residence: Rock Rise, Burngreave Road, Sheffield
J. Eyre's residence: Manor View, Andover Street, Sheffield
signed: Charles Hawksworth, John Eyre

Mr John Eyre being dead and Mr Charles Hawksworth having retired, the above marks were withdrawn and defaced (no date, probably 7.8.1873)

JKB * 7 August 1873
James Kebberling Bembridge, Plate worker
102 Nursery Street, Sheffield
J. K. Bembridge's residence: Western Bank, Sheffield
signed: J. K. Bembridge

 ** 20 December 1892
Hawksworth, Eyre & Co. Ltd, Plate workers
60 Rockingham Road, Sheffield
25 Bouverie Street, Fleet Street
signed: A. T. Smith, director, Rhine Hill, Stratford-on-Avon
T. A. Scott, director, Broomspring Lane, Sheffield

New address: 49 Holborn Viaduct, EC, 24 November 1897

 22 May 1900
Hawksworth, Eyre & Co. Ltd, Plate worker
60 Rockingham Street, Sheffield
49 Holborn Viaduct, London, EC
signed: Thos A Scott, managing director

4 November 1912
Hawksworth, Eyre & Co. Ltd, Silver workers
60 Rockingham Street, Sheffield
46A Holborn Viaduct, London, EC
H. Oliver's residence: 6 Avon Road, Walthamstow, Essex
directors: Harold Ernest Trubshaw, Henry Parish, Thomas A. Scott
signed: Henry Oliver, secretary

Removed to Golden House, Great Pulteney Street, London, W, 9 April 1915

A. C. Ridge appointed secretary, 28 June 1915

Removed to 19 Charterhouse Street, EC, 28 May 1920

This Sheffield firm of manufacturing silversmiths and platers, with Charles Hawksworth & John Eyre as its partners, was established in 1833 as the successor to the firm of Blagden, Hodgson & Co. Charles Hawksworth and John Eyre entered their first mark at the Sheffield Assay Office on 25 July 1833. It consisted of the initials 'HE' over '& Co' set in a quatrefoil surround. However, it was not until April 1866 that they entered their first mark at Goldsmiths' Hall, London.

When Charles Hawksworth and John Eyre dissolved their partnership in November 1869, the firm was continued by James Kebberling Bembridge, Thomas Hall and George Woodhouse. By the time J. K. Bembridge entered

148

his mark at Goldsmiths' Hall in August 1873, Thomas Hall, George Woodhouse and Charles Hawksworth had retired and John Eyre was dead, leaving J. K. Bembridge as sole partner. Soon after, J. K. Bembridge converted the firm into a limited liability company.

J. K. Bembridge had joined the firm when a boy and had been manager and director for 22 years by the time he died in November 1892. Following his death, the two new directors, A. T. Smith and T. A. Scott, entered their mark at Goldsmiths' Hall in December 1892, followed by Thomas Alfred Scott on his own in May 1900.

*Mark entered in two sizes.
**Mark entered in three sizes.

Hayne & Cater

* 5 July 1836
Samuel Hayne and Dudley Cater, Plate workers
16 Red Lion Street, Clerkenwell

* 12 April 1837 (Entry as for 5.7.1836)

26 May 1842 (Entry as for 5.7.1836)

1 October 1842 (Entry as for 5.7.1836)

* 5 December 1844
Samuel Hayne and Dudley Cater, Plate workers
manufactory: 16 Red Lion Street, Clerkenwell
S. Hayne's residence: 33 Great James Street, Bedford Row
D. Cater's residence: 16 Red Lion Street, Clerkenwell

* 25 January 1864
Samuel H. Hayne
16 Red Lion Street, Clerkenwell
residence: Sussex Lodge, 24 Finchley Road, St Johns Wood

149

This firm was established in 1780 by Thomas Wallis (No. 2) (silversmith and Goldsmith) of 54 Red Lion Street, Clerkenwell (see *Marks of London Goldsmiths and Silversmiths c.1697–1837*, revised edition 1988, pp. 348–9). By February 1810 he had entered into partnership with his former apprentice, Jonathan Hayne (silversmith, Citizen and Goldsmith), and they were trading as manufacturing silversmiths at 16 Red Lion Street. Thomas Wallis (No. 2) appears to have retired by 3 July 1821, this being when Jonathan Hayne entered his own mark at Goldsmiths' Hall and took over control of the firm.

Following the death of Thomas Wallis (No. 2) on 10 June 1836, Jonathan Hayne appears to have semi-retired, leaving the firm to be run by his son, Samuel Holditch Thomas Hayne, and a former apprentice, Dudley Frank Cater. They entered their partnership mark at Goldsmiths' Hall in July 1836, renaming the firm Hayne & Co. In October of that year, Jonathan Hayne was made an Assistant of the Goldsmiths' Company, and he eventually became Prime Warden in 1843. He died on 19 March 1848.

Dudley Frank Cater was the son of John Augustus Cater (gentleman deceased) of Guildford Street, Russell Square. He was apprenticed to Jonathan Hayne on 5 March 1823, but it was not until 5 October 1836 that he took up his freedom of the Goldsmiths' Company by Service, probably due to his having just become a partner of the firm. He was made a Liveryman in April 1842 and retired from the firm on 2 January 1864, eventually dying in the first half of the 1880s.

Samuel Holditch Thomas Hayne obtained his freedom of the Goldsmiths' Company by Patrimony on 1 April 1835, was made a Liveryman in December 1839 and became an Assistant in March 1850. However, for some reason he retired from the Goldsmiths' Company on 12 May 1854.

Following Jonathan Hayne's death on 19 March 1848, Samuel Holditch Thomas Hayne and Dudley Frank Cater continued running the firm under its new name of Hayne & Cater, manufacturing and wholesale silversmiths and silver spoon and fork makers.

With the retirement of Dudley Frank Cater on 2 January 1864, Samuel Holditch Thomas Hayne entered his own mark at Goldsmiths' Hall and continued trading as Samuel Hayne & Co. However, he became bankrupt in February 1865, and by January 1868 his premises at 16 Red Lion Street were occupied by the silversmith Robert Harper (see Robert Harper & Co.). Samuel Holditch Thomas Hayne died on 4 August 1887.

*Mark entered in two sizes.

Joseph Heming & Co.

* 22 July 1890
Joseph Heming, Small worker
28 Conduit Street, W
J. Heming's residence: 15 Thornton Hill, Wimbledon
signed: Joseph Heming

22 April 1897

** 12 June 1902
Joseph Heming and Company, Gold and Silver workers
28 Conduit Street, London, W
G. B. Heming's residence: Boscombe, Christchurch Road, Crouch End
signed: George B. Heming, partner

† 28 April 1904
Joseph Heming and Company, 28 Conduit Street, London, W
G. B. Heming's residence: Danes Cot, Hornsey Lane
signed: George Booth Heming, partner

*** 20 May 1912
Heming & Co. Ltd, Gold and Silver workers
28 Conduit Street, Regent Street, London
G. B. Heming's residence: Danes Cot, Hornsey Lane, Highgate
directors: George Booth Heming, Samuel Hook Partridge, Francis Harvey

5 December 1913
Heming & Co. Ltd, Gold and Silver workers
28 Conduit Street, Regent Street, London
S. H. Partridge's residence: Baruravie, Shepherds Hill, Highgate
directors: George Booth Heming, Samuel Hook Partridge, Francis Harvey

16 December 1913 (Entry as for 20.5.1912)

30 March 1922
director: Lawrence Vernon Brame
secretary: James Devonald Beynon

This firm of retail silversmiths and jewellers was established by Joseph Heming at 28 Conduit Street *circa* 1890. By June 1902 he had been joined in partnership by George Booth Heming, possibly a nephew. When Joseph Heming retired in December 1904, the firm was continued by his two partners, George Booth Heming and Samuel Hook Partridge.

George Booth Heming, jeweller, was the son of Thomas Heming and obtained his freedom of the Goldsmiths' Company by Redemption on 5 January 1898. He was made a Liveryman in January 1902 and an Assistant in December 1916. He became 4th Warden in 1921, 3rd Warden in 1922, 2nd Warden in 1923 and Prime Warden in 1924. He died on 24 September 1938.

In March 1912 the firm was converted into a limited liability company. It continued to trade as Heming & Co. Ltd until 1981 when it was amalgamated with William Bruford & Son Ltd of Exeter to form Bruford & Heming Ltd.

*Mark entered in two sizes.
**Mark entered in three sizes.
***Mark entered in four sizes.
†Mark entered in five sizes.

Robert Hennell & Sons

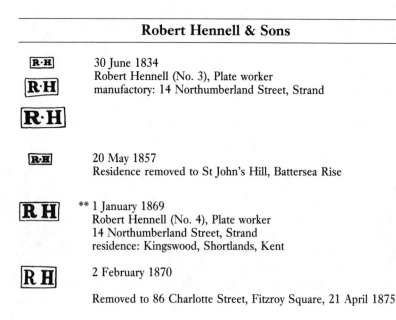

	30 June 1834
R·H	Robert Hennell (No. 3), Plate worker
R·H	manufactory: 14 Northumberland Street, Strand
R·H	

R·H	20 May 1857
	Residence removed to St John's Hill, Battersea Rise

R H	** 1 January 1869
	Robert Hennell (No. 4), Plate worker
	14 Northumberland Street, Strand
	residence: Kingswood, Shortlands, Kent

R H	2 February 1870

Removed to 86 Charlotte Street, Fitzroy Square, 21 April 1875

** 27 February 1877
James Barclay Hennell, Plate worker
86 Charlotte Street, Fitzroy Square
residence: Ifield Court, Mayow Road, Forest Hill

This firm was established by Robert Hennell (No. 2) (engraver, Citizen and Goldsmith) of 35 Noble Street in 1809 (see *Marks of London Goldsmiths and Silversmiths c.1697–1837*, revised edition 1988, pp. 175–6). His son, Robert Hennell (No. 3), joined him in the family business *circa* 1817 and, following the retirement of Robert Hennell (No. 2) on 25 May 1833, took over the firm of Robert Hennell & Son.

Robert Hennell (No. 3) was born in 1794, obtained his freedom of the Goldsmiths' Company by Patrimony on 7 May 1834 and was made a Liveryman in April 1842. Two of his sons were apprenticed to him and subsequently obtained their freedom of the Goldsmiths' Company. They were Robert Hennell (No. 4), apprenticed 1842, free 1849, and James Barclay Hennell, apprenticed 1843, free 1850. Following the freedom of the second son, the firm's name was changed to Robert Hennell & Sons.

In the 1851 Census return, Robert Hennell (No. 3) is described as a silversmith employing nine workmen and having a household consisting of his wife, Jane, aged 47 and five children. The children were: Jane, aged 26; Robert (No. 4), silver chaser, aged 24; James Barclay, silver plate worker, aged 23; Charles, aged 6 and Percy, aged 4.

Following the death of Robert Hennell (No. 3) in 1868, his two sons, Robert Hennell (No. 4) and James Barclay Hennell, took over the firm with Robert Hennell (No. 4) entering his mark at Goldsmiths' Hall in January 1869. Robert Hennell (No. 4) was born in 1826 and apprenticed to his father on 2 March 1842. He obtained his freedom of the Goldsmiths' Company by Service on 7 November 1849 and was made a Liveryman in May 1856. He officially retired from the family firm on 31 March 1877 and died on 11 November 1891. Following his official retirement in March 1877, his younger brother, James Barclay Hennell, continued running the firm, having already entered his own mark at Goldsmiths' Hall in February.

James Barclay Hennell was born in 1828 and apprenticed to his father on 1 February 1843. He obtained his freedom of the Goldsmiths' Company by Service on 6 February 1850 and was made a Liveryman in April 1859. With his retirement in 1887, the firm was sold to Holland, Aldwinckle & Slater, manufacturing silversmiths. James Barclay Hennell died on 5 August 1899. His son, Harold Barclay Hennell, became a silversmith and obtained his freedom of the Goldsmiths' Company by Patrimony on 2 February 1887.

**Mark entered in three sizes.

Robert George Hennell

RGH

circa 1844
(This mark is not recorded at Goldsmiths' Hall, although it was used by R. G. Hennell)

Robert George Hennell, jeweller, was born *circa* 1800–3 and died in 1884. He was the son of Samuel Hennell (silversmith, Citizen and Goldsmith) of Foster Lane and grandson of Robert Hennell (No. 1) (see *Marks of London Goldsmiths and Silversmiths c.1697–1837*, revised edition 1988, pp. 123, 177). In 1833 Robert George Hennell was trading from 5 Snow Hill, and in 1836 from 4 Southampton Street, Holborn. Although he never entered a mark at Goldsmiths' Hall, the unrecorded mark illustrated here was used by him on occasions.

Following his death in 1884, the business was continued by his sons, Edward Whittaker Hennell and Robert Montague Hennell, under the name of R. G. Hennell & Sons. In 1939 the firm was converted into a limited liability company. Today, the firm operates under the name of Hennell Ltd.

Francis Higgins & Son

F H

* 31 October 1817
Francis Higgins (No. 2), Plate worker
20 Cursitor Street, Chancery Lane

F·H

19 January 1821 (Entry as for 31.10.1817)

FH

18 February 1825 (Entry as for 31.10.1817)

F·H

7 August 1829 (Entry as for 31.10.1817)

FH

2 October 1829 (Entry as for 31.10.1817)

Removed to 47 Liquorpond Street, Grays Inn Road, 15 November 1834

F·H

3 December 1835
Francis Higgins (No. 2), Spoon maker
40 Kirby Street, Hatton Garden

154

FH * 14 June 1837 (Entry as for 3.12.1835)

FH 24 October 1843 (Entry as for 3.12.1835)

FH 14 October 1854 (Entry as for 3.12.1835)

FH * 30 June 1865 (Entry as for 3.12.1835)

F.H 1 April 1868
Francis Higgins (No. 2), Spoon maker
40 Kirby Street, Hatton Garden
residence: 24 Clarendon Road, Notting Hill

FH 16 October 1869
Removed to 9 Newman Street, Oxford Street

FH *

FH 23 June 1877

FH * 5 May 1880
Francis Higgins (No. 3), Spoon maker
9 Newman Street, Oxford Street

FH 5 August 1886
residence: Belle House, Hayes, Middlesex

FH 17 October 1889

FH 4 January 1898

This worker died in 1909 and the business was then converted
into a Limited Company. The next entry is F. Higgins and Son

F.H & S LTD 8 July 1909
F. Higgins and Son Ltd, Silver workers
9 Newman Street and 5–6 Newman Yard, Oxford Street,
London, W
J. Stonebridge's residence: 3 Elthorne Park Road, Hanwell, W

partners: Hortense Louise Higgins, Margaret Hortense Higgins
directors: Francis Joseph Higgins, Joseph Baines Stonebridge
secretary: Thomas Duggan

The Higgins family connection with the silversmithing trade commenced with James Higgins, the grandfather of Francis Higgins (No. 2). On 2 October 1782 James Higgins, a spoon polisher of Fore Street, London, apprenticed his son, Francis Higgins (No. 1), to John Manby (spoon maker, Citizen and Goldsmith) of Little Britain. This Francis Higgins (No. 1) was turned over to Stephen Adams (No. 1), a working goldsmith and Freeman of the Lorimers' Company, on 2 July 1783. However, when he obtained his freedom on 7 October 1789, it was of the Goldsmiths' Company, this being the Company of his original master, John Manby. There is no record of Francis Higgins (No. 1) having entered into business on his own account at any time during his working life.

His son, Francis (No. 2), was born in 1791 and apprenticed to George Smith (No. 4) (Citizen and Goldsmith) of Hosier Lane on 4 December 1805. At the time, Francis Higgins (No. 1) was recorded as a spoon maker and silversmith of Hosier Lane, so it could be that he was working for George Smith (No. 4). Because Francis Higgins (No. 1) was in 'poor circumstances' when his son was apprenticed to George Smith (No. 4), the apprenticeship fee of £7 14s 0d was paid by the charity of the Goldsmiths' Company. On 12 December 1826 Francis Higgins (No. 1) was elected a pensioner by the Court of Assistants of the Goldsmiths' Company, thereby granting him a sum of money per annum from the Company.

Francis Higgins (No. 2) obtained his freedom of the Goldsmiths' Company by Patrimony on 5 January 1814, and in October 1817 he entered his first mark having set up in business at 20 Cursitor Street. While at this address, he and his wife, Charlotte, had three children: Francis (No. 3) (b.1.9.1818), George Charles (b.13.4.1821) and Charlotte (b.24.6.1823). Francis Higgins (No. 2) remained in business for some 60 years, entering his last mark at Goldsmiths' Hall in June 1877. When he died on 5 February 1880 at the age of 89, his son, Francis Higgins (No. 3), took over sole control of the firm, entering his own mark at Goldsmiths' Hall.

Born in 1 September 1818, Francis Higgins (No. 3) was apprenticed to his father on 30 October 1832 but did not take up his freedom of the Goldsmiths' Company until 4 March 1857 when he acquired it by Patrimony. It seems that he worked for his father throughout this period of time. In 1859 he left his father's firm to become manager of the Portland Co. Ltd, which he, together with Harry Emanuel, a retail goldsmith of Hanover Square, and others, had just founded (see Portland Co. Ltd). This company was located in premises at 6 Riding House Street and had been set up to produce cutlery by an improved method of manufacture. Unfortunately it was not financially successful and went into voluntary liquidation in 1863. Francis Higgins (No. 3) was then out of work, and in December 1867 he filed his petition for bankruptcy. In 1868 he rejoined his father's firm as a partner, the firm's name being changed to Francis Higgins & Son. When his father died on 5 February 1880, Francis Higgins (No. 3) continued running the firm, entering his own mark at Goldsmiths' Hall. He was made a Liveryman of the Goldsmiths' Company in June 1882 and died at the age of 90 on 3 December 1908, not in 1909 as stated in the Register of Marks at Goldsmiths' Hall.

Following his death, his son, Francis Joseph Higgins, took over the firm. In June 1909 it was converted into a limited liability company, its directors being Hortense Louise Higgins, widow of Francis Higgins (No. 3); Margaret Hortense Higgins, daughter; Francis Joseph Higgins, son; and Joseph Baines Stonebridge, manager. Francis Joseph Higgins obtained his freedom of the Goldsmiths' Company by Patrimony on 9 June 1909 and was made a Liveryman in December 1919. He was not a craftsman, nor was he particularly interested in the family firm. He spent a total of 14 years' commissioned service in the British Army including the period of the two world wars. He became Captain in 1938, Major in 1944, and was discharged in 1949. He died on 25 July 1965.

Meanwhile, *circa* 1922, the firm of Francis Higgins & Son Ltd took over that of Holland, Aldwinckle & Slater, manufacturing silversmiths, and transferred it to 9 Newman Street. Then, in 1940, Francis Higgins & Son Ltd closed down and all its assets were sold.

*Mark entered in two sizes.

Richard Hodd & Son

| R H |
| W L |

29 August 1862
Richard Hodd (No. 1) and William Linley, Plate workers
manufactory: 31 Hatton Garden, London
R. Hodd (No. 1)'s residence: Stuart Villa, Wood Green, Tottenham
W. Linley's residence: 7 St Mark's Grove, Brompton

R H
W L   * 25 November 1863

R.H
R.H   ** 30 January 1872
          Richard Hodd (No. 1) and Richard Hodd (No. 2), Plate workers
          30 and 31 Hatton Garden
          R. Hodd (No. 1)'s residence: Stuart Villa, Wood Green,
          Tottenham
          R. Hodd (No. 2)'s residence: 71 Westbourne Road, North
          Barnsbury

      2 November 1881

      ** 12 February 1903
          R. Hodd & Son, Gold and Silver workers
          31 Hatton Garden
          George Ernest Hodd's residence: 59 Rutland Gardens,
          Harringay, N

Thomas Hutchinson Goodfellow, William Evans Tilley and Richard Hodd
(No. 1) established this firm of electroplaters at 31 Hatton Garden in 1849.
It traded under the name of Goodfellow, Tilley & Hodd until Tilley left the
partnership in 1854 and the firm's name was changed to Goodfellow &
Hodd.

In 1860 Goodfellow left the partnership and Richard Hodd (No. 1)
became the sole partner. He subsequently entered into partnership with
William Linley, trading under the name of Linley & Hodd, silversmiths and
electroplate manufacturers. They entered the firm's first mark at Goldsmiths' Hall in August 1862. At some later date, they were joined by Richard
Hodd (No. 1)'s son, Richard Hodd (No. 2), but following William Linley's
departure from the firm, this triple partnership was dissolved in January
1872. Richard Hodd (No. 1) and Richard Hodd (No. 2) then continued
running the firm under the name of Richard Hodd & Son, manufacturing
silversmiths and electroplaters.

In 1896 the firm came near to bankruptcy and had to seek repayment
arrangements with its creditors. By February 1903 George Ernest Hodd,
the son of Richard Hodd (No. 2), had taken over the firm as sole partner.
Today, the firm continues to trade as manufacturing silversmiths at 31
Hatton Garden.

*Mark entered in two sizes.
**Mark entered in three sizes.

5 December 1838
Henry Holland (No. 1), Plate worker
13 Smith Street, Northampton Square, Clerkenwell

13 May 1840

19 May 1840

23 November 1847

* 17 December 1849

* 25 October 1860
Henry Holland (No. 1), Plate worker
14 Northampton Square, Clerkenwell
residence: 5 Clarence Terrace, Albion Road, Stoke Newington

* 7 May 1863

16 February 1866 (Entry as for 25.10.1860)

Removed to 16 Jewin Crescent, Aldersgate Street, 7 July 1866

8 October 1869

25 January 1870

3 August 1876

* 30 September 1878
Henry Holland (No. 1), Plate worker
16 Jewin Crescent, Aldersgate Street
residence: 121 Albion Road, Stoke Newington

** 22 March 1880
John Aldwinckle and James Slater, Plate workers
1 Jewin Crescent and 49 Jewin Street
J. Aldwinckle's residence: 7 Compton Terrace
J. Slater's residence: 249 Camden Road

Removed to 18 Hosier Lane, EC, 13 August 1883

** 15 August 1884
John Aldwinckle and Thomas Slater, Plate workers
18 Hosier Lane, EC
J. Aldwinckle's residence: 7 Compton Terrace, Enfield N
T. Slater's residence: 249 Camden Road

** 13 December 1887

All these marks defaced, 7 February 1895

** 7 February 1895
Alfred Thomas Slater, Walter Brindley Slater and Henry Arthur
Holland, Silver workers
18 Hosier Lane, City, EC
A. T. Slater's residence: Fairlight, 8 Priory Road, West
Hampstead
W. B. Slater's residence: 39 Wolseley Road, Crouch End,
Hornsey
H. A. Holland's residence: Berisil, Sevenoaks, Kent

* 20 June 1900
All these marks cancelled 7 July 1902

* 7 July 1902
Holland, Aldwinckle and Slater, Silver workers
18 Hosier Lane, City, EC
A. T. Slater's residence: 40 Aberdare Gardens, West Hampstead,
NW

14 September 1903
Holland, Aldwinckle and Slater, Silver workers
18 Hosier Lane, Smithfield, EC
H. A. Holland's residence: Chevening, Worcester Road, Sutton

partners: Alfred Thomas Slater, Walter Brindley Slater, Henry
Arthur Holland

Alfred Thomas Slater having died, fresh punches were entered by
W. B. Slater and H. A. Holland, 20 October 1905

 †† 20 October 1905
Holland, Aldwinckle and Slater, Gold and Silver workers
13 to 20 Hosier Lane, West Smithfield, EC
W. B. Slater's residence: 19 Belsize Square, London, NW
partners: Henry Arthur Holland, Walter Brindley Slater

This firm of manufacturing silversmiths is thought to have been established
in 1838, the same year that Henry Holland (No. 1) entered his first mark
at Goldsmiths' Hall. At the time, he appears to have been in partnership
with Thomas Frercks (silversmith), trading as Holland & Frercks at 13
Lower Smith Street, Clerkenwell. Henry Holland (No. 1) was born in 1806
and his wife, Nancy, in 1801. They had two children, Henry Holland (No.
2), born in 1830, and Frances Holland, born in 1831.

When Thomas Frercks retired from the partnership at the age of 55 in
December 1841, Henry Holland (No. 1) continued working on his own at
the same address. Meanwhile his son, Henry Holland (No. 2), was
apprenticed to John Lommas Willson (silver chaser, Citizen and Goldsmith)
of 6 Brunswick Place, Grange Road, on 6 December 1843 and obtained his
freedom of the Goldsmiths' Company by Service on 5 February 1851. He
was then taken into partnership by his father, the firm's name being changed
to Henry Holland & Son.

In 1866 Henry Holland & Son bought the firm of Elizabeth Eaton & Son,
silver spoon and fork makers, and by 7 July it had moved into its premises
at 16 Jewin Crescent, Aldersgate Street (see Elizabeth Eaton).

On 30 September 1878 Henry Holland (No. 1) entered his final mark at
Goldsmiths' Hall. His signature against this mark is very shaky indeed,
indicating a lack of hand control, probably due to old age. He appears to
have retired or died within the next eighteen months for, on 22 March 1880,
a new mark was entered by John Aldwinckle and James Slater, the firm's
name having been changed to Holland, Son & Slater.

By May 1883 Henry Holland (No. 2) appears to have retired from the
firm, it being renamed Holland, Aldwinckle & Slater with James Slater's
sons, Alfred Thomas Slater and Walter Brindley Slater, as additional
partners. Also during that year, the firm of Chawner & Co., silver spoon
and fork manufacturers, was bought from the owner, George William
Adams (see George William Adams), and by 13 August 1883 its premises
at 18 Hosier Lane, Smithfield, were occupied by Holland, Aldwinckle &
Slater. In 1887 Holland, Aldwinckle & Slater also purchased the firm of
Robert Hennell & Sons, manufacturing silversmiths of 86 Charlotte Street,

Fitzroy Square.

In April 1884 James Slater retired from the firm, leaving his son, Alfred Thomas Slater, and John Aldwinckle as senior partners. Alfred Thomas Slater, manufacturing silversmith, obtained his freedom of the Goldsmiths' Company by Redemption on 7 April 1897. He was made a Liveryman in January 1902 and died on 26 April 1904 when only 48 years old. John Aldwinckle died on 27 June 1894, following which Henry Arthur Holland became a partner in the firm. Henry Arthur Holland was the son of Henry Holland (No. 2) and obtained his freedom of the Goldsmiths' Company by Patrimony on 6 July 1904. He was made a Liveryman in May 1910 and died on 8 April 1924.

Circa 1922 the firm was taken over by Francis Higgins & Son Ltd, manufacturing silversmiths, which transferred the firm to its own premises at 9 Newman Street, Oxford Street. Here, Holland, Aldwinckle & Slater continued to operate under its own name until 1932.

*Mark entered in two sizes.
**Mark entered in three sizes.
††Mark entered in six sizes.

D. J. & C. Houle

* 21 January 1842
Daniel (John) Houle and Charles Houle, Plate workers
24 Red Lion Street, Clerkenwell

2 November 1869
D. Houle's residence: 26 Stock Orchard Villas, Caledonian Road
C. Houle's residence: 24 The Grove, Hammersmith

23 October 1879
C. Houle's residence: Removed to 17 Sutherland Gardens, Harrow Road

23 September 1884
Charles Houle, Plate worker
24 Red Lion Street, Clerkenwell
C. Houle's residence: Halford House, Sutherland Place, Bayswater

Daniel John Houle and Charles Houle were two sons of John Houle

162

(silversmith) of 24 Red Lion Street, Clerkenwell. *Circa* 1811, John Houle established himself as a manufacturing silversmith at 24 Red Lion Street, entering his first mark at Goldsmiths' Hall on 10 April 1811. Presumably his two sons trained as silversmiths while working under him and subsequently joined him in partnership. By the beginning of 1842, they had taken over the running of the business, entering their first mark at Goldsmiths' Hall. In 1844 the firm's name was changed to John, Daniel & Charles Houle, then, in 1845, to Daniel & Charles Houle. John, Daniel and Charles Houle never became Freemen of the Goldsmiths' Company.

Daniel John Houle was born in 1818 and his wife, Jane (née Cranbrook), in 1829. They had four children, the eldest, Jane, being born in 1851. Charles Houle, who was born in 1820, married Emma Cranbrook, the sister of Jane Cranbrook. They had three children.

Following the death of Daniel John Houle on 16 May 1884, Charles Houle continued running the firm, entering his own mark at Goldsmiths' Hall. However, in 1885 he and the executors of Daniel John Houle's estate sold the firm to Charles Stuart Harris (silver spoon maker) of 29 Kirby Street, Hatton Garden. By 29 March 1886 Charles Stuart Harris had vacated his own premises and had moved into Houle's at 24 Red Lion Street.

*Mark entered in two sizes.

Hukin & Heath

* 19 November 1879
Jonathan Wilson Hukin and John Thomas Heath, Plate workers
Great Charles Street, Birmingham
19 Charterhouse Street, Holborn
J. W. Hukin's residence: Belle Vue Villa, Nunhead Lane,
Leamington

By virtue of a Power of Attorney dated 19 November 1879, I enter the marks of Jonathan Wilson Hukin and John Thomas Heath of Charles Street, Birmingham, silversmith. (Dated this) 19 day of November 1879 (by) John Thomas Heath of 19 Charterhouse Street, Holborn Circus, Attorney to the said Jonathan Wilson Hukin and John Thomas Heath

163

** 3 March 1886 (Entry as for 19.11.1879)

(Marks) all defaced 26.6.1886

 ** 21 June 1886
John Thomas Heath and John Harlshom Middleton, Small
workers
Great Charles Street, Birmingham
Charterhouse Street, EC
J. T. Heath's residence: Brasted Villa, 201 Brixton Hill
J. H. Middleton's residence: Stratford House, Olton, near
Birmingham

 ** 21 February 1896 (Entry as for 21.6.1886)

 4 June 1896 (Entry as for 21.6.1886)

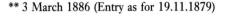 *** 2 December 1909
Hukin and Heath Limited, Gold and Silver workers
Imperial Works, Great Charles Street, Birmingham
19 Charterhouse Street, London, EC
F. P Heath's residence: Dunraven, 66 Compagne Gardens, West
Hampstead, NW
partners: John Thomas Heath, Frank Pearson Heath, John Wilson
Middleton

*** 28 April 1910 (Entry as for 2.12.1909)

This Birmingham firm of manufacturing silversmiths and electroplaters was
established by Jonathan Wilson Hukin *circa* 1855. On 19 November 1879
J. W. Hukin's partner, John Thomas Heath, entered the firm's mark for the
first time at Goldsmiths' Hall, London, where he listed the firm's premises
as, Great Charles Street, Birmingham (manufactory) and 19 Charterhouse
Street, London (showrooms). Also, *circa* 1879, J. W. Hukin and J. T. Heath
appointed Dr Christopher Dresser (1834–1904) as art adviser to the firm.
It is for its silver and electroplated goods produced to Dr Dresser's designs
that the firm is best known today.

When J. W. Hukin retired in March 1886, the firm was continued by the remaining partners, J. T. Heath and J. H. Middleton, who entered their partnership mark in June 1886.

In 1904 the firm was converted into a limited liability company under the name of Hukin & Heath Ltd, its directors being John Thomas Heath, Frank Pearson Heath, John Harlshom Middleton and John Wilson Middleton.

J. T. Heath died on 18 December 1910, aged 70, and J. H. Middleton retired or died at some date prior to 2 December 1909. The firm closed down in 1953.

*Mark entered in two sizes.
**Mark entered in three sizes.
***Mark entered in four sizes.

Hunt & Roskell

17 January 1839
John Samuel Hunt, Plate worker
** 17 Harrison Street, Grays Inn Road

* 30 December 1839
John Mortimer and John Samuel Hunt, Plate workers
17 Harrison Street, Grays Inn Road

*

* 25 February 1843

** 10 January 1844
John Samuel Hunt, Plate worker
17 Harrison Street, Grays Inn Road

* 22 November 1855
John Samuel Hunt, Plate worker
17 Harrison Street, Grays Inn Road

** 19 October 1865
John Hunt and Robert Roskell, Plate workers
26 Harrison Street, Grays Inn Road
residences: J. Hunt: 156 New Bond Street
R. Roskell: 22 Lancaster Gate, Bayswater, and Park House,
* Fulham

** 12 June 1882
Robert Roskell, Allan Roskell and John Mortimer Hunt, Plate
workers
26 Harrison Street, Grays Inn Road
156 New Bond Street
residences: R. Roskell: Park House, Fulham
A. Roskell: 156 New Bond Street
J. M. Hunt: 4 Airlie Gardens, Campden Hill

These marks were sent here to be defaced the 26 September
1889 the business having been transferred to Messrs Benson and
Webb

** 17 September 1889
Alfred Benson and Henry Hugh Webb, Plate workers
156 New Bond Street
manufactory: Harrison Street, Grays Inn Road
residences: A. Benson: Belsize Park, NW
H. H. Webb: Acacia Road, NW

1 December 1892 (Entry as for 17.9.1889)

These marks defaced 7 June 1894

* 7 June 1894
Alfred Benson and Arthur Henry Benson, Plate workers
156 New Bond Street

166

**26 Harrison Street
residences: A. Benson: Woodcote, Belsize Park
A. H. Benson: Ankerwyche House, Wraysbury near Staines

These marks defaced 4 August 1897

*** 25 August 1897
Hunt and Roskell Ltd, Gold and Silver workers
156 New Bond Street
26 Harrison Street, WC
25 Old Bond Street
62–64 Ludgate Hill
28 Royal Exchange
F. Hindon's residence: Longfield, Gordon Road, Ealing
director: Francis Hindon

All above marks were cancelled 28 March 1901. Defaced 1 April 1902

** 28 March 1901
Hunt and Roskell Ltd, Gold and Silver workers
156 New Bond Street
26 Harrison Street, WC
F. Hindon's residence: Longfield, Gordon Road, Ealing
director: Francis Hindon

29 March 1901 (Entry as for 28.3.1901)

* 4 June 1912
Hunt and Roskell Ltd, Gold and Silver workers
25 Old Bond Street, London, W
G. B. Whitworth's residence: Upper Gatton Park, Merstham (Surrey)
directors: Arthur Henry Benson, Alfred Benson, Geoffrey Budilent Whitworth, Alfred Douglas D. Benson

Hunt & Roskell was the continuation of an already established firm founded by the well-known silversmith, Paul Storr (see *Marks of London Goldsmiths and Silversmiths c. 1697–1837*, revised edition 1988, pp. 326–9). Paul Storr first entered into partnership with William Frisbee (silversmith, Citizen and Goldsmith) of 5 Cock Lane, Snowhill, in May 1792, but by 12 January 1793 he had set up on his own at 30 Church Street, Soho, from where he moved to 20 Air Street, St James in 1796. In 1807 he entered into a business agreement with the well-known retail firm of royal goldsmiths, Rundell, Bridge & Rundell of 32 Ludgate Hill. Under this agreement, Paul Storr, in partnership with Philip Rundell, John Bridge, Edmund Waller Rundell and

William Theed, set up a subsidiary firm of manufacturing silversmiths called Storr & Co. This firm was created primarily to manufacture goods for retailing by Rundell, Bridge & Rundell at its Ludgate Hill showrooms.

In February 1819 Paul Storr retired from the partnership and re-established himself as a separate business at 17 Harrison Street, Grays Inn Road, where he continued to trade as Storr & Co., working silversmiths. He entered into partnership with John Mortimer in 1822, renaming the firm Storr & Mortimer. Under their agreement, Storr concentrated on the manufacture of goods for Mortimer to sell in his shop at 13 New Bond Street. Then, *circa* 1826, Storr's nephew by marriage, John Samuel Hunt, joined the partnership. It seems that he had been working as a chaser in Storr's workshop for many years.

When Paul Storr retired in December 1838, the firm was renamed Mortimer & Hunt, its partners being John Mortimer, John Samuel Hunt and his son, John Hunt. Under this new partnership, John Samuel Hunt entered his first set of marks at Goldsmiths' Hall in 1839. Meanwhile, the firm's shop was relocated at 156 New Bond Street, although its manufactory remained at 17 Harrison Street.

As a result of John Mortimer's retirement in December 1843, John Samuel Hunt and John Hunt entered into partnership with Robert Roskell and Charles Frederick Hancock, changing the firm's name to Hunt & Roskell. The firm's addresses at the time were given as 156 New Bond Street (shop) and 26 Harrison Street (manufactory). In January 1849 Charles Frederick Hancock retired from the partnership and established his own firm of manufacturing silversmiths and jewellers at 39 Bruton Street (see Hancocks & Co.).

Following John Samuel Hunt's death on 20 May 1865, new marks were entered at Goldsmiths' Hall by John Hunt and Robert Roskell on 19 October 1865. Under this entry at Goldsmiths' Hall, the firm's manufactory was recorded for the first time as being at 26 Harrison Street. John Hunt obtained his freedom of the Goldsmiths' Company by Redemption on 5 February 1845 and was made a Liveryman in February 1850. When he died in November 1879, aged 68, the firm was continued by Robert Roskell, Allan Roskell and John Hunt's son, John Mortimer Hunt. John Mortimer Hunt obtained his freedom of the Goldsmiths' Company by Redemption on 7 October 1874 and was made a Liveryman in December 1879.

Following the death of Robert Roskell on 22 July 1888, Allan Roskell and John Mortimer Hunt dissolved their partnership in May 1889 and sold the firm to J. W. Benson, silversmiths and watch and clock makers of Ludgate Hill (see James William Benson). The new partners of Hunt & Roskell, Alfred Benson and Henry Hugh Webb, entered their marks at Goldsmiths'

Hall in September 1889.

In 1897 the two firms were converted into separate limited liability companies known as J. W. Benson Ltd and Hunt & Roskell Ltd. In 1911 Hunt & Roskell Ltd moved to 25 Old Bond Street, where it remained until *circa* 1965, but its manufactory continued to operate from 26 Harrison Street until destroyed by German bombing *circa* 1940. Hunt & Roskell subsequently became one of the Mappin & Webb Ltd group of companies, which was itself part of Sears Holdings Ltd. In 1990 Mappin & Webb Ltd was acquired by Asprey & Co.

*Mark entered in two sizes.
**Mark entered in three sizes.
***Mark entered in four sizes.

William Hutton & Sons

26 October 1863
William Hutton, Plate worker
High Street, Sheffield
13 Thavies Inn, Holborn
W. Hutton's residence: Claremont Place, Sheffield

* 11 June 1875
Robert Hutton, Plate worker
27 High Street, Sheffield
13 Thavies Inn, Holborn, London
R. Hutton's residence: Sharrow View, Sheffield

** 3 March 1880
Edward Hutton, Plate worker
27 High Street, Sheffield
13 Thavies Inn, Holborn, EC
E. Hutton's residence: 7 Heathfield Gardens, West Street, Hampstead

14 November 1881

15 September 1887

** 24 November 1887

169

** 9 January 1891
Ernest Hutton, Plate worker
West Street, Sheffield
13 Thavies Inn, Holborn
E. Hutton's residence: 48 Grange Crescent, Sheffield

Removed to 7 Farringdon Road, EC,
17 January 1894
signed: Chas W Blackman for Ernest Hutton

These marks erased 18.4.1894

** 5 April 1894
William Hutton & Sons, Plate workers
West Street, Sheffield
7 Farringdon Road (London)
H. Hutton (No. 1)'s residence: Tapton Croft, Sheffield
managing director: Herbert Hutton (No. 1)

22 May 1894

19 March 1896

16 November 1896 (Entry as for 5.4.1894)

* 4 May 1899
William Hutton & Sons Ltd, Silver workers
West Street, Sheffield
Hanley Street, Birmingham
7 Farringdon Road, EC
C. Blackman's residence: 102 Priory Road, West Hampstead
director: Charles W Blackman

22 June 1899

** 16 September 1901 (Entry as for 4.5.1899)

* 4 April 1902 (Entry as for 4.5.1899)

 23 October 1902 (Entry as for 4.5.1899)

 20 April 1903 (Entry as for 4.5.1899)

 24 July 1903
William Hutton & Sons Ltd, Silver workers
West Street, Sheffield
Hanley Street, Birmingham
9 Farringdon Road, EC
C. Blackman's residence: 102 Priory Road, West Hampstead
director: Charles W Blackman

 12 December 1903 (Entry as for 24.7.1903)

 9 May 1904
William Hutton & Sons Ltd, Silver workers
West Street, Sheffield
Hanley Street, Birmingham
7 Farringdon Road, London, EC
C. Blackman's residence: 102 Priory Road, West Hampstead
director: Charles W Blackman

* 18 October 1905 (Entry as for 9.5.1904)

*** 4 June 1913
William Hutton & Sons Ltd, Silver workers
7 Farringdon Road, London, EC
West Street, Sheffield
Hanley Street, Birmingham
S. C. Gibbs's residence: 153 Chevening Road, Brondesbury, NW
directors: Elford Pearse, Herbert Hutton, Robert Hutton, Sydney
Corah Gibbs, Wilfred Steel

** 2 July 1913 (Entry as for 4.6.1913)

 * 8 August 1913 (Entry as for 4.6.1913)

29 May 1914 (Entry as for 4.6.1913 but with S. C. Gibbs's
second residence listed as: Elm Lodge, Elstree, Herts.)

This firm of manufacturing silversmiths and platers was established by
William Carr Hutton at Sheffield in 1832. His father, William Hutton, born
in 1774, had become a silver plater and manufacturer of plated articles at
53 Park Street, Birmingham, in 1803. From 1812 to 1820 he had worked
at Paradise Street, during which time he was involved in two partnerships,
one called Rylands & Hutton, *circa* 1812, and the other, Hutton &
Houghton, from 1818 to 1820. In 1821 he was at Fleet Street, and from
1823 to 1842 at 130 Great Charles Street. He died on 2 May 1842 when
68 years old.

William Hutton had three sons, James, Joseph and William Carr, all of
whom worked for their father in the family business. William Carr Hutton
was born in 1803 and, having worked for his father for several years, moved
to Sheffield in 1832, where he set up his own firm at 58 Eyre Street, trading
as William Hutton, manufacturer of silver-plated articles. In 1833 his
premises were at 35½ Pinstone Street; in 1839 at 50 South Street, Moor;
in 1841 at 10 Surrey Street; and in 1845 at 27 High Street. The workshops
at this last address were rebuilt in 1853.

William Carr Hutton's brother James became the firm's representative in
London from 1833 to 1837, after which he moved to the Sheffield works
as a clerk. *Circa* 1845 he went to Canada as the firm's agent. Meanwhile,
circa 1843, William Carr Hutton's other brother, Joseph, was placed in
charge of the electroplating side of the business.

On 26 October 1863 William Carr Hutton entered his first mark at
Goldsmiths' Hall, London, giving the firm's addresses as High Street,
Sheffield (manufactory) and 13 Thavies Inn, Holborn, London (showrooms). He renamed the firm William Hutton & Son in 1864, and died,
aged 62, on 26 December 1865.

Following his death, the firm was continued by three of his sons, James
Edward Hutton, Robert Hutton and Herbert Hutton (No. 1). *Circa* 1870
the firm's name was further amended to William Hutton & Sons, and then,
in 1893, it was converted into a limited liability company. Also in 1893 it

took over the firm of Rupert Favell & Co., manufacturing silversmiths of Bucknall Street, New Oxford Street, London. Then, in 1902, it acquired the firm of Creswick & Co., manufacturing silversmiths of Arundel Street, Sheffield. The firm of William Hutton & Sons Ltd ceased manufacturing in 1930 when its goodwill was transferred to James Dixon & Sons Ltd of Sheffield.

William Carr Hutton had five sons, all of whom were educated at the Institution Sillig at Vevey, Switzerland. They were William Henry, James Edward, George, Robert and Herbert (No. 1). William Henry Hutton emigrated to Canada in 1860, where he joined his uncle, James Hutton. He married an American and died there in 1893. George Hutton, the third son, also went to Canada, where he died in 1864. Robert Hutton became a partner in the family firm at Sheffield. He retired from the firm in December 1879 and then moved to Bath in Somerset in 1883 or 1884. He died in June 1896.

Herbert Hutton (No. 1), born in 1843, joined his father's firm at Sheffield in 1864, where he eventually became a partner and so remained until his death in 1904. It was he who put Charles Blackman in charge of the London office in 1891 or 1892. Blackman, who became a director of the firm at some date prior to 1899, died on 29 April 1907. Herbert Hutton (No. 1) had a daughter who married a Colonel Elford Pearce, and he, following Herbert's death in 1904, joined the firm to represent the interests of his wife's branch of the family, who then owned 5/7ths of the firm's shares. Eventually Colonel Elford Pearce became chairman of the firm.

William Carr Hutton's second son, James Edward Hutton, was born in 1838. *Circa* 1860 he joined his father's firm, and subsequently moved to the London office where he developed the marketing side of the firm, promoting sales to retail jewellers and silversmiths in both the home and export markets. Eventually he became a senior partner, a position which he held until his death in 1890 when 52 years old. He had three sons who joined the family business: Ernest (by his first wife), Herbert (No. 2) and Robert Salmon. Ernest Hutton became a junior partner and developed the provincial business of the firm. He died in April 1907.

Herbert Hutton (No. 2) joined the firm at Sheffield in 1896, where he worked through all the various departments in the factory. *Circa* 1900 he moved to Birmingham to manage a small branch factory. On 29 July 1907 he took charge of the Sheffield factory as its managing director, and it was here that his brother, Robert Salmon Hutton, subsequently joined him. On 26 April 1923 Herbert Hutton (No. 2) retired as managing director, mainly due to rival family interests. Two years later, Herbert Hutton (No. 2)

173

became the manager of Messrs Josiah Williams & Co., a firm in Bristol, which he continued to run until the factory was destroyed in a blitz during the Second World War.

The third son, Robert Salmon Hutton, took a B.Sc. degree with first-class honours in chemistry at Victoria University, Manchester, in 1897. From 1898 to 1900 he carried out postgraduate research at Leipzig and Paris, and then, from 1900 to 1908, he was a lecturer in electrometallurgy at Manchester University, where in 1905 he obtained a Doctor of Science degree. In July 1907 he joined William Hutton & Sons Ltd, becoming a director of the firm based at Sheffield, where he concentrated on extending the export trade. In June 1917 he resigned from the firm in order to devote all his time to the Sheffield Flatware Co. Ltd, of which he was managing director. This company had been established in 1914 by William Hutton & Sons Ltd together with James Dixon & Sons, Walker & Hall and Barker Brothers Silversmiths Ltd. Robert Salmon Hutton continued in this position until 1921 when he became director of the British Non-Ferrous Metals Research Association. Then, in 1932, he became a professor of metallurgy at Cambridge University, where he researched into methods for preventing silver from tarnishing.

On 16 November 1932 he was elected by Special Grant to the Freedom and Livery of the Goldsmiths' Company, London. Then, on 19 February 1936, he was made an Assistant of the Company. He became 4th Warden in 1939, 3rd Warden in 1940, 2nd Warden in 1941 and Prime Warden in 1942. He died on 5 August 1970 when 94 years old.

*Mark entered in two sizes.
**Mark entered in three sizes.
***Mark entered in four sizes.

Frank Hyams Ltd

1 May 1903
Frank Hyams Ltd, Gold and Silver workers
128 New Bond Street, W
F. Hyams's residence: 65 Gloucester Terrace, Hyde Park, W
managing director: Frank Hyams

* 22 May 1903

† 3 February 1909
Frank Hyams Ltd, Gold and Silver workers
128 New Bond Street, London, W
E. J. Lowe's residence: Yeoveney, Ashford, Middlesex
secretary: Ernest J. Lowe

All these punches cancelled 5.2.1914
The next entry is that of E. J. Lowe

Frank Hyams originated from Dunedin, New Zealand. He founded his business of jewellers, silversmiths and gem dealers in 1902, registering it as a limited liability company. At the end of 1913 or early 1914, Frank Hyams Ltd closed and the business was continued by Ernest J. Lowe as successor to Frank Hyams Ltd. Lowe's premises were at 20 Grafton Street, New Bond Street.

*Mark entered in two sizes.
†Mark entered in five sizes.

George Ivory

G·I 8 January 1844
George Ivory, Plate worker
53 Compton Street, Clerkenwell

G I 20 October 1844

G·I * 10 June 1853
George Ivory, Plate worker
8 St James Walk, Clerkenwell

E·I 29 October 1860
Elizabeth Ivory, Plate worker
8 St James Walk, Clerkenwell

A·I * 19 July 1861
Alfred Ivory, Plate worker
8 St James Walk, Clerkenwell

Now called 27 St James Walk, 18 October 1880

George Ivory, the son of George Ivory (silversmith) of Compton Street, Clerkenwell, was apprenticed to Richard William Elliott (silversmith, Citizen and Goldsmith) of Compton Street on 6 February 1833 to learn the art of silversmith. He obtained his freedom of the Goldsmiths' Company by Service on 4 March 1840.

His brother, Charles Sage Ivory, was apprenticed to William Leavers (jeweller, Citizen and Goldsmith) of Duncan Place, City Road, on 1 March 1837 to learn the art of jeweller. He obtained his freedom of the Goldsmiths' Company by Service on 3 April 1844.

Having obtained his freedom in 1840, George Ivory (junior) may have continued working for Richard William Elliott and his father, William Elliott, until they retired from their silversmithing business *circa* 1844. By January 1844 George Ivory was trading as a silversmith with his own mark registered at Goldsmiths' Hall. Then, in 1860, he apparently emigrated, leaving the business at 8 St James Walk to be run by Mrs Elizabeth Ivory, silver plate manufacturer. At the time, his brother, Charles Sage Ivory, was also working at 8 St James Walk, this being the address he gave when taking over George Ivory's apprentice, George Charles Dexter, on 7 November 1860 on account of George Ivory having left England.

Mrs Elizabeth Ivory entered her mark at Goldsmiths' Hall in October 1860, but by 19 July 1861 the business had been taken over by Alfred Ivory, silver plate manufacturer. Alfred Ivory ceased trading *circa* 1882.

William Henry Jackson was apprenticed to George Ivory in 1851 and obtained his freedom in 1860.

*Mark entered in two sizes.

James Jackson & Son

JJ

13 February 1824
James Jackson, Case maker
22 Richmond Street, Old Street

24 August 1830
Removed to 10 Norman Street, St Lukes

(J J)

30 August 1832
New mark

JJ 28 June 1839
New mark

JJ
JJ 3 September 1842
Two new marks

JJ 11 May 1847
James Jackson, Silver case maker
6 Norman Street, St Lukes

J J 30 August 1849
New mark

JJ 24 August 1850
New mark broken

JJ 16 October 1850
New mark

JJ 21 July 1851
New mark

JJ 13 March 1865
New mark

J.J 25 August 1870
James Jackson, Case maker
36 Helmet Row, St Lukes

J.J 1 December 1873
New mark

This firm of watchcase manufacturers was founded by James Jackson (No. 1) (case maker, Citizen and Goldsmith) in 1785. Apprenticed on 1 July 1761, he obtained his freedom of the Goldsmiths' Company by Service on 10 April 1771. From his premises at 2 Bridgewater Street, Barbican, he entered two marks at Goldsmiths' Hall, one on 3 February 1785, the other on 12 July 1790. He died at some date prior to March 1794.

Three of his sons, Joshua, Samuel and James (No. 2), became Freemen of the Goldsmiths' Company. Joshua Jackson (watchcase maker) obtained his freedom by Patrimony on 6 February 1812. Samuel Jackson (silversmith) obtained his freedom by Service on 1 April 1795, having been apprenticed to his uncle, Joshua Jackson (Citizen and Goldsmith) of New Street, Cloth Fair, on 5 March 1788. James Jackson (No. 2) (watchcase maker) was

177

likewise apprenticed to his uncle, Joshua Jackson (goldsmith, Citizen and Goldsmith) of New Street, Cloth Fair, on 5 March 1794. For some unknown reason, James Jackson (No. 2) did not take up his freedom of the Goldsmiths' Company until 7 December 1825, and then by Patrimony. Possibly the reason was to enable him to accept his son, Joseph, as an apprentice in January 1826.

During this period of 'apprenticeship' (from 5.3.1794 to 7.12.1825), two of James Jackson's marks of 'JJ' in a rectangle were entered at Goldsmiths' Hall, one on 26 January 1805, the other on 14 February 1805. Both listed his address as 3 Church Row, St Lukes. Then, on 30 April 1816, he was recorded as having moved to 10 Norman Street, St Lukes. However, a new mark was registered on 13 February 1824 giving his address as 22 Richmond Street. This address was superseded on 24 August 1830 when he was again recorded as having moved to 10 Norman Street, St Lukes, although he was already at that address in January 1826 and November 1827 when two of his sons were apprenticed to him.

From here on the firm continued to trade from 10 Norman Street until 11 May 1847 when its address was given as 6 Norman Street. Then, on 25 August 1870, it was listed as 36 Helmet Row, St Lukes. The firm continued trading from this address until 1897.

James Jackson (No. 2) had five sons who became Freemen of the Goldsmiths' Company. They were Joseph, Samuel, George, William Henry and James (No. 3). Joseph Jackson (watchcase maker) was apprenticed to his father on 4 January 1826 and eventually obtained his freedom by Service on 7 January 1852. (Joseph's son was William Henry Jackson (silversmith) who entered into partnership with Walter Chase at 16 President Street in 1877. See William Henry Jackson.) Samuel Jackson (silversmith) was apprenticed to his father on 7 November 1827 and eventually obtained his freedom by Service on 2 October 1850. George Jackson (silversmith) was apprenticed to his father on 5 May 1830 and obtained his freedom by Service on 7 June 1837. William Henry Jackson (silversmith) was apprenticed to his father on 5 March 1834, and was then turned over to his brother, George Jackson (silversmith, Citizen and Goldsmith) of 13 Nelson Street, City Road, on 3 July 1839 due to his father having retired from business. He obtained his freedom by Service on 7 April 1841. James Jackson (No. 3) (silversmith) was apprenticed to his brother, William Henry Jackson (silversmith, Citizen and Goldsmith) of 26 Sydney Street, Goswell Road, on 2 October 1844 and obtained his freedom by Service on 3 December 1851.

William Henry Jackson

** 12 December 1877
William Henry Jackson and Walter Chase, Plate workers
16 President Street East, Goswell Road
residence: 4 Bruce Terrace, Lordship Lane, Wood Green

** 11 June 1883
William Henry Jackson, Plate worker
14 President Street, Goswell Road, EC
residence: 83 Crayford Road, Holloway

(Marks) defaced 17.7.1895

27 August 1883
Removed to 43 Spencer Street, Clerkenwell

* 6 May 1887
William Jackson and Peter Henderson Deere, Plate workers
43 Spencer Street, Clerkenwell
residence: 29 Linton Street, New North Road, Islington

** 26 May 1891

18 July 1895
William (Henry) Jackson, Plate worker
68 Moreland Street
residence: 25 Melgund Road, Highbury

25 July 1895

William Henry Jackson was the son of Joseph Jackson (watchcase maker, Citizen and Goldsmith) of 13 Nelson Street, City Road, and grandson of James Jackson (No. 2) (watchcase maker, Citizen and Goldsmith) of Norman Street, St Lukes. He was apprenticed to George Ivory (silversmith, Citizen and Goldsmith) of 53 Compton Street, Clerkenwell, on 5 March 1851 and obtained his freedom of the Goldsmiths' Company by Service on 4 January 1860. He and Walter Chase commenced trading as Jackson & Chase, silversmiths, at 16 President Street, Clerkenwell, in 1877. On 9 June 1883 they dissolved their partnership, following which William Henry

Jackson continued trading on his own.

In 1887 he entered into partnership with Peter Henderson Deere, trading as Jackson & Deere, silversmiths of 43 Spencer Street, Clerkenwell. Following the dissolution of their partnership in March 1895, he continued trading under his own name.

His son, Edmund Henry Jackson, was apprenticed to him on 4 November 1896 and obtained his freedom of the Goldsmiths' Company by Service on 2 December 1903.

William Henry Jackson appears to have retired or died in 1905 for, on 2 September 1905, Mary Jackson, sole partner in W. H. Jackson & Son, entered new marks at Goldsmiths' Hall. The firm eventually closed *circa* 1910.

*Mark entered in two sizes.
**Mark entered in three sizes.

Thomas Johnson (No. 1)

---

 19 January 1850
Thomas Johnson (No. 1), Small worker
10 Dyers Building, Holborn

Removed to 32 John Street, Bedford Row, Holborn, 3 January 1860

 15 October 1869

 15 November 1869

 8 March 1879

 10 November 1881

 * 7 May 1883
Two marks (of the four entered) defaced 19.2.1890

18 February 1890
Frederick Edmonds and Edward J. W. Johnson, Small workers
32 John Street, Bedford Row

6 March 1890 (Mark) erased 3.4.1891

3 April 1891 (Mark) erased 28.3.1892

*28 March 1892
Frederick Edmonds, Small worker
32 John Street, Bedford Row

 23 February 1897 (Mark) defaced 18.5.1898

Frederick Edmonds died 5 February 1898 the business afterwards carried on by his wife Mary Harris Edmonds

18 May 1898
Mary Harris Edmonds, Gold and Silver worker
32 John Street, Bedford Row, WC (Mark) cancelled 27.8.1898

The business of Mary Harris Edmonds (widow of Frederick Edmonds) trading as Johnson, Sons & Edmonds was on 27 August 1898 transferred to Messrs S. Mordan & Co. Ltd, 41 City Road, EC

Thomas Johnson (No. 1), who was born in 1817, established this firm of manufacturing silversmiths *circa* 1850. The firm specialised in dressing-case and travelling-bag fittings, silver flasks, card cases, snuff boxes, vinaigrettes and smelling bottles.

Circa 1875 the firm's name was changed to Thomas Johnson & Sons. However, when Frederick Edmonds joined the partnership in about 1878, it was renamed Johnson, Sons & Edmonds. The partners were Thomas George Johnson (retired January 1883), Thomas Johnson (retired March 1885), Edward J. W. Johnson (retired October 1891) and Frederick Edmonds (died 5 February 1898).

Following the death of Frederick Edmonds in 1898, his widow, Mary Harris Edmonds, continued running the firm. Then, on 27 August 1898, the firm was transferred to Sampson Mordan & Co. Ltd of 41 City Road, EC, where it became part of Mordan's firm.

*Mark entered in two sizes.

Thomas Johnson (No. 2)

23 October 1877
Thomas Johnson (No. 2), Small worker
51 Spencer Street, Clerkenwell

TJ 1 July 1880

T.J 17 January 1883

T.J 29 January 1891
Removed to 111 St John's Street Road, Clerkenwell

Removed to 19 Chadwell Street, Clerkenwell, EC, 14 August 1900

This worker having died, the business was carried on by his widow, Maria Johnson

M.J 23 November 1904
trading as T. Johnson, Stick mounter
business and residence: 19 Chadwell Street, Clerkenwell, EC
partner: Maria Johnson

Removed to 5 Middleton Square, Clerkenwell (business and residence), 24 June 1913

Succeeded by grandson, Arthur Ainsworth

Thomas Johnson (No. 2) commenced trading as a silversmith at 51 Spencer Street, Clerkenwell), in 1877, where he specialised in gold and silver mountings for walking sticks. Following his death in 1904, his widow, Maria Johnson, continued running the firm, trading as T. Johnson. In 1913 she moved to 5 Middleton Square, Clerkenwell, where the business was eventually taken over by her grandson, Arthur Thomas Ainsworth. He entered his mark of 'AA' in a double cusp at Goldsmiths' Hall on 10 June 1932, giving the firm's name as Arthur Ainsworth trading at 5 Middleton Square. His private residence was listed as 22 Bond Street, Holford Square.

Johnson & Springthorpe

 *** 12 December 1882
John Johnson and Alfred Springthorpe, Plate workers
20 Red Lion Street, Clerkenwell
J. W. Johnson's residence: 32 Emperors Gate, South Kensington, SW
A. Springthorpe's residence: Fair View, Bounds Green, New Southgate

(Marks) defaced 30.1.1885

30 January 1885
John Williams Johnson, Plate workers
20 Red Lion Street, Clerkenwell
J. W. Johnson's residence: 23 Sussex Villas, Kensington

*

(Marks) defaced 18.3.1887

** 18 March 1887
John Johnson and Matthew White, Plate workers
20 Red Lion Street, Clerkenwell
residence: 35A Russell Road, Kensington, W

(Marks) defaced 13.12.1887

** 13 December 1887
Matthew William White, Plate worker
20 Red Lion Street
residence: 9 Grays Inn Square

This firm is a continuation of Richards & Brown, silversmiths, of 20 Red Lion Street, Clerkenwell (see Richards & Brown). Following Edward Charles Brown's retirement from Richards & Brown, *circa* November 1882, the firm was taken over by John William Johnson and Alfred Springthorpe, who commenced trading as Johnson & Springthorpe, manufacturing gold and silversmiths.

On 17 January 1885 their partnership was dissolved, leaving John William Johnson to continue trading on his own. In 1886 he entered into partnership with Matthew William White, trading as Johnson & White.

On 31 October 1887 John William Johnson retired from the partnership, leaving Matthew William White to continue running the firm as Johnson & White until *circa* 1889.

*Mark entered in two sizes.
**Mark entered in three sizes.
***Mark entered in four sizes.

(J J.J W.)

5 February 1866
James Johnson and John (Charles) Walker, Gold workers
89 Aldersgate Street
residences: J. Johnson: 1 Grove Villa, Albion Grove, Stoke
Newington
J. Walker: 20 Hildrop Crescent, Camden Road

Removed to 80 Aldersgate Street, 19 February 1868

(J.J.J.W)

31 August 1871
(J. Walker) Removed to 14 Hildrop Road, Camden Road

(J.J.J.W)

* 29 February 1872

(J.J.JW)

4 October 1878
(J. Walker) Removed to Highfield Avenue Road, Crouch End

(W.W B.T)

** 11 December 1885
Walter (Crellin) Walker and Brownfield Tolhurst, Gold workers
80 Aldersgate Street, EC
residences: W. Walker: Oakleigh, Coolhurst Road, Crouch End,
N
B. Tolhurst: The Grange, Sidcup

(W.W B.T)

* 31 January 1893

(WW B.T)

30 November 1894

(W.W B.T)

** 26 February 1895

(W.W B.T)

1 July 1902
Walter (Crellin) Walker and Brownfield Tolhurst, Gold and Silver
workers
80 Aldersgate Street, EC
172 New Bond Street, W
residences: W. Walker: Percy Lodge, Winchmore Hill
B. Tolhurst: The Grange, Sidcup

5 November 1902
Walter (Crellin) Walker and Brownfield Tolhurst, (Entry as for 1.7.1902)

 12 February 1903
Walter (Crellin) Walker and Brownfield Tolhurst (Entry as for 1.7.1902)

 *

 20 February 1903

 ** 1 May 1908
Johnson, Walker & Tolhurst Ltd, Gold and Silver manufacturers
80 Aldersgate Street, EC
172 New Bond Street, W
E. E. Grimwood's residence: The Haven, East Avenue, Walthamstow, Essex
directors: Brownfield Tolhurst, Guy Walker, Ernest Alfred Walker, George Tolhurst
secretary: Ernest E. Grimwood

18 May 1909. New address:
21 Conduit Street, London, W

 * 26 June 1911
Johnson, Walker & Tolhurst Ltd, Gold and Silver workers
80 Aldersgate Street, EC
21 Conduit Street, London, W
E. E. Grimwood's residence: Elim, Lower Park, Loughton, Essex
directors: Ernest Alfred Walker, Guy Hamilton Walker, George Tolhurst, Edward Alfred Cox
secretary: Ernest E. Grimwood

 31 October 1911 (Entry as for 26.6.1911)

* 3 April 1912 (Entry as for 26.6.1911)

** 22 January 1914 (Entry as for 26.6.1911
but with E. E. Grimwood's residence as: Elim, Chase Court Gardens, Enfield)

This firm was established *circa* 1850 by James Johnson and John Charles Walker trading as Johnson & Walker. In 1856 they were listed as gold and silver refiners, but by 1867 they were wholesale dealers in bullion, jewellery and watches. At about this date George Edmeades Tolhurst joined the partnership and the firm was renamed Johnson, Walker & Tolhurst.

On 30 June 1885 the partnership between James Johnson, John Charles Walker and George Edmeades Tolhurst was dissolved. The firm was then continued by G. E. Walker in partnership with Walter Crellin Walker and Brownfield Tolhurst, still trading as Johnson, Walker & Tolhurst. G. E. Walker retired in June 1892 and Walter Crellin Walker died in November 1906.

By July 1902 the firm had acquired additional premises at 172 New Bond Street, but in 1909 these were relinquished and new premises were taken at 21 Conduit Street, Regent Street. The firm, by this time, had become a limited liability company and was listed as wholesale and export manufacturing goldsmiths and jewellers.

*Mark entered in two sizes.
**Mark entered in three sizes.

Jones & Willis

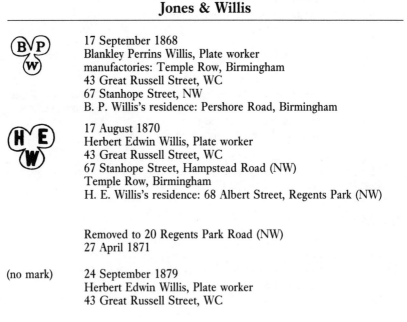

17 September 1868
Blankley Perrins Willis, Plate worker
manufactories: Temple Row, Birmingham
43 Great Russell Street, WC
67 Stanhope Street, NW
B. P. Willis's residence: Pershore Road, Birmingham

17 August 1870
Herbert Edwin Willis, Plate worker
43 Great Russell Street, WC
67 Stanhope Street, Hampstead Road (NW)
Temple Row, Birmingham
H. E. Willis's residence: 68 Albert Street, Regents Park (NW)

Removed to 20 Regents Park Road (NW)
27 April 1871

(no mark)   24 September 1879
Herbert Edwin Willis, Plate worker
43 Great Russell Street, WC

manufactory: 260, 262 and 264 Euston Road, NW
Temple Row, Birmingham
H. E. Willis's residence: Glenthorpe, Oakleigh Park, Whetstone

Removed to Aughtersoyle, Oakleigh Park, N, 1 May 1884

 12 September 1906
Jones and Willis Ltd, Gold and Silver worker
43 Great Russell Street, London, WC
79 Edmund Street, Birmingham
Concert Street, Bold Street, Liverpool
Eagle Works, Hornsey (N)
Church Works, Porchester Street, Birmingham
E. W. Willis's residence: Hazelwell Road, Putney, SW
directors: Walter Willis, Blankley H. Willis, William Percy Willis,
Edgar W. Willis, Lawrence W. Willis

This Birmingham firm specialised in the manufacture of church furnishings.
At the 1851 and 1862 Exhibitions, while trading as Newton, Jones & Willis,
the firm received bronze medals for embroidery. Later, it held warrant as
Church Furnishers to Queen Victoria. By 1868 the firm, now called Jones
& Willis, had expanded sufficiently to require factory and showroom
premises in London.

At the end of the nineteenth century, the firm could furnish a church
complete with organ cases, choir stalls, marble or wood reredoses, stained
glass, crosses, plate, candlesticks, paintings and carpets. Prior to 1906, the
firm was converted into a limited liability company, trading as Jones & Willis
Ltd, church furniture manufacturers, interior decorators, church plate,
clerical vestments, medieval metal workers, stone and wood carvers, glass
stainers, embroiderers, gas and electric fitters.

John James Keith

I·J·K   5 May 1824
John James Keith, Plate worker
26 Union Street, Hoxton New Town

Removed to 59 Britannia Terrace, City Road, 27 November 1834

I·J·K   1 October 1839

IJK / **IJK**	3 December 1845 John James Keith, Plate worker 59 Britannia Terrace, City Road, St Lukes
I·K	* 15 September 1848 John Keith, Plate worker 59 Britannia Terrace, City Road
	Removed to 41 Westmoreland Place, City Road, 12 September 1854
I·K R·S	* 29 January 1863 John Keith and Richard Stiff, Plate workers 41 Westmoreland Place, City Road 286 City Road
I·K	* 24 April 1863 John Keith, Plate worker 41 Westmoreland Place, City Road

John James Keith commenced trading in 1824. In 1829 he was recorded as being a working jeweller. Then, in 1843, he was appointed silversmith to the Ecclesiological Society, formerly the Cambridge Camden Society. This Society, under its scheme for the manufacture of church fittings, had appointed the architect and designer William Butterfield (1814–1900) as its agent, commissioning him to submit designs for approval by the Society's committee. Those approved were subsequently manufactured by John James Keith and, in later years, by his son, John Keith. However, in 1867 the Society terminated its contract with John Keith and appointed Barkentin & Krall, silversmiths, as its manufacturer.

In 1848 John Keith took over his father's business. Then, in December 1862 or January 1863, he took Richard Stiff into partnership. Following Richard Stiff's retirement in April 1863, John Keith continued on his own as an ecclesiastical silversmith.

John Keith's two sons, John and Walter Keith, were both apprenticed to John Bingham (silversmith, Citizen and Goldsmith) of 7 Murray Street, Hoxton, on 7 December 1864 and 5 December 1866 respectively, but neither obtained his freedom of the Goldsmiths' Company.

In October 1868 John Keith filed a petition for bankruptcy. Then, in 1870, his church plate manufacturing business together with him and his workmen were all taken over and absorbed by the firm of Cox & Sons, manufacturers of ecclesiastical metal work (see Cox & Sons).

In 1874 John Keith resigned from Cox & Sons and again set up on his own, this time at 6 Denmark Hill, Soho. However, by 1875 his business had been taken over by his son, Walter Keith, trading from the same address and using the name Keith & Co. Walter Keith subsequently entered his own mark at Goldsmiths' Hall on 27 July 1887. Also in 1887 he took over the firm of Figg & Co., manufacturing silversmiths, following the death of John Wilmin Figg in May 1886. Keith & Co. ceased trading *circa* 1929.

*Mark entered in two sizes.

Kilpatrick & Co.

* 8 April 1862
John Kilpatrick, Gold worker
2 Northampton Square, Clerkenwell
residence: Alton House, Highbury New Park

23 June 1862

Marks (above) defaced 23.7.1884

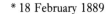

** 23 July 1884
John William Kilpatrick, Gold worker
2 Northampton Square, Clerkenwell
residence: 28 Daleham Gardens, Hampstead

* 18 February 1889

Circa 1846 John Kilpatrick commenced trading as a jeweller at 2 Northampton Square, Clerkenwell. Then, in 1853, he opened additional premises at 20 Queen Street, Melbourne, Australia, under the name of Kilpatrick & Co., gold and silversmiths, jewellers and watchmakers. It was not until April 1862 that he entered his first mark at Goldsmiths' Hall.

On 20 February 1873 he registered a mark at the Sheffield Assay Office under the name of John Kilpatrick & Co. of 2 Northampton Square, Clerkenwell. This mark was similar to the one entered at Goldsmiths' Hall,

London, on 23 June 1862.

Following his apparent retirement in 1884, the firm was continued by John William Kilpatrick, goldsmith. He entered his own mark at Goldsmiths' Hall on 23 July 1884 and a similar one at the Sheffield Assay Office on 11 February 1886, again under his own name.

The firm of Kilpatrick & Co. continued trading from 2 Northampton Square until 1895. In 1896 the firm subscribed to the Goldsmiths' Company Benevolent Society for the last time, giving its address as 34 Myddleton Street.

*Mark entered in two sizes.
**Mark entered in three sizes.

Lambert & Co.

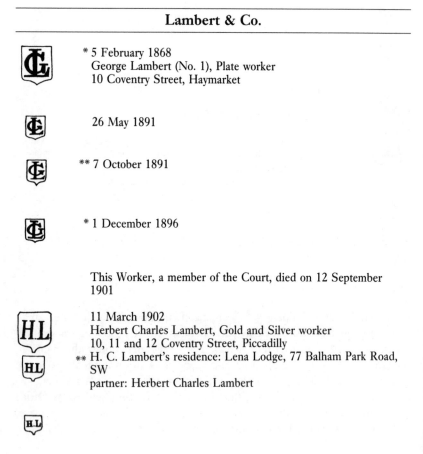

* 5 February 1868
George Lambert (No. 1), Plate worker
10 Coventry Street, Haymarket

26 May 1891

** 7 October 1891

* 1 December 1896

This Worker, a member of the Court, died on 12 September 1901

11 March 1902
Herbert Charles Lambert, Gold and Silver worker
10, 11 and 12 Coventry Street, Piccadilly
** H. C. Lambert's residence: Lena Lodge, 77 Balham Park Road, SW
partner: Herbert Charles Lambert

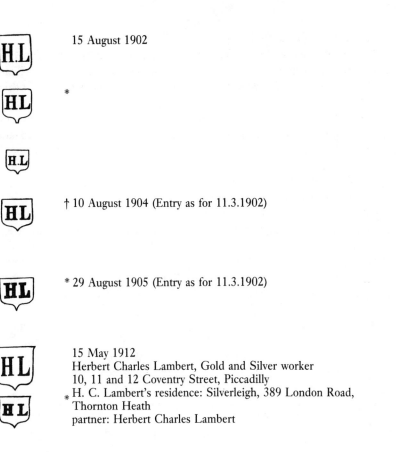

15 August 1902

*

† 10 August 1904 (Entry as for 11.3.1902)

* 29 August 1905 (Entry as for 11.3.1902)

15 May 1912
Herbert Charles Lambert, Gold and Silver worker
10, 11 and 12 Coventry Street, Piccadilly
* H. C. Lambert's residence: Silverleigh, 389 London Road,
Thornton Heath
partner: Herbert Charles Lambert

The founder of this well-known firm of retail jewellers and silversmiths was Francis Lambert (No. 1), born *circa* 1778. *Circa* 1800 he, together with Thomas Hamlet, opened a shop at 2 St Martin's Court, Leicester Square. Although Hamlet promised to enter into partnership with Francis Lambert (No. 1), the partnership did not materialise. Eventually Francis Lambert (No. 1) left and travelled abroad to Lisbon, where he opened a type of bazaar. It was not a success so he returned to England *circa* 1803, where he opened a shop selling jewellery and silver plate at 11–12 Coventry Street on the corner of Arundel Street. Also he took on William Rawlings as his manager, giving him a share of the profits. *Circa* 1819 he took William Rawlings into partnership, renaming the firm Lambert & Rawlings.

Francis Lambert (No. 1) and his wife, Caroline, are known to have had four children: Francis (No. 2), born 4.5.1810; Caroline Mary, born 3.5.1815; Harriett Walker, born 1.4.1821; and George, born 23.9.1823.

Francis Lambert (No. 1) obtained his freedom of the Goldsmiths' Company by Redemption on 17 March 1825 and was made a Liveryman in April 1827. Following his death on 2 February 1841, the firm was continued by William Rawlings and Francis Lambert (No. 2) together with his widowed mother, Caroline, as a sleeping partner.

Francis Lambert (No. 2) was apprenticed to his father, Francis Lambert (No. 1) (silversmith, Citizen and Goldsmith), on 2 November 1825 and obtained his freedom of the Goldsmiths' Company by Service on 7 November 1832. He was made a Liveryman in December 1839 and died on 21 February 1856 when only 45 years old. In the 1851 Census, he is recorded as a diamond and pearl merchant living at 10–12 Coventry Street together with his wife, Georgina, aged 36 and five children: Georgina, aged 7; Francis (No. 3), aged 6; William Rawlings, aged 5; Caroline, aged 4; and Alice Mary, aged 2. The two sons, Francis Lambert (No. 3) and William Rawlings Lambert, subsequently obtained their freedom of the Goldsmiths' Company by Patrimony in 1866 and 1868 respectively. A third son, Herbert Charles Lambert, was born *circa* 1852 and eventually became senior partner in the family firm.

When Caroline, the widow of Francis Lambert (No. 1), died in November 1860, her widowed daughter, Mrs Harriett Walker Rendle, acting as administrator of the estate, signed papers with William Rawlings dissolving the partnership on 29 April 1861. William Rawlings subsequently died later that year.

Meanwhile, since Francis Lambert (No. 2) was already dead, the firm was continued by his brother, George Lambert, trading under the name of Lambert & Co. George Lambert, the second son of Francis Lambert (No. 1), was apprenticed to his father on 4 July 1838, but following his father's death in February 1841, he was turned over to Francis Lambert (No. 2) (silversmith, Citizen and Goldsmith). George Lambert obtained his freedom of the Goldsmiths' Company by Service on 5 November 1845, was made a Liveryman in May 1856 and became an Assistant in February 1878. He became 4th Warden in 1884, 3rd Warden in 1885, 2nd Warden in 1886 and Prime Warden in 1887. His wife, Jemima, died on 20 January 1856, and in the 1861 Census George Lambert is recorded as a gold and silversmith and widower living at 10–12 Coventry Street with his 11-year-old son, George, who later died of pleurisy on 6 November 1872.

On 5 February 1868 the firm's mark was entered at Goldsmiths' Hall for the first time. By 1897 the firm was listed as goldsmiths, silversmiths, jewellers, diamond and pearl merchants, plate and jewellery valuers and clock and watch makers.

With the death of George Lambert on 12 September 1901, the firm was

continued by his nephew, Herbert Charles Lambert, the son of Francis
Lambert (No. 2). Herbert Charles Lambert obtained his freedom of the
Goldsmiths' Company by Patrimony on 7 May 1873 and was made a
Liveryman in March 1877. He became an Assistant in February 1904, 4th
Warden in 1910, 3rd Warden in 1911, 2nd Warden in 1912 and Prime
Warden in 1913. He died on 30 March 1924. His son, George Herbert
Lambert, also became a silversmith, obtaining his freedom by Patrimony in
1898 and becoming a Liveryman in 1905. He died on 25 March 1965.

In 1916 the firm was closed and absorbed by Harman & Co. Ltd of 177
New Bond Street, which then traded under the amended name of Harman
& Lambert.

*Mark entered in two sizes.
**Mark entered in three sizes.
†Mark entered in five sizes.

Latham & Morton

5 November 1898
Thomas Latham and Ernest Morton, Silver workers
115 and 116 Vyse Street, Birmingham
residences: T. Latham: 57 Soho Hill
E. Morton: 35 Wilson Road, Birmingham

2 December 1901
Thomas Latham and Ernest Morton, Silver workers
115 and 116 Vyse Street, Birmingham
residences: T. Latham: Alcocks Green, Wilson Road
E. Morton: Birchfields, near Birmingham

Thomas Latham and Ernest Morton established this firm in Birmingham
circa 1866, but it was not until November 1898 that they entered their first
mark at Goldsmiths' Hall, London. Thomas Latham retired in December
1904.

In 1913 the firm was listed as silver and electroplate makers. Then, in
July 1915, it was converted into a limited liability company.

Walter Latham & Son

25 February 1903
Walter Latham & Son, Silver workers
Brocco Works, Solly Street, Sheffield
9 Bartletts Buildings, Holborn Circus, EC
residences: W. Latham: 71 Rustlings Road, Sheffield
C. H. Latham: 39 Sheldon Road, Sheffield
partners: Walter Latham, Charles Henry Latham

* 25 May 1914
Walter Latham & Son, Silver workers
Brocco Works, Solly Street, Sheffield
9 Bartletts Buildings, Holborn Circus, EC
residences: W. Latham: 41 Penrhyn Road, Sheffield
E. W. Latham: Rose Cottage, Hatfield, near Doncaster
partners: Walter Latham, Ernest Walter Latham

This Sheffield firm was listed in 1893 as candlestick and candelabra manufacturers, then, in 1900, as silver and electroplated candlestick and candelabra manufacturers. In 1926 the firm was purchased by Frank Cobb & Co. of Howard Street, Sheffield.

*Mark entered in two sizes.

John Le Gallais

18 April 1849
John Le Gallais, Plate worker
2 Brook Street, Jersey

In 1834 John Le Gallais entered into partnership with Thomas de Gruchy. This partnership continued until 1849 when Thomas de Gruchy died. John Le Gallais then continued in business on his own until 1873 when he was succeeded by H. Hollinshed.

Charles Lias

I L
H L
C L

** 7 August 1823
John Lias (No. 2), Henry (John) Lias and Charles Lias, Plate
workers
8 Finsbury Street

I L
H L
C L

* 3 March 1828 (Entry as for 7.8.1823)

I·L
H·L
C·L

** 24 September 1830
John Lias (No. 2), Henry John Lias and Charles Lias, Plate
workers
8 Finsbury Street, St Lukes

I·L
H·L
C·L

26 August 1835 (Entry as for 24.9.1830)

C L

13 May 1837
Charles Lias, Plate worker
manufactory: 65 Crown Street, Finsbury Square

C·L

CL

23 August 1842

C L

1 March 1845

CL

26 October 1846

CL

Charles Lias, born *circa* 1800, was the son of John Lias (No. 2), silversmith
of 8 Finsbury Square and brother of Henry John Lias (No. 1) (silversmith,
Citizen and Goldsmith) (see *Marks of London Goldsmiths and Silversmiths
c.1697–1837*, revised edition 1988, pp. 206–10). Henry John Lias, having
obtained his freedom of the Goldsmiths' Company on 7 August 1816, joined
his father in partnership, trading as John Lias & Son. They entered their
joint mark at Goldsmiths' Hall on 14 March 1818.

Charles Lias, having presumably trained and worked under his father,
joined him and brother, Henry John Lias, in a triple partnership in 1823.
They entered their new marks at Goldsmiths' Hall in August 1823 and
amended the firm's name to John Lias & Sons.

In 1837 Charles Lias resigned from the partnership and set up in business as a silver spoon and plate manufacturer at 65 Crown Street, Finsbury Square, from where he entered his first marks at Goldsmiths' Hall. He appears to have retired or died at the beginning of 1847 since, on 24 February 1847, Judah Hart, spoon maker, entered his mark at Goldsmiths' Hall, giving the address of his manufactory as 65 Crown Street, Finsbury. On 3 September 1852 these premises were again taken over, this time by William Robert Smily, spoon maker.

*Mark entered in two sizes.
**Mark entered in three sizes.

John Lias & Son

* 19 May 1837
John Lias (No. 2) and Henry (John) Lias (No. 1), Plate workers manufactory and residence: 8 and 9 Finsbury Street, St Lukes

28 November 1839
John Lias (No. 2) and Henry (John) Lias (No. 1)

* 13 February 1843
John Lias (No. 2) and Henry (John) Lias (No. 1)

And a manufactory: 7 Salisbury Court, Fleet Street

30 July 1845
John Lias (No. 2) and Henry (John) Lias (No. 1)

Trading under the firm of John Lias and Son, 8 May 1848

** 7 February 1850
Henry John Lias (No. 1) and Henry John Lias (No. 2), Plate workers
manufactory: 7 Salisbury Court, Fleet Street
H. J. Lias (No. 1)'s residence: 138 Regents Park Terrace
H. J. Lias (No. 2)'s residence: 46 Myddleton Square Clerkenwell
(address deleted in Register at Goldsmiths' Hall)

30 August 1853

23 September 1856

196

13 September 1859

 * 21 February 1862
Henry John Lias (No. 1) and Henry John Lias (No. 2), Plate workers
manufactory: 7 Salisbury Court, Fleet Street
H. J. Lias (No. 1)'s residence: 18 Regents Park Terrace, Gloucester Gate

1 September 1864

13 September 1865

 1 July 1867

*

 5 December 1871
Henry John Lias (No. 1) and Henry John Lias (No. 2), Plate workers
7 Salisbury Court, Fleet Street
H. J. Lias (No. 1)'s residence: 18 Regents Park Terrace
H. J. Lias (No. 2)'s residence: 8 Greville Road, Kilburn Priory

Removed to St Bride's Street, Ludgate Circus

* 7 September 1875

** 18 January 1878
Henry John Lias (No. 2), Plate worker
31 St Bride's Street, Ludgate Circus
H. J. Lias (No. 2)'s residence: Fairlight, Willesden Lane, NW

*** 7 February 1879
Henry John Lias (No. 2) and James Wakely, Plate workers
31 St Bride's Street, Ludgate Circus
H. J. Lias (No. 2)'s residence: Greville House, Ferndale Park, Tunbridge Wells
J. Wakely's residence: 8 Glengall Terrace, Old Kent Road

(28 July 1884)
(Mark) defaced 1.10.1884

This firm of manufacturing silversmiths was founded in 1791 by John Lias (No. 1), silversmith and bucklemaker of 15 Great Sutton Street. He entered his first mark at Goldsmiths' Hall on 8 November 1791 followed by further marks in 1792 (with Dennis Charie) and 1794, after which he moved to premises at 8 Finsbury Street. However, subsequent marks registered from 13 July 1799 onwards were entered by John Lias, silversmith and plateworker, whose signature appears to be different from that of John Lias, bucklemaker. It is possible, therefore, that there were two John Liases: John Lias (No. 1), bucklemaker, and his successor, John Lias (No. 2), plateworker (see *Marks of London Goldsmiths and Silversmiths c.1697–1837*, revised edition 1988, pp. 206–10).

John Lias (No. 2) had two sons who became silversmiths. They were Henry John Lias (No. 1) and Charles Lias. Henry John Lias (No. 1) was apprenticed to Isaac Boorman (silversmith, Citizen and Goldsmith) of London on 1 February 1809 to learn the trade of silversmith. He obtained his freedom of the Goldsmiths' Company by Service on 7 August 1816 and subsequently joined his father in partnership, entering their first combined mark at Goldsmiths' Hall on 14 March 1818. Meanwhile, the firm's name was changed to John Lias & Son. Henry John Lias (No. 1) was made a Liveryman in June 1833 and an Assistant in March 1851. He became 4th Warden in 1858, 3rd Warden in 1859, 2nd Warden in 1860 and Prime Warden in 1861.

Although Charles Lias was never apprenticed through the Goldsmiths' Company, he joined his father and brother in partnership in 1823, the firm's name being amended to John Lias & Sons. New marks containing their three pairs of initials were entered at Goldsmiths' Hall on 7 August 1823 with further marks in 1828, 1830 and 1835 (see Charles Lias).

In May 1837 Charles Lias retired from the partnership and commenced trading on his own as a silver spoon and plate manufacturer at 65 Crown Street, Finsbury Square. Meanwhile, the family firm's name reverted to John Lias & Son with John Lias (No. 2) and Henry John Lias (No. 1) entering new marks at Goldsmiths' Hall. Further marks were entered in 1839 and 1843, in each case signed by both John Lias (No. 2) and Henry (John) Lias (No. 1). However, the entry of 8 May 1848, stating that the firm was trading under the name of John Lias & Son, was signed only by Henry (John) Lias (No. 1), presumably due to the retirement or death of John Lias (No. 2).

With the demise of John Lias (No. 2), the firm was continued by Henry John Lias (No. 1) in partnership with his son, Henry John Lias (No. 2), trading as Henry John Lias & Son.

Henry John Lias (No. 2) was apprenticed to his father, Henry John Lias

(No. 1) (silversmith, Citizen and Goldsmith), on 4 February 1840 to learn the trade of silversmith. He obtained his freedom of the Goldsmiths' Company by Service on 6 March 1850 and was made a Liveryman in July 1853. His partnership with his father continued until Henry John Lias (No. 1) died on 22 November 1877, following which he continued running the firm on his own. However, by 7 February 1879 he had entered into partnership with James Wakely. This new partnership continued until 1 October 1884 when he retired and James Wakely entered into partnership with Frank Clarke Wheeler (see Wakely & Wheeler). Henry John Lias (No. 2) died on 9 September 1906.

*Mark entered in two sizes.
**Mark entered in three sizes.
***Mark entered in four sizes.

Liberty & Co.

| IY&Cᵒ | * 8 February 1894 |

* 8 February 1894
Liberty & Co., Plate workers
142, 144, 148, 150, 218 & 222
Regent Street, London
J. W. Howe's residence: Strathearn, Greenhill Park, Harlesden
acting partner: J. W. Howe

** 28 April 1899
managing director and secretary: J. W. Howe

7 November 1900
managing director and secretary: J. W. Howe

This well-known department store was founded by Arthur Lasenby Liberty and opened on 17 May 1875 as an oriental warehouse. In 1894 it was turned into a limited liability company. By 1897 the store was trading in art furnishing fabrics and dress fabrics, silks, fans, shawls, carpets, furniture and imported porcelain and jewellery.

In 1899 the firm commenced manufacturing and retailing its own jewellery and silverware under the name of 'Cymric'. This was followed in 1901 by the launching of 'Tudric' pewterware. The manufacturer employed to produce these goods was the Birmingham firm of William Hair Haseler, manufacturing jewellers and silversmiths. In May 1901 a subsidiary company was formed, known as Liberty & Co. (Cymric) Ltd, to produce these goods from the designs of such artists as Bernard Cuzner, Archibold Knox and Rex Silver.

William Lister & Sons

17 July 1851
William Lister (No. 1), Plate worker
St Thomas Place, Newcastle
manufactory: 16 & 17 Mosley Street, Newcastle on Tyne
signed: William Lister (No. 1)

*** 10 August 1895
William Lister & Sons, Gold and Silver workers
9 Grey Street, Newcastle on Tyne
64 Hatton Garden, London EC
A. Burt's residence: 53 Larkspur Terrace, Newcastle on Tyne
director: Albert Burt

This Newcastle on Tyne firm was founded by William Lister (No. 1) in 1812. William Lister (No. 1) was apprenticed to Clement Gowland, watchmaker of Sunderland *circa* 1801 and commenced working as a watch and clock maker in Newcastle on Tyne in May 1812. By 1821, when he entered his first mark at the Newcastle on Tyne Assay Office, he was listed as a jeweller, silversmith, goldsmith and watchmaker. His first mark at Goldsmiths' Hall, London, was similar to that entered at Newcastle on Tyne in 1821.

On 28 August 1814 he married his master's daughter, Margaret Gowland. They had five children: Clement, baptised 21 January 1816; William (No. 2), born 1820; Margaret; Sarah; and Anne. Both Clement Lister and William Lister (No. 2) joined him in partnership *circa* 1841. William Lister (No. 2) died on 23 February 1859, aged 38; Margaret Lister (née Gowland), on 1 December 1867; William Lister (No. 1), on 3 November 1868; and Clement Lister *circa* 1874.

A. D. Loewenstark & Sons

A D L 4 November 1845
Abraham David Loewenstark, Small plate worker
49 Duke Street, Lincoln's Inn Fields

ADL 7 January 1846

ADL
ADL 26 October 1846
Removed to 10 Warwick Court, Holborn

Removed to 14 Duke Street, Aldgate, 22 November 1848

Removed to 1 Devereux Court, Essex Street, Strand, 26
November 1849

ADL 22 May 1855

ADL 8 October 1879

MDL * 10 December 1886
Marcus David Loewenstark, Small worker
135 Strand, WC
32 Aldgate, E

This firm of masonic jewellers was founded by Abraham David Loewenstark
in 1845. By 1860 the firm's name had changed to A. D. Loewenstark &
Son. Then, *circa* 1865, it became A. D. Loewenstark & Sons.

In December 1882 Marcus David Loewenstark, one of A. D. Loewen-
stark's sons, resigned from the firm to trade as a fancy goods dealer.
However, the business went into liquidation in March 1883, and by 1886
M. D. Loewenstark had rejoined the family firm, becoming the sole partner.

In 1883 the firm was trading as A. D. Loewenstark & Sons, masonic
jewellers, makers of naval, military and other medals and regalia, goldsmiths
and diamond merchants.

*Mark entered in two sizes.

Charles Maas

C . M 20 October 1883
Charles Maas, Small worker

13 Jewin Crescent, EC
residence: 3 The Terrace, Camden Square, NW

C.M   8 October 1884

C.M   28 September 1886

C.M   19 November 1888

C M

C.M   21 October 1889

C.M   12 August 1890

C M   24 September 1890
M M   Charles Maas and Marcus Maas, Small workers
13 Jewin Crescent, EC
residences: C. Maas: 3 The Terrace, Camden Square, NW
M. Maas: 36 Fairbridge Road, Upper Holloway, N

    6 June 1891
Charles Maas, Small worker
13 Jewin Crescent, EC
residence: 3 The Terrace, Camden Square, NW

22 February 1892

27 October 1892

C.M   16 June 1893

    30 January 1894

7 April 1894

C.M   26 March 1895

202

These punches with a crown have been cancelled at the request of Mr C. Maas as the Assay Office, Sheffield have written to him that the crown represents their hallmark and is objectionable, 28 February 1896

(CM) * 16 March 1896 (Entry as for 6.6.1891)

8 October 1910
Removed to 1A Aldermanbury Avenue, EC
residence: 182 Walm Lane, NW

(CM) 1 September 1911
One new mark

(CM) 21 February 1914
Charles Maas & Company, Gold and Silver worker
1A Aldermanbury Avenue, EC
residence: Walm Lane, Cricklewood, NW
partner: Charles Maas

This firm specialised in manufacturing and importing smokers' pipes of various types, including recherche and meerschaum. The firm's pipes were frequently silver-mounted, as were some of their smokers' accessories. In addition, they produced silver-mounted walking sticks.

Circa 1915 the firm was converted into a limited liability company.

*Mark entered in two sizes.

Gideon Paul Macaire

(G·P·M) 11 July 1854
Gideon Paul Macaire, Case maker
26 Myddleton Street, Clerkenwell

(R·G·M) 15 January 1857
Robert Gideon Macaire, Case maker
26 Myddleton Street, Clerkenwell

[GM]
[HD] 8 July 1867
Gideon (Paul) Macaire
and Hunter (Charles) Dewar, Case makers
26 Myddleton Street, Clerkenwell
H. Dewar's residence: 82 Caledonian Road, Clerkenwell

Gideon Paul Macaire first entered into partnership with Richard John Ball in 1806, trading as Ball & Macaire, watch-case makers (see Ball & Macaire). In 1853 Richard Macaire Ball joined their partnership, but in June 1854 it was dissolved, possibly as a result of the retirement or death of Richard John Ball. Richard Macaire Ball then continued in business under his own name at 31 Sudely Street, entering his mark at Goldsmiths' Hall on 13 July 1854 (see Richard Macaire Ball).

Meanwhile, Gideon Paul Macaire continued trading from 26 Myddleton Street under his own name. In January 1857 he retired, leaving the business to be continued by Robert Gideon Macaire. In 1867 Robert Gideon Macaire apparently retired or died and the business was again taken over by Gideon Paul Macaire, this time in partnership with Hunter Charles Dewar. Following Gideon Paul Macaire's death in April 1871, Hunter Charles Dewar continued working at 26 Myddleton Street, entering his own mark on 18 August 1871.

Alexander Macrae

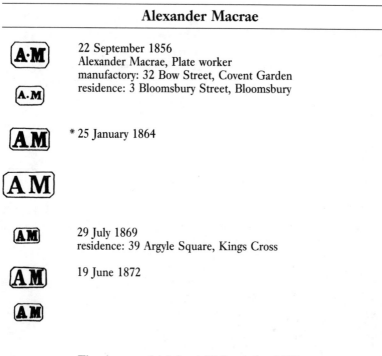

22 September 1856
Alexander Macrae, Plate worker
manufactory: 32 Bow Street, Covent Garden
residence: 3 Bloomsbury Street, Bloomsbury

* 25 January 1864

29 July 1869
residence: 39 Argyle Square, Kings Cross

19 June 1872

The above marks defaced 17 September 1878

*** 17 September 1878
Martin Goldstein, Plate worker
32 Bow Street, Covent Garden
residence: 22 Brunswick Street, Barnsbury Road, Islington

Removed to 17 Lisle Street, Leicester Square, 5 January 1882

Alexander Macrae established this business *circa* 1856, trading under his own name as a manufacturing silversmith. By 1870 he had entered into partnership with Martin Goldstein, changing the firm's name to Macrae & Goldstein, silversmiths.

In September 1878 Alexander Macrae retired or died, leaving Martin Goldstein to take over the firm and continue trading, this time under his own name. In 1886 he sold the firm to Cornelius Joshua Vander, the son of a silversmith and jeweller. Eventually the firm became C. J. Vander (see C. J. Vander).

*Mark entered in two sizes.
**Mark entered in four sizes.

Mallett & Son

 18 January 1887
Walter Ellis Mallett, Small worker
36 Milsom Street, Bath
residence: Summerdale, Greenway Lane, Bath

In 1862 John Mallett, retail jeweller, established this firm at 36 Milsom Street, Bath, Somerset. When his son, Walter Ellis Mallett, joined the firm *circa* 1874, its name was changed to Mallett & Son. Walter Ellis Mallett eventually took control of the firm, and in 1909 he opened a branch shop at 40 New Bond Street, London. John Mallett died *circa* 1907 and Walter Ellis Mallett on 3 September 1929. The firm was converted into a limited liability company, Mallett & Son (Antiques) Ltd, in 1938.

Mappin & Webb

27 February 1866
John Newton Mappin and George Webb, Plate workers

77–78 Oxford Street
71–72 Cornhill
residences: J. N. Mappin: Queens Road, Clapham Park
G. Webb: Victoria Road, Clapham Common

Removed to Mansion House Buildings, Poultry, 31 October 1871

17 February 1880
Removed to Southgate House, Southgate, N

 * 3 January 1882
John Newton Mappin, Plate workers
2 Queen Victoria Street, EC
late (of) 77–78 Oxford Street, WC
J. N. Mappin's residence: Norfolk Street, Sheffield

2 February 1883
158 Oxford Street
J. N. Mappin's residence: Southgate House, Southgate

* 25 February 1884 (Entry as for 2.2.1883)

13 November 1884 (Entry as for 2.2.1883)

* 24 April 1885 (Entry as for 2.2.1883)

*** 25 October 1886
35 King Street, Covent Garden

Removed to Winsley Works, Winsley Street, Oxford Street, 2
August 1889

Four marks above (entered 25.10.1886) defaced 21.7.1898

 ** 28 June 1897
John Newton Mappin trading as Mappin and Webb, Gold and
Silver worker

158–162 Oxford Street
18–22 Poultry
2 Queen Victoria Street Royal Works, Sheffield
J. N. Mappin's residence: Kensington House, Bayswater Hill, W

 ** 19 July 1898
Mappin and Webb, Silver worker
158 Oxford Street
2 Queen Victoria Street, EC
Winsley Street, Oxford Street, W
Norfolk Street, Sheffield
H. J. Mappin's residence: Headley Park, Epsom
partner: Herbert Joseph Mappin

 22 September 1898 (Entry as for 19.7.1898)

** 1 December 1899
Mappin and Webb Ltd, Gold and Silver workers
158 Oxford Street
2 Queen Victoria Street, EC
Winsley Street, W
Norfolk Street, Sheffield
J. Leahy's residence: 5 Riverside Villas, Teddington
director: James Leahy

The firm of Mappin and Webb having been turned into a Limited
Liability Company, the above punches (entered 1.12.1899) are
registered and all previous cancelled

** 3 January 1900 (Entry as for 1.12.1899)

18 July 1902
This entry is cancelled, the punches submitted for Registration
not being of the correct design (No marks are included with this
entry)

11 January 1904
Mappin and Webb Ltd, Gold and Silver workers
158–162 Oxford Street
2a Queen Victoria Street, EC
220 Regent Street
Winsley Works, W
Royal Works, Sheffield
Jardin Public, Nice
Public Library Buildings, Johannesburg
H. Portlock's residence: 42 Lordship Park, London, N
secretary: Henry Portlock

M W
&

10 August 1907
Mappin and Webb Ltd, Gold and Silver workers
158 Oxford Street, W
2 Queen Victoria Street, EC
220 Regent Street, W
Norfolk Street, Sheffield
H. J. Mappin's residence: Ifield Court, Crawley, Sussex
directors: John Newton Mappin, Walter John Mappin, Herbert
Joseph Mappin, Stanley A. Mappin, James Leahy, Walter T.
Haddock, James Gibson, Lindley Howlden

* 4 September 1907
Mappin and Webb Ltd, Gold and Silver workers
158–162 Oxford Street
2 Queen Victoria Street, EC
2 Winsley Street, W
Royal Works, Sheffield
Jardin Public, Nice
Norfolk House, Johannesburg
23 Boulevarde des Capucines, Paris
H. Portlock's residence: 50 Church Crescent, Cranley Gardens,
N
directors: John Newton Mappin, Herbert Joseph Mappin, Walter
John Mappin, Walter Thorpe Haddock, Herbert Lindley
Howlden, Robert James Gibson
secretary: Henry Portlock

8 February 1908 (Entry as for 4.9.1907 with following additional
residence:)
R. J. Gibson's residence: 87 Wimpole Street, W

* 29 May 1908
Mappin and Webb Ltd, Gold and Silver workers
158–162 Oxford Street
2 Queen Victoria Street, EC
2 Winsley Street, W
Royal Works, Sheffield
H. Portlock's residence: 50 Church Crescent, Cranley Gardens,
N
directors: John Newton Mappin, Walter John Mappin, Herbert J.
Mappin, Walter T. Haddock, Herbert L. Howlden, Robert J.
Gibson
secretary: Henry Portlock

(no mark)

28 June 1909
Mappin and Webb (1908) Ltd, Gold and Silver workers
158, 160 & 162 Oxford Street, W
220 Regent Street, W
2 Queen Victoria Street, EC
Winsley Works, 2 Winsley St, Oxford St, W

Royal Works, Norfolk Street, Sheffield
F. Waite's residence: 24 Third Avenue, Manor Park, Essex
directors: John Newton Mappin, Walter John Mappin, Herbert J.
Mappin, Stanley A. Mappin, Walter J. Haddock, Henry Portlock
secretary: Frederick Waite

MᴺWB
&   *** 16 September 1909
        Mappin and Webb (1908) Ltd (Entry as for 28.6.1909)

        27 May 1910. Joint secretaries: Frederick Waite, John Tyrrell
        Boyes

MᴺWB
&   ** 4 July 1910
        Mappin and Webb (1908) Ltd (Entry as for 28.6.1909 but with
        following secretary's residence:)
        J. T. Boyes' residence: 28 Beecroft Road, Brockley, SE

MᴺWB
&   * 18 January 1911
        Mappin and Webb (1908) Ltd, Gold and Silver workers
        158–162 Oxford Street, W
        220 Regent Street, W
        2 Queen Victoria Street, EC
        Winsley Works, 2 Winsley St, Oxford St, W
        Royal Works, Norfolk Street, Sheffield
        directors: J. N. Mappin: Headley Park, Epsom, Surrey; W. J.
        Mappin: 13 Herbert Crescent, Hans Place; H. J. Mappin: Ifield
        Court, Crawley, Sussex; S. A. Mappin: 12 Albert Hall Mansions,
        W; W. T. Haddock: Endcliffe Close, Sheffield; H. Portlock: 50
        Church Crescent, Cranley Gardens
        joint secretary:
        J. T. Boyes: 28 Beecroft Road, Brockley, SE

MᴺWB
&   * 21 March 1911
        Mappin and Webb (1908) Ltd (Entry as for 18.1.1911)

MNWB
&   13 April 1911
        Mappin and Webb (1908) Ltd (Entry as for 18.1.1911)

Mᴺ&WB 22 January 1912
        Mappin and Webb Ltd (Entry as for 18.1.1911 except Alexander
        Gordon MaGinnis added to list of directors and all directors'
        private addresses omitted)

MᴺWB
&   * 15 August 1912
        Mappin and Webb Ltd (Entry as for 18.1.1911 except directors'
        private addresses omitted but both joint secretaries' addresses
        included:) F. Waite: 24 Third Avenue, Manor Park, E
        J. T. Boyes: 28 Beecroft Road, Brockley, SE

6 May 1914
Mappin and Webb Ltd, Gold and Silver workers
158, 160 & 162 Oxford Street, W
220 Regent Street, W
2 Queen Victoria Street, EC
1 & 2 Winsley Street, W
Royal Works, Norfolk Street, Sheffield
directors: Walter J. Mappin, Herbert J. Mappin, Stanley A.
Mappin, Walter T. Haddock, Henry Portlock, Alex G. MaGinnis
joint secretaries: Frederick Waite, John T. Boyes

This well-known firm of manufacturing and retail silversmiths was founded by John Newton Mappin. He was the son of Joseph Mappin (No. 2), the founder of the firm Joseph Mappin, which later became Mappin Brothers (see Mappin Brothers).

When Joseph Mappin (No. 2) died *circa* 1841, he left his business to his four sons: Frederick Thorpe Mappin, Edward Mappin, Joseph Charles Mappin and John Newton Mappin. Frederick Thorpe Mappin, the eldest son, managed the firm until such time as his younger brothers came of age and could be brought into the firm. John Newton Mappin, being the youngest, was the last to be made a partner.

In 1851 the firm's name was changed to Mappin Brothers, but later there were disagreements between the brothers which resulted in both Frederick Thorpe Mappin and John Newton Mappin resigning from the firm in 1859.

John Newton Mappin then started his own plate and cutlery business called Mappin & Co. in October 1859. In 1860 he opened his first London shop at 77–78 Oxford Street. Having married a Miss Webb, he took his brother-in-law, George Webb, into partnership in 1864 and renamed the firm Mappin, Webb & Co. Then, in 1868, he amended the name to Mappin & Webb. Although George Webb died *circa* 1880, the firm's name remained unchanged until 1898 when it was converted into a limited liability company.

The firm registered its first maker's mark at the Sheffield Assay Office in May 1864, its address being listed as Eyre Street, Sheffield. Then, in February 1866, the firm's mark was entered at Goldsmiths' Hall, London, for the first time.

In 1869 John Newton Mappin commenced building himself new London premises in Cheapside and Poultry. Then, in 1886, he acquired the London firm of Stephen Smith & Son, which specialised in presentation silver, models and trophies. This firm, together with all its dies, tools and models, was moved to Oxford Street in 1889, where it was known as Winsley Works.

In 1898 Mappin & Webb was converted into a limited liability company trading as Mappin & Webb Ltd. As business grew, so agencies were opened in many countries. Retail shops were opened in Johannesburg, Nice, Paris, Biarritz, Monte Carlo, Lausanne, Rome, Copenhagen, Buenos Aires, Rio de Janeiro, São Paulo, Montreal and Bombay. Over the years, the firm received Royal Warrants from Queen Victoria, Edward VII, George V, Edward Prince of Wales and Queen Elizabeth II. It also received them from foreign royalty: the Emperor of Japan, King of Spain, King of Italy and King of the Netherlands.

In 1903 Mappin & Webb Ltd bought the firm of Mappin Brothers from the Goldsmiths & Silversmiths Co. Ltd of Regent Street. Thus John Newton Mappin was able to acquire his father's firm from which he himself had resigned in 1859.

John Newton Mappin had a daughter and four sons, two of whom became directors in the firm. They were Walter John Mappin and Herbert Joseph Mappin. The latter, who eventually became chairman, died in 1946. In 1913 John Newton Mappin died suddenly in the grounds of his home at Headley Park near Headley, Surrey, and the firm was carried on by his sons and members of the staff who had been made directors. However, by 1956 only two members of the family were still in the firm. They were J. N. Fraser, a grandson, and D. Harrison, a great-grandson of John Newton Mappin.

In 1919 Mappin & Webb Ltd acquired the firm of W. & G. Neal & Son, goldsmiths and silversmiths of 36 Skinner Street, Clerkenwell. In 1954 H. M. Oppenheim was elected to the board of directors, since when the firm has acquired J. W. Benson Ltd, Hunt & Roskell Ltd, the Brompton Silver Galleries, Nathan & Co. (Birmingham), Wilson & Sharp (Edinburgh), Bristol Goldsmiths Alliance (Bristol) and John Cameron & Sons Ltd (Kilmarnock). On 13 November 1959 Mappin & Webb Ltd took over Garrard & Co. and the Goldsmiths & Silversmiths Co. Ltd, thus bringing together three of the biggest retailers in the trade. In 1963 Mappin & Webb Ltd, Elkington & Co. Ltd and Walker & Hall Ltd amalgamated to form British Silverware Ltd, but this holding company closed down in 1971 due to industrial action. Mappin & Webb Ltd then became a member of Sears Holdings Ltd. In 1990 Sears Holdings Ltd sold Mappin & Webb Ltd to Asprey & Co. Ltd for £75m in exchange for a 13 per cent increase of their stake in Asprey & Co. Ltd to 38 per cent.

*Mark entered in two sizes.
**Mark entered in three sizes.
***Mark entered in four sizes.

(2 sizes)

* 9 December 1863
Edward Mappin and Joseph Mappin, Plate workers
222 Regent Street
67–68 King William Street, London
manufactory: Queens Works, Sheffield
E. Mappin's residence: Wharncliffe House, Kings Road, Clapham
J. Mappin's residence: The Ferns, Kings Road, Clapham Park

9 July 1867
manufactory: 406 Euston Road (London)

The above marks (entered 9.12.1863 and 9.7.1867) withdrawn
and two defaced. The business now carried on by Charles
Mappin, son of the above Edward Mappin deceased. (No date
given. Possibly March 1877 when Charles Mappin entered his
first mark at the Sheffield Assay Office)

** 10 April 1878
Charles Mappin, Plate worker
220 Regent Street
67 King William Street, London Bridge
manufactory: Queens Cutlery Works, Sheffield
C. Mappin's residence: 35 Dulwich Road, Herne Hill, SE

1 February 1884
Frederick Crockford and Charles Hickson, Plate workers
67–68 King William Street, EC
F. Crockford's residence: The Trossacks, Silverdale, Sydenham
C. Hickson's residence: Ashcroft, Ashdell Road, Sheffield

26 September 1884

* 9 August 1888
Removed to 35 St Pauls Churchyard

*

6 December 1892
Mappin Bros, Plate worker
220 Regent Street
66 Cheapside
Queens Works, Sheffield
J. Langman's residence: The Deanery, Great Marlow
partner for Mappin Bros: John L. Langman

30 May 1896 (Entry as for 6.12.1892)

11 April 1900
Mappin Bros, Gold and Silver workers
220 Regent Street
66 Cheapside
Queens Works, Sheffield
W. Gibson's residence: 47 Albion Street, Hyde Park, W
sole partner in Mappin Bros: William Gibson

21 June 1900 (Entry as for 11.4.1900)

17 July 1901 (Entry as for 11.4.1900)

The firm of Mappin Bros was amalgamated with Mappin & Webb Ltd about 1903–4

In 1816 Joseph Mappin (No. 1), an engraver, was recorded as working at Fargate, Sheffield. He was the son of Jonathan Mappin of Fargate, plate worker and engraver, working from about 1775 to 1797. Joseph Mappin (No. 1) had two sons: John Newton Mappin and Joseph Mappin (No. 2). John Newton Mappin became a brewer and subsequently founded Mappin's Brewery. He was a wealthy man when he died in 1883, and in his will he left his collection of paintings and £15,000 to finance the building of a civic art gallery in Sheffield to be known as the Mappin Art Gallery.

The other son, Joseph Mappin (No. 2), started his own business in Norfolk Street and Mulberry Street, Sheffield, with two partners whom he later bought out. The firm, trading as Joseph Mappin, specialised in the manufacture of pen knives, spring, sporting and table knives and razors.

213

Joseph Mappin (No. 2) died *circa* 1842, while still in his early 40s, and left the firm to his four sons, three of whom were minors, with instructions that the business could not be sold until the youngest son, John Newton Mappin, had been in the business for at least four years. These four sons were Frederick Thorpe Mappin, Edward Mappin, Joseph Charles Mappin and John Newton Mappin.

Frederick Thorpe Mappin, the eldest son, was born on 16 May 1821. Following his father's death he continued managing the firm of Joseph Mappin & Son, bringing in his younger brothers as active members when they came of age. In 1846 Joseph Mappin & Son acquired the firm of William Samson & Sons, cutlers of 105 Norfolk Street, Sheffield. In 1851 the firm changed its name to Mappin Brothers and moved to larger premises known as Queens Cutlery Works at Bakers Hill, Sheffield. About this time Mappin Brothers opened a shop in London, and for a while the firm had premises at 37 Moorgate Street, but in 1856 it moved to 67–68 King William Street. During the 1850s, the firm grew rapidly under Frederick's management, resulting in about 500 people being employed at the Queens Cutlery Works. Also, a large trade was built up through agencies in America, Canada, Australia and elsewhere. About this time the youngest brother, John Newton Mappin, became a partner, but soon dissensions arose among the four brothers, resulting in both Frederick Thorpe Mappin and John Newton Mappin leaving the firm.

Frederick Thorpe Mappin subsequently bought a steel mill in Sheffield, and became a director of the Sheffield Gas Company and the Midland Railway and a Liberal Member of Parliament. He was given a baronetcy for his services to the Liberal Party on 27 August 1886 and died on 19 March 1910.

John Newton Mappin started his own electroplating and cutlery business, trading as Mappin & Co. He subsequently changed its name to Mappin & Webb when he took his brother-in-law, George Webb, into partnership (see Mappin & Webb).

Meanwhile, the firm of Mappin Brothers continued to operate under the two remaining brothers, Edward Mappin and Joseph Charles Mappin. They first entered the firm's mark at the Sheffield Assay Office on 20 October 1859. In 1862 they opened a shop at 222 Regent Street, London, and the following year they registered their maker's mark at Goldsmiths' Hall, London. In 1865 a factory was opened at 406 Euston Road for manufacturing articles in silver and electroplate, but it was transferred to Sheffield in 1876. In 1870 the Regent Street shop was enlarged to include the adjacent shop, number 220. Later, the original shop at 222 Regent Street was closed.

When Joseph Charles Mappin retired on 31 March 1873, his brother, Edward Mappin, continued running the firm. Joseph Charles Mappin eventually died on 14 August 1901.

Upon Edward Mappin's death on 11 January 1875, his son, Charles Mappin, took over the firm, entering his own mark under the name of Mappin Bros at the Sheffield Assay Office in March 1877 and at Goldsmiths' Hall, London, in April 1878. He also brought two new partners into the firm. They were Frederick Crockford, a wealthy Maltese merchant, and Charles Hickson who came from a well-known Northampton family of bootmakers. They took a 25-year lease of the Sheffield works, but due to poor management the firm of Mappin Bros gradually declined. Charles Mappin eventually left the firm, and Crockford and Hickson entered their own marks under the name of Mappin Bros at the Sheffield Assay Office in December 1883 and at Goldsmiths' Hall, London, in February 1884. However, the firm continued to decline, and in 1889 Crockford and Hickson sold Mappin Bros to John L. Langman and William Gibson, a Belfast jeweller who had a controlling interest in the Goldsmiths & Silversmiths Company (see Goldsmiths & Silversmiths Co. Ltd).

W. Gibson and J. L. Langman had previously entered their own partnership marks at the Sheffield Assay Office in February 1881 and April 1883, giving their address as 112 Regent Street, London. In January 1890 they registered new partnership marks at Sheffield consisting of 'WG' over 'JLL' and 'WG JLL', but this time under the name of Mappin Bros of Bakers Hill, Sheffield, this being the address of the Queens Works factory.

W. Gibson and J. L. Langman continued to register marks under their own names at Goldsmiths' Hall throughout the 1890s (see Goldsmiths & Silversmiths Co. Ltd), while at the same time still maintaining Mappin Bros as a separate entity. In July 1893 a new Mappin Bros mark was entered at Sheffield followed by similar marks at Goldsmiths' Hall, London, in December 1892 and May 1896.

In 1899 the firm of Mappin Bros was taken over by the Goldsmiths & Silversmiths Company. In 1900 and 1901 further Mappin Bros marks were entered at Goldsmiths' Hall by William Gibson, the sole partner.

In 1903 the Goldsmiths & Silversmiths Company sold its interest in Mappin Bros to the firm of Mappin & Webb (see Mappin & Webb), which had been founded by John Newton Mappin in 1860. Thus John Newton Mappin acquired his father's firm of which he had last been a member some 43 years earlier, and Mappin Bros became a part of Mappin & Webb.

*Mark entered in two sizes.
**Mark entered in three sizes.

Gilbert Marks

* 14 March 1896
Gold and Silver worker
21 Dingwall Road, Croydon

Removed to The Quest, Hazeldean Road, East Croydon, 7 August 1896

Gilbert Marks was the son of Sarah (née Walker) and John George Marks, a wine shipper's manager of Croydon, Surrey. His parents were married in June 1860 and Gilbert Marks was born on 1 April 1861, the eldest of five brothers and one sister who died at the age of three. From May 1871 to August 1878, he attended Whitgift School, Croydon, where he excelled at sport and won several academic prizes including the Drawing Prize for four consecutive years. On leaving school, he spent the next seven years working for Johnson, Walker & Tolhurst, a firm of manufacturing silversmiths. Meanwhile, he continued living with his parents at 115 Waddon New Road, Croydon. *Circa* 1885 he joined the firm of Masurel & Fils of 66 Coleman Street, EC. Then, on 12 March 1888, he married 23-year-old Florence Elizabeth Ford.

About this time, he set up his own silversmithing workshop, where he produced silverware by hand, much of it decorated with repoussé. From 1895 to 1901 he regularly exhibited his work at a series of exhibitions held by Johnson, Walker & Tolhurst at 80 Aldersgate Street, EC. On 15 January 1904 he was admitted to the Holloway Sanitorium, Virginia Water, suffering from syphilis which he had originally contracted some sixteen years earlier. He died on 5 February 1905 and was buried on 9 February in the Queen's Road Cemetery, Croydon.

*Mark entered in two sizes.

Martin, Hall & Co. Ltd

24 November 1853
John Roberts and Ebenezer Hall, Plate workers
manufactory: Shrewsbury Works, Broad Street Park, Sheffield
showrooms: 15 Bouverie Street, Fleet Street
residence: Abbeydale Villa, Abbeydale Road, near Sheffield

** 30 May 1863
Richard Martin and Ebenezer Hall, Plate workers
Broad Street Park, Sheffield
residence: Brincliffe Villa, Abbeydale Park, Sheffield

(Marks) cancelled 9.1.1880

* 9 January 1880
Richard Martin and Ebenezer Hall, Plate workers
Shrewsbury Works, Broad Street Park, Sheffield
‡ 28 Bouverie Street, Fleet Street, London
R. Martin's residence: 12 Collingham Road, South Kensington,
SW
E. Hall's residence: Abbeydale Park, Abbeydale, near Sheffield

17 October 1884
‡ Removed to 22 Ely Place, Holborn (This asterisked note applies
to the vacation of previous premises at 28 Bouverie Street only)

These marks withdrawn 24.2.1896

*** 24 February 1896
Richard Martin and Ebenezer Hall, Silver workers
Shrewsbury Works, Broad Street Park, Sheffield
22 Ely Place, Holborn, London EC
186 St Vincent Street, Glasgow
16–18 Castlereagh Street, Sydney, NSW
R. Martin's residence: 10 Porchester Terrace, Hyde Park, W
E. Hall's residence: Abbeydale Park, Dore, near Sheffield

*** 11 May 1904
Martin, Hall and Co. Ltd, Silver workers
Shrewsbury Works, Sheffield
22 Ely Place, London
186 St Vincent Street, Glasgow
18 Ludgate Hill, Birmingham
R. Martin's residence: 10 Porchester Terrace, Hyde Park, W
E. Hall's residence: Abbeydale Park, Dore, near Sheffield
partners: Richard Martin, Ebenezer Hall

** 14 February 1912
Martin Hall and Co. Ltd, Gold and Silver workers
Shrewsbury Works, Broad Street, Sheffield
Audrey House, Ely Place, Holborn, London
18 Ludgate Hill, Birmingham
Gordon Chambers, 90 Mitchell St, Glasgow
residences: 99 Rustlings Road, Sheffield

217

12 Coverdale Road, Brondesbury
directors: Alfred Maxfield, Hy Wilkins, Philip Wake, Richard
Martin, John M. Ensell, F. Newton

John Roberts appears to have been the founder of this Sheffield firm of manufacturing silversmiths and platers. Originally he was in partnership with Henry Wilkinson, trading as Wilkinson & Roberts. Following Henry Wilkinson's resignation from the partnership in 1836, he continued working on his own, taking on Ebenezer Hall as an apprentice. Ebenezer Hall, who was born at Middleton-by-Wirksworth, Derbyshire, in 1820, was apprenticed to him in 1836 and subsequently joined him in partnership in 1846, the firm's name being amended to Roberts & Hall. On 19 April 1847 they entered their first mark at the Sheffield Assay Office. This was followed by their first mark at Goldsmiths' Hall, London, in November 1853.

In 1854 Roberts & Hall amalgamated with the firm of Martin & Naylor, and Richard Martin of the latter firm joined them in partnership to form Martin, Hall & Co. At the same time, John Roberts appears to have semi-retired and Ebenezer Hall's brother, Joshua Hall, joined the partnership. He was the father of J. F. Hall, one of the founders of Sibray, Hall & Co. (see Sibray, Hall & Co). John Roberts eventually retired on 1 January 1857. On 9 February 1854 the firm's new mark of 'M H' over '& Co' was entered at the Sheffield Assay Office, and in 1866 the firm was converted into a limited liability company.

By 1880 Richard Martin was apparently residing in London, initially at South Kensington and then, by 1896, at Hyde Park. Presumably he was responsible for supervising the London branch of the firm while Ebenezer Hall remained responsible for the Sheffield factory.

With the death of Ebenezer Hall in 1911 at the age of 91, a board of directors continued running the firm. Prior to 1914 the firm had some 750 employees, but following the end of the First World War, the number of employees dropped to about 500. During the 1920s business gradually declined until, in 1929, a receiver was appointed. The firm eventually went into liquidation in 1936.

*Marks entered in two sizes.
**Marks entered in three sizes.
***Marks entered in four sizes.

Thomas Mitchell & Co.

T M
I B
T M

21 February 1831
Thomas Mitchell, James Burden and Thomas Merrifield, Plate workers
Bath
By virtue of Power of Attorney I enter the mark of Thomas Mitchell, James Burden, Thomas Merrifield all of the City of Bath this 21 February 1831. (signed) George Frederick Bult, Attorney to the said firm

T M
T M

17 June 1845
Thomas Mitchell and Thomas Merrifield, Plate workers
23 Kingsmead Terrace, Bath

This firm of silversmiths appears to have been founded *circa* 1831 by Thomas Mitchell, James Burden and Thomas Merrifield at 23 Kingsmead Terrace, Bath, Somerset. Although Thomas Merrifield is listed in directories as being at 10 King Street, Bath, between 1826 and 1846, he was also working in partnership with James Burden and Thomas Mitchell by February 1831, this being when their combined mark was entered at Goldsmiths' Hall, London, by George Frederick Bult[1] acting on their behalf.

From 1837 to 1841 James Burden is listed as being at 6 Paradise Street, Wells Road. In June 1845 the remaining partners, Thomas Mitchell and Thomas Merrifield, entered their second mark at Goldsmiths' Hall, London. On this occasion they signed the entry personally instead of appointing an attorney to sign on their behalf. The firm continued to trade as Thomas Mitchell & Co., silversmiths, but by 1852 the sole partner listed is Mrs Mitchell, silversmith and water gilder.

1. George Frederick Bult was the son of James Bult (silversmith, Citizen and Goldsmith) and grandson of Thomas Bult (yeoman) of Kingston, Somerset. He obtained his freedom of the Goldsmiths' Company by Patrimony on 4 August 1824 and was made a Liveryman in April 1827. He died on 26 December 1861. His father, James Bult, was a partner in the London firm of Godbehere, Wigan & Bult, manufacturing silversmiths of 86 Cheapside from *circa* 1800 onwards. *Circa* 1841 James Bult, Philip Bult and George Frederick Bult set up as bankers, trading as James Bult & Co. at 85–86 Cheapside. James Bult died on 13 May 1846.

SM

9 June 1823
Sampson Mordan (No. 1), Small worker
22 Castle Street, City Road

SM·GR

30 April 1824
Sampson Mordan (No. 1) and Gabriel Riddle, Plate workers
22 Castle Street, City Road

S M

4 January 1837
Sampson Mordan (No 1), Small worker
22 Castle Street, City Road

SM

13 April 1843
Sampson Mordan (No. 2), Small worker
22 Castle Street, City Road

S.M

8 October 1880
Six new marks (all same size)
Removed to 41 City Road
By virtue of a Power of Attorney dated 7 October 1880, I enter
the Marks of Sampson Mordan of 41 City Road, London.
(signed) Silversmith, Edmund George Johnson of 41 City Road,
London, Attorney to the said Sampson Mordan

Marks erased 16.6.(1890)

S.M & Co

16 June 1890
S. Mordan and Co., Small workers
41 and 43 City Road
72 Cheapside

S.M & Co

* residence: 12 Birchington Road, Crouch End
partner: H. L. Symonds

S.M&Co

28 November 1895
41 and 43 City Road

residence: Brenton, Cyprus Road, Finchley
partner: H. L. Symonds

S M&Co

20 August 1902
S. Mordan and Co. Ltd, Silver workers
41 City Road
residence: Montrose, Hendon Lane, Finchley, N
managing director: H. L. Symonds

(Mark) cancelled 15.6.1928

[SM&Co]	21 March 1904 S. Mordan and Co. Ltd, Gold and Silver workers 41 City Road, EC 9 Warwick Street, Regent Street, W residence: Montrose, Hendon Lane, Finchley managing director: Harry Lambert Symonds
S.M & Co	** 7 September 1905 S. Mordan and Co. Ltd, Gold and Silver workers 41 City Road, EC 11 Warwick Street, Regent Street, W residence: Montrose, Hendon Lane, Finchley managing director: Harry Lambert Symonds

(Marks) cancelled 15.6.1928

[SM&Co]   31 August 1906 (Entry as for 7.9.1905)

11 August 1925
S. Mordan and Co. Ltd residence: Sunnyside, Hornchurch
director: Margery Doris Symonds

(Mark) cancelled 15.6.1928

Born in 1790, Sampson Mordan (No. 1) patented his invention for a propelling pencil called the Ever-Pointed Pencil on 20 December 1822. He entered his first mark at Goldsmiths' Hall in June 1823 then joined Gabriel Riddle in partnership in 1824. With the dissolution of their partnership in December 1836, Sampson Mordan (No. 1) continued trading on his own as S. Mordan & Co., manufacturers of Ever-Pointed pencils, portable pens, smelling bottles, inkstands, etc. He and his wife, Elizabeth, had five children: Sampson (No. 2), Augustus, Emma, Francis (who founded the firm of Francis Mordan & Co.) and Charles.

With the death of Sampson Mordan (No. 1) in early 1843, the firm was continued by his two sons, Sampson Mordan (No. 2) and Augustus Mordan. At a later date, they were joined by Edmund George Johnson who, in October 1880, entered marks at Goldsmiths' Hall on behalf of Sampson Mordan (No. 2) who had retired to Paris. Sampson Mordan (No. 2) died in Paris in May 1881, leaving his share of the firm to Augustus Mordan.

In June 1890 Harry Lambert Symonds was listed as partner in the firm, and then, in August 1902, as managing director. In 1898 the firm was converted into a limited liability company trading as S. Mordan & Co. Ltd. Also, in 1898 it took over the firm of Johnson, Sons & Edmonds of 32 John Street.

On 11 August 1925 it was recorded at Goldsmiths' Hall that Margery Doris Symonds, residing at Sunnyside, Hornchurch, was the firm's sole director. On 15 June 1928 all of the firm's remaining marks were cancelled. In December 1941 the firm's factory in City Road was destroyed by German bombing and the firm ceased trading. The firm's patents were bought by a pencil manufacturer, Edward Baker, who was later taken over by the Yard-o-Lead Pencil Co.

*Mark entered in two sizes.
**Mark entered in three sizes.

Nathan & Hayes

G N / R H	22 August 1893
	George Nathan and Ridley Hayes, Plate workers
	285 Icknield Street, Birmingham
	G. Nathan's residence: 53 Carlisle Road, Birmingham
	R. Hayes's residence: 131 Church Hill Road, Birmingham

(no mark)   27 May 1908
Nathan & Hayes, Silver workers
Howard Street, Birmingham
G. Nathan's residence: 13 Hatton Garden, London
partners: George Nathan, Ridley Hayes

George Nathan and Ridley Hayes founded this Birmingham firm of manufacturing silversmiths in 1885. The firm was taken over by S. Blackensee & Son Ltd at some time during the 1920s. George Nathan died in 1935, aged 80.

Nayler Brothers

    11 September 1908
Alfred Walter Nayler, Silver worker
5 Denmark Hill, Charing Cross Road, WC
residence: 126 Lyndhurst Road, Peckham, SE
partner: Alfred Walter Nayler

15 November 1909
Nayler Brothers, Silver workers
5 Denmark Hill, Charing Cross Road, WC
A. W. Nayler's residence: 126 Lyndhurst Road, Peckham
W. E. Nayler's residence: 48 Stuart Road, Peckham Rye
partners: Alfred Walter Nayler, William Edwin Nayler

1 June 1911
Removed to 46 Greek Street, Soho, W
W. E. Nayler's residence: 391 Wandsworth Road, Clapham, SW

21 July 1914
Nayler Brothers, Silver workers
38a Broad Street, Golden Square, WC
W. E. Nayler's residence: 391 Wandsworth Road, Clapham, SW
partners: Alfred Walter Nayler, William Edwin Nayler

This firm was founded by Alfred Walter Nayler, chaser, in 1908. He subsequently entered into partnership with his brother, William Edwin Nayler, at some date prior to 15 November 1909. On 2 November 1927 William Edwin Nayler obtained his freedom of the Goldsmiths' Company by Redemption. He was made a Liveryman in January 1931 and died on 24 December 1949.

The firm is still trading as Nayler Brothers (Silversmiths) Ltd, under the directorship of C. T. Smith and his wife, the daughter of William Edwin Nayler.

Ollivant & Botsford

24 September 1896
Charles Wright Botsford and James Wall Botsford, Gold and Silver workers
12 and 14 St Ann Street, Manchester
C. W. Botsford's residence: Heatherdale, Alexandra Road South, Manchester
J. W. Botsford's residence: Barnfield, Ashton-on-Mersey, near Manchester

* 28 September 1901
Ollivant and Botsford, Gold and Silver workers
12 and 14 St Ann Street and Police Street, Manchester
C. W. Botsford's residence: Heatherdale, Alexandra Road South, Manchester

Oᵀ**&B**ᴰ 21 November 1903
Ollivant and Botsford, Gold and Silver workers
12 and 14 St Ann Street and 3 Police Street, Manchester
J. W. Botsford's residence: Barnfield, Ashton-on-Mersey,
Cheshire
partners: James Wall Botsford, Charles Wright Botsford

Oᵀ**&B**ᴰ 17 September 1912 (Entry as for 21.11.1903 except James Wall
Botsford is the sole partner)

This Manchester firm of silversmiths was founded in 1789 by Thomas Ollivant, plate worker, trading under his own name. Later it became Ollivant, Sons & Nephew. Then, *circa* 1855, John Josiah Ollivant entered into partnership with John William Botsford and the firm was renamed Ollivant & Botsford. With the death of John Josiah Ollivant in 1868, John William Botsford continued the firm, still trading under the name of Ollivant & Botsford, goldsmiths, silversmiths, jewellers, electroplaters and watch and chronometer manufacturers.

By 1896 the partners were Charles Wright Botsford and James Wall Botsford. In 1933 the firm was converted into a limited liability company, trading as Ollivant & Botsford Ltd, the name under which it still operates today.

*Mark entered in two sizes.

Pairpoint Brothers

E·P 27 September 1848
Edward Pairpoint, Plate worker
44 Whitcomb Street, Leicester Square

E·P 5 December 1848
Removed to 16 Litchfield Street, Soho

E·P 14 March 1851
Edward Pairpoint, Plate worker
44 Greek Street, Soho

E·P
G.W 22 February 1856
Edward Pairpoint and George Wood, Plate workers
44 Greek Street, Soho
G. Wood's residence: 2 Francis Villas, Grange Road, Canonbury

23 February 1859
Edward Pairpoint, Plate worker

2 February 1864

* 21 August 1866

J P
F P
6 February 1879
John Pairpoint, Frank Pairpoint, Plate workers
57 King Street, Soho Square
residence: Providence Cottage, Enfield Lane, Hornsey

Removed to 47 Rupert Street, Haymarket, 20 September 1879

Removed to 80A Dean Street, Soho

A P
F P
A P
** 10 March 1909
Pairpoint Brothers, Gold and Silver workers
80 Dean Street, 14 Richmond Buildings, W
residence: 73 Hamilton Terrace, St Johns Wood Road, NW
partners: Alfred James Pairpoint, Francis William Pairpoint,
Arthur Walter Pairpoint

This firm was founded by Edward James Pairpoint at 44 Whitcomb Street, Leicester Square, in September 1848. He moved to 16 Litchfield Street in December 1848 and subsequently to 44 Greek Street. He was born *circa* 1825, the son of William Pairpoint, water gilder, who founded the firm of William Pairpoint & Sons Ltd. Edward James Pairpoint and his wife, Eliza (b.1825), had five children: Edward John (b.1848), William Henry (b.1850), Alfred James (b.1852), Eliza Ann (b.1854), and Francis William (b.1858). The property at 44 Greek Street served as both business and residential premises for him and his family, and in 1861 it additionally housed Walter Alexander Pairpoint, aged 24, together with his wife, Janealine, and baby daughter, Ellen Maria.

In early 1856 Edward James Pairpoint entered into partnership with George Wood, the firm being renamed Pairpoint & Wood, manufacturing silversmiths. This partnership was dissolved in January 1859 and E. J. Pairpoint continued trading on his own as Edward Pairpoint until he became bankrupt in 1879. The firm was then taken over by John Pairpoint and Frank Pairpoint, trading as Pairpoint Brothers, silversmiths.

In 1904 the firm was under the control of three new partners: Alfred

J. Pairpoint, Francis W. Pairpoint and Arthur W. Pairpoint. Both Alfred J. Pairpoint and Francis W. Pairpoint were the sons of Edward James Pairpoint. Alfred J. Pairpoint died in January 1937 and Francis W. Pairpoint in December 1945.

*Mark entered in two sizes.
**Mark entered in three sizes.

Pearce & Sons Ltd

 * 19 August 1897
Pearce & Sons, Gold and Silver workers
13 Commercial Street, Leeds
34 Gallowtree Gate, Leicester
residences: John Pearce: 69 Potternewton Lane, Leeds
William Pearce: Clifton Park, Ilkley
Henry Pearce: 4 New Street, Huddersfield

 27 September 1897

 * 7 March 1906
Pearce & Sons, Gold and Silver workers
Bond Street, Leeds
Lendal, York
Gallowtree Gate, Leicester
J. Pearce's residence: Ingledene, Roundhay, Leeds
directors: John Pearce, William Pearce

6 November 1906
directors: John Pearce, William Pearce, Charles Brook
secretary: Tom Archer Pearce

 17 July 1911
Pearce & Sons Ltd, Gold and Silver workers
Bond Street, Leeds
Lendal, York
 Gallowtree Gate, Leicester
T. A. Pearce's residence: Exton, Ilkley
directors: John Pearce, William Pearce, Charles Brook
secretary: Tom Archer Pearce

226

* 15 April 1913
Pearce & Sons Ltd, Gold and Silver workers
Bond Street, Leeds
Lendal, York
Gallowtree Gate, Leicester
A. H. Pearce's residence: Chellow Dene, Gledhow Wood Grove, Leeds
directors: John Pearce, John Pearce Jr, Charles Brook, Arthur H. Pearce

15 October 1913 (Entry as for 15.4.1913)

*

This Leeds firm of retail silversmiths and jewellers was founded in the mid-nineteenth century. The firm's mark was entered for the first time at Goldsmiths' Hall, London, in August 1897, listing the partners as John, William and Henry Pearce. In 1898 the firm moved to Bond Street, Leeds, and then, in 1904, branch premises were opened at Lendal, York.

By March 1906 Henry Pearce had left the firm and set up in business on his own, trading as H. Pearce & Son of New Street, Huddersfield. This firm eventually closed down in 1934.

During 1906 Pearce & Sons was converted into a limited liability company, trading as Pearce & Sons Ltd.

*Mark entered in two sizes.

Peard & Jackson (later Hart, Son, Peard & Co.)

13 February 1866
Thomas Peard, Plate worker
159 High Holborn
residence: 15 Trafalgar Square, Twickenham

23 March 1866
Removed to 53–58 Wych Street, Strand
T. Peard's residence: 4 Brook Street, Hanover Square

 19 November 1869

 26 April 1882
90–91 Drury Lane, London
Grosvenor Works, Grosvenor Street, Birmingham

Removed to 88–91 Drury Lane, 17 July 1894

 6 September 1906
Hart, Son, Peard & Co. Ltd, Silver workers
138–140 Charing Cross Road, London, WC
Grosvenor Works, Birmingham
C. J. Hart's residence: Highfield Gate, Birmingham
T. Peard's residence: 13 Princes Avenue, Finchley
directors: Charles Joseph Hart, Thomas Peard

 11 July 1911
Hart, Son, Peard & Co. Ltd, Gold and Silver workers
138–140 Charing Cross Road, London, WC
Grosvenor Works, Grosvenor Street West, Birmingham
W. J. Peard's residence: Ermynville, Fortis Green Road, East
Finchley, London, N
director: William James Peard

10 June 1914 Removed to Commerce House, 70–86 Oxford
Street, W
residence: 40 Fortis Green Avenue, East Finchley, N

11 November 1920
Removed to 28 Berners Street, W1
director: William James Peard

Thomas Peard was apprenticed to an ironmonger in Bideford, Devon.
Having completed his apprenticeship, he joined the firm of Joseph Hart &
Sons, ironmongers of 53 Wych Street, London, in 1853. In 1860 he left
the firm and set up in business on his own. Not long after, he entered into
partnership with Frederick Jackson, trading as Peard & Jackson.

In February 1866 Thomas Peard entered his first mark at Goldsmiths'
Hall, giving the firm's address as 159 High Holborn. The firm at this time
was listed as being manufacturers of medieval art metal works, smiths, iron
and brass founders and finishers and hot water and gas fitters.

By 23 March 1866 Peard & Jackson had amalgamated with Thomas

Peard's old firm of Joseph Hart & Son, wholesale, retail and manufacturing ironmongers of 53–58 Wych Street (see Joseph Hart & Son). This new firm traded as Hart, Son, Peard & Co. with Charles Hart in charge of the Grosvenor Works at Birmingham, Thomas Peard the London manufactory and showrooms, and Frederick Jackson the firm's finances.

Circa 1905 the firm was converted into a limited liability company, trading as Hart, Son, Peard & Co. Ltd with Thomas Peard and Charles Joseph Hart as directors. The firm was still in existence in 1920 at 28 Berners Street, Oxford Street.

Frederick Perry

* 13 March 1873
Frederick Perry and William Frederick Curry, Plate workers
39 St John Street Road, Clerkenwell
residences: F. Perry: 18 Sudeley Street, City Road
W. Curry: 7 St George's Terrace, Liverpool Road

Manufactory removed to 1 Upper Gloucester Street, Clerkenwell (undated)

1 November 1880
Frederick Perry, Plate worker
25 Thornhill Road, Barnsbury N

Removed to 375 City Road, Islington, 26 November 1889

4 May 1893

Removed to 17 Tyndale Place, Upper Street, Islington, 5 March 1894

Frederick Perry and William Frederick Curry, trading as Perry & Curry, silversmiths, entered their partnership mark at Goldsmiths' Hall in 1873. *Circa* 1874 they moved from 39 St John Street Road, Clerkenwell, to new working premises at 1 Upper Gloucester Street, Clerkenwell.

When they dissolved their partnership in September 1875, W. F. Curry remained at the Upper Gloucester Street premises while F. Perry moved to 25 Thornhill Road, Barnsbury, from where he later entered his own mark at Goldsmiths' Hall. Meanwhile, W. F. Curry entered his mark on 24 March 1879 (see William Frederick Curry).

*Mark entered in two sizes.

S. J. Phillips

 ** 1 July 1901
Solomon Joel Phillips, Silver worker
113 New Bond Street, W
38 Wimpole Street, W

This well-known firm was founded in 1869 by Solomon Joel Phillips at 66 Regent Street, London. In 1874 he moved to 113 New Bond Street where he built up the firm as retail silversmiths, jewellers, diamond merchants and dealers in antique plate.

When Solomon J. Phillips died on 17 July 1908, the firm was continued by his son, Edmund Avigdor Phillips. Edmund A. Phillips obtained his freedom of the Goldsmiths' Company by Redemption on 3 June 1931. He died in 1934 when 55 years old. Today the firm is still trading as S. J. Phillips at 139 New Bond Street, W1.

**Mark entered in three sizes.

George Frederick Pinnell

GFP
GFP | 27 September 1830
George Frederick Pinnell
21 Well Street, Jewin Street

GFP | 10 November 1840
Removed to 18 Red Cross Square

GFP | 10 February 1841

GFP | 23 November 1841

GFP | 4 July 1842

Dead (G. F. Pinnell) and mark defaced 7.2.1852

J·P | * 6 February 1852
Jane Pinnell, Plate worker
18 Red Cross Square, City

George Frederick Pinnell, the son of John Pinnell (gentleman) of Islington, was apprenticed to William Barrett (silversmith, Citizen and Goldsmith) of 3 Great Deans Court, St Martins-le-Grand, on 4 October 1815 to learn the trade of silversmith. However, upon completing his apprenticeship, he did not take up his freedom of the Goldsmiths' Company. Presumably he continued working for William Barrett.

Circa 1830 he commenced in business as a small worker at 21 Well Street, Jewin Street. However, with the death of William Barrett in 1831, he acquired Barrett's premises at 18 Red Cross Square, Cripplegate, and probably his business as well. On 5 October 1831 he obtained his freedom of the Goldsmiths' Company by Service.

George Frederick Pinnell's brother, Edward Pinnell, was likewise apprenticed to William Barrett (silversmith, Citizen and Goldsmith) of 18 Red Cross Square, Cripplegate, on 1 June 1825 to learn the trade of silversmith. Following Barrett's death, he was turned over to George Frederick Pinnell (silversmith, Citizen and Goldsmith) of 18 Red Cross Square on 2 November 1831, but it was not until 5 November 1856 that he took up his freedom of the Goldsmiths' Company by Service. Presumably he continued working for his brother during those intervening years.

Following George Frederick Pinnell's death in late 1851 or early 1852, the business was continued by his widow, Jane Pinnell, trading as silversmith and polisher.

Edward Pinnell's son, Edward George Pinnell, was apprenticed to George Frederick Pinnell (silversmith, Citizen and Goldsmith) on 2 February 1848, but as a result of the latter's death he was turned over to his widow, Jane Pinnell, on 7 April 1852. There is no record of him obtaining his freedom of the Goldsmiths' Company.

Jane and George Frederick Pinnell had a son, George Frederick Pinnell, who obtained his freedom of the Goldsmiths' Company by Patrimony on 6 July 1859.

*Mark entered in two sizes.

Henry Hodson Plante

6 September 1864
Joseph Hirons, Henry Hodson Plante and Rowland Bourne, Plate workers
54–56 Frederick Street Works, Birmingham
4 (41?) Hatton Garden, London
R. Bourne's residence: Laburnam Grove, Edgbaston

* 19 April 1887
Henry Millington Harwood and Henry Hodson Plante, Plate workers
185 and 187 Newhall Street, Birmingham
12 Hatton Garden, EC
H. M. Harwood's residence: Oakfield, Lordswood Road, Harbourne
H. H. Plante's residence: Stafford House, Wylde Green, Erdington

22 August 1894
Emily Catherine Plante, Silver worker
55 Frederick Street, Birmingham
residence: Canterbury Place, Chester Road, near Birmingham

(P&B) ** 31 October 1906
Plante & Bannister, Gold and Silver workers
3 Regent Place, Regent Street, W
H. H. Plante's residence: Drayton Lodge, Shortlands, Kent
H. E. Bannister's residence: 60 Edith Road, West Kensington
partners: Henry Hodson Plante, Harry Edward Bannister

This firm dissolved Partnership in 1908 and the next entry is that of H. H. Plante

(H·H·P) ** 5 November 1908
H. H. Plante, Gold and Silver worker
3 Regent Place, Regent Street, W
residence: Rupert House, Alma Road, Herne Bay
partner: Henry Hodson Plante

(H·H·P) ** 16 May 1911
H. H. Plante, Gold and Silver worker

(H·H·P) * 3 Regent Place, Regent Street, W
residence: 70 Beacon Road, Herne Bay (Kent)
partner: Henry Hodson Plante

Circa 1860 Henry Hodson Plante entered into partnership with Joseph Hirons and Rowland Bourne, thereby establishing the firm of Hirons, Plante & Bourne, silversmiths and electroplaters at 54–56 Frederick Street, Birmingham, and 41 Hatton Garden, London. Prior to this date, Joseph Hirons had been in partnership with Joseph Woodward as wholesale jewellers at 11 Upper Hockley Street, Birmingham, but this partnership had been dissolved in July 1860.

In June 1878, Rowland Bourne resigned from the partnership, leaving Joseph Hirons and Henry Hodson Plante as the remaining partners. They continued trading as Hirons, Plante & Co., silversmiths and electroplaters at 54–56 Frederick Street, Birmingham and 12 Hatton Garden, London, until Joseph Hirons retired in January 1882. Henry Hodson Plante then continued trading on his own as H. H. Plante & Co., manufacturers of electroplated goods at 55 Frederick Street and 12 Hatton Garden. However, at some date prior to August 1894, he appears to have relinquished control of H. H. Plante & Co. since, on 22 August 1894, a new mark was entered at Goldsmiths' Hall, London, by the firm's sole partner, Emily Catherine Plante.

In 1897 H. H. Plante & Co. of 55 Frederick Street, Birmingham, was converted into a limited liability company, trading as H. H. Plante & Co. Ltd, goldsmiths, silversmiths, jewellers, electroplaters, gilders and manufacturers of works of art. Its directors were Albert H. Plante, Albert Grinder and Henry P. Macklin. In 1899 this company sold its stock at Frederick Street, after which it apparently closed down.

Meanwhile, at some date between 1883 and 1886, Henry Hodson Plante entered into partnership with Henry Millington Harwood and Walter Andrew Harrison of Harwood, Son & Harrison, silversmiths and spoon makers at 185–187 Newhall Street, Birmingham, and Russell Chambers, Bedford Street, London. Under this new partnership, the firm was renamed Harwood, Plante & Harrison, silversmiths and electroplaters at 185–187 Newhall Street, Birmingham, and 12 Hatton Garden, London.

In June 1886 Walter Andrew Harrison resigned from the partnership, leaving Henry Millington Harwood and Henry Hodson Plante to continue trading as Harwood & Plante, electroplate manufacturers at 185–187 Newhall Street and 12 Hatton Garden. In October 1892 their partnership was dissolved and the firm continued trading as Harwood & Son, silversmiths, spoon makers and electroplate manufacturers at 185–187 Newhall Street until some date between 1894 and 1899, after which the premises were occupied by Norton & White, electroplate manufacturers.

Circa 1906 Henry Hodson Plante once again became a partner in a firm of silversmiths. This time he entered into partnership with Harry Edward Bannister, trading as Plante & Bannister at 3 Regent Place, Regent Street, London. In March 1908 Henry Hodson Plante and Harry Edward Massingham, the current partners in Plante & Bannister, dissolved their partnership. At the time, the firm was trading as goldsmiths, silversmiths, jewellers, chronometer makers and watch and clock makers. Henry Hodson Plante then continued trading on his own as H. H. Plante. In 1915 he moved to 12 Bury Street, St James, London.

*Mark entered in two sizes.
**Mark entered in three sizes.

The Portland Co. Ltd

---

* 22 August 1859
Francis Higgins (No. 3), Spoon maker
6 Riding House Street, Portland Place
signed: Francis Higgins Jr

* 3 December 1859
signed: Francis Higgins Jr

The Portland Co. Ltd was founded in January 1859 by Harry Emanuel, retail goldsmith of Hanover Square, Francis Higgins (No. 3) (silversmith, Citizen and Goldsmith) of 6 Riding House Street, Elliot Grasett of 6 Chesham Street, Charles M. Lushington of 9 Mansfield Street, Reginald B. K. Hugeseen of Faversham, Kent, Edwin W. Streeter of 6 Toriano Avenue, Holloway, and Charles Martin of 28 Bucklersbury. The company was set up to produce cutlery by an improved method of manufacture, for which Harry Emanuel had taken out a patent in 1856.

During 1859 Francis Higgins (No. 3) left his father's firm, F. Higgins & Son, silver knife, fork and spoon manufacturer, to become manager of the Portland Co. Ltd. Unfortunately the company was not a financial success and went into voluntary liquidation in 1863. In the Post Office Directories for 1860, 1861 and 1862, Francis Higgins (No. 3) is recorded as silver spoon and fork maker and manager of the Portland Co. Ltd of 6 Riding House Street. In 1863 he is recorded as before, but with additional premises at 4 and 5 Riding House Street and 48 Fenchurch Street. In 1864 there is no mention of the Portland Co. Ltd and the Riding House Street premises are occupied by Wright & Mansfield, cabinet makers.

Following the demise of the Portland Co. Ltd in 1863, Francis Higgins (No. 3)'s financial circumstances declined to such an extent that, in December 1867, he was obliged to file his petition for bankruptcy. However, in 1868 he rejoined his father's firm as a partner and eventually took over the firm when his father died in 1880 (see Francis Higgins & Son).

*Mark entered in two sizes.

R. Pringle & Sons

(R P)
17 January 1862
Robert Pringle (No. 1), Gold worker
44 St John's Square, Clerkenwell
residence: 19 Great Percy Street, Bagnigge Wells Road

Removed to 17 Wilderness Row, Clerkenwell, 13 February 1863

Now called 21 Wilderness Row, Clerkenwell (This note has been added later)

(R·P)
25 October 1871
Removed to 42 Clerkenwell Road
(This was previously named 21 Wilderness Row)

(R·P)
11 February 1874

(R·P)
25 March 1874

(R·P)
11 December 1884 (Marks) defaced 10 June 1890

(RP)

(R·P)
*** 10 June 1890
Robert Pringle (No. 1), Gold worker
40 and 42 Clerkenwell Road
39 Halford Square

Removed to 36 Arundel Square, N
17 March 1896

Owing to the retirement of Robert Pringle from the firm of R. Pringle and Sons, new punches were entered by R. Pringle Junior, 14 March 1907.

*** 14 March 1907
Robert Pringle and Sons, Gold and Silver workers
40 and 42 Clerkenwell Road
and 20 Great Sutton Street, EC
residence: Hillside, 107 Crouch Hill, N
partner: Robert Pringle (No. 2)

 ** 20 April 1907 (Entry as for 14.3.1907)

 ** 18 March 1909 (Entry as for 14.3.1907)

 24 March 1910 (Entry as for 14.3.1907)

 ** 24 November 1910 (Entry as for 14.3.1907)

Robert Pringle (No. 1) was born in 1836, the son of Robert Pringle, a working jeweller who had set up in business in London *circa* 1835. By 1852 Robert Pringle had established himself as a gilt jeweller at 9 Amwell Street, Clerkenwell.

His son, Robert Pringle (No. 1), subsequently inherited the business and in 1862 entered his first mark at Goldsmiths' Hall, giving 44 St John's Square, Clerkenwell, as his working premises. By 1877 he had increased his business to become a wholesale manufacturer and dealer in jewellery and electroplate, selling gem and fancy rings, gold and silver chains, earrings, brooches, gold and silver pencil cases, general electroplate, plated spoons, forks, tea sets, prize cups and unmanufactured gold, silver and plating.

Following a long illness, he recuperated during 1879–80 by taking a sea voyage to New Zealand and back. Returning to London, fully recovered, he commenced expanding his business. By now his sons were assisting him, and *circa* 1882–3 he renamed the firm Robert Pringle & Co. In 1884 he acquired and occupied the adjoining property at 40 Clerkenwell Road. By 1890 each of his sons was a manager of a department within the firm: Robert (No. 2), the refinery department; William, the silversmithing department;

James, the bullion department; and Edwin, the watch department. In April 1899 Robert Pringle (No. 1) took his son Robert Pringle (No. 2) into partnership, at the same time changing the firm's name to Robert Pringle & Sons.

Following his father's death on 23 June 1907, Robert Pringle (No. 2) took over the firm and entered into partnership with his brothers, William, James and Edwin. Robert Pringle (No. 2) died on 14 December 1942.

In 1931 the firm was converted into a limited liability company, trading under the name of Robert Pringle & Sons (London) Ltd.

**Mark entered in three sizes.
***Mark entered in four sizes.

Edwin Charles Purdie

26 August 1876
Edwin Charles Purdie, Plate worker
29 Gloucester Street, Clerkenwell
residence: 14 Thornhill Crescent, Barnsbury

28 September 1876

Removed to 9 Cobourg Street, Clerkenwell, 21 June 1881

11 January 1883
Said to be broken (This mark was entered due to the old punch having broken)

Removed to 5 Sun Street, Finsbury Square, 3 July 1883

* 21 February 1895

In 1883 Edwin Charles Purdie took over the firm of Thomas Smily, silversmith, at 5 Sun Street, Finsbury Square, moving into the premises by 3 July 1883. From 1884 to *circa* 1902, he traded as Edwin Charles Purdie & Co., wholesale silversmith.

*Mark entered in two sizes.

L. J. Purdie & H. A. Purdie

10 October 1873
Lewis James Purdie
and Henry Alfred Purdie, Plate workers
2 Whiskin Street, Clerkenwell
residence: 12 Everilda Street, Islington

In 1885 Lewis James Purdie, silversmith, was trading at 70 Wynyatt Street, Goswell Road, Clerkenwell.

On 1 February 1893 Alfred Henry Purdie, the son of Henry Alfred Purdie of 99 Compton Buildings, Goswell Road, was apprenticed to Alfred Robert Godfrey (silver plate gilder, Citizen and Goldsmith) of 31 Great Sutton Street, Clerkenwell. Alfred Henry Purdie obtained his freedom of the Goldsmiths' Company by Service on 3 October 1900.

Ramsden & Carr

(RN&CR) 15 February 1898
Omar Ramsden and Alwyn Charles Ellison Carr, Gold and Silver workers
Stamford Bridge Studios, Fulham Road, SW
signed: A. C. E. Carr, partner

(RN&CR) 9 May 1900
signed: Omar Ramsden, partner

(RN&CR) 15 July 1901
Ramsden and Carr, Gold and Silver workers
St Albert Studios, Albert Bridge Road, London SW
signed: Alwyn C. E. Carr, Omar Ramsden

Removed to St Dunstans Studio, Seymour Place, Fulham Road, SW, 11 September 1905

Partnership dissolved December 1918

Omar Ramsden was born on 21 August 1873, the son of Norah (née Ibbotson) and Benjamin Woolhouse Ramsden, engraver, of 16 Fir Street, Nether Hallam, Walkley, Sheffield. In 1879 his father was trading as Benjamin W. Ramsden & Co., manufacturers of silver and electroplate fish carvers, fish eaters, dessert spoons, knives, scoops, etc. at Rockingham

Works, 124 Rockingham Street, and also as stationer at 270 South Road, Sheffield.

For some reason, Omar Ramsden spent seven years of his childhood in America, but having returned to England, he was apprenticed to a Sheffield firm of silversmiths in 1887. In 1890 he began attending evening classes at the Sheffield School of Art, where he met Alwyn C. E. Carr.

Alwyn Charles Ellison Carr was born on 8 August 1872, the eldest son of Emily (née Ellison) and Charles Carr of Pitsmoor, Sheffield. Alwyn Carr was educated at the Pitsmoor National School, then at the Sheffield Central Higher Grade School for three years and finally at the Sheffield School of Art. In 1893 he won a Sheffield Corporation Scholarship tenable at the Sheffield School of Art. In 1894 this same scholarship was won by Omar Ramsden.

Omar Ramsden's father, Benjamin, appears to have died *circa* 1895, but his mother, Norah, survived until 1930. Apparently Omar Ramsden had no desire to take over his father's business for, in 1897, having won an open competition for designing a new mace for the City of Sheffield, he enlisted Alwyn Carr's help for its manufacture. They entered into partnership and moved to London. Their workshop was a dilapidated building in Fulham Road, Chelsea, which they called Stamford Bridge Studios. The mace was completed and presented in 1899, but it is thought that the actual silversmithing work was that of either Alwyn Carr or an experienced assistant, since Omar Ramsden almost certainly never did any actual manufacturing work on the silverware produced in their workshop.

With Alwyn Carr's financial support, they were able to plough their profits back into the business so that the firm gradually flourished and expanded. In 1901 the studio moved as a separate entity to Albert Bridge Road, Battersea. From here it moved to Seymour Place, Fulham Road in 1905.

In 1914 Alwyn Carr enlisted in the Artist's Rifles, and in March 1915 he was granted a commission in the Royal Artillery Service Corps. He served in France during the First World War as 2nd Lieutenant and then Lieutenant until June 1915 when he was gazetted Captain. In July 1918 he was invalided out of the army with the honorary rank of Captain, and after some months of illness he tried to return to the old partnership with Omar Ramsden. Ramsden, however, had continued to run the firm during the war years with considerable success, profiting from war memorials, etc. to such an extent that Carr's financial support was no longer required. Also, Ramsden had formed a close friendship with a Mr and Mrs Downes-Butcher, much to Carr's resentment. In December 1918 the partnership between Omar Ramsden and Alwyn Carr was dissolved with Ramsden retaining St Dunstan's Studio and the workshop while Carr established himself in the former studio of Sir Hamo Thornycroft, sculptor. Here he worked as a silversmith and designer of wrought iron during the 1920s. He died on 22 April 1940 aged 67.

After the dissolution of their partnership, Omar Ramsden's business continued to expand. During the 1930s he employed about 20 assistants. Much of the firm's expansion was due to the business acumen of the formidable Mrs Downes-Butcher (née Annie Emily Berrife), whom Omar Ramsden had married following her husband's death.

Omar Ramsden was a founder member of the Art Workers Guild and chairman of the Church Crafts League. On 16 January 1929 he was elected to the freedom and Livery of the Goldsmiths' Company by Special Grant. He died in August 1939.

John Henry Rawlings

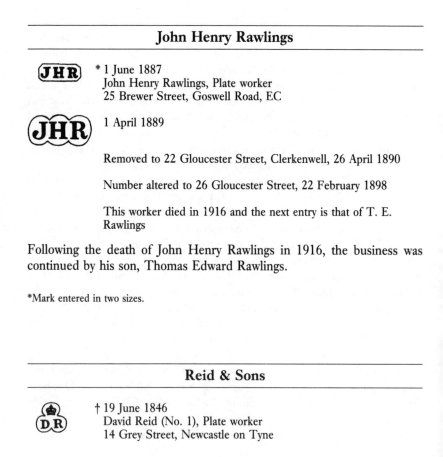

* 1 June 1887
John Henry Rawlings, Plate worker
25 Brewer Street, Goswell Road, EC

1 April 1889

Removed to 22 Gloucester Street, Clerkenwell, 26 April 1890

Number altered to 26 Gloucester Street, 22 February 1898

This worker died in 1916 and the next entry is that of T. E. Rawlings.

Following the death of John Henry Rawlings in 1916, the business was continued by his son, Thomas Edward Rawlings.

*Mark entered in two sizes.

Reid & Sons

† 19 June 1846
David Reid (No. 1), Plate worker
14 Grey Street, Newcastle on Tyne

15 September 1885
Christian John Reid, Plate worker
41 Grey Street, Newcastle on Tyne
C. J. Reid's residence: Oakfield, Benwell, Newcastle on Tyne

** 28 February 1901
Reid & Sons, Gold and Silver workers
41 Grey Street and 48 Grainger Street, Newcastle on Tyne
residences: T. A. Reid: 83 Hunters Road, Newcastle
F. J. Langford: 35 Edwards Road, Whitley
C. L. Reid: 1 Wardle Terrace, Newcastle
partners: Thomas Arthur Reid, Francis James Langford, Christian
Leopold Reid

* 29 June 1909
Reid & Sons, Gold and Silver workers
Gem Buildings, Blackett Street, Newcastle
C. L. Reid's residence: 26 Highbury, Newcastle on Tyne
partners: Thomas Arthur Reid, Christian Leopold Reid, William
Septimus Leete

(Marks) defaced 7.9.1938

* 9 July 1909 (Entry as for 29.6.1909)

This Newcastle upon Tyne firm was founded in 1778 by Christian Ker
Reid, a working silversmith. He was born in 1756 and died on 18 September
1834. (For Christian Ker Reid's marks from 1815 to 1834, see *Marks of
London Goldsmiths and Silversmiths c.1697–1837*, revised edition 1988, p.
266).

Following his death, the firm was continued by his three sons in
partnership: William Ker Reid, David Reid (No. 1) and Christian Bruce
Reid. At the time, William Ker Reid was already running his own firm of
manufacturing silversmiths in London (see Edward Ker Reid), so he is more
likely to have taken only an advisory role within the firm. (For William Ker
Reid's marks from 1812 to 1828, see *Marks of London Goldsmiths and
Silversmiths c.1697–1837*, revised edition 1988, p. 268).

In 1843 the firm moved from 12 Dean Street to 14 Grey Street,
Newcastle, where it remained until early this century. On 6 December 1845
Christian Bruce Reid retired from the partnership, leaving his two brothers
to continue running the firm. They were joined by David Reid (No. 1)'s
son, Christian John Reid. Meanwhile, the firm continued trading as Reid &

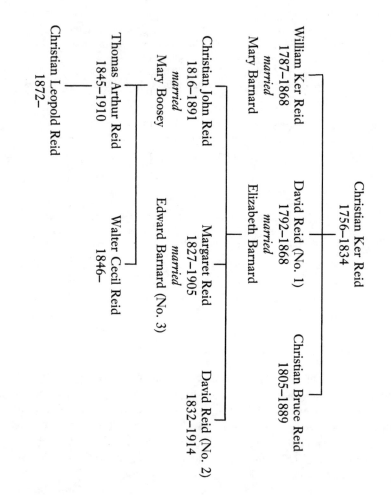

Christian Ker Reid
1756–1834

William Ker Reid
1787–1868
married
Mary Barnard

David Reid (No. 1)
1792–1868
married
Elizabeth Barnard

Christian Bruce Reid
1805–1889

Christian John Reid
1816–1891
married
Mary Boosey

Margaret Reid
1827–1905
married
Edward Barnard (No. 3)

David Reid (No. 2)
1832–1914

Thomas Arthur Reid
1845–1910

Walter Cecil Reid
1846–

Christian Leopold Reid
1872–

Sons, goldsmiths, silversmiths, jewellers and watchmakers.

On 31 March 1858 William Ker Reid retired, leaving David Reid (No. 1) and his son, Christian John Reid, to continue running the firm. At the time, William Ker Reid's own firm in London was already being run by his son, Edward Ker Reid.

Following David Reid (No. 1)'s death in 1868, Christian John Reid was joined by his two sons, Thomas Arthur Reid and Walter Cecil Reid, together with Christian John Reid's brother, David Reid (No. 2). On 31 July 1882 David Reid (No. 2) retired, and in 1891 Christian John Reid died, leaving the firm to be continued by his two sons, Thomas Arthur Reid and Walter Cecil Reid in partnership with Francis James Langford.

Following Walter Cecil Reid's retirement on 1 April 1895, Thomas Arthur Reid's son, Christian Leopold Reid, became a partner. By 1909 Francis James Langford had disappeared from the partnership to be replaced by William Septimus Leete. With the death of Thomas Arthur Reid in 1910, the partners were reduced to Christian Leopold Reid and William Septimus Leete.

In 1930 the firm was converted into a limited liability company trading as Reid & Sons Ltd. In 1967 the firm became a subsidiary of the Northern Goldsmiths Co. Ltd.

The following details relate to members of the Reid family, previously mentioned.

William Ker Reid was born in 1787, the son of Christian Ker Reid, silversmith. He married Mary Barnard, the daughter of Edward Barnard (No. 1) (silversmith, Citizen and Goldsmith) of Paternoster Row, London, on 11 February 1812. She was born on 25 April 1792 and died on 24 October 1845. They had thirteen children, seven boys and six girls, of whom only seven lived beyond the age of thirteen. The eldest surviving boy was Edward Ker Reid, one of twin boys. The other twin died when fourteen months old. William Ker Reid obtained his freedom of the Goldsmiths' Company by Redemption on 2 November 1814 and was made a Liveryman in April 1818. On 1 January 1853 his son, Edward Ker Reid, took over the London firm and then, on 31 March 1858, William Ker Reid retired from Reid & Sons. He died on 1 February 1868 aged 81.

David Reid (No. 1) was born on 26 March 1792, the son of Christian Ker Reid, silversmith. On 26 August 1815 he married Elizabeth Barnard, the daughter of Edward Barnard (No. 1) (silversmith, Citizen and Goldsmith) of Paternoster Row, London. Presumably David Reid (No. 1) had originally met Elizabeth through family relations, since David's brother, William Ker Reid, had already married Elizabeth's sister, Mary. Elizabeth was born on 4 May 1794 and died on 8 June 1870. They had ten children, four boys and six girls, including Christian John Reid and David Reid (No. 2), both of whom became partners in Reid & Sons. Another of their children was Margaret, born in 1827, who married her cousin, Edward Barnard (No. 3), silversmith, in 1853 (see Edward Barnard & Sons). David Reid (No. 1) died on 7 February 1868 aged 75, only six days after the death of his brother, William Ker Reid. One wonders if news of his brother's death brought about his own.

Christian Bruce Reid, the son of Christian Ker Reid (silversmith), was born in 1805 and died in 1889.

Christian John Reid, the son of Elizabeth and David Reid (No. 1) (silversmith), was born on 12 November 1816. On 19 September 1840 he married Mary Boosey, the daughter of Thomas Boosey, who was a cousin of David Reid (No. 1). Mary and Christian John Reid had nine children, four boys and five girls, of whom only four survived beyond 32 years of age. These four included Thomas Arthur Reid and Walter Cecil Reid, both of whom became partners in the firm. Christian John Reid died on 19 April 1891 and his wife, Mary, in April 1903.

Thomas Arthur Reid, the son of Mary and Christian John Reid, retail silversmith, was born on 13 February 1845. In 1871 he married Ida Selby. They had three children, two boys and a girl, including Christian Leopold Reid, who subsequently became a partner in the firm. Thomas Arthur Reid died in 1910.

Walter Cecil Reid, the son of Mary and Christian John Reid, retail silversmith, was born on 21 August 1846. He married Helen Sandeman in April 1877, by whom he had five children, four boys and a girl.

Christian Leopold Reid, the son of Ida and Thomas Arthur Reid, was born on 19 December 1872. He married his cousin, Nora Sandeman. She was born on 18 November 1875 and died on 16 August 1924.

*Mark entered in two sizes.
**Mark entered in three sizes.
†Mark entered in five sizes.

Edward Ker Reid

 ** 31 July 1855
Edward Ker Reid, Plate worker
manufactory: 5 Bream's Buildings, Chancery Lane
E. K. Reid's residence: 3 Brooksby Street, Liverpool Road, Islington

Removed to 4 Gough Square, Fleet Street, 23 June 1874

E·K·R 1 January 1883

EKR ** 12 January 1883

Edward Ker Reid was born on 24 October 1821, the son of Mary (née Barnard) and William Ker Reid. His maternal grandfather was the silversmith Edward Barnard (No. 1), who established the firm of Edward Barnard & Sons of London, and his paternal grandfather was the silversmith Christian Ker Reid, who founded the firm of Reid & Sons of Newcastle upon Tyne. His father, William Ker Reid, was born in 1787 and married Mary Barnard, the daughter of Edward Barnard (No. 1), on 11 February 1812. She was born on 25 April 1792 and died on 24 October 1845. They had thirteen children, seven boys and six girls, of whom only seven lived beyond the age of thirteen. The eldest surviving boy was Edward Ker Reid, one of twin boys. The other twin, William Ker Reid junior, died when fourteen months old. In 1832 they had another son, also named William Ker Reid, who was apprenticed to his brother, Edward Ker Reid, on 6 May 1846. This William Ker Reid died on 27 May 1855 when 23 years old without having obtained his freedom.

In 1812 William Kerr Reid (senior) joined Joseph Cradock in partnership at 67 Leather Lane, and on 8 June 1812 they entered their joint mark at Goldsmiths' Hall. On 2 November 1814 William Ker Reid obtained his freedom of the Goldsmiths' Company by Redemption. He was made a Liveryman in April 1818. In 1825 he dissolved his partnership with Joseph Cradock and set up in business on his own account at 5 Bream's Buildings, Chancery Lane (for William Ker Reid's marks from 1812 to 1828, see *Marks of London Goldsmiths and Silversmiths c.1697–1837*, revised edition 1988, p. 268).

In 1834 William Ker Reid's father, Christian Ker Reid, died, leaving the Newcastle firm to be run by William Ker Reid and his two brothers, David Reid (No. 1) and Christian Bruce Reid. Since William Ker Reid was already running his own firm of manufacturing silversmiths in London, it is likely that his role in the Newcastle firm of Reid & Sons was advisory only.

On 1 June 1836 William Ker Reid's son, Edward Ker Reid, was apprenticed to his father to learn the trade of silversmith. He obtained his freedom of the Goldsmiths' Company by Patrimony on 2 November 1842 and was made a Liveryman in December 1848. On 26 August 1847 he married Anna Barnard, the eldest daughter of John Barnard (No. 1)

245

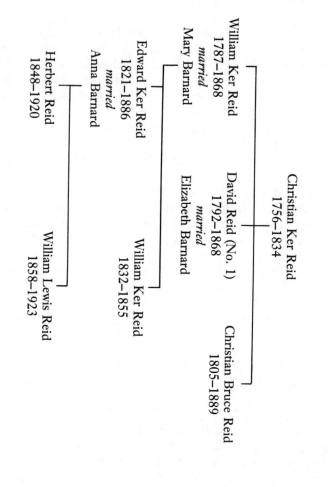

Christian Ker Reid
1756–1834

William Ker Reid
1787–1868
married
Mary Barnard

David Reid (No. 1)
1792–1868
married
Elizabeth Barnard

Christian Bruce Reid
1805–1889

Edward Ker Reid
1821–1886
married
Anna Barnard

William Ker Reid
1832–1855

Herbert Reid
1848–1920

William Lewis Reid
1858–1923

(silversmith, Citizen and Goldsmith). They were cousins, both being the grandchildren of Edward Barnard (No. 1). She was born on 19 January 1827 and died on 18 June 1898. They had ten children, five boys and five girls. The eldest son, Herbert Reid, was born on 8 June 1848 and apprenticed to John Barnard (No. 1) on 2 July 1862 to learn the trade of silversmith. He obtained his freedom of the Goldsmiths' Company by Patrimony on 7 July 1869 and died on 9 October 1920. Another son, William Lewis Reid, was born on 2 September 1858 and obtained his freedom of the Goldsmiths' Company by Patrimony on 3 March 1880. He died on 2 April 1923.

Circa 1847 William Ker Reid entered into partnership with his son, Edward Ker Reid, at the same time changing the firm's name to W. K. Reid & Son. Then, on 1 January 1853, he retired from the partnership, leaving Edward Ker Reid to continue running the firm. In 1855 the firm's name was changed to Edward Ker Reid, remaining as such until the firm's closure *circa* 1886.

On 31 March 1858 William Ker Reid retired from the firm of Reid & Sons of Newcastle. He died on 1 February 1868 aged 81.

In 1874 the firm of Edward Ker Reid moved to 4 Gough Square, Fleet Street, where it traded as silver plate manufacturers until its closure following the death of Edward Ker Reid on 10 February 1886.

**Marks entered in three sizes.

Manoah Rhodes & Sons Ltd

** 12 August 1893
Ackroyd Rhodes, Plate worker
31 St Bride Street, Ludgate Circus, London
A. Rhodes's residence: 2 St Hildas, Frizinghall, Bradford

*** 28 August 1895
Removed to 64 Hatton Garden, London

18 December 1907
Manoah Rhodes & Sons Ltd, Silver workers
45 Kirkgate, Bradford
A. Rhodes's residence: Brieryfield House, Frizinghall, Bradford
partner: Ackroyd Rhodes

** 30 June 1910
Manoah Rhodes & Sons Ltd, Silver workers
45 Kirkgate, Bradford
A. Rhodes's residence: 1167 Grangefield Avenue, Thornbury, Bradford
partner: Ackroyd Rhodes

** 4 August 1910
Manoah Rhodes & Sons Ltd, Gold and Silver workers
45 Kirkgate, Bradford
A. Rhodes's residence: 1167 Grangefield Avenue, Thornbury, Bradford
managing director & secretary: Ackroyd Rhodes

This worker died in 1915 and the next entry is that of F. C. M. S. Rhodes

This Bradford firm of silversmiths is thought to have been established in the 1830s. In 1888 the firm was converted into a limited liability company, trading as Manoah Rhodes & Sons Ltd with Thomas Ackroyd Rhodes (otherwise known as Ackroyd Rhodes) as managing director.

On 7 January 1907, the firm's mark was entered at the Sheffield Assay Office, giving its address as Kirkgate, Bradford. Following Ackroyd Rhodes's death in 1915, the firm was continued by F. C. M. S. Rhodes.

**Mark entered in three sizes.
***Mark entered in four sizes.

Richards & Brown

* 16 May 1844
George John Richards, Plate worker
26½ Sekforde Street, Clerkenwell

7 June 1845

Removed to 35 Whiskin Street, Clerkenwell, 13 April 1849

Removed to 20 Red Lion Street, Clerkenwell, 28 April 1852

* 16 April 1855

GR

 * 13 July 1857
George Richards and Edward Brown, Plate workers
20 Red Lion Street, Clerkenwell
G. J. Richards's residence: Willow Lodge, West Green Road,
Tottenham

 ** 16 October 1865

 ** 25 April 1867
Edward Charles Brown, Plate worker
20 Red Lion Street, Clerkenwell

10 July 1871

This firm was established *circa* 1843 by George John Richards, the son of William Richards (silversmith, Citizen and Goldsmith). William Richards had been apprenticed to John Gwyn Holmes (silversmith, Citizen and Goldsmith) of Clerkenwell Green on 4 December 1805 then turned over by consent to John Clarke (silversmith, Citizen and Lorimer) of Clerkenwell Green on 4 November 1807. He had obtained his freedom of the Goldsmiths' Company by Service on 3 March 1813.

George John Richards, born *circa* 1817, obtained his freedom of the Goldsmiths' Company by Patrimony on 6 February 1839 and was made a Liveryman in June 1864. He entered his first mark at Goldsmiths' Hall in 1844, trading as a silversmith at 26½ Sekforde Street.

On 5 March 1845 Edward Charles Brown, the son of Henry Brown (deceased) of Copenhagen Street, Islington, was apprenticed to George John Richards (silversmith, Citizen and Goldsmith). Edward Charles Brown obtained his freedom of the Goldsmiths' Company by Service on 7 April

1852 and was made a Liveryman in January 1875.

Circa 1857 George John Richards took Edward Charles Brown into partnership. At the same time, the firm's name was changed to Richards & Brown, silversmiths.

Following George John Richards' retirement on 30 March 1867, Edward Charles Brown continued trading as Richards & Brown, wholesale silversmiths. George John Richards died on 23 August 1876. *Circa* November 1882 Edward Charles Brown retired, leaving the firm to be continued by John Williams Johnson and Alfred Springthorpe. They entered their mark at Goldsmiths' Hall on 12 December 1882 (see Johnson & Springthorpe). Edward Charles Brown died on 20 January 1883.

George John Richards had two brothers, William Henry Richards (engraver) and Charles Edwin Richards (silversmith). They obtained their freedom of the Goldsmiths' Company by Patrimony on 4 January 1837 and 6 April 1847 respectively. Also, George John Richards had a son, Matthew Wilks Richards (average adjuster), who obtained his freedom by Patrimony on 3 October 1877. William Comyns was apprenticed to George John Richards in 1849 and obtained his freedom in 1856 (see William Comyns & Sons).

Edward Charles Brown had two sons, Edward Charles Brown (chartered accountant) and Spencer Douglas Brown (surveyor and land agent), both of whom obtained their freedom of the Goldsmiths' Company by Patrimony on 5 July 1898. In the archives at Goldsmiths' Hall there is a letter from Edward Charles Brown junior dated 26 February 1938, stating that George John Richards was his uncle as well as being his father's partner in Richards & Brown.

*Mark entered in two sizes.
**Mark entered in three sizes.

Roberts and Belk

2 June 1865
Samuel Roberts and Charles Belk, Plate workers
Furnival Works, Sheffield
28 Ely Place, Holborn (London)
S. Roberts's residence: Sharrow Mount, Sheffield
C. Belk's residence: Kenwood Bank, Sheffield

8 January 1878

**

** 5 July 1883
Charles Belk, Plate worker
Furnival Works, Sheffield
Gresham House, 24 Holborn Viaduct, London
C. Belk's residence: Kenwood Bank, Sheffield

** 21 March 1901
C. Belk's residence: Holmwood, Eccleshall, Sheffield

Charles Belk died during 1905 and the next entry is that of
Roberts & Belk Ltd

** 13 March 1906
Roberts & Belk Ltd, Silver workers
Furnival Works, Sheffield
24 Holborn Viaduct, London
193 Clarence Street, Sydney, NSW
D. F. Bell's residence: Martin, Cherry Orchard Road,
Bromley Common, Kent
directors: Walter Patrick Belk, secretary
Duncan F. Bell, London director
Frank E. Hallam

This Sheffield firm of silversmiths was founded in 1809 as Furniss, Poles & Turner of Furnival Street, its mark of 'MF & Co' in a rectangular surround being registered at the Sheffield Assay Office on 20 December 1810. *Circa* 1825 the firm was taken over by William Briggs and then, in 1845, it passed to Samuel Roberts and Joseph Slater, trading as Roberts & Slater. The firm's mark of 'R & S' in a rectangular surround was registered at the Sheffield Assay Office on 1 September 1845. Joseph Slater retired on 1 July 1858 and was subsequently replaced by another William Briggs who had joined the firm *circa* 1841, but it was not until September 1859 that a new mark of 'R & B' in a rectangular surround was registered at the Sheffield Assay Office under the name of Roberts & Briggs.

On 30 June 1863 the partnership between Roberts and Briggs was dissolved. By February 1864 Samuel Roberts had entered into partnership

251

with Charles Belk, trading as Roberts & Belk, and had registered a new mark of 'R & B' in a rectangular surround at the Sheffield Assay Office. In June 1865 the firm entered its mark for the first time at Goldsmiths' Hall, London.

Samuel Roberts retired on 1 July 1879, and on 17 July 1879 a new mark of 'CB' over 'EP' in a square surround, representing Charles Belk and E. Parkin, was entered at the Sheffield Assay Office.

Samuel Roberts was born in 1809 and died in September 1885. Charles Belk was born in 1840 and died in November 1904, not during 1905 as stated in the register of marks at Goldsmiths' Hall.

In 1901 the firm was converted into a limited liability company with Charles Belk and his son, Walter Patrick Belk, as directors. Walter Patrick Belk, born on 18 March 1872, trained as an architect and became a Fellow of the Royal Institute of British Architects. He obtained his freedom of the Goldsmiths' Company by Special Grant on 13 February 1929 and was made a Liveryman at the same ceremony. In 1961 he sold the firm of Roberts & Belk Ltd to C. J. Vander Ltd, manufacturing silversmiths of 14A St Cross Street, Hatton Garden. He died in August 1963.

**Mark entered in three sizes.

Rosenthal, Jacob & Co.

J·L·R	13 September 1867 Judah Louis Rosenthal, Gold worker 53 Greek Street J. L. Rosenthal's residence: 355 Oxford Street
	Removed to 4 Southampton Street, Fitzroy Square, 19 May 1876
JLR	24 July 1879
JR SJ	31 May 1881 Judah Rosenthal and Samuel Jacob, Gold workers 4 Southampton Street, Fitzroy Square S. Jacob's residence: 68 Colvestone Crescent, Dalston
JR SJ	
JR SJ	17 October 1882

252

JR / SJ

2 December 1885
S. Jacob's residence: removed to 13 Goldhurst Road, South Hampstead

JR / SJ

JR / SJ

29 June 1889

J R

20 September 1892
Julius Rosenthal, Plate worker
23 Southampton Street, Fitzroy Square

JR

LR

10 January 1896
Loewe Rosenthal, Silver worker
21 Southampton Street, Fitzroy Square

Removed to 48 Potsdown Road, Maida Vale, 8 December 1896
(L. Rosenthal's residence)

LR

7 May 1901

Julius Loewe Rosenthal, alias Judah Louis Rosenthal, established this business in 1867, trading as a goldsmith at 53 Greek Street. In 1876 he moved premises to 4 Southampton Street, and then, in 1881, he entered into partnership with Samuel Jacob, trading as Rosenthal, Jacob & Co., art workers in silver and manufacturers of hand mirrors, hand brushes, various small works and jewellery. This partnership was dissolved in September 1892 with Samuel Jacob moving to 22 Air Street, Regent Street, and Julius Rosenthal trading from 23 Southampton Street as Rosenthal & Co., silversmiths.

In June 1895 Rosenthal & Co. was closed down due to Julius Rosenthal's debts. Following his bankruptcy and public examination, it seems he may have recommenced trading in January 1896, but this time as an 'assistant' to his son, Loewe Judah Rosenthal, who entered marks at Goldsmiths' Hall in 1896 and 1901. This new firm traded under the name of Loewe Rosenthal. Loewe Judah Rosenthal obtained his freedom of the Goldsmiths' Company by Special Grant on 4 December 1901. He was a manufacturing silversmith and a member of the City Imperial Volunteers.

John Round & Son Ltd

20 October 1888
Joseph Ridge, Plate worker
Tudor Street, Sheffield
residence: 340 Gessop Street, Sheffield
partner: Joseph Ridge, manager to John Round & Son Ltd,
Sheffield

* 4 June 1894
John Round & Son Ltd, Plate workers
Tudor Works, Tudor Street, Sheffield
114 and 115 Holborn, EC

28 January 1898
Joseph Ridge, Gold and Silver worker
Tudor Works, Tudor Street, Sheffield
residence: 9 Clarkson Street, Sheffield

4 April 1901
Two new marks
J. Ridge's residence: 30 Oakholme Road, Sheffield

London address: 20 High Holborn, WC

This Sheffield firm of manufacturing silversmiths, electroplaters and Britannia metal workers was established by John Round in 1847. Prior to that date he was an employee of William Hutton, electroplate manufacturer of 27 High Street, Sheffield.

In 1847 John Round commenced trading on his own account at a house with attached workshop in Tudor Street, Sheffield. Initially he manufactured spoons and forks only, but the business grew so rapidly that he was frequently having to acquire additional premises. Having taken his son, Edwin, into partnership, he renamed the firm John Round & Son. Meanwhile, the firm continued to expand until it was manufacturing all types of silver and electroplated goods.

In July 1874 the firm was converted into a limited liability company trading as John Round & Son Ltd, its directors being Henry Pawson, Joseph Gamble and J. W. Barber. John Round having retired, he received shares in the firm in return for the continued use of his name. He died on 18 March 1877.

In January 1886 John Round & Son Ltd absorbed the firm of Ridge, Allcard & Co., electroplate manufacturers of Lion Works, Eyre Lane,

Sheffield. One of this firm's partners, Joseph Ridge, was made manager of John Round & Son Ltd, a position he continued to hold until early in 1911. He died in 1919 when 74 years old. Meanwhile his elder son, Alfred Ridge, became a director of Hawksworth, Eyre & Co. Ltd, manufacturing silversmiths, in 1915.

*Mark entered in two sizes.

A. B. Savory & Sons

7 September 1833
Adey Bellamy Savory, Joseph Savory (No. 2) and Albert Savory (No. 1), Plate workers and spoon makers
14 Cornhill
Factories at 15 Gee Street, Goswell Street and at 5 Finsbury Place South

5 July 1834
Adey Bellamy Savory, Joseph Savory (No. 2) and Albert Savory (No. 1)
14 Cornhill
Factories at 15 Gee Street, Goswell Street and at 5 Finsbury Place South

2 January 1835
Joseph Savory (No. 2) and Albert Savory (No. 1), Plate workers
14 Cornhill
Factory at 5 Finsbury Place South
Trading under the firm of A. B. Savory & Sons

14 November 1835
Joseph Savory (No. 2) and Albert Savory (No. 1)
14 Cornhill

22 December 1841
Joseph Savory (No. 2) and Albert Savory (No. 1), Spoon makers
9 and 14 Cornhill
5 Finsbury Place South
Trading under the firm of A. B. Savory & Sons

255

J S
A S

J S
A S

18 January 1844
Joseph Savory (No. 2) and Albert Savory (No. 1)
9 and 14 Cornhill
5 Finsbury Place South
J. Savory's residence: Elm Field, Upper Clapton
A. Savory's residence: Hale End, Walthamstow, Essex

J S
A S

J S
A S

29 June 1846
Joseph Savory (No. 2) and Albert Savory (No. 1), Spoon makers
9 & 14 Cornhill
5 Finsbury Place South
J. Savory's residence: Elm Field, Upper Clapton
A. Savory's residence: Hale End, Walthamstow, Essex

J.S
A.S

** (No date. Entered between 29 November and 4 December 1854. Marks subsequently defaced)

Trading under the firms of A. B. Savory & Sons and T. Cox Savory & Co.

J
A S H
E

*** 5 March 1880
Joseph Savory (No. 3), Albert Savory (No. 2), Horace Savory and Ethelbert Savory, Plate workers
11 and 12 Cornhill
18 Red Lion Street
J. Savory (No. 3)'s residence: Buckhurst Park, Sunninghill, Berks
A. Savory (No. 2)'s residence: Potters Park, Chertsey
H. Savory's residence:
Canes Wood, Weybridge
E. Savory's residence: Clifton Downs, Sidcup, Kent

(Marks) defaced 15.10.1884

JSH

** 14 October 1884
Joseph Savory (No. 3) and Horace Savory, Plate workers
11 and 12 Cornhill, EC
18 Red Lion Street, EC
J. Savory (No. 3)'s residence: Buckhurst Park, Sunninghill, Berks
H. Savory's residence: Ranmore Lodge, Guildford

Marks produced and defaced 14 April 1893

This firm was founded *circa* 1812 by Adey Bellamy Savory, the son of Joseph Savory (No. 1) (Citizen and Goldsmith). Joseph Savory (No. 1) had been apprenticed to James Hunt (Citizen and Goldsmith) on 2 July 1760 and had obtained his freedom of the Goldsmiths' Company by Service on 3 February 1768.

Adey Bellamy Savory obtained his freedom of the Goldsmiths' Company by Patrimony on 6 October 1802, but did not enter his first mark at Goldsmiths' Hall until 14 February 1826. He entered subsequent marks on 13.10.1826, 11.11.1826, 11.11.1829, 3.4.1830 and 26.1.1832 (for illustrations of these marks, see *Marks of London Goldsmiths and Silversmiths c.1697–1837*, revised edition 1988, p. 290).

In 1833 he changed the firm's name to A. B. Savory & Sons, entering new marks at Goldsmiths' Hall in partnership with two of his sons, Joseph Savory (No. 2) and Albert Savory (No. 1). It seems that his sons took over control of the firm towards the end of 1834, following which they entered their own partnership mark in 1835.

Adey Bellamy Savory had four sons: Thomas Cox Savory, Joseph Savory (No. 2), Albert Savory (No. 1) and Adey Bellamy Savory junior, all of whom obtained their freedom of the Goldsmiths' Company by Patrimony. Adey Bellamy Savory junior obtained his freedom on 3 March 1841 and traded at 46 Cornhill as a bookseller, stationer and dressing-case maker.

Thomas Cox Savory obtained his freedom by Patrimony on 2 December 1829, by which time he was already trading at 54 Cornhill as Thomas Cox Savory & Co., silversmiths. This was the same address as used by his father, Adey Bellamy Savory, from *circa* 1826 until 1833. Thomas Cox Savory had already entered his first mark at Goldsmiths' Hall on 13 September 1827 with further marks on 2.11.1827 and 27.1.1832 (for illustrations of these marks, see *Marks of London Goldsmiths and Silversmiths c.1697–1837*, revised edition 1988, p. 292).

Joseph Savory (No. 2) was born on 24 July 1808 and died on 16 December 1879. His wife, Mary Caroline, was born on 21 July 1818 and died on 7 January 1887. Both Joseph Savory (No. 2) and his brother, Albert Savory (No. 1), obtained their freedoms by Patrimony on 4 December 1833.

Circa 1854 the firms of A. B. Savory & Sons and Thomas Cox Savory & Co. were united, apparently under one ownership, but continued to trade under their own names. In 1866 they were converted into a limited liability company, trading as the Goldsmiths' Alliance Ltd.

From August 1855 to September 1865, silverware produced by A. B. Savory & Sons was stamped with the mark of William Smily, and from October 1865 to March 1880 with that of his son, Samuel Smily. Apparently, William Smily was working for A. B. Savory & Sons in the 1830s and 1840s. He then became manager of Savory's factory in 1855, a position he held until his death on 9 September 1865. His son, Samuel Smily, then took over as manager, a position he retained until his retirement in March 1880.

On 5 March 1880, new marks were entered by the next generation of the Savory family. Joseph Savory (No. 3) and Ethelbert Keston Savory were the sons of Joseph Savory (No. 2), while Albert Savory (No. 2) and Horace Savory were the sons of Albert Savory (No. 1).

Joseph Savory (No. 3) was born on 23 July 1843 and educated at Harrow. He obtained his freedom of the Goldsmiths' Company by Patrimony on 2 December 1874 and was made a Liveryman in December 1880. He was Sheriff of London and Middlesex in 1882–3 and became Alderman of London for the Langbourn Ward in 1883. In 1888 he married Helen Pemberton Leach, the daughter of Lt.-Col. Sir George Archibald Leach KCB, RE. In 1890–1 he was Lord Mayor of London, and in 1891 he was created a baronet. As Sir Joseph Savory, he sat as Member of Parliament for Westmoreland North from 1892 to 1900 when he was defeated. He died on 1 October 1921, and his widow, Helen Pemberton, on 4 November 1939.

Ethelbert Keston Savory, Albert Savory (No. 2) and Horace Savory obtained their freedoms by Patrimony on 2 December 1874, the same day as Joseph Savory (No. 3). Horace Savory was made a Liveryman in June 1882 and died on 23 July 1937.

The firm continued trading until early in 1893 when it was voluntarily closed down and its stock sold at Christie's. Shortly afterwards, the business was disposed of to the Goldsmiths & Silversmiths Co. Ltd of 112 Regent Street.

*Mark entered in three sizes.
**Mark entered in four sizes.

Searle & Co.

(W.H.S)   *** 28 March 1899
Walter Henry Searle, Gold and Silver worker
78–79 Lombard Street, EC
W. H. Searle's residence: 47 Tremadoc Road, Clapham

(W.H.S)   *** 6 July 1899

* 4 July 1901
Walter Henry Searle (Entry as for 28.3.1899)

*

22 November 1906
Searle and Company, Gold and Silver workers
78–79 Lombard Street, London, SW
W. H. Searle's residence: 17 Cavendish Gardens, Clapham Park, SW
director: Walter Henry Searle

Walter H. Searle went out of the firm of Searle & Co. in 1907

20 March 1908
Searle and Company, Gold and Silver workers
78–79 Lombard Street, London, EC
residence: Pobruan, Seaford, Sussex
directors: Frank Eady, Arthur Borlase Eady

† (No date. Some time in June 1908)
Searle and Company (Entry as for 20.3.1908)

This firm was founded by Walter Henry Searle *circa* 1893. In 1895 he moved to 78–79 Lombard Street where he traded as Searle & Co., silversmiths and jewellers. In 1897 he entered into partnership with Frank Eady and Arthur Borlase Eady, but continued to trade under the name of Searle & Co. This partnership was dissolved on 29 April 1907 due to Walter Henry Searle having used several thousands of pounds of the firm's money to speculate on the Stock Exchange.

Following Walter Henry Searle's retirement from Searle & Co., the firm was continued by Frank Eady and his brother, Arthur Borlase Eady. With the death of Frank Eady on 30 January 1909, Searle & Co. was acquired from his widow, Ida Eady, and Arthur Borlase Eady. It was then converted into a limited liability company, trading as Searle & Co. Ltd. Its directors were Arthur Borlase Eady and W. T. Leviansky.

Frank Eady (jeweller, Citizen and Goldsmith), the son of Thomas William Eady (goldsmith, jeweller, Citizen and Goldsmith), obtained his freedom of the Goldsmiths' Company by Patrimony on 4 July 1877. He was made a Liveryman in December 1880 and an Assistant in June 1898. He became

4th Warden in 1902, 3rd Warden in 1903, 2nd Warden in 1904 and Prime Warden in 1905.

Arthur Borlase Eady (diamond broker, Citizen and Goldsmith), the son of Thomas William Eady (goldsmith, jeweller, Citizen and Goldsmith) obtained his freedom of the Goldsmiths' Company by Patrimony on 7 December 1881 and was made a Liveryman in February 1887. He died on 3 December 1940.

Frank Eady and Arthur Borlase Eady came from a long line of Freemen of the Goldsmiths' Company. Their great-grandfather, William Eady, was a Freeman of the Company at the end of the eighteenth century. Their grandfather, William Eady (jeweller, Citizen and Goldsmith), was apprenticed to their great-grandfather on 1 April 1807 and obtained his freedom by Service on 4 January 1815. He was made a Liveryman in February 1831 and died in April 1865.

Their father, Thomas William Eady, and uncle, Henry John Eady, both became goldsmiths and jewellers and both obtained their freedoms of the Goldsmiths' Company by Patrimony on 6 January 1847. H. J. Eady was made a Liveryman in July 1851 followed by T. W. Eady in May 1856. However, T. W. Eady died first, on 7 January 1892, followed by H. J. Eady exactly six months later, on 7 July 1892.

*Marks entered in two sizes.
***Marks entered in four sizes.
†Marks entered in five sizes.

Arthur Sibley

18 March 1853
Arthur Sibley, Plate worker
8 Pleasant Row, Pentonville Hill

Address renamed: 224 Pentonville Road, 11 January 1858

Removed to 15 Upper Charles Street, Goswell Road, 9 May 1860

Arthur Sibley was born on 6 June 1817, the son of Mary and Richard Sibley (No. 1) (silversmith, Citizen and Goldsmith) of Red Lion Street, Clerkenwell. (For illustrations of Richard Sibley (No. 1)'s marks, see *Marks of London Goldsmiths and Silversmiths c.1697–1837*, revised edition 1988, p. 302). On 6 July 1831 Arthur Sibley was apprenticed to his father to learn

260

the trade of silversmith. Following his father's death in 1836, he was not turned over to another Freeman of the Goldsmiths' Company to complete his apprenticeship; instead he obtained his freedom of the Goldsmiths' Company by Patrimony on 5 June 1839.

Having obtained his freedom, it seems likely that he continued working with his brother, Richard Sibley (No. 2), who had already taken over the family business following their father's death. In 1853 Arthur Sibley set up on his own account as a plate worker at 8 Pleasant Row, Pentonville Hill. In 1860 he moved to 15 Upper Charles Street, where he is listed as a silversmith until 1879.

Richard Sibley (Nos 2 and 3)

23 February 1836
Mary Sibley and Richard Sibley (No. 2), Plate workers
30 Red Lion Street, Clerkenwell

15 March 1837
Richard Sibley (No. 2), Spoon maker
30 Red Lion Street, Clerkenwell

21 June 1839
Removed to 10 Dufours Place, Broad Street, Golden Square

Removed to 30 Poland Street, Oxford Street, 6 September 1853

Removed to 18 Poland Street, Oxford Street, 30 July 1858

Removed to 13 Oxford Market, Oxford Street, 2 July 1862

10 July 1880
Richard Sibley (No. 3), Plate worker
3 Great Titchfield Street
residence: 25 Langham Street, Portland Place

Richard Sibley (No. 2), born *circa* 1807, was the son of Mary and Richard Sibley (No. 1) (silversmith, Citizen and Goldsmith) of Red Lion Street, Clerkenwell (see *Marks of London Goldsmiths and Silversmiths c.1697–1837*, revised edition 1988, p. 302). On 7 February 1821 he was apprenticed to his father to learn the trade of silversmith. He obtained his freedom of the

Goldsmiths' Company by Service on 4 February 1829, following which it is presumed he continued working with his father.

Following his father's death in early 1836, Richard Sibley (No. 2) and his mother, Mary, entered into partnership to continue running the family business. By 15 March 1837, however, Richard Sibley (No. 2) was trading on his own. His brother, Arthur Sibley, born in 1817, obtained his freedom of the Goldsmiths' Company by Patrimony on 5 June 1839 (see Arthur Sibley). Presumably he remained working in the family business until setting up on his own in early 1853. At about this time, Richard Sibley (No. 2) entered into partnership with Joseph Waple, trading as Sibley and Waple, manufacturing silversmiths, but this partnership was dissolved on 13 August 1853.

In the Census return for 1861, Richard Sibley (No. 2), aged 54, is described as a working silversmith employing five men and two boys. At the time, he was residing at 18 Poland Street together with his wife, Fanny, aged 39, and their two children, Fanny, aged 15, and Richard (No. 3), aged 5.

In 1862 he moved premises to 13 Oxford Market, where he remained until 1880. However, from 1874 Francis Boone Thomas was likewise giving this address as his premises when entering marks at Goldsmiths' Hall (see F. B. Thomas & Co.) Also, numerous articles of silverware have been noted bearing Sibley's maker's mark and Thomas's name as retailer. Therefore, it seems likely that, over a period of several years, Richard Sibley (No. 2) was manufacturing silverware to order for retailing by F. B. Thomas & Co.

In July 1880 new marks were entered at Goldsmiths' Hall by Richard Sibley (No. 3), trading from 3 Great Tichfield Street. Born *circa* 1856, he was the son of Fanny and Richard Sibley (No. 2) and obtained his freedom of the Goldsmiths' Company by Patrimony on 6 November 1878. It seems likely that he took over his father's business at this time.

Sibray, Hall & Co

 ** 20 May 1880
Frederick Sibray and Job Frank Hall, Plate workers
St Mary's Road, Sheffield
residences: F. Sibray: Eccleshall, Sheffield
J. F. Hall: Fitzwalter House, Sheffield

These marks erased 5.6.1893

1 June 1893
Job Frank Hall, Plate worker
† Fitzwalter Works, 111 St Mary's Road, Sheffield
30 Ely Place, London

20 February 1900
J. F. Hall having in January 1900 disposed of his interest in the
firm of Sibray, Hall & Co. Ltd to another director, C. C. Pilling

** 20 February 1900
Charles Clement Pilling, Silver worker
111 St Mary's Road, Sheffield
30 Ely Place, London
residence: Beauchief, Sheffield
Trading as Sibray, Hall & Co. Ltd

This Sheffield firm of manufacturing silversmiths was founded by Frederick
Sibray and Job Frank Hall *circa* 1878. They entered their first mark,
consisting of 'FS' over 'JH', at the Sheffield Assay Office on 28 October
1878, trading as Sibray, Hall & Co. at Fitzwalter Works, 111 St Mary's
Road, Sheffield. In 1880 they entered their first marks at Goldsmiths'
Hall, London, and *circa* 1890 they opened a London showroom at 30 Ely Place.

Following Frederick Sibray's death in 1891, the firm was continued by
Job Frank Hall in partnership with Charles Clement Pilling. In 1896 the
firm was converted into a limited liability company, trading as Sibray, Hall
& Co. Ltd, its directors being J. F. Hall, C. C. Pilling and G. Pilgrim.

Following Job Frank Hall's retirement in January 1900, the company was
continued by Charles Clement Pilling.

**Marks entered in three sizes.
†Mark entered in five sizes.

W. & G. Sissons

25 July 1864
Henry Smith, Plate worker
8 Duke Street, Adelphi, WC
residence: Knights Park, Kingston, Surrey

* 15 February 1866
William Sissons (No. 2) and George Sissons, Plate workers
9 Eyre Street, Sheffield
8 Duke Street, Adelphi (London)

* 22 February 1887
Walter Sissons and Charles Sissons, Plate workers
77 St Mary's Road, Sheffield
34 Southampton Street, Strand (London)
W. Sissons's residence: 32 Beatrice Road, Stroud Green, N
C. Sissons's residence: 110 Upperthorpe, Sheffield

21 January 1896 Removed to 3 Charterhouse Street, Holborn
Circus, EC
75–77 St Mary's Road, Sheffield
W. Sissons's residence: 80 Graham Road, Ranmoor, Sheffield
C. Sissons's residence: 34 St Mary's Road, Sheffield

This Sheffield firm of manufacturing silversmiths was founded *circa* 1784 by Samuel Roberts and George Cadman, trading as Roberts, Cadman & Co. By 1841 the firm was trading as Roberts, Smith & Co., but this partnership was dissolved in 1848 and the firm continued as Smith, Sissons & Co. with Evan Smith and William Sissons (No. 1) as partners. On 6 November 1858 this partnership was dissolved and the firm continued under William Sissons (No. 2) and George Sissons, trading as W. & G. Sissons. On 2 December 1858 they entered their first mark, 'WS' over 'GS', at the Sheffield Assay Office. In 1864 the firm's mark was entered for the first time at Goldsmiths' Hall, London, by Henry Smith using his own initials. By 1887 the firm's partners were Walter Sissons, who died in 1941, and Charles Sissons.

During the early part of this century the firm gradually diversified into other types of metal work. In 1943 the manufacturing silversmiths side of the firm was transferred to a subsidiary company trading as Bell Reproductions Ltd, while the parent company, W. & G. Sissons Ltd, specialised in manufacturing articles in stainless steel and other sheet metals.

*Mark entered in two sizes.

Samuel Smily (No. 1)

---

* 17 October 1865
Samuel Smily (No. 1), Plate worker

18 Red Lion Street, Clerkenwell
residence: 12 Chapel Street, Barnsbury

Removed to 19 Red Lion Street, 1 April 1880

Samuel Smily (No. 1) was born in 1825, the son of William Smily (silversmith, Citizen and Goldsmith). He was apprenticed to his father, of 5 Finsbury Place South, Clerkenwell, on 1 January 1840 to learn the art of silversmith and obtained his freedom of the Goldsmiths' Company by Service on 1 December 1847. In December 1869 he was made a Liveryman of the Goldsmiths' Company.

Having obtained his freedom, it is presumed that he continued working with his father at 5 Finsbury Place South, manufacturing silverware for retailing by A. B. Savory & Sons (see A. B. Savory & Sons). In the 1851 Census return, he is recorded as residing at 38 Sekforde Street, Clerkenwell, with his wife, Mary Ann, aged 26.

Circa 1855 his father, William Smily, became works manager for A. B. Savory & Sons, a position he held until his death (see William Smily). In April 1865 William Smily moved to 18 Red Lion Street, Clerkenwell, where he died on 9 September. Samuel Smily (No. 1) then took over his father's position as works manager for A. B. Savory & Sons. At the time, his working address was recorded as being 18 Red Lion Street. This address was subsequently listed in 1880 by A. B. Savory & Sons as its own factory. Unlike his father, Samuel Smily (No. 1) does not appear to have resided at 18 Red Lion Street since he had separate residential premises at 12 Chapel Street, Barnsbury.

On 1 April 1880 Samuel Smily (No. 1) retired from A. B. Savory & Sons, moving next door to 19 Red Lion Street. He died on 28 July 1882, leaving an estate of about £2,400. At the time of his death, he was described as a farmer and goldsmith, with the following three residences: Camps Farm, Green Leaves, Nazeing, Essex (inherited from his mother); St Helier's, Brook Road, Upper Clapton; and 19 Red Lion Street, Clerkenwell.

He and his wife, Mary Ann, are known to have had a daughter, Mary Ann, and a son, Samuel (No. 2), born in 1860. Samuel Smily (No. 2) was apprenticed to his father (silversmith, Citizen and Goldsmith), of 18 Red Lion Street, Clerkenwell, on 2 December 1874. He obtained his freedom of the Goldsmiths' Company by Service on 5 April 1882, giving his address at the time as St Helier's, Brook Street, Upper Clapton. Since he never entered his mark at Goldsmiths' Hall, it seems unlikely that he traded on his own as a silversmith. He died in 1930.

*Mark entered in two sizes.

Thomas Smily

** 10 July 1858
Thomas Smily, Plate and spoon maker
65 Crown Street, Finsbury Square

** 20 January 1863
Thomas Smily, Plate worker
65 Crown Street, Finsbury‡
residence: 32 Wellington Street, Barnsbury

‡now called 5 Sun Street, Finsbury, 7 March 1870

30 October 1866
residence:
Removed to Cumberland Villa, Albion Road, Holloway Road

*

26 April 1870

*

Business transferred to Purdie (no date)

Thomas Smily was born in 1827, the son of William Smily (silversmith, Citizen and Goldsmith) of 5 Finsbury Place South, Clerkenwell. He was apprenticed to his father on 5 May 1841 to learn the art of silversmith and obtained his freedom of the Goldsmiths' Company by Service on 4 October 1848. At the time, his address was recorded as being 5 Finsbury Place South, this being both the family residence and his father's place of work.

Having obtained his freedom, it is presumed that he continued working with his father and then with his brother, William Robert Smily, who was running his own business as spoon maker and plate manufacturer at 65 Crown Street, Finsbury Square, from 1852 (see William Robert Smily).

On 24 May 1858 William Robert Smily died at the age of 34. Following his death, Thomas Smily took over the business, but still continued to trade under the name of W. R. Smily.

Early in 1883 Thomas Smily disposed of the business to Edwin Charles Purdie, wholesale silversmith, who moved into the premises at 5 Sun Street by 3 July 1883 (see Edwin Charles Purdie). Meanwhile, Thomas Smily emigrated to Canada, where he died in 1918 aged 91.

*Mark entered in two sizes.
**Mark entered in three sizes.

William Smily

WS * 20 August 1855
William Smily, Plate worker
5 Finsbury Place South

WS * 28 January 1856

Removed to 18 Red Lion Street, Clerkenwell, 25 April 1865

William Smily was born in 1792, the son of James Smily (brassfounder deceased) of Barbican, London. On 5 July 1809 he was apprenticed to Joseph Preston (silver spoon and fork maker, Citizen and Goldsmith) of Hulls Terrace, City Road, Middlesex, to learn the art of silver spoon and fork maker. Following Joseph Preston's death, he was turned over to Thomas Wallis (No. 2) (working silversmith, Citizen and Goldsmith) of 16 Red Lion Street, Clerkenwell, on 5 April 1815. He did not take up his freedom of the Goldsmiths' Company upon completion of his apprenticeship, it being another fifteen years before he obtained it by Service on 5 May 1830. Since his address at the time was recorded as Gee Street, Goswell Street, it is likely he had recently commenced working for A. B. Savory & Sons. This firm first listed 15 Gee Street and 5 Finsbury Place South as being the addresses of its two factories in 1833 (see A. B. Savory & Sons).

Although Pigots Directory for 1832–4 lists William Smily, spoon maker, at 15 George Street, he was still residing and working at Gee Street in 1833 when his son, William Robert Smily, was apprenticed to him. By the end of 1834 A. B. Savory & Sons no longer listed Gee Street as being one of its premises, and William Smily was next recorded in January 1840 residing and working at 5 Finsbury Place South, another of Savory's factories. Here, the premises consisted of a large Georgian town house complete with cast-iron railings and steps up to the front door and outbuildings at the rear, which, presumably, were converted to workshop use. The property has since been demolished to make way for an office block (River Plate House near Broad Street station).

William Smily resided at 5 Finsbury Place South with his wife, Caroline Elizabeth, their three sons, William Robert, Samuel (No. 1) and Thomas, their daughter, Sarah, and a housekeeper cousin. Sarah Smily was a delicate child and eventually died of a fit while still young.

William Robert Smily was apprenticed to his father in 1833 and obtained his freedom in 1840. He entered his first mark at Goldsmiths' Hall in 1842 (see William Robert Smily).

Samuel Smily (No. 1) was apprenticed to his father in 1840 and obtained his freedom in 1847. He likewise worked for A. B. Savory & Sons (see Samuel Smily (No. 1)).

Thomas Smily was apprenticed to his father in 1841 and obtained his freedom in 1848. He entered his first mark in 1858 (see Thomas Smily).

Circa 1855 William Smily became works manager for A. B. Savory & Sons, entering his own marks at Goldsmiths' Hall in 1855 and 1856. These marks were used on silverware manufactured for the firm. Two such articles of silverware noted are a salver of 1862 and a teapot of 1865, both bearing William Smily's mark and stamped 'A. B. Savory & Sons'.

In April 1865 he moved to 18 Red Lion Street, Clerkenwell (now called Britton Street), where he died on 9 September 1865 leaving an estate of over £5,000. Since this address was listed by A. B. Savory & Sons in 1880 as being the firm's factory, it seems likely that William Smily used it for both manufacturing and residential purposes in 1865. Following his death, the vacant post of works manager at 18 Red Lion Street was taken by his son, Samuel Smily (No. 1). Under the terms of his father's will, he had inherited all of his father's books, tools, implements and trade patterns.

In later life, William Smily indulged in experimental farming. This he pursued at Camp Farm, Nazeing, Essex, which he owned and later bequeathed to his widow, Caroline Elizabeth. The farm subsequently became the Smily family's 'country residence', used for summer holidays until sold by William Smily's grandson, Samuel Smily (No. 2), in 1912.

*Mark entered in two sizes.

William Robert Smily

(WRS)   3 March 1842
William Robert Smily, Spoon maker
7 Seaward Street, Goswell Street

WRS   31 July 1844

Removed to 9 Camomile Street, City (no date)

(WRS)   30 May 1846

WRS   17 August 1847

Removed to 65 Crown Street, Finsbury Square, 3 September 1852

(WRS)   23 November 1852
(WR S)   William Robert Smily, Spoon maker
65 Crown Street, Finsbury Square

(WRS)   29 January 1857

(WRS)   30 May 1857
(WR)

William Robert Smily was born in 1823, the son of William Smily (spoon maker, Citizen and Goldsmith) of Gee Street, Goswell Street, Clerkenwell. He was apprenticed to his father on 2 January 1833 to learn the art of spoon maker and obtained his freedom of the Goldsmiths' Company by Service on 2 December 1840. His address at the time was 5 Finsbury Place South, this being both the family residence and his father's manufacturing premises.

In 1842 William Robert Smily established his own business, trading as W. R. Smily, spoon maker, at 7 Seaward Street, Goswell Street. *Circa* 1844 he moved to 9 Camomile Street, where he traded as a manufacturing silversmith. Then, in 1852, he moved to 65 Crown Street, Finsbury Square, where he traded as a silver spoon and fork maker, plate manufacturer and dealer in second-hand plate. These premises had previously been occupied by Charles Lias, spoon maker and plate manufacturer, from 1837 to 1847 (see Charles Lias) and by Judah Hart, spoon maker, from 1847 to 1852 (see

Judah Hart).

William Robert Smily died on 24 May 1858, aged 34, leaving an estate of over £7,000. Following his death, his business was continued by his brother, Thomas Smily, who entered his own mark at Goldsmiths' Hall on 10 July 1858, although continuing to trade under the name of W. R. Smily (see Thomas Smily).

William Robert Smily had two sons, William Robert (silver chaser) and Alfred (printer), both of whom obtained their freedom of the Goldsmiths' Company by Patrimony. William Robert Smily (silver chaser) was born in 1845 and obtained his freedom on 5 May 1869. Later, he emigrated to Australia, where he died in 1887. Alfred Smily (printer) obtained his freedom on 3 May 1871. Both sons at the time of their freedoms gave their residential address as 70 Malvern Road, Dalston.

James Smith & Sons

J.S	15 December 1877 James Smith, Small worker 467 Oxford Street 5 Hemmings Row 47 Moorgate Street 2 Savile Row
J . S	26 January 1881
J.S	3 February 1881
J.A.S	25 February 1881 James Albert Smith, Small worker 59 Oxford Street 5 Hemmings Row 47 Moorgate Street 2 Savile Row Bond Street Arcade
J.A.S	8 March 1881
J.A.S	16 February 1881
J.A.S.	29 August 1881
J.A.S.	4 October 1881

J.A.S	21 March 1882
J.A.S	27 January 1883
JAS	7 May 1883
J.A.S	8 October 1883 James Albert Smith, Small worker 59 New Oxford Street residence: 72 New Oxford Street
J.A.S	12 November 1883 (Entry as for 8.10.1883)
J.A.S	7 July 1884 (Entry as for 8.10.1883)
J·A·S	1 December 1885
JS&Ss	** 11 July 1904 James Smith & Sons, Gold and Silver stick mounters 57–59 New Oxford Street 72 New Oxford Street 1 Fouberts Place, Regent Street, W 1 Savile Place, Regent Street, W T. F. Smith's residence: 72 New Oxford Street, London, WC partners: Thomas Francis Smith, Robert Ernest Smith
JS&Ss	8 December 1913 James Smith & Sons, Gold and Silver mounters 57–59 New Oxford Street, WC 1 Savile Place, Regent Street, London, W T. F. Smith's residence: Trigarthen, 30 The Ridgeway, Golders Green partners: Thomas Francis Smith, Robert Ernest Smith

This firm of walking-stick mounters was founded by James Smith *circa* 1840, but it was not until December 1877 that he entered his first mark at Goldsmiths' Hall. At the time of his last entry on 3 February 1881, his signature was very shaky and it seems likely that he retired or died soon after, for on 25 February 1881 his son, James Albert Smith, entered his own mark at Goldsmiths' Hall for the first time.

James Albert Smith continued running the firm, still trading as James Smith & Sons, umbrella and walking-stick makers and stick mounters in gold and silver. *Circa* 1900 he emigrated to Tasmania with his daughter and two of his sons to start farming. Meanwhile, his various businesses in London were looked after by his other sons. Two of them, Thomas Francis Smith and Robert Ernest Smith, were appointed partners in James Smith & Sons and entered fresh marks in July 1904.

Today, the firm is still operating as umbrella and walking-stick manufacturers at 53 New Oxford Street.

**Mark entered in three sizes.

Samuel Smith & Son

S.S

23 February 1893
Samuel Smith, Gold and Silver workers
6 Grand Hotel Buildings, Trafalgar Square
9, 51, 85 Strand, WC
68 Piccadilly
residence: Lavington, Putney Heath

SS

26 June 1896

SS

24 June 1898

SS

SS   *

SS

21 March 1899

SS

SS

SS

(No date. *Circa* January/February 1909)
The Association of Diamond Merchants, Jewellers and Silversmiths, Gold and Silver workers
6 Grand Hotel Buildings, Trafalgar Square
Samuel Smith's residence: The Croft, Totteridge, Herts

SS

(This) Worker did not attend to complete, so entry was cancelled 22.7.1914

272

This firm of manufacturing watchmakers, jewellers and silversmiths was watchmakers to the Admiralty, producing non-magnetisable watches, split seconds chronographs and four-dial non-magnetic chronographs. Although the firm was trading as early as 1885, it did not register its first mark at Goldsmiths' Hall until 1893. In 1899 the firm was converted into a limited liability company, trading as Samuel Smith & Son Ltd.

The firm also traded as the Diamond Merchants' Alliance, otherwise known as the Association of Diamond Merchants, Jewellers & Silversmiths. This subsidiary firm was likewise converted into a limited liability company in 1899.

By 1913 the parent company had received Royal Warrants for the manufacture of speed indicators.

When the firm went into voluntary liquidation in 1930, a portion of the business was acquired by S. Smith & Sons (Motor Accessories) Ltd. This firm subsequently became S. Smith & Sons (England) Ltd and, eventually, Smith Industries Ltd.

*Mark entered in two sizes.

S. W. Smith & Co.

24 February 1882
Samuel Watton Smith, Plate worker
57 Cambridge Street, Birmingham
residence: 67 Wheeleys Road, Birmingham

9 June 1882
40 Whitfield Street, London
residence: 16 George Street, Birmingham

Removed to 1 Dyers Buildings, Holborn, EC, 8 February 1887

* 8 September 1897
Samuel Watton Smith, Silver worker
57 Cambridge Street, Birmingham
20 High Holborn, London
12–13 Grays Inn Chambers

** 7 November 1900
Samuel Watton Smith and Company, Silver workers
57 Cambridge Street, Birmingham
20 High Holborn, London
12–13 Grays Inn Chambers

S.W.S & Co   signed: John B. Carrington, partner in S. W. Smith & Co.

Removed to 32 Brewer Street, Golden Square, W, 29 January 1907
signed: W. Carrington Smith, partner in S. W. Smith & Co.

(no mark)   20 July 1910
S. W. Smith & Co., Gold and Silver workers
Cambridge Street, Birmingham
6 Great Pulteney Street, Golden Square, W
W. C. Smith's residence: 105 Lancaster Gate, W
signed: W. Carrington Smith, sole partner in S. W. Smith & Co.

This Birmingham firm of manufacturing silversmiths and platers was founded by Samuel Watton Smith. In 1882, as representative of S. W. Smith & Co., he entered into partnership with John Bodman Carrington representing G. R. Collis & Co., manufacturing silversmiths of 57 Cambridge Street, Birmingham, and 130 Regent Street, London. At the time, J. B. Carrington was also sole partner at Carrington & Co., retail and manufacturing silversmiths, likewise of 57 Cambridge Street and 130 Regent Street. Apparently both G. R. Collis & Co. and Carrington & Co. were under his control and were sharing the same premises in Birmingham and London while still trading as separate firms (see G. R. Collis & Co. and Carrington & Co.).

Under the terms of the partnership between Samuel Watton Smith and John Bodman Carrington, S. W. Smith & Co. appears to have taken over G. R. Collis & Co.'s factory at 57 Cambridge Street, where it continued to manufacture goods for sale by both G. R. Collis & Co. and Carrington & Co. at their Regent Street showrooms. At the same time, the factory also supplied goods to S. W. Smith & Co.'s own showroom at 40 Whitfield Street, London. This showroom was moved to 1 Dyers Buildings, Holborn, in February 1887 and then to 20 High Holborn by September 1897.

On 31 December 1888 the partnership between Samuel Watton Smith and John Bodman Carrington was dissolved, possibly due to S. W. Smith's retirement. J. B. Carrington then continued as partner, running both S. W. Smith & Co. and G. R. Collis & Co., together with Carrington & Co.

In 1893 G. R. Collis & Co. was absorbed by Carrington & Co. Then, on 1 January 1906, J. B. Carrington retired from S. W. Smith & Co. and Carrington & Co., leaving both firms to be continued by William Carrington

Smith. William Carrington Smith, the son of Thomas Smith, obtained his freedom of the Goldsmiths' Company by Redemption on 2 January 1901. He was made a Liveryman in April 1904 and died on 25 March 1924.

*Mark entered in two sizes.
**Mark entered in three sizes.

Stephen Smith & Son

* 23 May 1850
Stephen Smith and William Nicholson, Plate workers
manufactory: 12 Duke Street, Lincolns Inn Fields
S. Smith's residence: 2 Dacre Terrace, Blackheath
W. Nicholson's residence: 4 Loudoun Villas, St John's Wood

7 September 1850 (Entry as for 23.5.1850)

** 2 January 1865
Stephen Smith, Plate worker
Duke Street, Lincolns Inn Fields
residence: Morden Road, Blackheath Park

Removed to 35 King Street, Covent Garden, 16 March 1867

* 23 July 1872
35 King Street, Covent Garden

24 October 1878
35 King Street, Covent Garden

* 31 December 1880
35 King Street, Covent Garden

11 May 1882
35 King Street, Covent Garden

18 December 1884
Stephen Smith, Plate worker
35 King Street, Covent Garden
residence: Morden Road, Blackheath Park

Stephen Smith was born in 1822, the son of Susannah (née Pellatt) and Benjamin Smith (No. 2) (silversmith, Citizen and Goldsmith). His paternal grandfather was Benjamin Smith (No. 1) (silversmith, Citizen and Goldsmith) who established this firm at Lime Kiln Lane, Greenwich, in 1802 with financial backing from his partner, Digby Scott (see *Marks of London Goldsmiths and Silversmiths c.1697–1837*, revised edition 1988, pp. 305–8). Digby Scott, born in 1753, died at Royal Hill, Greenwich, on 20 November 1816, aged 62, leaving a widow and one daughter.

Benjamin Smith (No. 1) manufactured extensively for the well-known firm of Rundell & Bridge, later Rundell, Bridge & Rundell. In 1816 he entered into partnership with his son, Benjamin Smith (No. 2), trading as Benjamin Smith & Son. After a long illness of over a year, he died on 28 August 1823, leaving his son, Benjamin Smith (No. 2), to continue running the firm.

Born on 6 October 1793, Benjamin Smith (No. 2) was apprenticed to his father on 6 July 1808 and obtained his freedom of the Goldsmiths' Company by Service on 3 January 1821. In 1817 he married Susannah, the daughter of Apsley Pellatt, glass manufacturer, of The Friars, Lewes, Sussex. They had eight sons and two daughters. The eight sons were: Benjamin Frederick, b.1819; Stephen, b.1822; Henry, b.1823; Apsley, b.1825; George Maberly, b.1831; Thomas, b.1833; Joseph Brandram, b.1835; and Herbert Jowett, b.1837.

In 1840 Benjamin Smith (No. 2) entered into an agreement with George Richards Elkington, the founder of the well-known firm of Elkington & Co., electroplaters and manufacturing silversmiths (see Elkington & Co.). Under this agreement, Elkington supplied Smith with electroplated goods for sale in London in return for two-thirds of the profits. In 1841 it was agreed that Smith could manufacture the electroplated goods in London, giving Elkington two-thirds of the profits, while Elkington would establish similar premises in Birmingham, giving Smith one-third of the profits. As a result, electroplating workshops were opened at 45 Moorgate Street, London.

However, since Benjamin Smith (No. 2) failed to keep these and other subsequent agreements, Elkington terminated them all in 1849 and took over the London electroplating workshops at 45 Moorgate Street. Also in 1849 his daughter, Emma Elizabeth Elkington, married one of Smith's sons, Apsley Smith (copper smelter). It seems that they took over the running of the electroplating works on behalf of G. R. Elkington. Meanwhile, Benjamin Smith (No. 2) became bankrupt in early 1850 and died in May of that year.

His son, Stephen Smith, took over the remains of the firm, but had to enter into partnership with William Nicholson in order to obtain financial backing. They traded as Smith, Nicholson & Co., manufacturing silversmiths and electroplaters. Nicholson retired in December 1864 and died on 23 December 1867, leaving Stephen Smith to continue on his own. Stephen Smith then took his son, Stephen Pellatt Smith, into partnership, trading as Stephen Smith & Son.

In 1886 Stephen Smith sold the firm to Mappin & Webb, manufacturing silversmiths. They maintained it under its own name until 1889 when the King Street premises were closed and the firm was moved to 158–162 Oxford Street, where it became part of Mappin & Webb.

Stephen Smith, born in 1822, obtained his freedom of the Goldsmiths' Company by Patrimony on 3 April 1867, was made a Liveryman in December 1873 and became an Assistant in November 1877. He became 4th Warden in 1882, 3rd Warden in 1883, 2nd Warden in 1884 and Prime Warden in 1885. He died on 20 February 1890 when 67 years old. In 1847 he married Mary Sophia, the daughter of John Greaves of Radford, Warwickshire. Their son, Stephen Pellatt Smith, obtained his freedom of the Goldsmiths' Company by Redemption on 5 January 1887. He was made a Liveryman in November 1886 and died on 22 December 1905. Mary Sophia Smith lived on until 20 November 1906.

Returning to Stephen Smith's brothers, the following information is recorded.

Benjamin Frederick Smith was educated at Trinity College, Cambridge. He became Archdeacon of Maidstone and a Canon of Canterbury Cathedral. In 1846 he married Harriet Anne, only daughter of Thomas Ward of Moreton Morrell, Warwickshire, and died on 25 March 1900.

Henry Smith married Rosa Sophia, daughter of Robert Knaggs MD of Melbourne, in 1852 and died in 1896.

Apsley Smith married Emma Elizabeth, daughter of George Richards Elkington of Woodbrooke, Northfield, Worcestershire, in 1849. Emma died in 1893 and Apsley in 1905.

George Maberly Smith was educated at Caius College, Cambridge. He became Rector of Penshurst, Kent, and honorary Canon of Canterbury Cathedral. In 1863 he married Emily Harriet, eldest daughter of Maxwell Macartney MD of Rosebrook, County Armagh.

Thomas Smith, born on 23 March 1833, married Ann Eliza, daughter of Frederick Parbury of Lancaster Gate, Hyde Park, London, on 27 August 1862. She died on 9 February 1879. Thomas became a Fellow of the Royal College of Surgeons. He was made Surgeon Extraordinary to HM Queen Victoria, honorary Serjeant-Surgeon to HM King Edward VII and consultant surgeon to St Bartholomew's Hospital and King Edward VII's Hospital for Officers. On 6 September 1897 he was created a baronet, thereafter known as Sir Thomas Smith KCVO of Stratford Place, London.

277

Herbert Jowett Smith married Emily, daughter of the Reverend William Wilson, on 10 June 1862. He became a silversmith, obtaining his freedom of the Goldsmiths' Company by Patrimony on 3 April 1867. He died in 1899.

*Mark entered in two sizes.
**Mark entered in three sizes.

William Somersall

R A **W S**	26 July 1824 Richard William Atkins and William Nathaniel Somersall, Plate workers 11 Bridgewater Square
R A **W S**	31 March 1825
R A **W S**	6 February 1830
W S	10 May 1838 William Somersall, Plate worker 11 Bridgewater Square
W B **W S**	* 10 April 1839 William Brown (No. 1) and William Somersall, Plate workers 53 Bartholomew Close
W·S	21 January 1851 William Somersall Removed to 31 Kirby Street, Hatton Garden

In 1824 William Somersall, full name William Nathaniel Somersall, entered into partnership with Richard William Atkins. They traded as plate workers until early 1838 when R. W. Atkins apparently retired or died, leaving W. N. Somersall to continue on his own. In 1839 he entered into partnership with William Brown (No. 1), trading as plate workers from W. Brown's premises at 53 Bartholomew Close (see William Brown (No. 1)).

When this partnership was dissolved in 1843, W. Brown (No. 1) continued trading from the same address while W. N. Somersall moved to

278

31 Kirby Street, where he was listed as a working silversmith until *circa* 1852.

*Mark entered in two sizes.

Spink & Son

** 11 May 1887
John Marshall Spink, Plate worker
2 Gracechurch Street, EC
residence: Fernleigh, Sevenoaks, Kent

* 11 March 1892

6 April 1894

31 December 1895

** 6 March 1911
Spink & Son Ltd, Gold and Silver workers
17–18 Piccadilly, W
6 King Street, St James, SW
J. M. Spink's residence: Taormina, Carew Road, Eastbourne

*** 18 November 1913
Spink & Son Ltd, Gold and Silver workers
17–18 Piccadilly, W
6 King Street, St James, SW
J. M. Spink's residence: Taormina, 4 Carew Road, Eastbourne, Sussex
partner: John Marshall Spink

In 1841 Marshall Spink, silversmith and jeweller, was trading at Gracechurch Street as Marshall Spink & Son, but by 1852 the firm's name had changed to Spink & Son. By 1871 the firm was under the control of John Spink and his son, John Marshall Spink. Soon after, his other two sons joined the partnership. They were Samuel Martin Spink and Charles Frederick Spink.

Following John Spink's retirement in 1886, his three sons continued running the firm, still trading as Spink & Son, jewellers and silversmiths.

279

John Marshall Spink, as senior partner, entered his first mark at Goldsmiths' Hall on behalf of the firm in May 1887. In 1892 the firm acquired additional premises at 17–18 Piccadilly, but continued to retain its Gracechurch Street premises until 1906. By now the firm was listed as manufacturing goldsmiths, silversmiths, bullion dealers, diamond and pearl merchants, appraisers, wholesale and retail buyers of second-hand jewels, silver plate, gold and silver coins and medals.

In 1903 the firm was converted into a limited liability company with the three brothers, J. M. Spink, S. M. Spink and C. F. Spink as directors. J. M. Spink resigned as chairman and company secretary in 1932 and was declared bankrupt the following year. He died on 2 March 1943, aged 87.

S. M. Spink's son, Harold Hans Marshall Spink (gold and silversmith), obtained his freedom of the Goldsmiths' Company by Redemption on 2 June 1936. He was made a Liveryman in January 1938 and died on 26 October 1958.

*Mark entered in two sizes.
**Mark entered in three sizes.
***Mark entered in four sizes.

Harold Stabler

 * 23 May 1913
Harold Stabler, Gold and Silver worker
34 Upper Mall, Hammersmith, W
H. Stabler's residence: 34 Upper Mall, Hammersmith, W

Harold Stabler, designer, silversmith and jeweller, was born in Westmoreland in 1872. He became head of metal work at the Keswick School of Industrial Art, but left in 1902 when 30 years old. After moving to London he subsequently became a teacher at the Royal College of Art. He and his wife, Phoebe, an enameller, lived at 34 Upper Mall, Hammersmith.

*Mark entered in two sizes.

E. H. Stockwell

 * 16 May 1865
E. H. Stockwell, Small worker
15 Greek Street, Soho

9 August 1881

19 October 1882

20 November 1885

Edward H. Stockwell, born *circa* 1840, was the son of Jemima and Henry William Stockwell, jeweller, of 15 Greek Street (see Henry William Stockwell). With the death of his father in 1865, the business passed to his widowed mother, Jemima, but Edward took over the running of the business.

By 1869 he was trading as Edward Stockwell, ornamental metal worker, and by 1894 as ornamental gold, silver and metal manufacturer. Presumably he retired or died during 1894 since his business at 15 Greek Street was taken over by William Tiebzsch, who entered his own mark on 9 July 1894 from the same address.

*Mark entered in two sizes.

Henry William Stockwell

11 November 1859
Henry Stockwell, Small worker
15 Greek Street, Soho

Born *circa* 1805, Henry William Stockwell entered into partnership with Joseph Holt in the late 1820s, trading at Berwick Street, Soho, as jewellers, modellers and chasers. This partnership was dissolved in 1838.

By 1851, at the age of 46, he was trading as a jeweller at 8 Frith Street, Soho, where he lived with his wife, Jemima, aged 36, and their children, Edward, aged 11, Jemima, aged 9, and Jessie, aged 4. Later, he moved to 15 Greek Street, from where he entered his only mark at Goldsmiths' Hall.

He appears to have died in 1865, leaving the business to his widow, Jemima, but with his son, Edward, running the business on her behalf (see E. H. Stockwell).

E.W.S   3 April 1873
Edwin William Streeter, Gold worker
37 Conduit Street
Coach & Horses Yard, Savile Row
residence: The Mount, Primrose Hill Road

E.W.S
EWS   19 March 1878
18 New Bond Street

E W S   22 November 1882
EWS

E W S   24 February 1898
Edwin William Streeter, Gold worker
18 New Bond Street, W
residence: 2 Park Crescent, Portland Place

** 27 July 1899
Streeter & Co. Ltd, Gold and Silver workers
18 New Bond Street, W
residence: 2 Park Crescent, Portland Place, W
managing director: Edwin W. Streeter

17 October 1899 (Entry as for 27.7.1899)

Edwin William Streeter was born at Wrotham, Kent, in 1834. In 1858 he entered the employment of Harry Emanuel, retail jeweller and goldsmith, where he became manager (see Emanuel Brothers). In 1859 he joined Harry Emanuel, Francis Higgins (No. 3) and others to found the Portland Co. Ltd (see Portland Co. Ltd). This company was established to manufacture cutlery by an improved method. Unfortunately it failed and the company went into voluntary liquidation in 1863. *Circa* 1868 he left Emanuel and set up on his own at 37 Conduit Street, trading as Edwin W. Streeter, goldsmith and diamond merchant. When Harry Emanuel retired from business in 1873, Edwin W. Streeter bought the lease of his old employer's premises at 18 New Bond Street, moving in during December.

In 1884 he decided to retire and offered the whole of his stock of diamond ornaments, 18 carat gold work, English keyless lever watches and Japanese art work at reduced prices. However, instead of retiring, he took on partners prepared to inject money into the firm, and in 1885 he renamed the firm Streeter & Co.

Edwin W. Streeter was a Member of the Anthropological Institute and a Fellow of the Royal Geographical Society. He wrote three books related to his business: *The Great Diamonds of the World, Precious Stones and Gems* and *Pearls and Pearling Life.*

In 1895 the firm was converted into a limited liability company, trading under the name of Streeter & Co. Ltd, goldsmiths, silversmiths, jewellers, diamond and pearl merchants, dealers in precious stones, ivory works of art, articles of vertu, furniture, antiques and ornaments. Edwin W. Streeter was chairman and managing director of the new company with Lt.-Col. Arthur Collins, G. E. J. Manners and Capt. F. G. J. Manners as directors and Cecil Foljambe Streeter as secretary. In 1904 Edwin W. Streeter retired from the firm, and by early 1905 the company's premises and goodwill had been transferred to the United Investment Corporation on behalf of Lacloche Frères of 15 Rue de la Paix, Paris. By 1913 Streeter & Co. Ltd had been transferred to Kirby & Bunn, jewellers, at 17 Cork Street, London.

**Mark entered in three sizes.

William Summers

|WS| 16 March 1826
William Summers, Gold worker
19 Little Britain

|CR|WS| ** 6 April 1829
Charles Rawlings and William Summers, Small workers
Brook Street, Holborn

Removed to 10 Great Marlborough Street, Regent Street, 9 January 1839

|CR|WS| ** 2 December 1840
Charles Rawlings and William Summers
Marks defaced 7.12.1863

(WS) ** 7 December 1863
William Summers, Small worker
10 Great Marlborough Street

(W S)
(WS)

William Summers having died, the business was discontinued.
The son, H. Summers, afterwards registered, 18 July 1905

William Summers was born on 11 October 1804, the son of Kathrine and Thomas Summers (Citizen and Goldsmith). Having obtained his freedom of the Goldsmiths' Company by Patrimony on 1 March 1826, he entered his first mark at Goldsmiths' Hall, giving his address as 19 Little Britain. In 1829 he entered into partnership with Charles Rawlings at 9 Brook Street, Holborn, trading as Rawlings & Summers, goldsmiths and silversmiths. Charles Rawlings had first entered his mark at Goldsmiths' Hall on 3 July 1817, since when he had been working on his own as a goldsmith and silversmith (for previous marks of Charles Rawlings from 1817 to 1826, see *Marks of London Goldsmiths and Silversmiths c.1697–1837*, revised edition 1988, p. 263).

In 1839 Rawlings & Summers moved to premises at 10 Great Marlborough Street, from where the firm continued to trade as working goldsmiths and silversmiths. In February 1850 William Summers was made a Liveryman of the Goldsmiths' Company.

Following the death of Charles Rawlings on 9 October 1863, the firm was continued by William Summers, still trading as Rawlings & Summers. William Summers had four sons, William, Edward, James Lea and Henry, all of whom obtained their freedom of the Goldsmiths' Company by Patrimony between 1858 and 1866.

When William Summers died on 15 January 1890, aged 85, his son, Henry Summers, continued running the firm until June 1897 when it officially closed down due to Henry's retirement as the surviving partner. Henry Summers subsequently re-registered at Goldsmiths' Hall as a gold and silver worker on 18 July 1905. No mark was entered, but he listed both his business and private addresses as 26 Crockerton Road, Upper Tooting.

**Mark entered in three sizes.

Charles Taylor & Son

---

11 January 1837
Charles Taylor and Thomas Terrett Taylor, Plate workers
High Street, Bristol

By Virtue of a Power of Attorney bearing the date 6 January 1837 from Charles Taylor, I enter his Mark as also my own as his

284

Partner and carrying on business under the firm of Charles
Taylor & Thomas Terrett Taylor
signed: Charles Taylor, Thomas Terrett Taylor

Charles Taylor was the son of William Taylor (yeoman) of Clearwell, Gloucestershire. He was apprenticed to John Tanner (jeweller) on 10 March 1796, but did not take up his freedom of the City of Bristol until 28 August 1812. *Circa* 1805 he set up in business as a goldsmith and jeweller at 37 High Street, Bristol. In 1837 he took his son, Thomas Terrett Taylor, into partnership, trading as Charles Taylor & Son, working jewellers and goldsmiths at 9 High Street, Bristol. In 1848 the firm moved to 30 College Green, Bristol.

From *circa* 1857 Thomas Terrett Taylor was additionally in partnership with George Carley and Philip Bettle, trading as George Carley & Co., wholesale watch manufacturers at 30 Ely Place, Holborn Circus, London. Thomas Terrett Taylor retired from this partnership in 1870.

Charles Taylor died on 17 November 1861, aged 80, leaving the remaining partners, Thomas Terrett Taylor, George Carley and John James Peters to continue the firm of Charles Taylor & Son. George Carley retired from the partnership in 1867. Later, the firm continued trading as John J. Peters & Co. until incorporated into the Bristol Goldsmiths Alliance *circa* 1884 (see Bristol Goldsmiths Alliance).

One well-known firm of manufacturing silversmiths which supplied Charles Taylor & Son with goods during the mid-nineteenth century was Edward Barnard & Sons. In 1855 one single order of silverware received from Edward Barnard & Sons amounted to 1,798 troy ounces.

William Theobalds (No. 1)

W.T

W.T

14 January 1829
William Theobalds (No. 1), Plate worker
3 Lovells Court

Removed to 7 Salisbury Court, Fleet Street, 20 November 1829

    * 23 January 1834

15 July 1834

 † 12 February 1835
William Theobalds (No. 1), Plate and spoon worker
7 Salisbury Court, Fleet Street
3 Lovells Court, Paternoster Row

 * 30 June 1835
William Theobalds (No. 1) and Lockington Bunn, Plate and
spoon workers
7 Salisbury Court, Fleet Street

 *** 27 February 1836
William Theobalds (No. 1), Plate and spoon worker
7 Salisbury Court, Fleet Street

 ** 24 June 1838
William Theobalds (No. 1) and Robert Metcalfe Atkinson, Plate
and spoon workers
7 Salisbury Court, Fleet Street

 24 October 1838

 ** 28 October 1839

 ** 1 January 1841
William Theobalds (No. 1), Plate and spoon worker
7 Salisbury Court, Fleet Street

This firm appears to have been established at some date prior to 1829 by William Theobalds (No. 1) together with his son, William Theobalds (No. 2).

Born *circa* 1780, William Theobalds (No. 1) was the son of William Theobalds (loop spinner) of Croydon, Surrey. He was apprenticed to Richard Crossley (goldsmith, Citizen and Goldsmith) on 2 October 1793. Richard Crossley died in April 1815, but William Theobalds (No. 1) did not take up his freedom of the Goldsmiths' Company by Service until 7 November 1821, listing his address as Charles Street, Blackfriars Road. Normally he would have completed his apprenticeship in late 1800, at about the time that his son, William Theobalds (No. 2), was born.

Born *circa* 1801, William Theobalds (No. 2) was the son of William Theobalds (No. 1) (silversmith, Citizen and Goldsmith). He was apprenticed to John Kerschner (silver spoon maker, Citizen and Goldsmith) of Clerkenwell Green, Middlesex, on 6 November 1815. At the time, his father, William Theobalds (No. 1), was already residing at Charles Street, Christchurch, Surrey. On 5 April 1820 William Theobalds (No. 2) was turned over by mutual consent to Charles Eley (silversmith, Citizen and Goldsmith) of Lovell's Court, Paternoster Row, and he obtained his freedom of the Goldsmiths' Company by Service on 3 December 1823, listing his address as Charles Street.

In January 1829 William Theobalds (No. 1) entered his first mark at Goldsmiths' Hall, trading frm 3 Lovell's Court, Paternoster Row. It seems that his son, William Theobalds (No. 2), was already working with him at the time. The premises at 3 Lovell's Court had been occupied previously by Charles Eley's brother, William Eley (No. 2), from January 1825 to December 1826 and probably to December 1828 (see *Marks of London Goldsmiths and Silversmiths c.1697–1837*, revised edition 1988, p. 120–1). Meanwhile, the adjoining premises at 2 Lovell's Court had been occupied by Charles Eley from January 1825 until December 1828 when William Eaton (No. 2) had taken them over (see *Marks of London Goldsmiths and Silversmiths c.1697–1837*, revised edition 1988, p. 111). By 20 November 1829 William Theobalds (No. 1) had moved to 7 Salisbury Court, but at the same time he still occupied 3 Lovell's Court until some date between February and June 1835.

In June 1835 he entered into partnership with Lockington St Lawrence Bunn, trading as William Theobalds & Co., silversmiths. This partnership was not dissolved officially until September 1836, although William Theobalds (No. 1) had already entered marks on his own at Goldsmiths' Hall in February 1836.

In 1838 he entered into partnership with Robert Metcalfe Atkinson, but in December 1840 it was dissolved and he continued on his own, trading as William Theobalds & Co., silversmiths.

In the 1841 Census return for 7 Salisbury Court, the residents listed include: William Theobalds (No. 1), silversmith, aged 60; William Theobalds (No. 2), silversmith, aged 40; Hannah Theobalds, aged 60; Susanna Theobalds, aged 45; two apprentices aged 15 and others.

It seems that the firm was taken over by John Lias & Son, manufacturing silversmiths, who occupied the premises on or before 13 February 1843 (see John Lias & Son).

*Mark entered in two sizes.

**Mark entered in three sizes.
***Mark entered in four sizes.
†Mark entered in five sizes.

F. B. Thomas & Co.

** 13 May 1874
Francis Boone Thomas, Plate workers
153 New Bond Street
13 Oxford Market

** 17 March 1875

16 November 1887

Mr F. B. Thomas, a member of the Court of Assistants, died in 1900, his business being subsequently carried on by his nephews Messrs C. H. Townley and John William Thomas

*** 24 July 1901
Charles Henry Townley and John William Thomas, Silver workers
153 New Bond Street
1 & 2 Bruton Street, W
residences: C. H. Townley: Riseholm, Purley, Surrey
J. W. Thomas: 172 Belsize Road, S. Hampstead

11 February 1902

* 4 March 1903 (Entry as for 24.7.1901)

288

** 26 July 1910
F. B. Thomas & Company, Gold and Silver workers
153 New Bond Street, W
residence: J. W. Thomas: 172 Belsize Road, NW
partners: Charles Henry Townley, John William Thomas

This firm was established during the second half of the eighteenth century. In 1848 it came under the sole control of John William Thomas (No. 1), the son of John Thomas. John William Thomas (No. 1) obtained his freedom of the Goldsmiths' Company by Redemption on 7 January 1835 and was made a Liveryman in December 1839. He became an Assistant in November 1851 and died in May 1852. Following his death, his two sons, John William Thomas (No. 2) and Francis Boone Thomas, took control of the firm, trading as J. W. Thomas & Son or alternatively known as J. W. & F. B. Thomas, retail silversmiths.

John William Thomas (No. 2), the son of John William Thomas (No. 1) (silversmith, Citizen and Goldsmith), was apprenticed to his father on 6 May 1840 to learn the art of silversmith. He obtained his freedom of the Goldsmiths' Company by Service on 2 June 1847, was made a Liveryman on 29 July 1853 and died *circa* 1862–7.

Francis Boone Thomas, the son of John William Thomas (No. 1) (silversmith, Citizen and Goldsmith), was apprenticed to his father on 3 February 1847 to learn the art of silversmith. Due to the death of his father in May 1852, he was turned over to John William Thomas (No. 2) (goldsmith, Citizen and Goldsmith) of 153 New Bond Street on 3 November 1852. He obtained his freedom of the Goldsmiths' Company by Service on 1 March 1854, was made a Liveryman in April 1859 and became an Assistant in October 1871. He became 4th Warden in 1878, 3rd Warden in 1879, 2nd Warden in 1880 and Prime Warden in 1881.

Following the death of his brother, John William Thomas (No. 2), *circa* 1862–7, Francis Boone Thomas assumed control of the firm, changing its name to F. B. Thomas & Co. He entered his first mark at Goldsmiths' Hall in May 1874, listing 153 New Bond Street as the firm's showrooms and 13 Oxford Market as its manufactory. However, 13 Oxford Market was the working premises of Richard Sibley (No. 2), manufacturing silversmith, from 1862 to 1880 and it seems he supplied F. B. Thomas & Co. with goods over a considerable period of time (see Richard Sibley (Nos 2 and 3)).

Circa 1896 Francis Boone Thomas took his two nephews, Charles Henry Townley and John William Thomas (No. 3), into partnership. Meanwhile, the firm continued to trade as F. B. Thomas & Co., but as manufacturing goldsmiths, jewellers, silversmiths and watchmakers.

Charles Henry Townley, the son of Charles Augustus Townley

(deceased), was apprenticed to Francis Boone Thomas (goldsmith, Citizen and Goldsmith) to learn the art of goldsmith on 6 January 1864. He obtained his freedom of the Goldsmiths' Company by Service on 1 February 1871, was made a Liveryman in January 1875 and became an Assistant in December 1901. He became 4th Warden in 1907, 3rd Warden in 1908, 2nd Warden in 1909 and Prime Warden in 1910. He died on 19 August 1924.

John William Thomas (No. 3), the son of John William Thomas (No. 2) (silversmith, Citizen and Goldsmith deceased), obtained his freedom of the Goldsmiths' Company by Patrimony on 6 June 1877 and was made a Liveryman in December 1880. He joined the firm in 1896 and died on 2 August 1951 aged 94.

On 27 June 1900 Francis Boone Thomas died, aged 71, leaving the firm to be continued by his two nephews, Charles Henry Townley and John William Thomas (No. 3). *Circa* 1919 John William Thomas (No. 3), who by then was the sole partner, took his son into the firm. Following the son's death in 1941, the firm closed down.

*Mark entered in two sizes.
**Mark entered in three sizes.
***Mark entered in four sizes.

Tiffany & Co.

[A.W.F]   29 February 1892
Albert William Fearearyear, Plate worker
221 and 221A Regent Street
A. W. Fearearyear's residence: 71 Gascony Avenue, West Hampstead

22 February 1894
Removed to private address: 25 Ulysses Road, West Hampstead, NW

(AWF)   26 August 1898
One new mark
A. W. Fearearyear's residence: 28 Agamemnon Road, West Hampstead, NW

[A.W.F]   20 January 1913
Tiffany & Company, Gold and Silver worker

(AWF) 221 Regent Street, London, W
A. W. Fearearyear's residence: 4 Acland Road, Willesden Green, N
manager: Albert William Fearearyear

7 July 1922
Removed to (private address): 103 Anson Road, Cricklewood, SW

6 November 1923
Removed to (business address): 23 & 25 Maddox Street, Regent
Street, W

This American firm of manufacturing and retail goldsmiths, silversmiths and
jewellers first opened a London branch in 1868. Then, in 1891, it opened
a shop at 221 Regent Street under the management of Albert William
Fearearyear.

In 1923 the London branch moved to 23 and 25 Maddox Street. Later
it moved to 44 New Bond Street, where it remained until its closure *circa*
1941.

Tucker & Edwards

J·T 20 November 1868
John Tucker, Plate worker
180 Stanhope Street, Hampstead Road

J.T 11 December 1868

Removed to 58 William Street, Regent's Park, 5 April 1869

J·T R·E ** 11 August 1870
John Tucker and Robert Edwards, Plate workers
58 William Street, Regent's Park
manufactory: 17 King Street, Clerkenwell

J.T R.E 6 September 1870
John Tucker and Robert Edwards

J.T ** 27 July 1871
John Tucker, Plate worker
17 King Street, Clerkenwell
residence: 58 William Street, Regent's Park

John Tucker entered his first mark at Goldsmiths' Hall in November 1868. In 1870 he entered into partnership with Robert Walter Edwards, trading as Tucker & Edwards, manufacturing silversmiths. This partnership was dissolved on 17 July 1871, following which John Tucker continued manufacturing at 17 King Street while residing at 58 William Street.

**Mark entered in three sizes.

Unite & Sons

8 July 1886
George Richard Unite, Small worker
65 Caroline Street, Birmingham
* 11 Thavies Inn, EC (London)
residence: Blackwell Court, Bromsgrove (Birmingham)

4 July 1889

George Unite was apprenticed to the Birmingham silversmith, Joseph Willmore, in 1810. He was first recorded in London as a silversmith in 1852 with premises at 16 Thavies Inn, Holborn. This address was also being used at the time by the Birmingham gold and silver manufacturers, Nathaniel Mills & Sons and Joseph Willmore & Co.

In 1854 he was trading from 65 Caroline Street, Birmingham, as George Unite, manufacturing silversmith. Then, on 4 July 1861, he entered his mark at the Sheffield Assay Office for the first time.

In 1880 he was trading as George Unite & Sons, manufacturers of dessert knives and forks, fish carvers, cake carvers, salt cellars and spoons, fruit spoons, napkin rings, various cups, cigar and cigarette cases, dram flasks, snuff boxes, card cases, bells, trowels, pocket communion services, inkstands, etc.

It was George Richard Unite who entered the firm's mark at Goldsmiths' Hall, London, for the first time in 1886. Following his death on 19 October 1896, the remaining partners, Edward Willoughby Unite and William Oliver Unite, dissolved their partnership in January 1897. In 1928 George Unite

& Sons and William Lyde amalgamated and were converted into a limited liability company trading as George Unite & Lyde Ltd.

*Mark entered in two sizes.

Vander & Hedges

13 June 1887
John Gotlieu Vander and John Hedges, Small workers
26 New Bond Street
residences: J. G. Vander: 30 Lansdowne Gardens
J. Hedges: 26 New Bond Street

The partnership by J. G. Vander and John Hedges was dissolved in January 1896

17 January 1896
John Gotlieu Vander, Gold and Silver worker
26 New Bond Street
residence: Tunnel Woods, Watford

* 11 March 1904
John Vander, Gold and Silver worker
26 New Bond Street, London, W
residence: The Paddocks, Haywards Heath, Sussex

John Vander died early in 1910 and the business of Vander and Hedges, formerly E. Tessier was afterwards carried on by A. M. Parsons and F. H. Parsons under the title of Vander and Hedges, 26 April 1910

** 29 April 1910
Vander & Hedges, Gold and Silver workers
26 New Bond Street, London, W
residence: Beechcroft, Chorley Wood, Bucks
partners: Arthur Martin Parsons, Frank Herbert Parsons

** 23 May 1910
Vander & Hedges (Entry as for 29.4.1910)

* 2 August 1911
Vander & Hedges (Entry as for 29.4.1910)

This firm is the continuation of an earlier one established *circa* 1857 by Henry Thomas Louis Tessier and Edward Tessier, trading as Henry and Edward Tessier, goldsmiths, jewellers and silversmiths. Following the dissolution of their partnership in December 1869, Edward Tessier continued running the firm at 26 New Bond Street until his death in 1875. The firm was then acquired by John Gotlieu Vander (Vanderpump) and John Hedges, who traded as Vander & Hedges. Following the dissolution of their partnership in January 1896, John Gotlieu Vander continued trading as Vander & Hedges. This remained the firm's name until *circa* 1915.

John Gotlieu Vander was born *circa* 1845, the son of Sarah (née Ogborn) and James Vanderpump, jeweller and silversmith. He was one of five children, the others being Cornelius Joshua, b.1837; Thomas John, b.1839; William Lewis, b.1841; and Sarah Agnes, b.1853. It was Cornelius Joshua Vander who subsequently acquired the firm of Macrae & Goldstein, silversmiths, and then proceeded to trade as C. J. Vander, manufacturing silversmiths (see C. J. Vander).

Following the death of John Gotlieu Vander in early 1910, the firm was continued by Arthur Martin Parsons and Frank Herbert Parsons. F. H. Parsons died in 1934 and A. M. Parsons in 1943, aged 84. A. M. Parsons' son, Herbert Martin Parsons, b.1892, obtained his freedom of the Goldsmiths' Company by Redemption on 4 March 1925, his occupation being listed as goldsmith, silversmith and jeweller. He was made a Liveryman in January 1928 and an Assistant in 1939. He became 4th Warden in 1945, 3rd Warden in 1946, 2nd Warden in 1947 and Prime Warden in 1948. He died in 1981.

In 1920 the firm was converted into a limited liability company, trading as Tessiers Ltd. The firm still continues today.

*Mark entered in two sizes.
**Mark entered in three sizes.

C. J. Vander

* 18 October 1886
Cornelius Joshua Vander
17 Lisle Street, Soho
residence: 97 Gloucester Road, Camberwell
marks defaced 25.11.1904

Joshua Vander died early in 1904. The (firm) was afterwards carried on by his sons Henry Vander and Alfred Vander

* 24 November 1904
C. J. Vander, Gold and Silver workers
17 Lisle Street, Leicester Square, WC
residences: H. Vander: 205 Wellmeadow Road, Hither Green, SE
A. Vander: 150 Erlanger Road, New Cross, SE
partners: Henry Vander, Alfred Vander

Removed to 12 Betterton Street, Drury Lane, 18 April 1907
residences: H. Vander: 7 Spencer Gardens, Eltham
A. Vander: 11 Gourock Road, Eltham

This firm is the continuation of an earlier one founded by Alexander Macrae (see Alexander Macrae). *Circa* 1870 Alexander Macrae entered into partnership with Martin Goldstein, changing the firm's name to Macrae & Goldstein, silversmiths. Martin Goldstein took over sole control of the firm in 1878 and commenced trading under his own name. At the time, the firm was located at 32 Bow Street, but later it moved to 17 Lisle Street.

In 1886 the firm was purchased by Cornelius Joshua Vander (Vanderpump) who proceeded to trade under the name of C. J. Vander, manufacturing silversmith. Cornelius Joshua Vander was born on 25 July 1837, the son of Sarah (née Ogborn) and Thomas James Vanderpump, jeweller and silversmith. He was one of five children, one of whom was John Gotlieu Vander who subsequently acquired the firm of Edward Tessier, silversmith and jeweller (see Vander & Hedges).

On 22 December 1861 Cornelius Joshua Vander married Mary Ann Kimber, daughter of Charles Kimber, cellarman. Following the death of C. J. Vander early in 1904, the firm was continued by his sons, Henry and Alfred Vander. Henry Vander's sons, Henry and Arthur, and Alfred Vander's son, Norman, joined the firm *circa* 1926.

Circa 1930 the firm was converted into a limited liability company, trading as C. J. Vander Ltd. Around 1948 the firm acquired the use of old steel box-dies owned by the Goldsmiths & Silversmiths Co. Ltd. Originally these dies had been used by various firms such as Eley, Fearn & Chawner; Chawner & Co.; William Eaton; Elizabeth Eaton; Francis Higgins & Sons Ltd; Holland, Aldwinckle & Slater. They had been inherited by the Goldsmiths & Silversmiths Co. Ltd through numerous takeovers and mergers over the years.

In 1958 the firm acquired the tableware dies and patterns of Atkin Brothers (Silversmiths) Ltd of Sheffield when the firm went into liquidation (see Atkin Brothers). *Circa* 1965 C. J. Vander Ltd purchased the Sheffield firms of Roberts & Belk Ltd, manufacturing silversmiths; William Bush & Son; and Benton Brothers, casters.

In 1971 C. J. Vander Ltd acquired some of the dies and tools of Mappin & Webb Ltd from British Silverware Ltd when it ceased to trade. British Silverware Ltd had been created in 1963 by the amalgamation of Mappin & Webb Ltd, Elkington & Co. Ltd and Walker & Hall Ltd.

*Mark entered in two sizes.

J. C. Vickery

 25 April 1899
John Collard Vickery, Gold and Silver worker
181 & 183 Regent Street, London, W
residence: Leighholme, Leigham Avenue, Streatham

 2 May 1899

J.C.V ** 22 May 1901 (Entry as for 25.4.1899)

J.C.V * 14 April 1902 (Entry as for 25.4.1899)

J.C.V * 26 June 1903 (Entry as for 25.4.1899)

John Collard Vickery first entered into partnership with Arthur Thomas Hobbs at 183 Regent Street *circa* 1890. Following the dissolution of this partnership in 1891, J. C. Vickery continued on his own. By 1897 he was trading as J. C. Vickery, dressing-case and travelling-bag maker, stationer, jeweller and silversmith.

*Mark entered in two sizes.
**Mark entered in three sizes.

Wakely & Wheeler

*** 7 February 1879
Henry John Lias (No. 2) and James Wakely, Plate workers
31 St Bride's Street, Ludgate Circus
residences: H. J. Lias (No. 2): Greville House, Ferndale Park,
Tunbridge Wells
J. Wakely: 8 Glengall Terrace, Old Kent Road

(28 July 1884) (Mark) defaced 1.10.1884

*** 1 October 1884
James Wakely and Frank Clarke Wheeler, Plate workers
31 St Bride's Street, Ludgate Circus, EC
residences: J. Wakely: 25 Glengall Road, Old Kent Road
F. Wheeler: 6 Rothsay Villas, Richmond, Surrey

13 June 1891
residences: J. Wakely: 323 Southampton Road, Old Kent Road,
SW
F. Wheeler: Sunny Side, St James Road, Sutton, Surrey

New address; 64 Hatton Garden, EC, 12 February 1895

All markes defaced 20.2.1895

** 20 February 1896
James Wakely and Frank Clarke Wheeler, Silver workers
64 Hatton Garden
residences: J. Wakely: Uplands, Audley Road, North Dulwich
F. Wheeler: 1 Lisgar Terrace, West Kensington

* 18 January 1906
Wakely & Wheeler, Silver workers
64 Hatton Garden, EC
residences: J. Wakely: 43 Alleyn Park, West Dulwich
F. Wheeler: 1 Lisgar Terrace, West Kensington
partners: James Wakely, Frank C. Wheeler

** 27 April 1909
Wakely & Wheeler, Gold and Silver workers
27 Red Lion Square, London
14 Fade Street, Dublin
residences: F. Wheeler: 1 Stanway Gardens, Acton Hill, W
A. Wakely: 32 Camden Hill Road, Upper Norwood
E. Wakely: 25 Copley Park, Streatham, SW
partners: Frank Clarke Wheeler, Arthur Day Wakely, Edward
James Wakely

This firm is the continuation of an earlier one founded in 1791 by John Lias (No. 1) (see *Marks of London Goldsmiths and Silversmiths c.1697–1837*, revised edition 1988, pp. 206–10). With the death of Henry John Lias (No. 1) on 22 November 1877, his son, Henry John Lias (No. 2), continued running the firm, entering his own marks on 18 January 1878 (see John Lias & Son). However, by 7 February 1879 he had entered into partnership with James Wakely, trading as Lias & Wakely, silver plate manufacturers. This partnership continued until 1 October 1884 when Henry John Lias (No. 2) retired and James Wakely entered into partnership with Frank Clarke Wheeler, trading as Wakely & Wheeler, silversmiths and silver plate manufacturers.

Frank Clarke Wheeler was the son of Robert John Wheeler (Assistant Secretary to the Royal Geographical Society) of Eltham, Kent, who had died at some date prior to F. C. Wheeler's apprenticeship. Frank Clarke Wheeler was apprenticed to Henry John Lias (No. 2) (silverplate manufacturer, Citizen and Goldsmith) of St Bride's Street, Ludgate Hill, on 6 May 1874. The premium of £50 was paid to his master by the Drapers' Company out of Mr Samuel Pennoyer's Charity. Having obtained his freedom of the Goldsmiths' Company by Service on 6 July 1881, Frank Clarke Wheeler remained working for the firm of Lias & Wakely while residing at 6 Rothsay Villas, Richmond Hill. By 1 October 1884 he had entered into partnership with James Wakely.

On 27 April 1909 the firm's partners were recorded as Frank Clarke Wheeler and James Wakely's sons, Arthur Day Wakely and Edward James Wakely. Presumably James Wakely had retired or died by this date. In 1916 Frank Clarke Wheeler died in Dublin, leaving the firm to be continued by A. D. Wakely, E. J. Wakely and P. W. Adams.

Arthur Day Wakely, born in 1881, was apprenticed to Frank Clarke Wheeler (silversmith, Citizen and Goldsmith) on 3 May 1899 to learn the art of silversmith. He obtained his freedom of the Goldsmiths' Company by Service on 4 May 1904, was made a Liveryman in May 1921 and became an Assistant in October 1931. He became 4th Warden in 1936, 3rd Warden in 1937, 2nd Warden in 1938 and Prime Warden in 1939.

His brother, Edward James Wakely, born in 1883, was apprenticed to Frank Clarke Wheeler (silversmith, Citizen and Goldsmith) on 7 March 1900 to learn the art of silversmith. He obtained his freedom of the Goldsmiths' Company by Service on 5 April 1905 and was made a Liveryman in July 1912. Following his death on 26 April 1937, the firm was continued by his brother, A. D. Wakely. After A. D. Wakely's death on 7 December 1958, the firm was acquired by Padgett & Braham Ltd.

A. D. Wakely had two sons, Robert James Wakely and David Hellyar

Wakely, who became freemen of the Goldsmiths' Company. Robert James Wakely, born in 1914, obtained his freedom by Patrimony on 9 April 1936 and was made a Liveryman in July 1940. David Hellyar Wakely, born in 1919, obtained his freedom by Patrimony on 1 March 1950 and died on 30 December 1969.

*Mark entered in two sizes.
**Mark entered in three sizes.
***Mark entered in four sizes.

Walker & Hall

[JEB] ** 8 June 1877
John Edward Bingham, Plate worker
Electro Works, Howard Street, Sheffield
residence: West Lea, Ranmoor

[JEB] 2 May 1884
Marks defaced 10.11.1893

[WR&HL] 10 November 1893
[WR&HL] Walker & Hall, Plate workers
Howard Street, Sheffield
45 Holborn Viaduct, London
residence: West Lea, Sheffield
senior partner: John E. Bingham

[W&H] *** 13 November 1903
Walker & Hall, Gold and Silver workers
Howard Street, Sheffield
45 Holborn Viaduct, London
24–34 Paradise Street, Liverpool
86 Deansgate, Manchester
A. E. Bingham's residence: Ranmoor Grange, Sheffield
directors: John Edward Bingham, Albert Edward Bingham

[W&H] 28 August 1906
Walker & Hall, Gold and Silver workers
Howard Street, Sheffield
45 Holborn Viaduct, London, EC
24–34 Paradise Street, Liverpool
86 Deansgate, Manchester
146 Briggate, Leeds
8 Gordon Street, Glasgow
17 South St Andrew Street, Edinburgh

60 Grey Street, Newcastle upon Tyne
100 St Mary Street, Cardiff
10 Royal Avenue, Belfast
39 Saville Street, Hull
1 Clare Street, Bristol
364 Little Collins Street, Melbourne
416 George Street, Sydney
Grenfell Street, Adelaide
Cape Lines Buildings, Cape Town
directors: Sir John Edward Bingham, West Lea, Ranmoor,
Sheffield, Albert Edward Bingham, Ranmoor Grange, Sheffield

13 May 1907 (Entry as for 28.8.1906 except addresses in
Melbourne, Sydney, Adelaide and Cape Town are omitted)

26 November 1907
Walker & Hall, Gold and Silver workers
Howard Street, Sheffield
45 Holborn Viaduct, London
J. E. Bingham's residence: West Lea, Ranmoor, Sheffield
directors: John Edward Bingham, Albert Edward Bingham

* 27 November 1913
Walker & Hall, Gold and Silver workers
Electro Works, Sheffield
45 Holborn Viaduct
165 Fenchurch Street, London, EC
Sir J. E. Bingham's residence: West Lea, Ranmoor, Sheffield
directors: Sir John Edward Bingham, Albert Edward Bingham

This Sheffield firm of electroplaters was established *circa* 1845 by George
Walker in partnership with William Robson and Samuel Coulson, trading
as Walker & Co. Following William Robson's retirement in 1848, Henry
Hall joined the partnership, the firm being renamed Walker, Coulson &
Hall, electroplaters and gilders. With Coulson's retirement in 1853, the firm
was continued by the two remaining partners, trading as Walker & Hall.

On 8 May 1862 the firm's mark of 'W & H' in a rectangular surround
was entered for the first time at the Sheffield Assay Office. Later, George
Walker's nephew, John Edward Bingham, joined the partnership, and in
January 1865 George Walker retired, leaving H. Hall and J. E. Bingham to
continue running the firm. J. E. Bingham was elected Master of the
Sheffield Cutlers' Company in 1881 and was subsequently created a
baronet. He died on 18 March 1915.

On 22 October 1867 the two partners entered their mark at the Sheffield

Assay Office. This mark consisted of the initials 'HH &' over 'JEB' in a rectangular surround. With Henry Hall's retirement in January 1873, J. E. Bingham assumed sole control of the firm, entering his own mark of 'JEB' in a rectangular surround at the Sheffield Assay Office on 7 September 1873. He then took his brother, Charles Henry Bingham, into partnership and they entered their joint mark of 'JEB' over 'CHB' in a rectangular surround at the Sheffield Assay Office on 4 May 1876. Born in 1848, C. H. Bingham had joined Walker & Hall in 1865 and become a partner in 1873. He was elected Master of the Sheffield Cutlers' Company in 1894.

In 1877 J. E. Bingham reverted to using his own initials for the firm's marks. This occurred in June when he entered 'JEB' marks for the first time at Goldsmiths' Hall, London, and in November when he again entered similar marks at the Sheffield Assay Office.

In 1890 J. E. Bingham's son, Albert Edward Bingham, came of age and joined his father in partnership. He succeeded to the baronetcy upon the death of his father in 1915 and died in 1945, aged 76.

In 1892 Walker & Hall purchased the firm of Henry Wilkinson & Co. Ltd, manufacturing silversmiths, of which J. E. Bingham was already a director (see Henry Wilkinson & Co.). In 1920 the firm became a limited liability company, trading as Walker & Hall Ltd. The directors were: Sir Albert Edward Bingham, Bt., Herbert Ward, William Webb, John Coulson Riddle, George Reeves Slater, John Douglas and Arthur Neale Lee, with Edward Percy Gilbert as secretary.

In 1963 Walker & Hall Ltd combined with Mappin & Webb Ltd and Elkington & Co. Ltd to form British Silverware Ltd. However, due to industrial action, this company closed down in 1971 and Walker & Hall Ltd was revived as a retail firm only under the control of the Mappin & Webb Ltd group.

*Mark entered in two sizes.
**Mark entered in three sizes.
***Mark entered in four sizes.

Henry Godfrey Webb

---

 8 August 1838
Henry (Godfrey) Webb and Joseph (Charles) Webb, Gold case makers
5 Skinner Street, Clerkenwell

H W **J W**	5 August 1841
H W	3 July 1847 Henry (Godfrey) Webb, Case maker 8 Skinner Street, Clerkenwell
	Removed to St John Street Road, Clerkenwell, 3 April 1873
HW	6 November 1879
	Defaced 4 June 1887
F·W **W·W**	4 January 1887 Frederick Webb and Walter Webb, Gold workers 33 St John Street Road residence: 16 Southborough Park, Brixton Street
	Address changed to 265 St John Street, EC, 26 September 1905

In August 1838 Henry Godfrey Webb and Joseph Charles Webb entered their first partnership mark as watch-case makers, trading from 5 Skinner Street, Clerkenwell. In 1841 they were listed as watch-case and dial makers. Following the dissolution of their partnership on 28 June 1847, J. C. Webb moved to 10 Woodbridge Street, where he continued working as a watch-case maker, entering his mark at Goldsmiths' Hall on 7 July 1847 (see Joseph Charles Webb).

Meanwhile, H. G. Webb continued trading as a watch-case maker at 8 Skinner Street. Apparently he moved to 33 St John Street Road in early 1873, where he remained in business until succeeded by Frederick Webb and Walter Webb in 1887. They continued trading as watch-case makers until *circa* 1908.

Joseph Charles Webb

H W **J W**	8 August 1838 Henry (Godfrey) Webb and Joseph (Charles) Webb, Gold case makers 5 Skinner Street, Clerkenwell
H W **J W**	5 August 1841

302

JCW
7 July 1847
Joseph Charles Webb, Case maker
10 Woodbridge Street, Clerkenwell

[JCW]
27 February 1850

[JCW]
26 June 1850

Removed to 53 Spencer Street, Clerkenwell, 25 April 1854

[JCW]
17 May 1855

Trading as watch-case makers from 5 Skinner Street, Clerkenwell, Henry Godfrey Webb and Joseph Charles Webb entered their first mark at Goldsmiths' Hall in August 1838. This partnership was dissolved on 28 June 1847, leaving H. G. Webb to continue working as a watch-case maker at 8 Skinner Street (see Henry Godfrey Webb). Meanwhile, J. C. Webb moved to 10 Woodbridge Street, Clerkenwell, from where he entered his mark at Goldsmiths' Hall in July 1847.

In 1854 he moved to 53 Spencer Street, where in 1856 he was listed as a gold case maker. About this time, he entered into partnership with Frederick Holmes, trading as Holmes & Co., watchmakers. This partnership was dissolved on 16 April 1859.

D. & J. Wellby

[I W]
25 June 1834
John Wellby (No. 1), Gold worker
57 King Street, Soho

[IW]
30 November 1837

[DW / JW]
[DW / JW]
23 February 1863
Daniel Wellby‡ and John (Henry) Wellby, Gold workers
* manufactory: 57 King Street, Soho Square
residences: D. Welby: 2 Porchester Terrace, Bayswater
J. Wellby: 3 Albion Road, St Johns Wood

‡Removed to 7 Arundel Gardens, Kensington Park, W
(residence)

Factory removed to 20 Garrick Street, Covent Garden, WC, 19 September 1866

 8 February 1873
Residences removed to: D. Wellby: Bedford Hill, Balham
J. Wellby: Lawrie Park, Sydenham

 17 October 1879
Daniel Wellby and John H. Wellby, Gold workers
20 Garrick Street, Covent Garden
residences: D. Wellby: Clapham Common
J. Wellby: 12 Russell Square

 7 December 1887

 ** 10 December 1896

 10 March 1910
D. & J. Wellby Ltd, Gold and Silver workers
18 & 20 Garrick Street, Covent Garden, WC
* residence: H. Wellby: 96 West Hill, Sydenham
directors: John Henry Wellby, Edward Henry Wellby, Howard Wellby, secretary

In 1827 John Wellby (No. 1) was recorded in partnership with Joseph Clement at 57 King Street, Soho, trading as refiners and jewellers. In June 1834 he entered his own mark at Goldsmiths' Hall for the first time, presumably having taken over the business. He continued to trade as a refiner, being described as such in 1836, 1841 and 1852.

After a period of over 25 years since the previous entry, new marks were entered at Goldsmiths' Hall in February 1863 by Daniel Wellby and John (Henry) Wellby. From here on the firm continued to expand, and by the 1890s it was trading as diamond merchants, wholesale jewellers and dealers in plate. Manufacturing silversmiths who supplied D. & J. Wellby with goods during this period included Edward Barnard & Sons, C. J. Vander, Edward Brown, and Aldwinckle, Holland & Slater.

In 1897 the firm was converted into a limited liability company, trading as D. & J. Wellby Ltd, assayers, refiners, jewellers and dealers in gold, silver and platinum. The directors were Daniel Wellby, John Henry Wellby,

Edward Henry Wellby and Howard Wellby. On 10 July 1897 the firm's mark was entered at the Sheffield Assay Office for the first time. This mark was similar to that entered at Goldsmiths' Hall, London, on 10 December 1896. The firm continued to trade until 1973 when it closed down.

Howard Wellby was born in 1867 and died in 1934. John Henry Wellby died on 2 August 1917, aged 83, leaving two sons already working for the firm. They were Edward Henry Wellby and Edwin Victor Wellby. E. H. Wellby eventually became chairman of the firm and died in 1940. E. V. Wellby (silversmith and Captain in City Imperial Volunteers) obtained his freedom of the Goldsmiths' Company by Special Grant on 1 May 1901 and was made a Liveryman in April 1905. He became an Assistant in 1923, 4th Warden in 1927, 3rd Warden in 1928, 2nd Warden in 1929 and Prime Warden in 1930. He died on 3 February 1950.

His son, Guy Sinclair Wellby, was born in 1906 and joined the firm in 1926. He obtained his freedom of the Goldsmiths' Company by Special Grant on 7 October 1931, being recorded at the time as a diamond merchant and silversmith. He was made a Liveryman in June 1931 and an Assistant in 1951. He became 4th Warden in 1962, 3rd Warden in 1963, 2nd Warden in 1964 and Prime Warden in 1965. He died on 29 June 1989.

*Mark entered in two sizes.
**Mark entered in three sizes.

West & Son

* 16 August 1879
(Langley) Archer West, Plate worker
18 College Green, Dublin

By virtue of a Power of Attorney dated 30 June 1879, I enter eight marks of Archer West of 18 College Green, Dublin, Plate worker, this 16 August 1879. James Crossley, Attorney to the said Archer West

12 December 1879

** 1 January 1894
Langley Archer West, Plate worker
18 & 19 College Green, Dublin

These marks cancelled on 25 March 1901

** 14 April 1902
West & Son, Gold and Silver workers
18 & 19 College Green (Dublin)
14 Fade Street (Dublin)
9 Fleet Street (Dublin)
L. A. West's residence: 89 Merrion Square, Dublin
C. H. Lawson's residence: Solent, Kimmage Road, Torenure,
Co. Dublin
signed: Langley Archer West, Charles Howard Lawson

** 18 October 1911
West & Son, Gold and Silver workers
18 & 19 College Green
14 Fade Street
9 Fleet Street, Dublin
L. A. West's residence: Mount Offaly, Greystones,
County Wicklow
partners: Langley Archer West, George William Thornley,
George Crowly

** 16 July 1912 (Entry as for 18.10.1911)

Established in the eighteenth century, this Dublin firm of silversmiths traded as Matthew West and subsequently as Matthew West & Sons during the first half of the nineteenth century. In 1877 James West, the firm's current proprietor, died, leaving the business to his son, Langley Archer West. He continued running the firm of West & Son, trading as goldsmiths, jewellers and watchmakers.

On 21 February 1902 the firm's mark was entered at the Sheffield Assay Office for the first time. This mark was similar to that entered at Goldsmiths' Hall on 14 April 1902.

Langley Archer West died in 1932.

*Mark entered in two sizes.
**Mark entered in three sizes.

Thomas Whitehouse

4 January 1848
Thomas Whitehouse, Small worker
9 Wellington Street, Goswell Street

TW   15 April 1850

TW   * 17 April 1850

     Removed to 12 Smith Street, Northampton Square, 10 May 1856

T.W   24 October 1862

T.W   29 November 1877
     residence: 43 Sparsholt Road, Crouch Hill

TW   9 December 1881

T.W   18 July 1883

TW   8 February 1886
     Thomas Whitehouse, Small worker
     12 Smith Street, Northampton Square, E6
     residence: 43 Sparsholt Road, Crouch Hill

T.W   24 March 1891

TW   5 November 1891

     Thomas Whitehouse died 30 January 1900 (year incorrectly
     stated, date was actually 30.1.1898). The next entry is that of
     Percy Horace Arthur Whitehouse

Having entered his initial mark at Goldsmiths' Hall in January 1848, Thomas Whitehouse was first listed as a silversmith in 1852. He subsequently built up a business specialising in the manufacture of fittings, spring tops, etc. for bags and dressing cases. In 1897 he was listed as a silversmith and manufacturer of silver fittings for dressing cases and bags. Following his death on 30 January 1898, the firm was continued by Percy Horace Arthur Whitehouse. In 1913 and 1916 the firm was trading as Whitehouse Brothers, manufacturing silversmiths.

*Mark entered in two sizes.

307

Samuel Whitford (No. 2)

 * 27 September 1856
Samuel Whitford (No. 2), Small worker
4 Porter Street, Soho

 5 July 1866

Removed to 36 Gerrard Street, Soho, 14 April 1882

Born on 22 January 1818, Samuel Whitford (No. 2) was the son of Harriet (née Colliver) and Samuel Whitford (No. 1) (silversmith). His father first entered his mark at Goldsmiths' Hall in 1800 and continued trading as a silversmith until his death at some date prior to September 1856.

Following his father's death, Samuel Whitford (No. 2) entered his own mark while trading from his deceased father's premises at 4 Porter Street, Soho. In early 1882 he moved to 36 Gerrard Street, Soho. Later he moved to 58 Frith Street, Soho, where he apparently worked as a hospital secretary as well as a manufacturing silversmith. In 1891 his private residence was 2 Elm Villas, Lower Park, Loughton, Essex.

*Mark entered in two sizes.

John James Whiting and John Whiting

 7 October 1833
John James Whiting, Spoon maker
19 Myrtle Street, Hoxton

 30 October 1833

J W 10 March 1834

 18 September 1834

11 May 1840

 24 August 1842

Removed to 107 Bunhill Row, St Lukes, 5 July 1845

 8 May 1846

 22 December 1847

 14 March 1855
John Whiting, Spoon maker
107 Bunhill Row, St Lukes

7 November 1857
John Whiting
107 Bunhill Row, St Lukes

*

John James Whiting (spoon maker) entered his first mark at Goldsmiths'
Hall in October 1833, trading from 19 Myrtle Street. He remained at this
address until 1845 when he moved to 107 Bunhill Row. These premises
had previously been occupied by Hester Bateman, William Bateman (No.
1) and Bateman & Ball, manufacturing silversmiths, until 1843, following
which they were occupied by Benjamin Carr, horse-hair manufacturer, until
1845.

In December 1847 J. J. Whiting entered his final mark at Goldsmiths'
Hall. His signature against this entry was written with a shaky hand
indicating lack of control, possibly due to some illness. However, in 1852
he was still trading as a silver spoon and fork manufacturer.

Following his death *circa* 1855, his son, John Whiting, continued running
the business. John Whiting was succeeded at 107 Bunhill Row by George
Whiting (spoon maker) who entered his own mark at Goldsmiths' Hall on
30 December 1858.

*Mark entered in two sizes.

309

Henry Wilkinson & Co.

 * 23 June 1857
Henry Wilkinson, Plate worker
manufactory: Norfolk Street, Sheffield
warehouse: 4 Bolt Court, Fleet Street, London
residence: Endcliffe Hall near Sheffield

 26 June 1857

 6 November 1879
This mark (two marks as illustrated) was used by John Brashier
after the death of Mr Henry Wilkinson

The above six marks were defaced 8 November 1879

 † 6 November 1879
John Brashier, Plate worker
20 Norfolk Street, Sheffield
4 Bolt Court, Fleet Street
residence: 105 Isledon Road, Finsbury Park

Removed to Eley House, 13 Charterhouse Street, EC, 7
November 1887

These five marks erased 3 October 1890

*** 3 October 1890
Henry Wilkinson & Co. Ltd, Plate workers
13 Charterhouse Street, Holborn Circus
signed: John Edward Cutler

*** 17 March 1892
Henry Wilkinson & Co., Plate workers
13 Charterhouse Street, Holborn Circus
signed: John E. Bingham, senior partner

This Sheffield firm of manufacturing silversmiths was established *circa* 1830. Trading as Henry Wilkinson & Co., the firm's mark was entered for the first time at Goldsmiths' Hall, London, by Henry Wilkinson in June 1857. At the time, the firm's London premises at 4 Bolt Court served as showrooms as well as being used for warehouse purposes.

In 1872 the firm was converted into a limited liability company trading as Henry Wilkinson & Co. Ltd.

Following the death of Henry Wilkinson, the firm was continued by John Brashier who entered his mark at Goldsmiths' Hall in November 1879. In October 1890 new marks were entered at Goldsmiths' Hall by John Edward Cutler. By March 1892 John Edward Bingham had become senior partner in the firm. He was also senior partner in the Sheffield firm of Walker & Hall, manufacturing silversmiths and platers, having joined the firm *circa* 1864 (see Walker & Hall). During 1892 the firm of Henry Wilkinson & Co. Ltd went into liquidation and was acquired by Walker & Hall.

*Mark entered in two sizes.
***Mark entered in four sizes.
†Mark entered in five sizes.

Josiah Williams & Co.

18 January 1883
George Maudsley Jackson, Plate worker
* 18 St Augustus Parade, Bristol
residence: 4 Burlington Buildings, Redland, Bristol

26 February 1884
9 Thavies Inn (London)
Two (marks) in use some time before they were registered

Three (marks) defaced 7.1.1892

7 January 1892
(Marks) defaced 21.11.1894

26 May 1892

311

GMJ 29 November 1892
Removed to Three Queens Lane, Redcliff Road, Bristol
25 Thavies Inn, Holborn Circus (London)
residence: 38 Lower Redland Road, Bristol

 GMJ * 13 November 1894

 GMJ 10 December 1895
George Maudsley Jackson, Plate worker
Three Queens Lane, Redcliff Road, Bristol
25 Thavies Inn, Holborn Circus
residence: 38 Lower Redland Road, Bristol

GJ DF ** 22 March 1897
George Maudsley Jackson and David Landsborough Fullerton,
Silver workers
Three Queens Lane, Bristol
25 Thavies Inn, London
Jackson's residence: 38 Lower Redland Road, Bristol
Fullerton's residence: 21 Clarendon Road, Bristol
signed: D. L. Fullerton, partner in firm of Jackson & Fullerton

10 March 1915
These Workers (partners) dissolved partnership in March 1915
and the next entry is that of D. L. Fullerton

From *circa* 1846 to 1853 this Bristol firm of silversmiths was under the control of Robert Williams and his two sons, James and Josiah, all of whom were trading as Robert Williams & Sons. When Robert Williams retired in 1853, the firm was continued by his two sons, trading as James & Josiah Williams, but by 1877 only Josiah Williams remained, trading as Josiah Williams & Co. He subsequently entered into partnership with George Maudsley Jackson and retired in 1879, leaving G. M. Jackson to continue running the firm under the name of Josiah Williams & Co. Josiah Williams died on 9 October 1894.

In 1883 G. M. Jackson entered his mark at Goldsmiths' Hall, London, for the first time. Then, in 1884, he took over premises at 9 Thavies Inn for use as showrooms. By 1897 he had entered into partnership with David Landsborough Fullerton, trading as Jackson & Fullerton. Their partnership continued until dissolved in March 1915, presumably due to the retirement or death of G. M. Jackson. D. L. Fullerton then entered his own mark at

Goldsmiths' Hall on 10 March 1915 and continued trading as Josiah Williams & Co. He died on 24 April 1930.

Circa 1925 the firm was converted into a limited liability company, trading as Josiah Williams & Co. (Bristol) Ltd. It closed down in 1940.

*Mark entered in two sizes.
**Mark entered in three sizes.

Wilson & Davis

27 June 1870
Frederick Wilson and William Davis, Plate workers
10 Hatton Garden
F. Wilson's residence: 11 Park Villas, Park Road, Holloway
Davis's residence: 156 Great Portland Street

* 28 February 1883
Frederick Wilson, Small workers
10 Hatton Garden, EC
F. Wilson's residence: Spencer House, Adelaide Road, Surbiton, Surrey

27 September 1886

13 November 1902
Frederick Wilson & Co., Silver workers
9, 11 and 13 Cavendish Street, Sheffield
9 Hatton Garden, London
W. S. Legge's residence: 37 Berkeley Road, Crouch End
signed: W. S. Legge, partner

This firm's factory was located at Hatton Works, Eyre Street, Sheffield, the firm's partners being Frederick Wilson and William (Pittman) Davis, trading as Wilson & Davis, silversmiths and electroplaters.

Following the dissolution of their partnership on 1 February 1883, Frederick Wilson began trading as Frederick Wilson & Co., electroplate manufacturers, silversmiths, silver cutlers and nickel silver spoon and fork makers. In 1895 Frederick Wilson committed suicide and the firm was continued by W. S. Legge, another partner. At some date between 1902 and 1910, the firm was converted into a limited liability company, trading as Travis, Wilson & Co. Ltd, electroplate manufacturers.

*Mark entered in two sizes.

Horace Woodward & Co. Ltd

25 October 1866
Horace Woodward, Plate worker
Great Charles Street, Birmingham
41 Hatton Garden, London
H. Woodward's residence: 37 Wellington Road, Edgbaston, Birmingham

18 March 1870
Removed to (?Arnscot) House, Arthur Road, Edgbaston, Birmingham

H. Woodward's residence: Holborn Viaduct, London, 7 May 1873

** 30 July 1883
Edgar Finley and Hugh Taylor, Plate workers
E. Finley's residence: 8 Charlotte Road, Edgbaston
H. Taylor's residence: 22 Wellington Road, Edgbaston, Birmingham

19 December 1884
38 Holborn Viaduct, London, EC

22 November 1888

These marks were defaced 11.10.1893 (refers to all Finley & Taylor marks)

* 11 October 1893
Horace Woodward & Co. Ltd, Plate workers
38 Holborn Viaduct (London)
Atlas Works, Paradise Street, Birmingham
H. Taylor's residence: 6 Penfold Street, Streatham
signed: Hugh Taylor, director

9 May 1894
signed: Hugh Taylor, director

3 December 1900
signed: Matthew Hollins, managing director

*** 18 February 1902
Horace Woodward & Co. Ltd, Silver workers
38 Holborn Viaduct, London, EC
Atlas Works, Paradise Street, Birmingham
M. Hollins's residence: 174 Heathfield Road, Handsworth, Birmingham
signed: M. Hollins

*** 2 February 1903
Horace Woodward & Co. Ltd, Gold and Silver workers
38 Holborn Viaduct, London, EC
Atlas Works, Paradise Street (Birmingham)
102 Vyse Street (Birmingham)
H. E. Taylor's residence: 51 Blenheim Road, Moseley, Birmingham
signed: H. E. Taylor, secretary

This Birmingham firm of manufacturing silversmiths and platers was established by George Cartwright and Joseph Hirons, trading as Cartwright & Hirons. *Circa* 1853 Horace Woodward joined the partnership, the firm's name being changed to Cartwright, Hirons & Woodward, electroplate manufacturers and silversmiths. At the time, the firm was trading from 138–139 Great Charles Street, Birmingham, and 41 Hatton Garden, London.

In 1859 the partnership with Joseph Hirons was dissolved and the firm continued trading as Cartwright & Woodward. Then, in 1865, George Cartwright retired, leaving Horace Woodward to continue trading on his own as Horace Woodward & Co.

Following the retirement or death of Horace Woodward *circa* 1883, the firm was continued by Edgar Finley and Hugh Taylor, still trading as Horace Woodward & Co. In 1893 the firm was converted into a limited liability company, trading as Horace Woodward & Co. Ltd with Hugh Taylor as director. By December 1900 Matthew Hollins was the firm's managing director.

In 1919 the firm was acquired by Adie Brothers Ltd, manufacturing silversmiths. This firm entered its mark at Goldsmiths' Hall, London, on 3 December 1919.

*Mark entered in two sizes.
**Mark entered in three sizes.
***Mark entered in four sizes.

John Yapp & Co.

 17 June 1846
John Woodward and John Yapp junior, Plate workers
manufactory: 13 Bread Street, Birmingham
warehouse: 11 Thavies Inn, London
J. Woodward's residence: 42 Lower Camden Street (Birmingham)
J. Yapp's residence: 17 Camden Street, Birmingham

This firm was the continuation of Joseph Willmore & Co., a Birmingham firm of silversmiths (see *Marks of London Goldsmiths and Silversmiths c.1697–1837*, revised edition 1988, p. 362). Joseph Willmore entered his mark at Goldsmiths' Hall, London, on 21 February 1805 and again on 14 March 1840. In 1834 he entered into partnership with John Yapp and John Woodward, trading as Joseph Willmore & Co., otherwise Willmore, Yapp & Woodward, goldsmiths.

Joseph Willmore retired in 1844, leaving John Yapp (junior) and John Woodward to continue the firm. Following John Woodward's retirement or death *circa* 1852, John Yapp, in partnership with John Richard Chinn, continued running the firm, trading as John Yapp & Co., jewellers and silversmiths. This partnership was dissolved in 1854, leaving John Yapp to continue on his own.

London Assay Office Hallmarks

Standard Mark (Lion Passant)

Denotes a minimum silver content of 92.5 per cent. This mark (for Sterling Standard silver) is used by all Assay Offices in England. It has been struck on English silverware since 1544.

Britannia Mark

Denotes a minimum silver content of 95.84 per cent. This mark (for Britannia Standard silver) was introduced in 1697 and remained in compulsory use until 1720 when the Sterling Standard was restored. The Britannia Standard continues as an optional alternative and is still used occasionally.

Assay Office Mark (or Town Mark)

This indicates the Assay Office at which the assaying and hallmarking were carried out. The Leopard's Head mark illustrated here represents the London Assay Office and appears on articles of gold and Sterling Standard silver. From 1975 onwards, it also appears on platinum articles.

The mark is often found on provincial silver where it appears in addition to the provincial town mark.

In May 1822 the London Assay Office introduced the uncrowned

Leopard's Head for use on all articles of gold and silver. However, for some unknown reason, this mark is occasionally found on spoons bearing the date letter for 1821, whereas all other articles of 1821 apparently bear the crowned Leopard's Head.

Lion's Head Erased

Prior to 1975, this was an Assay Office mark used in conjunction with the Britannia mark on articles of Britannia Standard. In the London Assay Office, it replaced the Leopard's Head as Town mark when the Britannia Standard was introduced in 1697, but in other English Assay Offices, it was used together with the appropriate Town mark. It was withdrawn from use at the end of 1974.

Sovereign's Head (or Duty Mark)

This indicates that excise duty was paid on the article of gold or silverware bearing it. The duty was collected by the Assay Office on behalf of the Commissioners of Stamps (later the Inland Revenue).

The mark was introduced in 1784 and remained in use until 1890 when the duty was abolished. When first introduced on 1 December 1784, the mark was an incuse Sovereign's Head. Subsequently, it was changed to a raised Sovereign's Head in May 1786. This means that articles bearing the date letter 'i' for 1784 will only have the incuse Sovereign's Head if they were assayed during the period from December 1784 to May 1785 inclusive.

Date Letter Mark

This indicates the year in which the article was hallmarked. At the London Assay Office, this mark was changed during May of each year up until the end of 1974. Thus each Date Letter covered a portion of two calendar years. On 1 January 1975 the changeover was standardised for all the Assay Offices whereby it occurs on 1 January of each year.

Prior to 1974, a twenty-letter alphabet was always used by the London Assay Office.

'Drawback' Mark

This mark was in use for less than eight months, from 1 December 1784 to 24 July 1785. The mark constitutes an incuse figure depicting Britannia and was stamped by the Assay Office on articles intended for export.

Normally a manufacturer paid excise duty to the Assay Office on all articles as they were assayed, at a rate of 8 shillings per ounce on gold and 6 pence per ounce on silver. When a manufacturer later specified that an article was to be exported, the duty was 'drawn back' and repaid to him, this transaction being indicated on the finished article by the incuse Britannia mark.

The actual stamping of the mark on finished articles was abandoned after such a short period because of the damage it could cause to the finished article. However, the manufacturer continued to be reimbursed for the duty he had paid on the article that was to be exported.

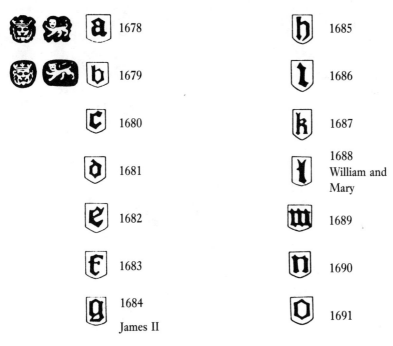

a 1678	**h** 1685
b 1679	**l** 1686
c 1680	**k** 1687
d 1681	**l** 1688 William and Mary
e 1682	**m** 1689
f 1683	**n** 1690
g 1684 James II	**o** 1691

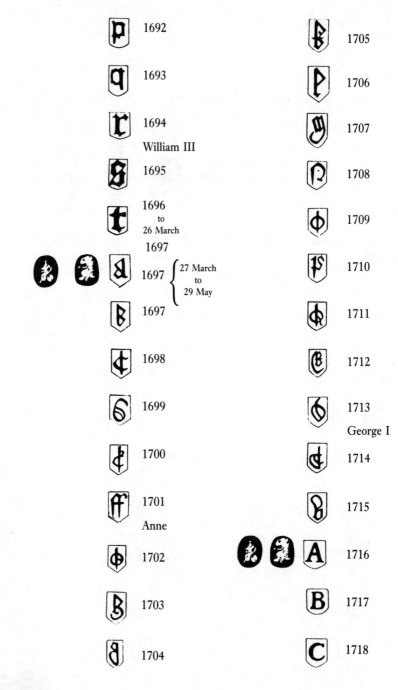

1692

1693

1694
William III

1695

1696
to
26 March
1697

1697 { 27 March
to
29 May

1697

1698

1699

1700

1701
Anne

1702

1703

1704

1705

1706

1707

1708

1709

1710

1711

1712

1713
George I

1714

1715

1716

1717

1718

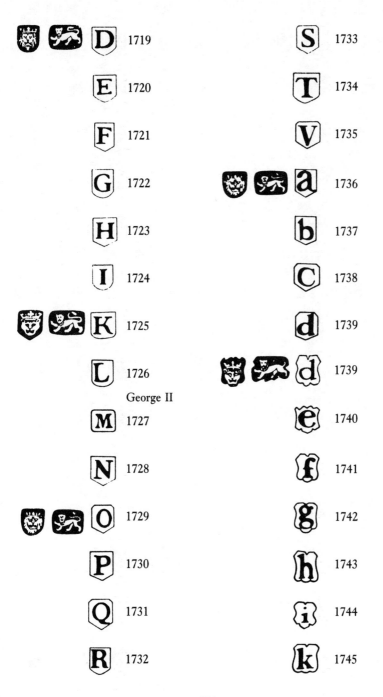

D 1719

E 1720

F 1721

G 1722

H 1723

I 1724

K 1725

L 1726

George II

M 1727

N 1728

O 1729

P 1730

Q 1731

R 1732

S 1733

T 1734

V 1735

a 1736

b 1737

C 1738

d 1739

d 1739

e 1740

f 1741

g 1742

h 1743

i 1744

k 1745

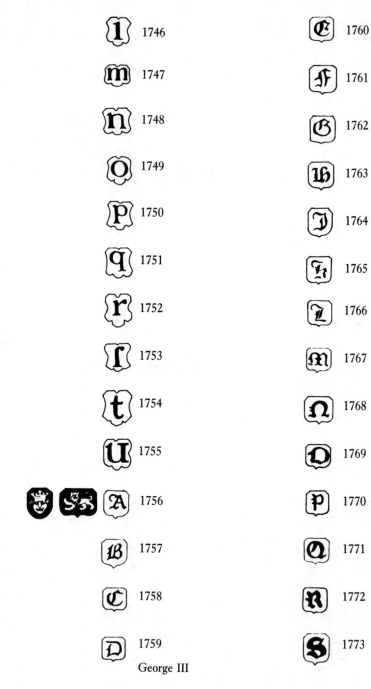

𝔩	1746	𝕰	1760
𝔪	1747	𝕱	1761
𝔫	1748	𝕲	1762
𝔬	1749	𝕳	1763
𝔭	1750	𝕴	1764
𝔮	1751	𝕶	1765
𝔯	1752	𝕷	1766
𝔰	1753	𝕸	1767
𝔱	1754	𝕹	1768
𝔲	1755	𝕺	1769
𝕬	1756	𝕻	1770
𝕭	1757	𝕼	1771
𝕮	1758	𝕽	1772
𝕯	1759	𝕾	1773

George III

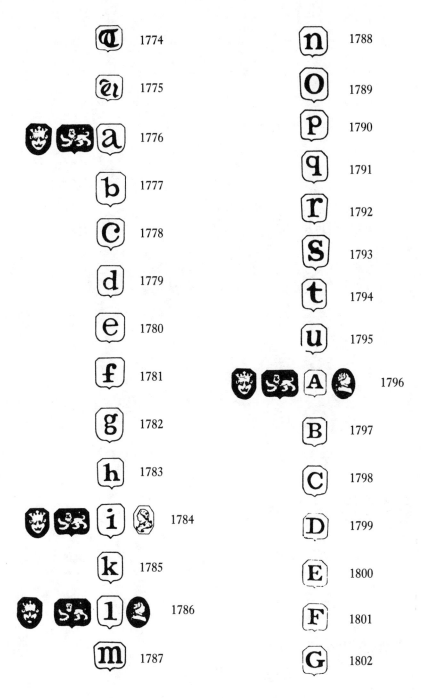

	1774		1788
	1775		1789
	1776		1790
	1777		1791
	1778		1792
	1779		1793
	1780		1794
	1781		1795
	1782		1796
	1783		1797
	1784		1798
	1785		1799
	1786		1800
	1787		1801
			1802

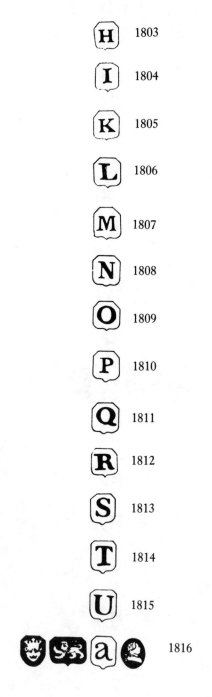

H 1803

I 1804

K 1805

L 1806

M 1807

N 1808

O 1809

P 1810

Q 1811

R 1812

S 1813

T 1814

U 1815

a 1816

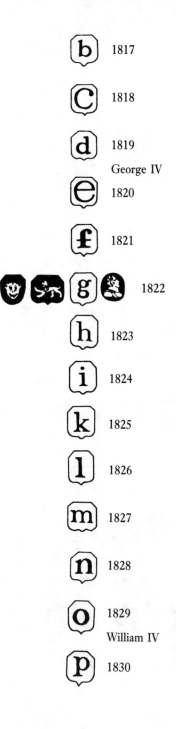

b 1817

C 1818

d 1819

George IV
e 1820

f 1821

g 1822

h 1823

i 1824

k 1825

l 1826

m 1827

n 1828

o 1829

William IV
p 1830

324

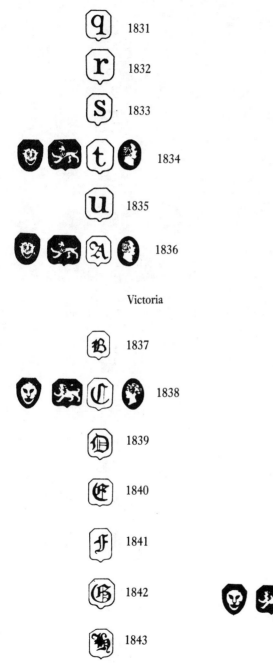
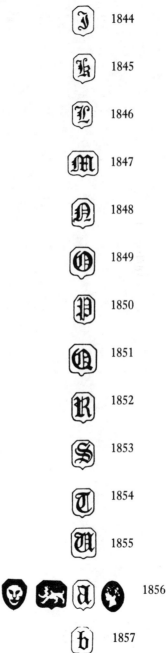

q 1831

r 1832

s 1833

t 1834

u 1835

A 1836

Victoria

B 1837

C 1838

D 1839

E 1840

F 1841

G 1842

H 1843

J 1844

K 1845

L 1846

M 1847

N 1848

O 1849

P 1850

Q 1851

R 1852

S 1853

T 1854

U 1855

A 1856

b 1857

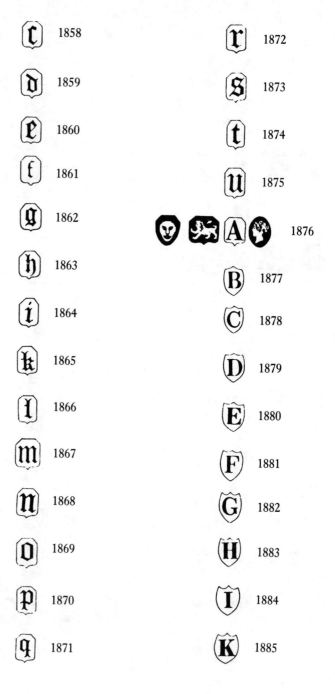

c 1858

d 1859

e 1860

f 1861

g 1862

h 1863

i 1864

k 1865

l 1866

m 1867

n 1868

o 1869

p 1870

q 1871

r 1872

s 1873

t 1874

u 1875

A 1876

B 1877

C 1878

D 1879

E 1880

F 1881

G 1882

H 1883

I 1884

K 1885

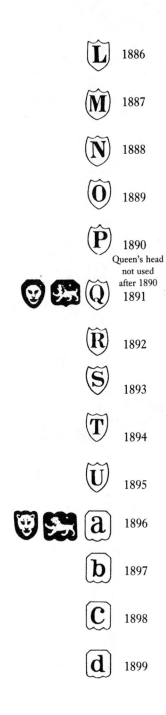

L 1886

M 1887

N 1888

O 1889

P 1890

Queen's head
not used
after 1890

Q 1891

R 1892

S 1893

T 1894

U 1895

a 1896

b 1897

c 1898

d 1899

e 1900

Edward VII

f 1901

g 1902

h 1903

i 1904

k 1905

1 1906

m 1907

n 1908

o 1909

George V

p 1910

q 1911

r 1912

s 1913

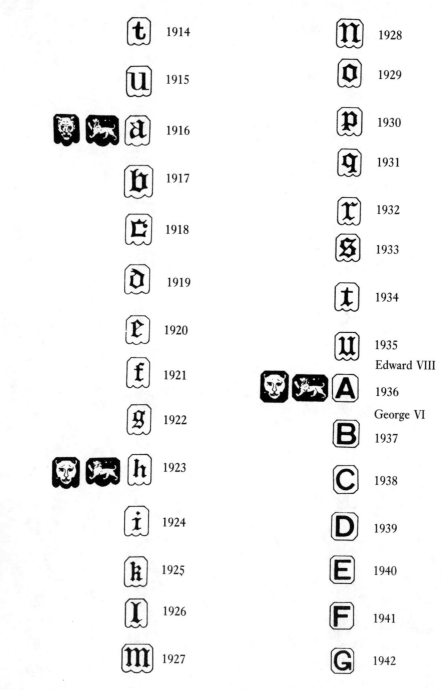

𝖙 1914	𝕹 1928
𝖚 1915	𝕺 1929
𝖆 1916	𝕻 1930
𝖇 1917	𝕼 1931
𝖈 1918	𝕽 1932
𝖉 1919	𝕾 1933
𝖊 1920	𝕿 1934
𝖋 1921	𝖀 1935 Edward VIII
𝖌 1922	A 1936 George VI
𝖍 1923	B 1937
𝖎 1924	C 1938
𝖐 1925	D 1939
𝖑 1926	E 1940
𝖒 1927	F 1941
	G 1942

328

H	1943	C	1958
I	1944	d	1959
K	1945	e	1960
L	1946	f	1961
M	1947	g	1962
N	1948	h	1963
O	1949	i	1964
P	1950	k	1965
Q	1951 Elizabeth II	l	1966
R	1952	m	1967
S	1953	n	1968
T	1954	o	1969
U	1955	p	1970
a	1956	q	1971
b	1957	r	1972

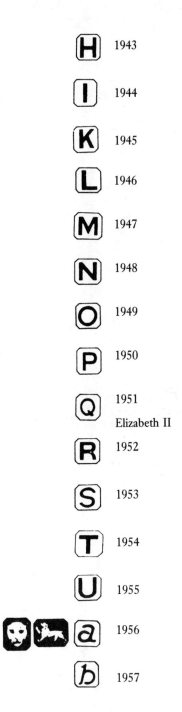

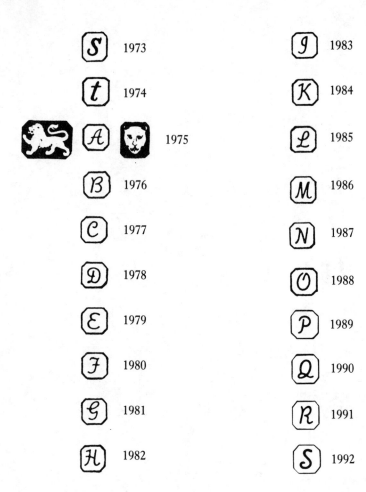

S 1973

t 1974

A 1975

B 1976

C 1977

D 1978

E 1979

F 1980

G 1981

H 1982

I 1983

K 1984

L 1985

M 1986

N 1987

O 1988

P 1989

Q 1990

R 1991

S 1992

Index of Makers' Marks

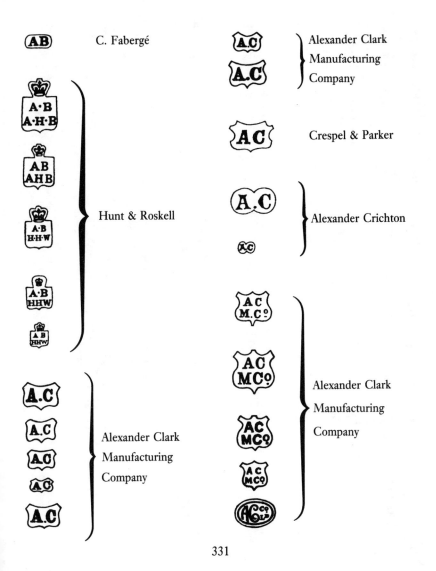

AB	C. Fabergé

Hunt & Roskell

Alexander Clark Manufacturing Company

Alexander Clark Manufacturing Company

Crespel & Parker

Alexander Crichton

Alexander Clark Manufacturing Company

 Asprey & Co. Ltd

Crespel & Parker

A D L

A. D. Loewenstark
& Sons

A·I   George Ivory

Alexander Macrae

Vander & Hedges

    Pairpoint Brothers

Manoah Rhodes
& Sons Ltd

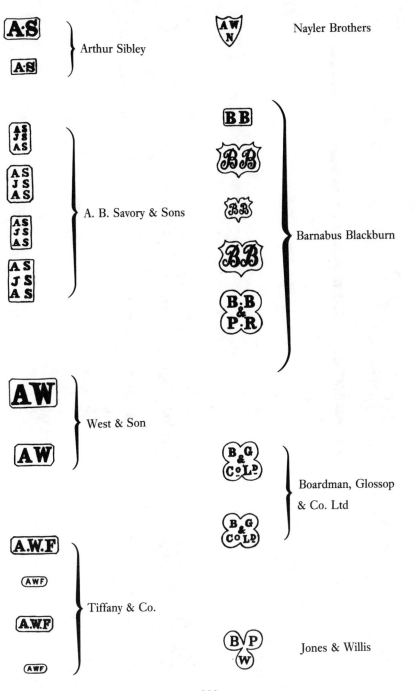

Arthur Sibley

Nayler Brothers

A. B. Savory & Sons

Barnabus Blackburn

West & Son

Boardman, Glossop & Co. Ltd

Tiffany & Co.

Jones & Willis

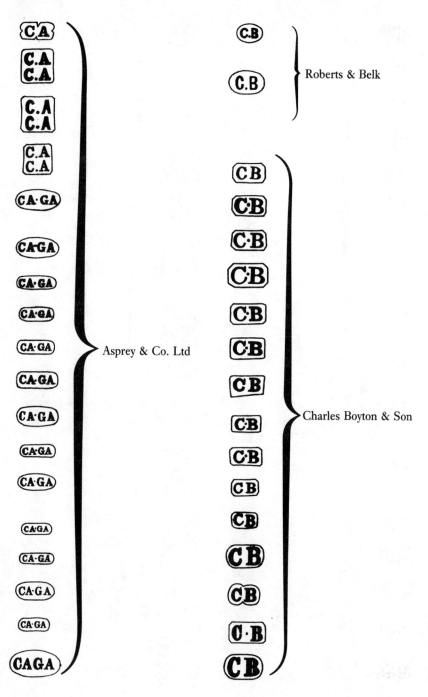

Roberts & Belk

Asprey & Co. Ltd

Charles Boyton & Son

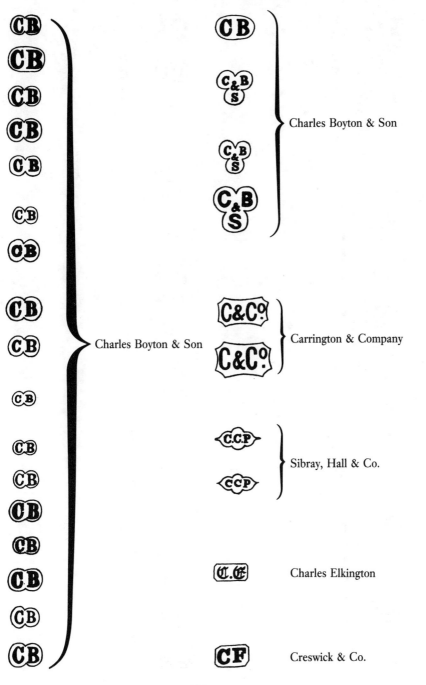

Charles Boyton & Son

Charles Boyton & Son

Carrington & Company

Sibray, Hall & Co.

Charles Elkington

Creswick & Co.

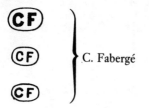 C. Fabergé

 Joseph Hart & Son

 D. J. & C. Houle

Hawksworth, Eyre & Co. Ltd

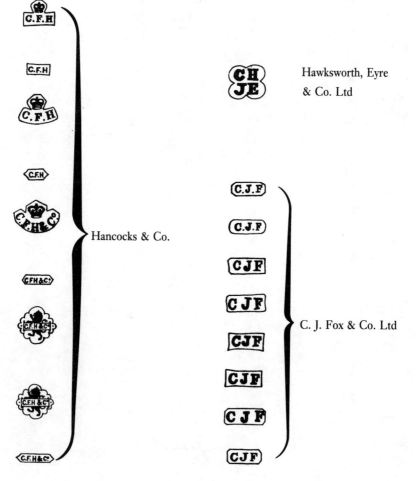

Hancocks & Co.

C. J. Fox & Co. Ltd

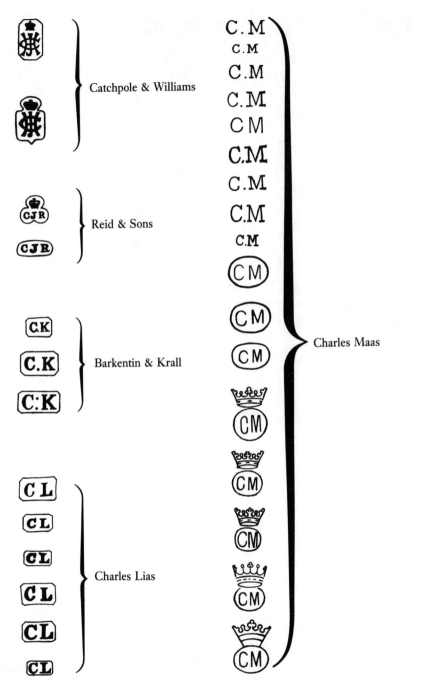

Catchpole & Williams

Reid & Sons

Barkentin & Krall

Charles Lias

C.M
C.M
C.M
C.M
C M
C.M
C.M
C.M
C.M

Charles Maas

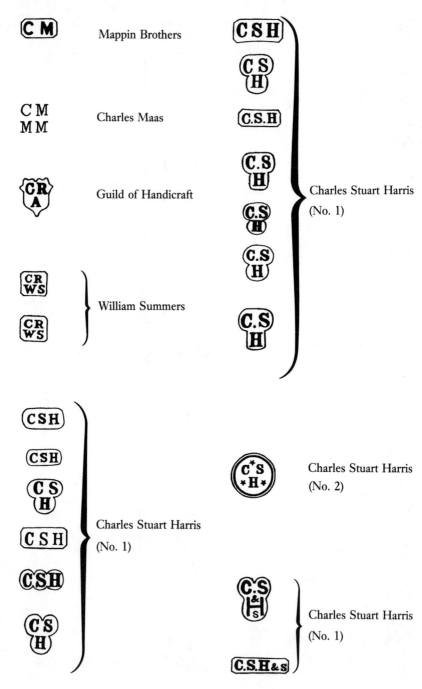

C M — Mappin Brothers

C M / M M — Charles Maas

CRA — Guild of Handicraft

CR WS / CR WS — William Summers

CSH (group) — Charles Stuart Harris (No. 1)

CSH (group) — Charles Stuart Harris (No. 1)

C*S*H — Charles Stuart Harris (No. 2)

C.S H&s / C.S.H&s — Charles Stuart Harris (No. 1)

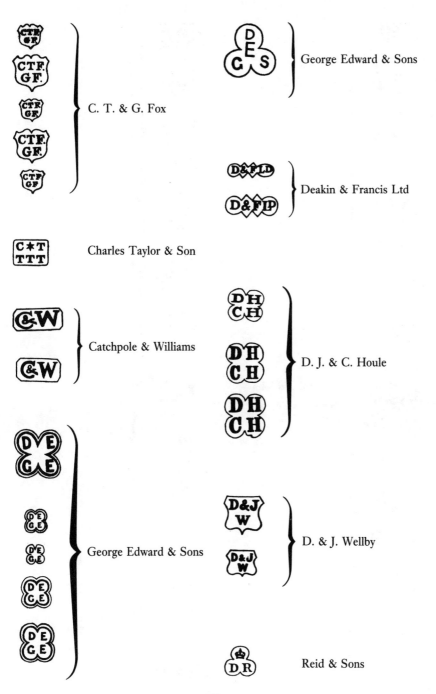

C. T. & G. Fox

George Edward & Sons

Deakin & Francis Ltd

Charles Taylor & Son

Catchpole & Williams

D. J. & C. Houle

George Edward & Sons

D. & J. Wellby

Reid & Sons

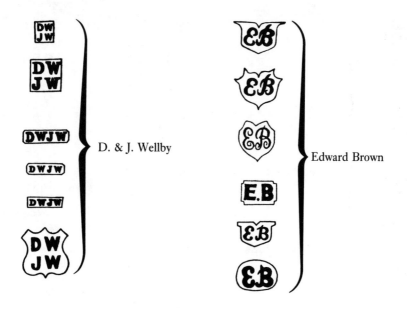 D. & J. Wellby

Edward Brown

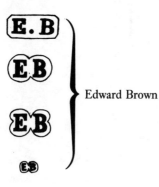 Edward and John
Septimus Beresford

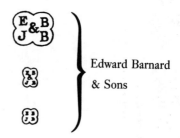 Edward Barnard
& Sons

Edward Brown

 Edward and John
Septimus Beresford

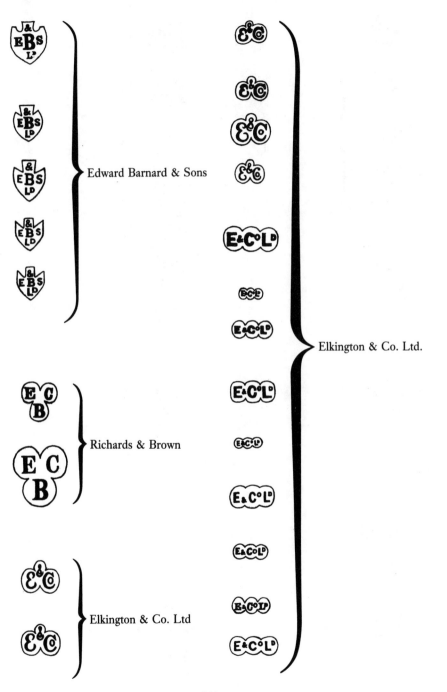

Edward Barnard & Sons

Richards & Brown

Elkington & Co. Ltd

Elkington & Co. Ltd.

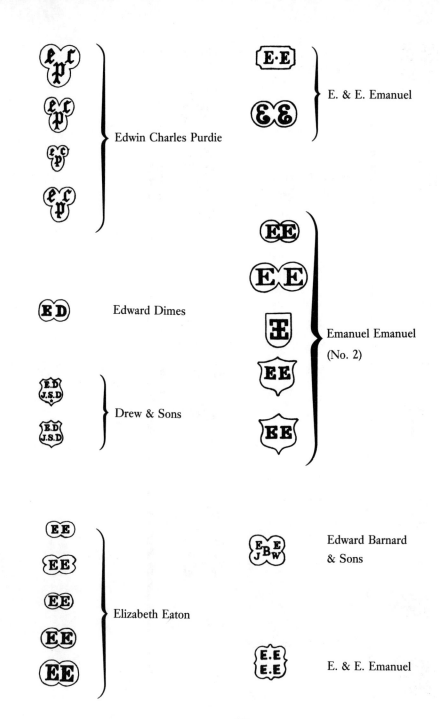

Edwin Charles Purdie

E. & E. Emanuel

Edward Dimes

Emanuel Emanuel
(No. 2)

Drew & Sons

Elizabeth Eaton

Edward Barnard
& Sons

E. & E. Emanuel

Edwards & Son

 Elizabeth Eaton

 Horace Woodward & Co. Ltd

William Hutton & Sons

EHS
EHS
EHS
EHS
} E. H. Stockwell

George Sherwood
Edward

 George Ivory

 } William Hutton & Sons

 Edward Barnard & Sons

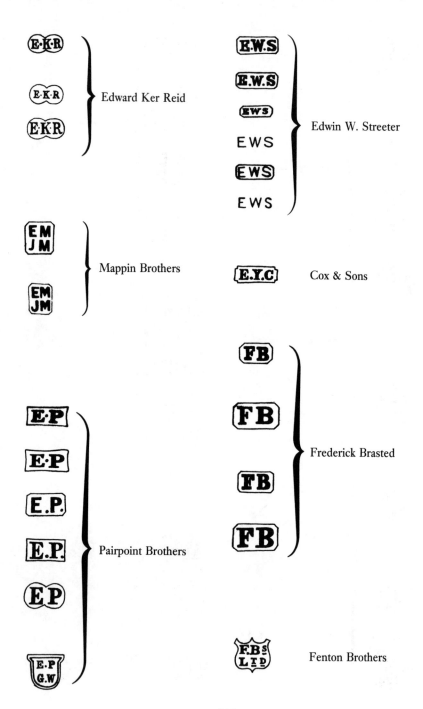

Edward Ker Reid

Edwin W. Streeter

Mappin Brothers

Cox & Sons

Pairpoint Brothers

Frederick Brasted

Fenton Brothers

F. B. Thomas & Co.

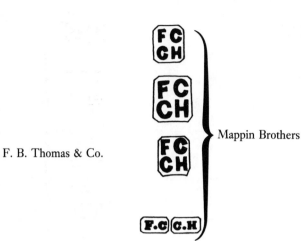

Mappin Brothers

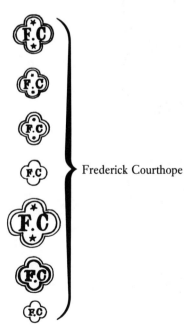

Frederick Courthope

Francis David Dexter

Blunt & Wray

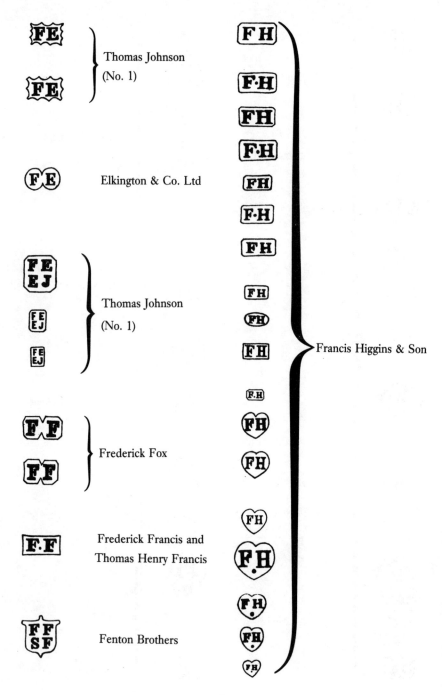

Thomas Johnson
(No. 1)

Elkington & Co. Ltd

Thomas Johnson
(No. 1)

Frederick Fox

Frederick Francis and
Thomas Henry Francis

Fenton Brothers

Francis Higgins & Son

Frederick Perry

 The Portland Co. Ltd

Frederick Perry and William Frederick Curry

 Brockwell & Company

 Sibray, Hall & Co.

Frank Hyams Ltd

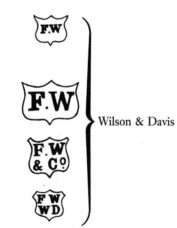 Wilson & Davis

 Francis Higgins & Son

Bristol Goldsmiths Alliance

 Henry Godfrey Webb

347

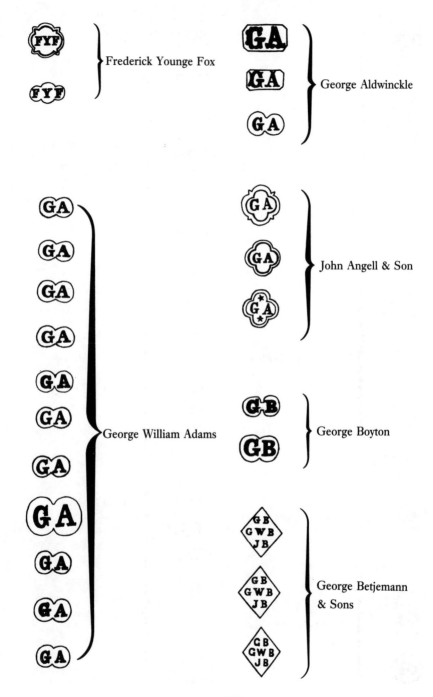

Frederick Younge Fox

George Aldwinckle

George William Adams

John Angell & Son

George Boyton

George Betjemann & Sons

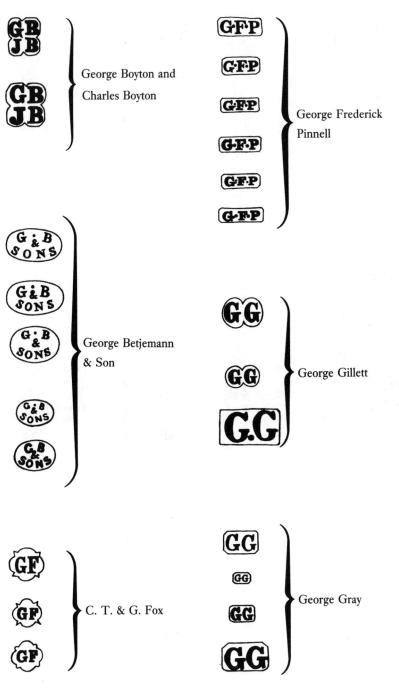

George Boyton and
Charles Boyton

George Frederick
Pinnell

George Betjemann
& Son

George Gillett

C. T. & G. Fox

George Gray

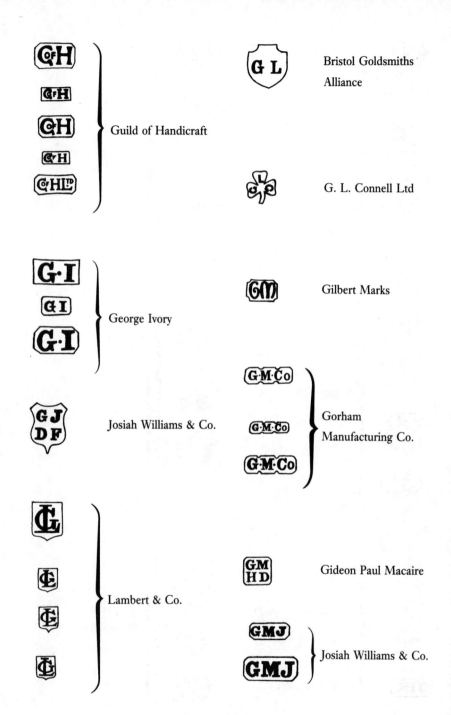

Guild of Handicraft

George Ivory

Josiah Williams & Co.

Lambert & Co.

Bristol Goldsmiths Alliance

G. L. Connell Ltd

Gilbert Marks

Gorham Manufacturing Co.

Gideon Paul Macaire

Josiah Williams & Co.

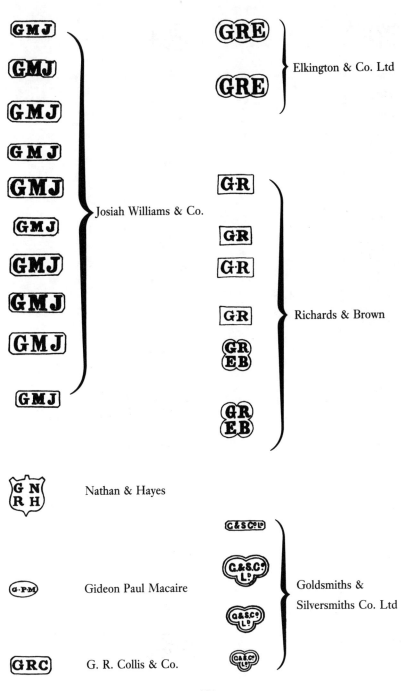

GMJ
GMJ
GMJ
GMJ
GMJ
GMJ — Josiah Williams & Co.
GMJ
GMJ
GMJ
GMJ

GRE
GRE — Elkington & Co. Ltd

G·R
GR
G·R
G·R
GR EB
GR EB — Richards & Brown

GNRH — Nathan & Hayes

G·P·M — Gideon Paul Macaire

GRC — G. R. Collis & Co.

G&SCºLᴰ
G.&S.Cº Lᴰ
G.&S.Cº Lᴰ
G&SCº Lᴰ — Goldsmiths & Silversmiths Co. Ltd

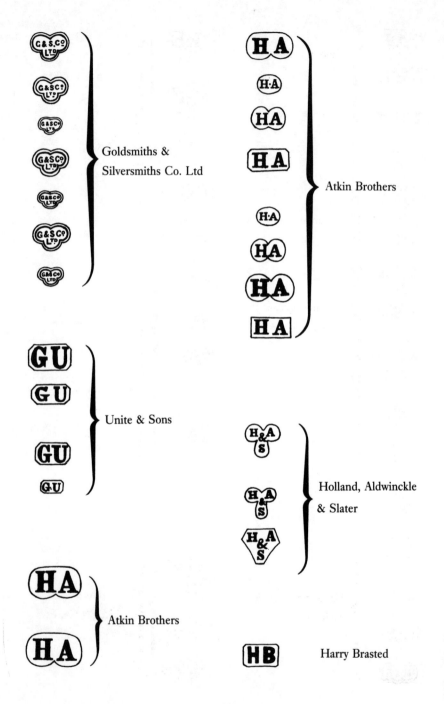

Goldsmiths & Silversmiths Co. Ltd

Atkin Brothers

Unite & Sons

Holland, Aldwinckle & Slater

Atkin Brothers

Harry Brasted

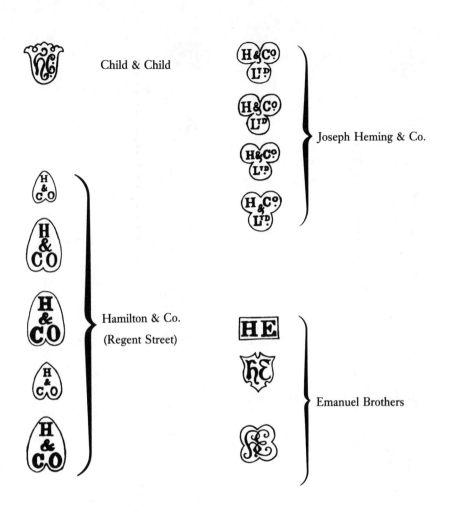

Child & Child

Joseph Heming & Co.

Hamilton & Co.
(Regent Street)

Emanuel Brothers

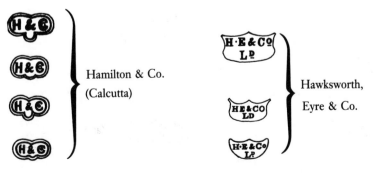

Hamilton & Co.
(Calcutta)

Hawksworth,
Eyre & Co.

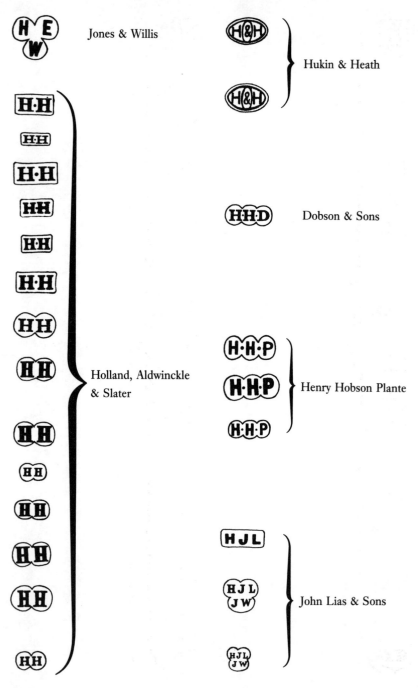

Jones & Willis

Hukin & Heath

Dobson & Sons

Holland, Aldwinckle & Slater

Henry Hobson Plante

John Lias & Sons

354

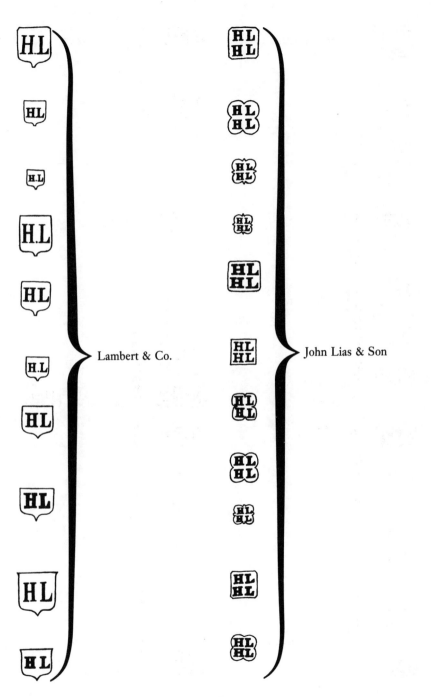

Lambert & Co.

John Lias & Son

Henry Hodson Plante   Harris Bros

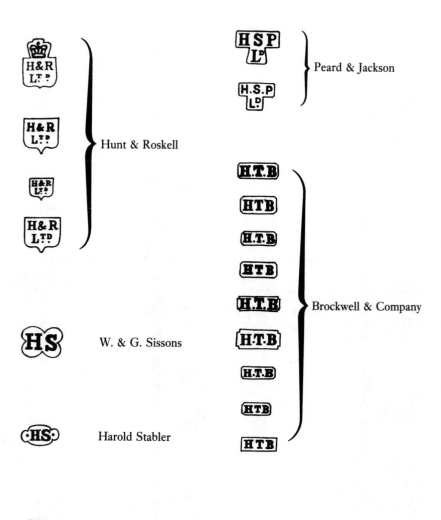

Hunt & Roskell

Peard & Jackson

W. & G. Sissons

Brockwell & Company

Harold Stabler

 Henry William Stockwell

 C. J. Vander

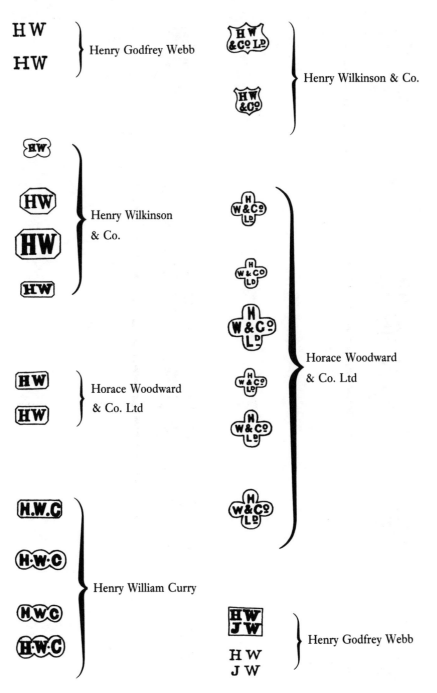

HW

HW } Henry Godfrey Webb

Henry Wilkinson & Co.

Henry Wilkinson
& Co.

Horace Woodward
& Co. Ltd

Horace Woodward
& Co. Ltd

Henry William Curry

Henry Godfrey Webb

H W
J W

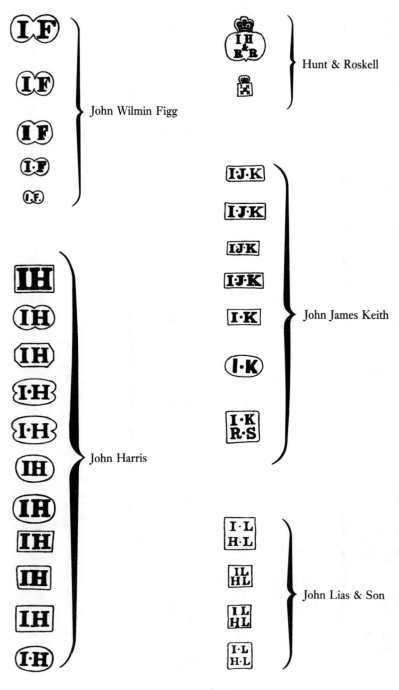

John Wilmin Figg

Hunt & Roskell

John James Keith

John Harris

John Lias & Son

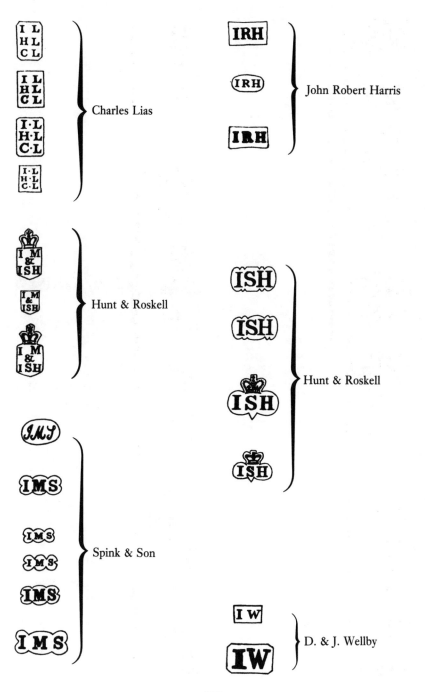

Charles Lias

John Robert Harris

Hunt & Roskell

Hunt & Roskell

Spink & Son

D. & J. Wellby

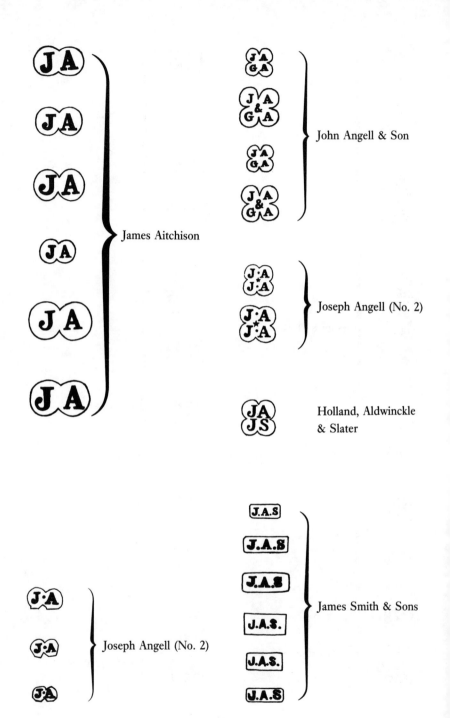

James Aitchison

John Angell & Son

Joseph Angell (No. 2)

Holland, Aldwinckle
& Slater

James Smith & Sons

Joseph Angell (No. 2)

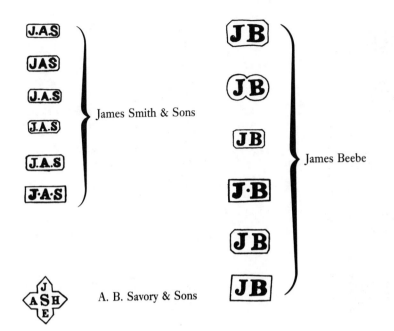

James Smith & Sons

James Beebe

A. B. Savory & Sons

Holland, Aldwinckle & Slater

James Boyton

Barkentin & Krall

Henry Wilkinson & Co.

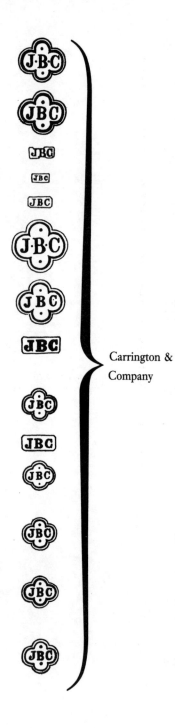

 Thomas Bradbury
& Sons

 Frederick Brasted

Robert Hennell & Sons

Carrington &
Company

 Cartier

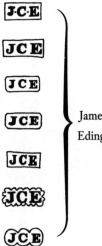 James Charles
Edington

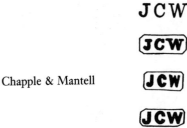

Chapple & Mantell

Joseph Charles Webb

Creswick & Co.

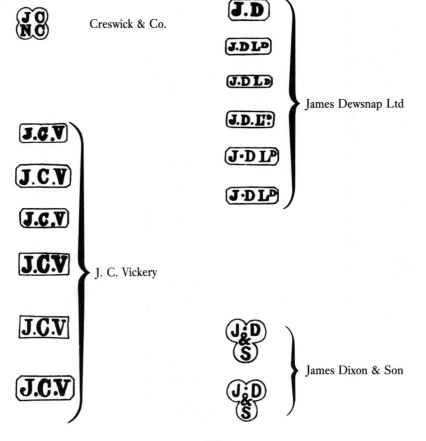

J. C. Vickery

James Dewsnap Ltd

James Dixon & Son

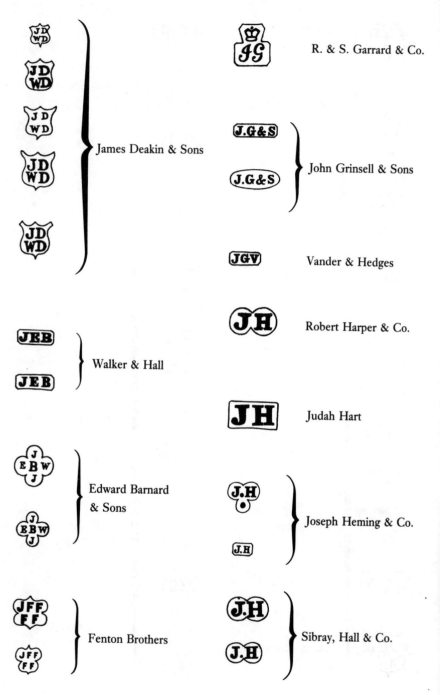

James Deakin & Sons

R. & S. Garrard & Co.

John Grinsell & Sons

Vander & Hedges

Walker & Hall

Robert Harper & Co.

Judah Hart

Edward Barnard & Sons

Joseph Heming & Co.

Fenton Brothers

Sibray, Hall & Co.

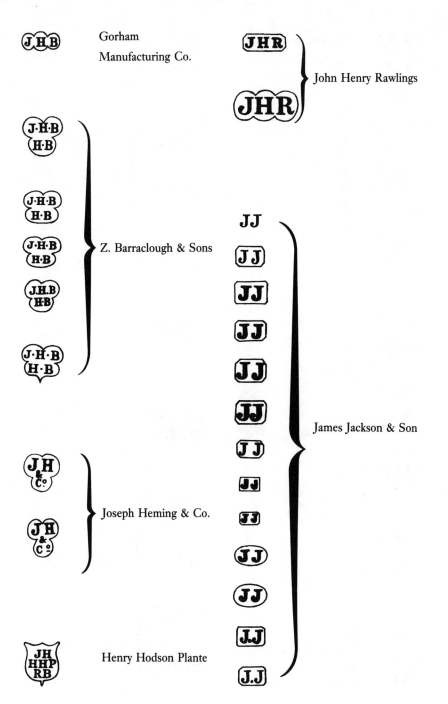

Gorham
Manufacturing Co.

John Henry Rawlings

Z. Barraclough & Sons

JJ

James Jackson & Son

Joseph Heming & Co.

Henry Hodson Plante

Johnson &
Springthorpe

 John Le Gallais

 Johnson, Walker
& Tolhurst

Rosenthal, Jacob & Co.

Johnson &
Springthorpe

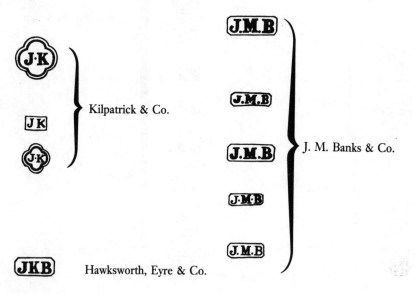

Kilpatrick & Co.

J. M. Banks & Co.

JKB Hawksworth, Eyre & Co.

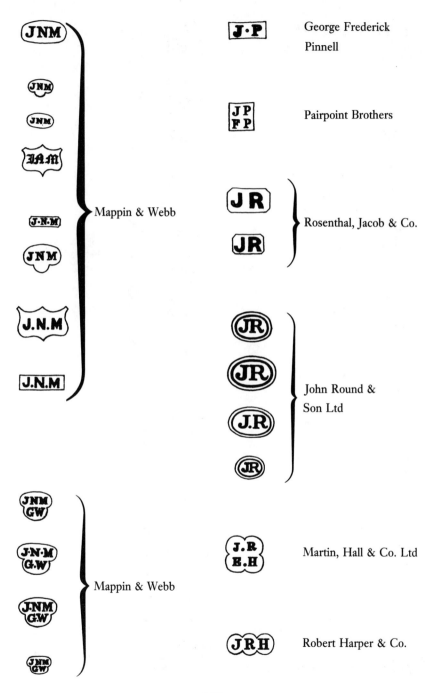

Mappin & Webb

George Frederick
Pinnell

Pairpoint Brothers

Rosenthal, Jacob & Co.

John Round &
Son Ltd

Mappin & Webb

Martin, Hall & Co. Ltd

Robert Harper & Co.

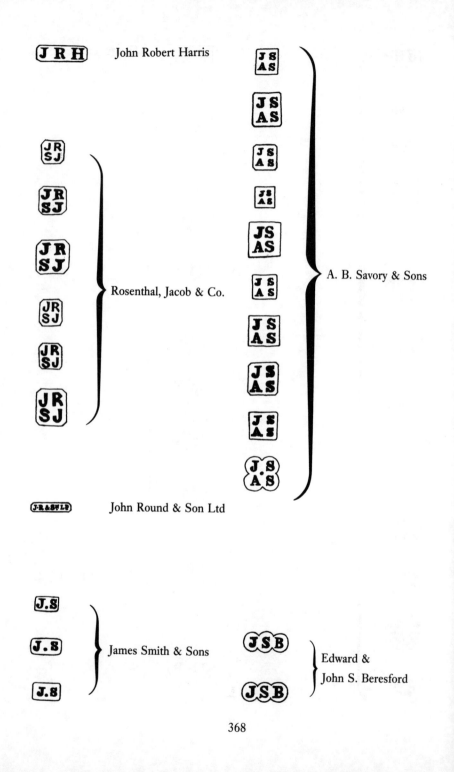

J R H   John Robert Harris

Rosenthal, Jacob & Co.

A. B. Savory & Sons

J·R·&S¥L?   John Round & Son Ltd

James Smith & Sons

Edward &
John S. Beresford

A. B. Savory & Sons

  Vander & Hedges

 } James Smith & Sons

$J.V$ C. J. Vander

  Vander & Hedges

} Tucker & Edwards

} Hukin & Heath

John James Whiting
and John Whiting

  } Tucker & Edwards

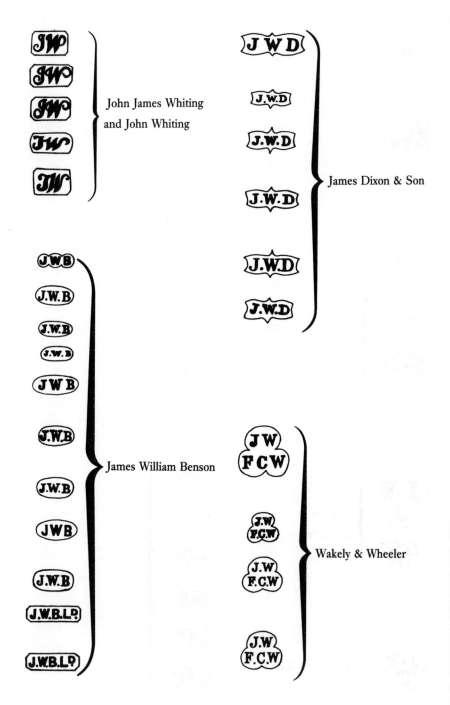

John James Whiting
and John Whiting

James Dixon & Son

James William Benson

Wakely & Wheeler

370

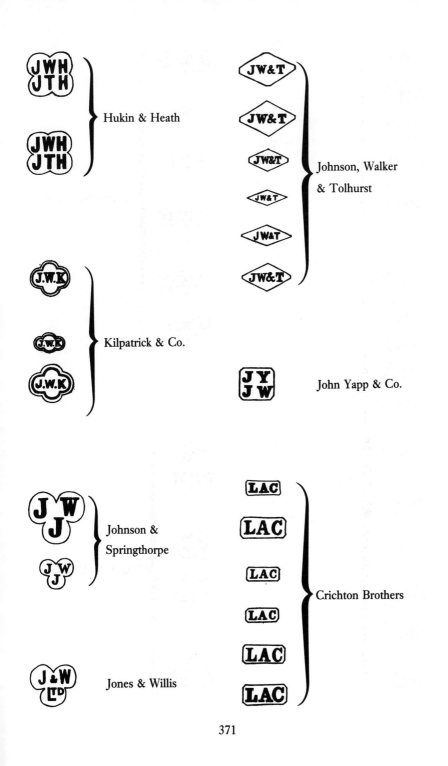

Hukin & Heath

Johnson, Walker
& Tolhurst

Kilpatrick & Co.

John Yapp & Co.

Johnson &
Springthorpe

Crichton Brothers

Jones & Willis

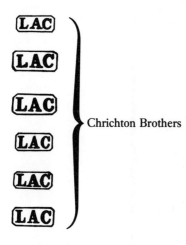 Chrichton Brothers

 George William Adams

 A. D. Loewenstark
& Sons

 Thomas Johnson (No. 1)

 West & Son

Emanuel Brothers

 L. J. Purdie and
H. A. Purdie

Rosenthal, Jacob & Co.

 Alexander Macrae

 Liberty & Co.

 Martin, Hall & Co. Ltd

372

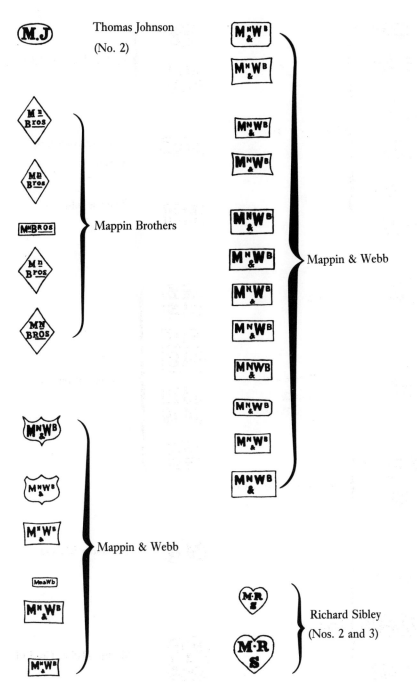

Thomas Johnson
(No. 2)

Mappin Brothers

Mappin & Webb

Mappin & Webb

Richard Sibley
(Nos. 2 and 3)

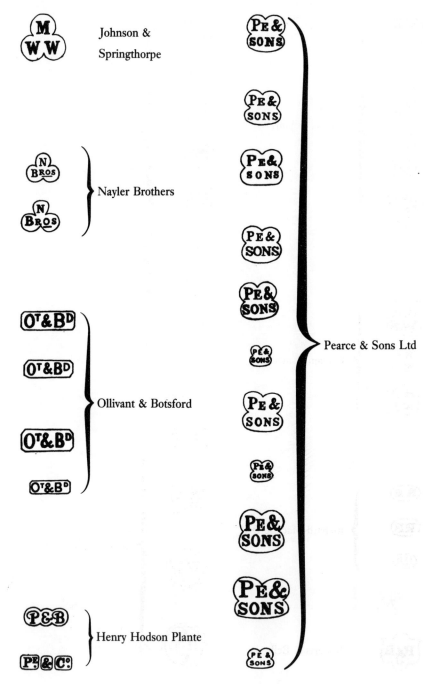

Johnson &
Springthorpe

Nayler Brothers

Ollivant & Botsford

Henry Hodson Plante

Pearce & Sons Ltd

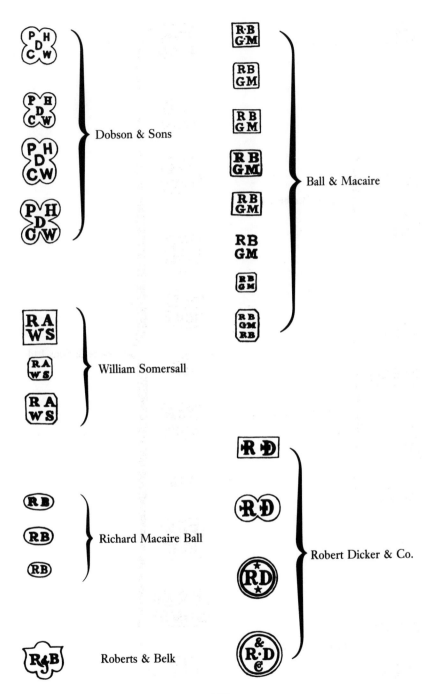

Dobson & Sons

William Somersall

Richard Macaire Ball

Roberts & Belk

Ball & Macaire

Robert Dicker & Co.

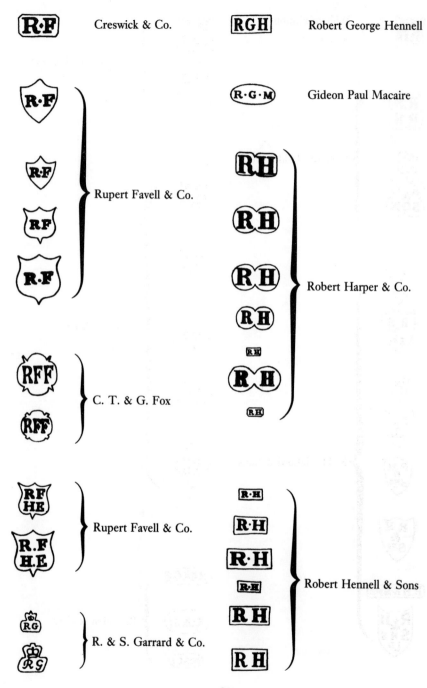

Creswick & Co.

Robert George Hennell

Gideon Paul Macaire

Rupert Favell & Co.

Robert Harper & Co.

C. T. & G. Fox

Rupert Favell & Co.

R. & S. Garrard & Co.

Robert Hennell & Sons

376

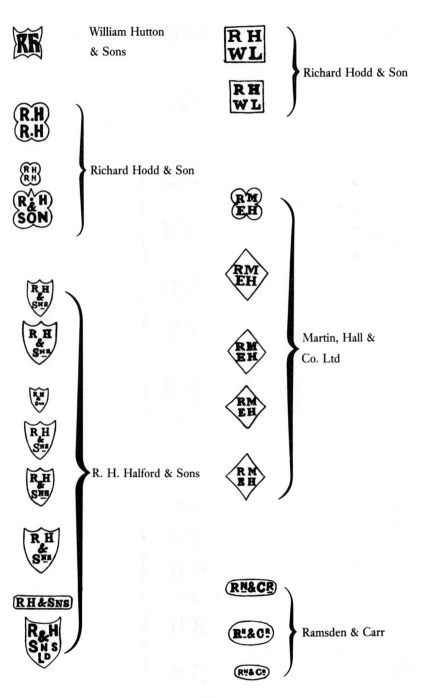

William Hutton
& Sons

Richard Hodd & Son

Richard Hodd & Son

Martin, Hall &
Co. Ltd

R. H. Halford & Sons

Ramsden & Carr

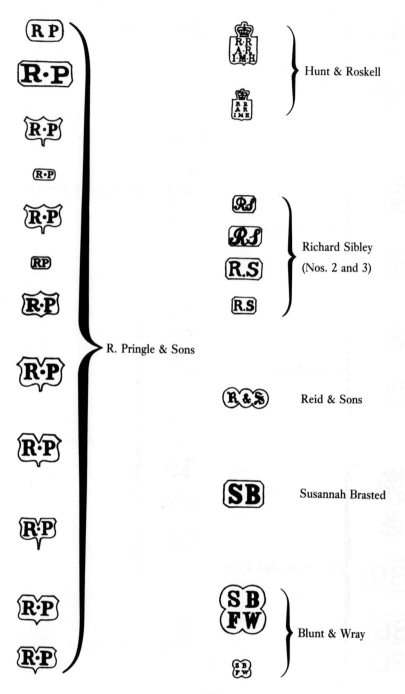

R. Pringle & Sons

Hunt & Roskell

Richard Sibley
(Nos. 2 and 3)

Reid & Sons

Susannah Brasted

Blunt & Wray

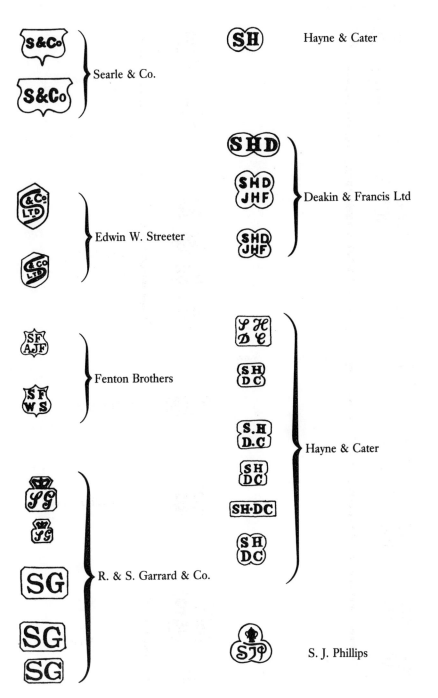

Searle & Co.

Hayne & Cater

Edwin W. Streeter

Deakin & Francis Ltd

Fenton Brothers

Hayne & Cater

R. & S. Garrard & Co.

S. J. Phillips

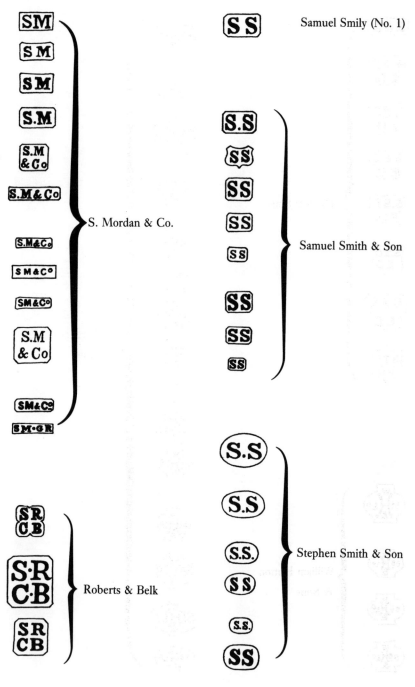

S. Mordan & Co.

Samuel Smily (No. 1)

Samuel Smith & Son

Stephen Smith & Son

Roberts & Belk

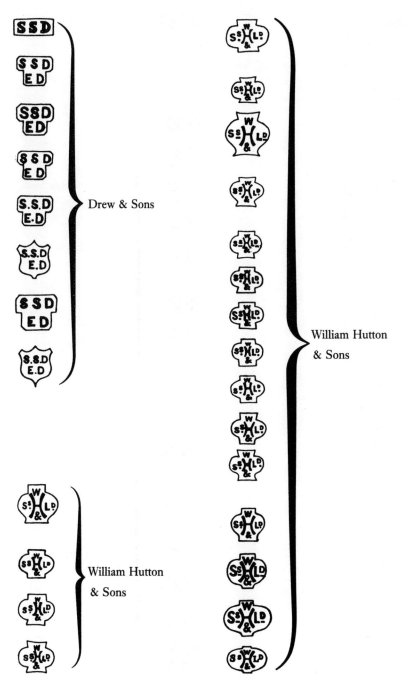

Drew & Sons

William Hutton
& Sons

William Hutton
& Sons

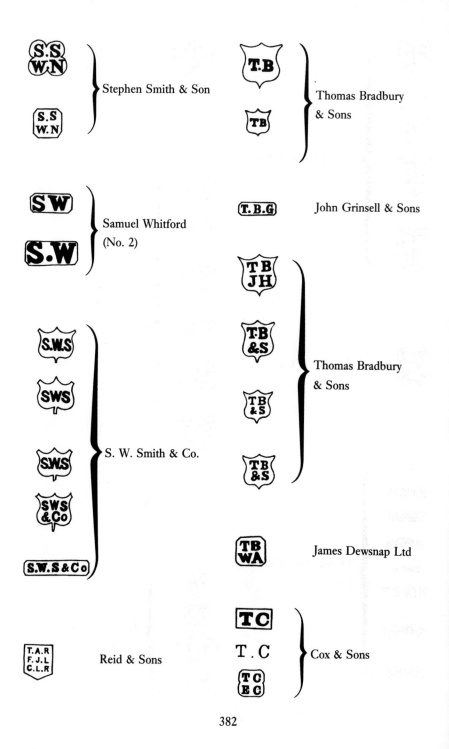

S.S W.N
S.S W.N } Stephen Smith & Son

T.B
TB } Thomas Bradbury & Sons

SW
S.W } Samuel Whitford (No. 2)

T.B.G   John Grinsell & Sons

S.W.S
SWS
SWS
SWS &Co
S.W.S & Co } S. W. Smith & Co.

TB JH

TB &S
TB &S
TB &S } Thomas Bradbury & Sons

TB WA   James Dewsnap Ltd

TC
T.C
TC EC } Cox & Sons

T.A.R F.J.L C.L.R   Reid & Sons

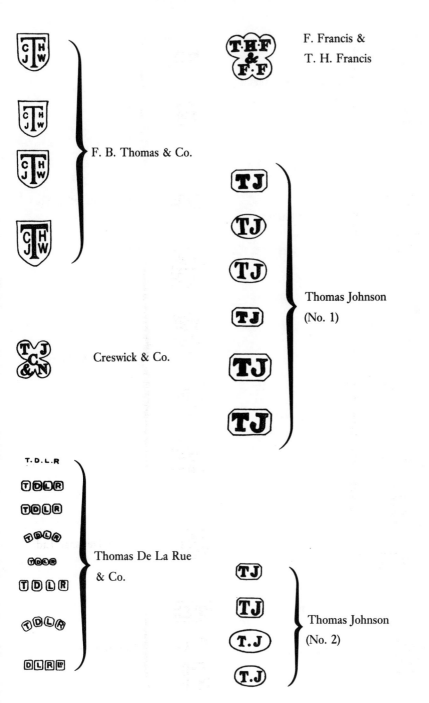

F. Francis &
T. H. Francis

F. B. Thomas & Co.

Thomas Johnson
(No. 1)

Creswick & Co.

Thomas De La Rue
& Co.

Thomas Johnson
(No. 2)

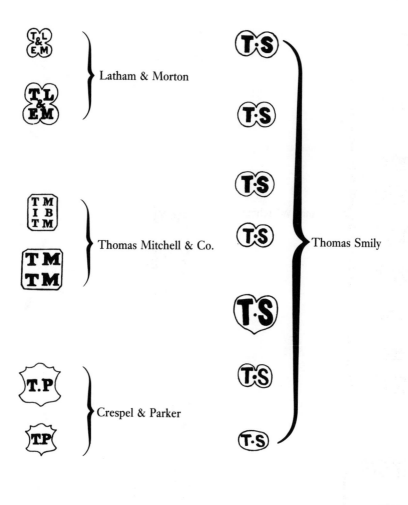

Latham & Morton

Thomas Mitchell & Co.

Crespel & Parker

Thomas Smily

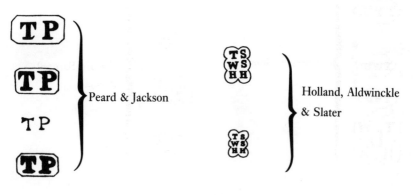

Peard & Jackson

Holland, Aldwinckle
& Slater

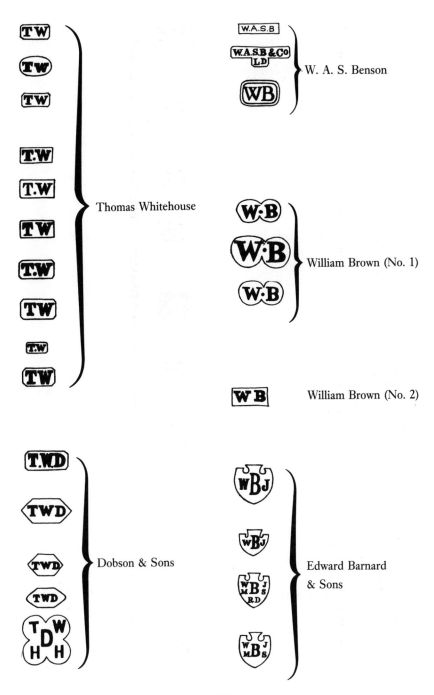

Thomas Whitehouse

W. A. S. Benson

William Brown (No. 1)

William Brown (No. 2)

Dobson & Sons

Edward Barnard
& Sons

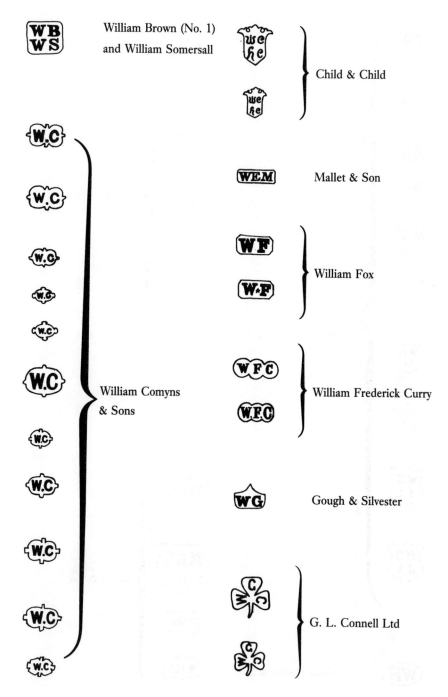

William Brown (No. 1) and William Somersall

Child & Child

Mallet & Son

William Fox

William Comyns & Sons

William Frederick Curry

Gough & Silvester

G. L. Connell Ltd

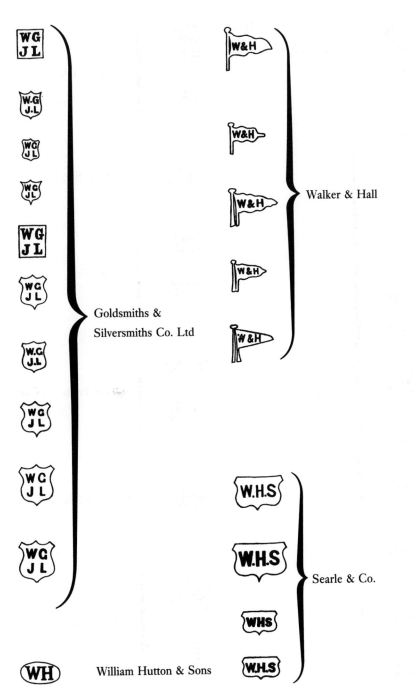

Goldsmiths &
Silversmiths Co. Ltd

Walker & Hall

Searle & Co.

William Hutton & Sons

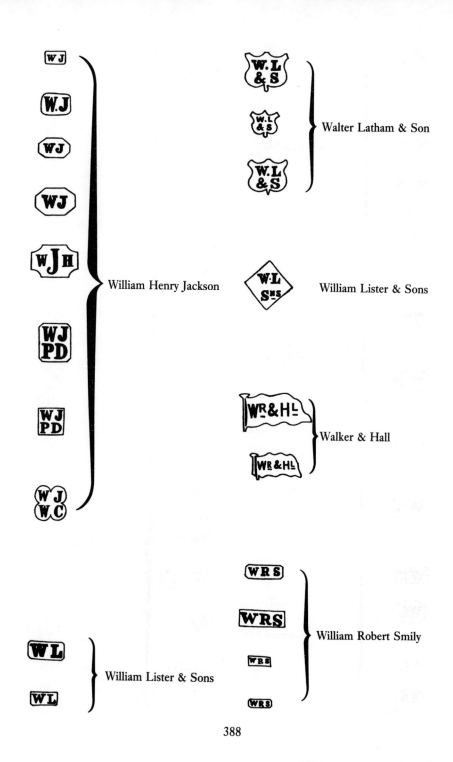

William Henry Jackson

Walter Latham & Son

William Lister & Sons

Walker & Hall

William Robert Smily

William Lister & Sons

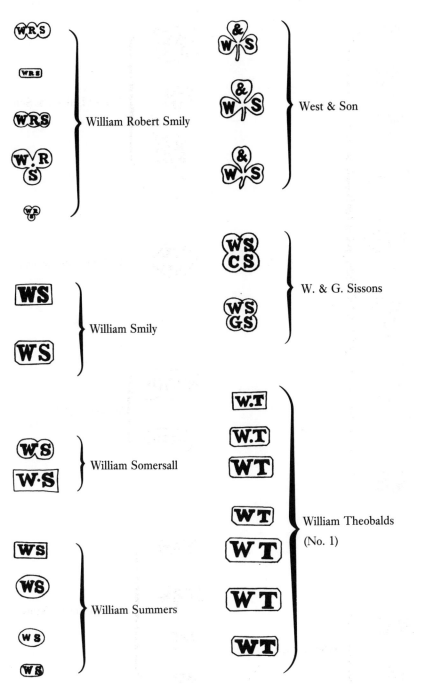

William Robert Smily

West & Son

William Smily

W. & G. Sissons

William Somersall

William Summers

William Theobalds (No. 1)

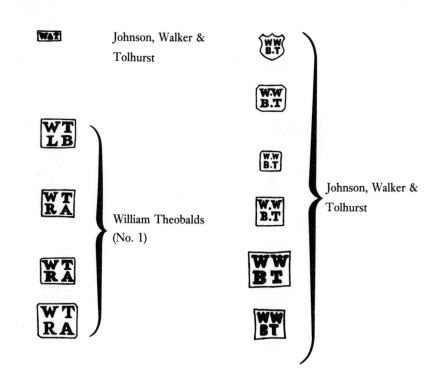

Johnson, Walker & Tolhurst

William Theobalds (No. 1)

Johnson, Walker & Tolhurst

Wakely & Wheeler

Johnson, Walker & Tolhurst